LAND AND LIFE

From photograph by K. J. Pelzer, September, 1935.

Carl O Sauer

"*Locomotion should be slow, the slower the better; and should be often interrupted by leisurely halts to sit on vantage points and stop at question marks.*"

Infra, p. 400.

LAND
AND
LIFE

A SELECTION FROM THE WRITINGS OF
CARL ORTWIN SAUER

EDITED BY
JOHN LEIGHLY

UNIVERSITY OF CALIFORNIA PRESS
BERKELEY AND LOS ANGELES · 1967

University of California Press
Berkeley and Los Angeles, California
Cambridge University Press
London, England
© 1963 by The Regents of the University of California
Library of Congress Catalog Card Number 63-21069
(First Paper-bound Edition)
Printed in the United States of America

Contents

Introduction

Geography as a subject of instruction in American universities has a respectable age, but neither its curricula nor the investigations carried on by its academic representatives have become standardized. This situation, though disadvantageous in some respects, is fortunate in others. The professor of geography has the freedom of an extremely wide field, in almost any part of which he may find fruitful soil awaiting cultivation. One consequence of the freedom that the scholarly geographer enjoys is that the work of any one man is a peculiarly individual contribution, often overlapping but slightly that of his colleagues. Moreover, in the absence of an accepted pattern of scholarly activity, differences in intellectual quality among the practitioners of geography are more conspicuous than in more standardized fields of learning. If the pedestrian mind appears more heavy-footed here than elsewhere, the first-class mind finds room for longer and higher flights.

The present volume brings together some of the products of a first-class mind. The circumstance that Carl Sauer has elected to work, and has worked freely and imaginatively, in an ill-defined and unspecialized field of scholarship makes his writings of interest to an audience more inclusive than the group in which the structure of learned institutions places him. All who share in any degree Sauer's concern with the quality of human life on the earth will find in his work enlightenment and stimulation. I write "human life"; but human life can not exist without the interposition, between it and the inorganic constituents of our planet, of the complex web of plant and animal life that sustains it. Sauer has therefore had to concern himself with nonhuman life on the earth as well. Hence the general title of the volume, the alliterative conjunction of "land" and "life" that Sauer, without ostentation or self-consciousness, has used more than once in his writings.

Carl Sauer probably needs no introduction to many of the readers of this book. To others a few biographical facts may be useful. He was born in Warrenton, Missouri, December 24, 1889, the son of a teacher in Central Wesleyan College, a now defunct German Methodist college in Warrenton. In his boyhood his parents placed him in a school at Calw, a town in western Württemberg at the eastern foot of the Schwarzwald. In this school he received better instruction than did most of his midwestern contemporaries. The advantage he gained from this instruction enabled him to earn the A.B. degree at Central Wesleyan before his nineteenth birthday, and the Ph.D. in geography at the University of Chicago before his twenty-sixth. The next phase of his academic career was similarly accelerated: he advanced from the rank of instructor to that of professor at the University of Michigan in the seven years from 1915 to 1922. In 1923 he came to the University of California, Berkeley, as professor of geography, which position he held until his retirement in 1957. During most of this time he was chairman of the Department of Geography at Berkeley. Soon after coming to California he began his scholarly exploration of Mexico, and in the course of time pushed his investigations still farther into the American lands south of the United States.

When Sauer was a graduate student, the University of Chicago provided the only significant graduate program in geography in the United States. It was a good program, directed by R. D. Salisbury, whose memory Sauer cherishes, like all who studied under Salisbury. Salisbury was a geologist and geomorphologist, but by the time when Sauer was a student the program in geography at Chicago had already assumed the form, including work in economic and human geography, that became a model for other and younger American departments. In later years many American academic departments of geography have almost or entirely abandoned interest in the physical earth. Most of Sauer's scholarly work has been done in human geography, but he has never permitted his feet, or those of his students, to lose contact with the sustaining surface of the earth. The instruction he received at Chicago included much more than courses in geography; the ideas derived from outside the department in which he was inscribed that recur most frequently in his writings are from plant ecology, which he studied under H. C. Cowles. His reconstructions of past relations of man to vegetation, for example, represented in the papers grouped as Part III of this volume, rest on interpretations of the ecology of plants. Moreover, he makes much use of ecological analogies in his discussions of human groups and cultures. In human geography the dominant theme in the United States in Sauer's student days was that geography is concerned with "influences" exerted by the physical attributes of the earth on human beings, including their cultures. Ellen Churchill Semple, the most learned and eloquent expositor of the doctrine of "influences," lectured at Chicago. Sauer heard her lectures, and maintained until her death a warm personal friendship with her; but though environmentalism left some traces in his earliest writings it does not dominate them.

Doctrines of mechanical determinism, whether environmental or other, appeal primarily to those who look on human beings as objects moved by some remote and impersonal power, whose remoteness and impersonality are shared in some degree by the exponents of such doctrines. Sauer is incapable of looking at his fellow men from any such Olympian distance. In writing about people on the earth, he views them with sympathy, in the truest etymological sense of that word. In the preface to his doctoral dissertation, on the Ozark highlands of his native Missouri, he wrote: "The people who move upon the scene of this account are homefolks one and all." These people were "homefolks" by virtue of the place of his birth and upbringing. But when in later years he has had occasion to write of people among whom he first came as a stranger he has made "homefolks" of them, too, by sympathetic involvement in their every-day activities, however humble. In "The Road to Cíbola," included in Part II of the present volume, worthies dead four hundred years, perhaps especially the rascally Fray Marcos and the ill-fated Negro Esteban, are warmly present, not mere names in crabbed Spanish handwriting. In his reconstructions of life in "the farther reaches of human time," to which much of his writing in the last two decades has been devoted, and which provide the papers included here as Part IV, his first aim is to recapture in his imagination the daily activities of the primitive household, the fundamental unit in the ecology as well as in the wider social structure of humanity. He evokes the image of the solicitous mother, providing for the needs of her offspring and extending her maternal care to the young of other animals, thus laying the foundations of the cultivation of plants and the domestication of animals. Except for the Promethean gift of fire, to which Sauer has also given attention in one article included in Part IV, these techniques, acquired in the remote dawn of human prehistory, remain for him the greatest cultural accomplishments of mankind. More than anything else, his appreciation of simple people living in close contact with inorganic nature and in symbiosis with plants and animals distinguishes Sauer's writing about man on the earth. It was nurtured by his association with such people in Missouri, in Kentucky, and especially in the out-of-the-way parts of Mexico in which he spent much time in the nineteen-twenties and -thirties. His Pleistocene people are, indeed, extrapolations to simpler cultural conditions of humble folk he has observed in Latin America.

Closely related to Sauer's sympathetic involvement in the everyday affairs of simple people is a strong ethical bent. Once in a conversation with him an economist colleague supported his side of a conflict of opinion with the remark, intended to clinch his argument, "I am an economist." Sauer replied, with equal assurance, "We are moralists." The ethic Sauer has had most frequent occasion to avow, as in the penultimate paragraph of "The Education of a Geographer," here reproduced as the final paper in Part V, is an ethic of responsibility for man's terrestrial inheritance, which has suffered such appalling depletion under the impact of technology. His abhorrence of irresponsible destruction of the bounty and beauty of the earth led him into his principal public services: in his Michigan days a leading part in the establishment of the Michigan Land Economic Survey, and in the nineteen-thirties an active participation in the work of the fledgling Soil Conservation Service. An international Symposium on Man's Role in Changing the Face of the Earth held at Princeton, New Jersey, in 1955, for whose organization Sauer was largely responsible, provided the occasion for his most mature utterance on this theme. His principal contribution to this symposium has recently been republished elsewhere [1]; hence nothing from it is included here.

Whoever reads much in Sauer's writings finds, in fact, that Sauer has always been concerned with man's role in changing, intentionally or unintentionally, the face of the earth in directions determined by his immediate needs. These changes are most conspicuous when men move into new dwelling places. The words "pioneer" and "frontier"

---

[1] "The Agency of Man on the Earth," *in* Philip L. Wagner and Marvin W. Mikesell, edits., Readings in Cultural Geography (Chicago, 1962), pp. 539–557; reprinted from William L. Thomas, Jr., edit., Man's Role in Changing the Face of the Earth (Chicago, 1956), pp. 49–69.

are among the ones that recur most frequently in Sauer's writings. In his pages people are usually on the move or establishing themselves in new surroundings. They burn the grass and trees, plant in newly cleared woodland, break the prairie sod, seek the best places for their houses, adapt as well as they can the local resources to their inherited or newly discovered needs. When in his earlier years Sauer wrote of settled districts in the Middle West, as in the first two items in Part I of the present collection, he gave as close attention to the conditions of establishment of settlement as to those that obtained at the time when he was making his observations in the field. The shaping of the cultural landscape is a cumulative process, each stage of which conditions the next one; the first stage is therefore the most critical one. Writing of the formerly Spanish territories in North America, as in the material included here in Part II, Sauer is mainly concerned with the probing and prospecting of the Spaniards northward from the site of their first foothold. His primitive human beings move tentatively into new areas. try out new foods and new ways of providing for themselves, and follow the migrations of plants and animals in the wake of the retreating ice sheets. Consciousness of the frontier has been with him from the beginning: he recalls, in "Homestead and Community on the Middle Border," in Part I, boyhood memories of "movers" passing westward in their wagons through Missouri, and family traditions from the time of his grandparents, when the Middle West itself was still a frontier.

An omnivorous and retentive reader, Sauer has always reflected intellectual influences arising far beyond the ideas current in American academic geography. In the preface to his doctoral dissertation he cites, as examples he wished to emulate in that work, French regional monographs, which he still commended in later programmatic writings. The authors whose points of view are recognizable for the longest time in his work are Friedrich Ratzel and Eduard Hahn. The Ratzel whose thinking recurs in Sauer's is the author, in particular, of the second volume of the *Anthropogeographie,* not the one interpreted—or misinterpreted—by Miss Ellen Semple. This second volume has the subtitle "Die geographische Verbreitung des Menschen," in which the word "Verbreitung" carries not only the static meaning of "distribution," but also the kinetic connotation of "spreading" from initial points of establishment, such as is observed in organisms other than man. Hahn directed Sauer's attention to the symbiosis implied in the bringing of plants under cultivation and animals under domestication. These influences emanating from the world of scholarship articulate closely with interests prompted by his personal experience and observations.

The sequence of Sauer's substantive writings, which may be followed in the chronologic order of his bibliography, represents a consistent unfolding of interests within a broad but recognizable field as the years brought him time and opportunity for accumulated observation and reflection. The direction and rate of his movement from one object of investigation to another have been of his own choosing, without regard to the artificial boundaries that divide learning. Occasionally he has accorded recognition to these boundaries, however, and from his nominal place within them has addressed words of admonition to his colleagues. Four such admonitory utterances make up Part V of this book. The first of these, "The Morphology of Landscape," is included because of the impact it had upon American academic geography. It was an attempt on Sauer's part to define for geography a firm position within the general field of scholarship. Many others have participated in the quest for such a position, rarely with as much learning as Sauer brought to it. This and other methodological writings by Sauer from the middle nineteen-twenties had one salutary effect: they gave the death blow to the doctrine of environmental determinism that had dominated American geography since the turn of the century. The positive effect of this paper was, unfortunately, to stimulate a spate of detailed descriptions of small areas written in the ensuing twenty years, which had little value, either scholarly or practical. Long before the echoes of "The Morphology of Landscape" died away in departments of geography Sauer had outgrown his temporary inclination to define geography by setting narrow limits to it. In his two ceremonial addresses to the Association of American Geographers included in Part V, "Foreword to Historical Geography" and "The Education of a Geographer," he expressly repudiates most of the doctrines he propounded in the "Morphology," and commends to his colleagues principles and objects of investigation as free and inclusive as the ones he himself has pursued. In "Folklore of Social Science," addressed to a wider audience, he inveighs against a more recent mechanistic heresy than environmental determinism: the investigation of human beings and their behavior by mechanical processes of organization and computation. This departure from humane scholarship is as repugnant to him as the one he demolished many years earlier.

A temperament such as Sauer's inevitably finds distasteful much of American culture in the twentieth century, with its blatancy, haste, and crowding. He has consistently avoided matters that command immediate but temporary attention, except in his efforts to salvage something of our imperiled earthly heritage. He has found escape from the obtrusive ugliness of our culture, which does not spare the academic community, in the exploration of remote times and places. That kind of withdrawal is familiar in American intellectual history; one needs to think only of Henry Thoreau and John Muir as examples. It is equally in this American tradition that its bearers bring back to those that have ears to hear words of wisdom and warning. It is a risky venture to try to summarize in a few words the fruits of an inquiring and catholic mind active through many years; but if one hazards such a distillation of what Carl Sauer has learned and taught, it can be expressed approximately thus: There is such a thing as a humane use of the earth; the simpler cultures are less destructive of the terrestrial basis of man's existence than is our present technology; and the possessors of modern technology may find in the past experiences of man on the earth guidance toward a balance of the capacities of the land with the requirements of life that gives some promise of permanence.

The present volume is by no means a collection culled from Sauer's complete works. He is still producing learned papers, and in all probability there are articles still unpublished or unwritten that would, if they were available, deserve a place in a selection such as this. The papers and extracts presented here reflect, however, the wide range of matters with which Sauer has been concerned through nearly fifty years. Selection of the material for this kind of book depends on the availability of papers of moderate length or of passages in longer works that can survive excision. The least representative section of the volume is Part II, based on the work that has occupied more of Sauer's time in the field and has yielded more pages in his publications than has any other part of his scholarly activity. Most of his writings on Mexico and adjoining parts of the United States are too long to be included, and are not readily divisible. The reader who would follow Sauer along other Mexican trails than "The Road to Cíbola" must be referred to these longer works, which are listed in the bibliography that follows the main body of the volume.

I have touched the original published text of these selections as lightly as possible, limiting myself to changes in punctuation and the correction of a few obvious errors. References to literature, which are often sketchy in Sauer's writings, are completed and put into a uniform style. In "Foreword to Historical Geography" I have supplied citations of literature that was familiar to the audience to which it was originally addressed, but may not be to all readers of this volume. I am indebted to Miss Eleanor Blum, of the University of Illinois, Urbana, for help with obscure topographic literature cited imperfectly in the original publication of "Conditions of Pioneer Life in the Upper Illinois Valley" and inaccessible to me in Berkeley.

Grateful acknowledgment is due the following institutions for their generous permission to republish material to which they hold the copyright:

The American Geographical Society of New York, for "The Personality of Mexico," "Early Relations of Man to Plants," "A Geographic Sketch of Early Man in America," and "The End of the Ice Age and Its Witnesses," all of which were originally published in *Geographical Review*.

The University of Minnesota, for "Folkways of Social Science," from: *The Social Sciences at Mid-century: Essays in Honor of Guy Stanton Ford;* published for the Social Science Research Center of the Graduate School by the University of Minnesota Press, Minneapolis; copyright 1952 by the University of Minnesota.

JOHN LEIGHLY

Berkeley, California,
January, 1963.

PART I

The Midland Frontier

Conditions of Pioneer Life in the
Upper Illinois Valley

PROBLEM OF THE PRAIRIES

The newly arrived emigrant found himself in a region to which his old home offered few parallels. In spite of the voluminous advice of guide books for emigrants, he was a stranger in a strange land. One of the great problems that confronted the settler from the wooded hills of New England was the almost level and nearly treeless prairie, which covered much of the state.

The prairies of Illinois are essentially the uneroded, drift-covered upland, and the wooded lands are chiefly narrow belts, marginal to the valleys of the streams. At the time of settlement, the woods and the prairies were distributed as follows:[1] (1) Southern Illinois was chiefly woodland, with small detached prairies in the interstream areas. (2) South and west of a line from Rock Island to Peoria, and thence to Champaign, mixed woodland and prairie prevailed, the proportion of prairie to woodland increasing away from the Mississippi Valley. (3) North and east of this line the land was mostly prairie. East-central and northern Illinois were covered by a younger till sheet than the country to the west and south, and hence the northeastern part of the state is less dissected by streams and also has less timber. The belt of woodland along the Illinois Valley divides this region into two parts, the eastern of which was known as the Grand Prairie. (4) The extreme northwestern part of the state, which remained unglaciated, was a wooded area.

The counties of the upper Illinois Valley belong to the third of

Geography of the Upper Illinois Valley and History of Development. Illinois State Geological Survey, Bulletin 27, 1916, pp. 153–163.

[1] "Map of Illinois Showing Its Prairies, Woods, Swamps and Bluffs," *in* Frederick Gerhard, Illinois as It Is (Chicago and Philadelphia, 1857). Redrawn as Figure 35, p. 69, of Harlan H. Barrows, Geography of the Middle Illinois Valley, Illinois State Geol. Survey, Bulletin 15, 1910.

the divisions mentioned, in which the valleys of the Illinois and
its tributaries formed the largest timbered area. The pioneer in
this region had the choice of homesteading in the timber, or at its
margin, or out on the open prairie. During the first years, homesteads were taken up in the timber or along its edge; the open prairie
was avoided, and many thought it must always remain waste land.
In 1821 a man sent to explore the upper Illinois Valley for a colonization site reported that he had found there no site suited for such
a purpose.[2] Even in 1834 a traveler wrote of the desolation of these
plains.[3] Some of the objections to the prairie were based on super-
stitions that were soon dispelled, others were due actually to adverse
conditions. Some of the objections were: (1) One of the early super-
stitions held that the prairie was a desert, unable to support any
vegetation other than native grasses. The absence of timber was
considered an evidence of the poverty of the land. This idea was
expressed by Monroe in a letter to Jefferson: "A great part of the
territory is miserably poor, especially that near Lake Michigan and
Erie, and that upon the Mississippi and Illinois consists of extensive
plains which have not had from appearances, and will not have, a
single bush upon them for ages. The districts therefore within which
these fall will perhaps never contain a sufficient number of inhabitants
to entitle them to membership in the Confederacy."[4] This notion
soon was disproved, as the settlers became acquainted with the rich
black soil and the luxuriance of the grassy growth upon it. (2) Another prejudice, less readily discredited, pictured the winter climate
of the prairies as too severe for human habitation. Wonderful tales
of the bitter western winters circulated through the country for
years. In Hoffman's "A Winter in the Far West" are painted dole-
ful pictures of the winter climate, and emphasis is placed on the
prodigious effect of the freezing winds from the Rocky Mountains
which "do sorely ruffle; for many a mile about, there's scarce a
bush." "The general impression was that only the timber belts would
ever be inhabited. The prairie, swept by the fires of summer and
the piercing blasts of winter, seemed little better than a desert, and
for several years there was not a cabin in Grundy County, built more

---

[2] Elmer Baldwin, History of La Salle County, Illinois (Chicago, 1877),
pp. 76–78.

[3] C. F. Hoffman, A Winter in the Far West, Vol. 1 (London, 1835), pp.
239–240.

[4] S. M. Hamilton, edit., The Writings of James Monroe, Vol. 1 (New
York, 1898), p. 117.

[5] O. L. Baskin & Co., publ., History of Grundy County, Illinois (Chicago,
1882), p. 148.

than 100 yards from the timber." [5] The belief that the prairie was treeless because of the severity of the winter remained prevalent for some time. (3) The tall grasses of the prairie were highly inflammable when dry, and the danger from fires was great to the first prairie homesteads. A prairie fire, once started, might sweep over miles of the nearly flat surface faster than man could ride. In numerous instances houses and crops were destroyed by such fires. (4) The matted roots of the prairie grasses formed a tough, heavy sod which the pioneer found difficult to break with the weak tools and the few draft animals in his possession. Heavier plows were made presently, and in a few years a plow was developed with a mouldboard shaped especially to turn the heavy sod. In a few years also, the farmer's stock had increased so that he no longer was handicapped by a lack of working animals. (5) The apparent lack of water on the prairie deterred settlers. Only after some time did they discover that water was accessible by shallow wells almost everywhere on the prairie. (6) In areas remote from wooded valleys, the lack of wood formed an insuperable barrier to settlement. Timber for buildings, fences, fuel, tools, and other purposes was an absolute necessity. (7) The large prairies were unavailable for settlement so long as the only means of transportation was by wagon or horseback. The cost of hauling farm products to market and of getting necessities not produced on the farm limited the pioneer settlements to sections which could ship by some waterway.

For these and other reasons, the settlement of the prairie was difficult. In the timbered belt, on the other hand, conditions were favorable for homesteading. Cultivable land was to be had in the creek bottoms, and at the edge of the prairies, where the sod was less heavy than farther from the timber. The hillsides furnished many springs of good water. Near them the frontiersman generally built his cabin and his barn. The valley slopes also sheltered buildings from prairie fires and winter winds. Above all, here was timber in abundance, and here, in most cases, the pioneer had easy access to water routes.

The pioneer was thus limited by the conditions of his environment to the timbered areas. The first homes were built in or along the edge of the best timber.[6] Even now, descendants of some of the first settlers speak of "the old homestead down in the timber," which has been abandoned in most cases for a modern home well out on the prairie. A number of large timbered valleys favored the early settlement of La Salle County, and their absence retarded settle-

---

[6] Elmer Baldwin, *op. cit.,* p. 87.

ment in Grundy County. In La Salle County the first pioneers settled in the valleys of the Illinois, the Big Vermilion, and the Fox. A dozen families that settled along the timber of Nettle and Au Sable creeks in the early thirties formed the nucleus of settlement in Grundy County. In Putnam County, immigration "spread over the country in every direction, like a flood, so that nearly every grove of timber soon found an inhabitant." [7] In Bureau County, the earliest settlements were along the timber of Bureau Creek.[8] The northern and western parts of Bureau County, the southern and northwestern parts of La Salle County, and the northern part of Grundy County are all open prairie, and these sections were not settled until years later. In the rest of the region the expansion of settlement from woodland to the adjacent prairie came about easily and naturally.

IMPROVEMENT OF THE HOMESTEAD

In all his activities the pioneer had to adapt himself to his new surroundings. Institutions and methods brought from the East were modified to meet the needs of his altered conditions.

The establishment of a "claim" required at first merely that the settler cultivate and harvest a crop, the amount thereof not being specified. "A rail fence of four lengths was often seen on the prairie, the ground enclosed, spaded over, and sowed in wheat." [9] The right to land was secured by its possession. Most of the people living in the region were homesteaders, and they banded together, when occasion demanded, for the protection of their interests against land speculators. If a settler failed to file a pre-emption claim, his neighbors saw that he had the opportunity to bid in his land at the minimum price when it was offered for sale. Speculators were handled roughly by settlers if they attempted to bid in improved claims. By the primitive law of the pioneer, every settler had a right to the place on which he had located, and anyone who interfered was apt to meet with violence.[10]

The first improvement that the settler provided was shelter for himself and his goods. In a few days he could build a log cabin with

---

[7] Samuel Augustus Mitchell, Illinois in 1837 (Philadelphia, 1837), p. 100.
[8] H. F. Kett & Co., publ., The Voters and Tax-payers of Bureau County, Illinois (Chicago, 1877), p. 87.
[9] Elmer Baldwin, op. cit., p. 131.
[10] Ibid.

the ready help of his neighbors. "Let a man and family go into any of the frontier settlements, get a shelter or even camp out, call upon the people to aid him, and in three days from the start he will have a comfortable cabin, and become identified as a settler." [11] Cabin-raising offered an opportunity to the neighbors for miles around for a welcome holiday to relieve the monotony of the frontier life. In most cases the materials for the cabin were secured on the homestead. Rudely hewn logs were used for the walls, and logs more carefully split provided the puncheon floor, if there was such a luxury. Wooden pins were used instead of nails, and at the corners of the cabin the logs were secured by being notched and fitted into each other. Cracks in the wall were chinked with clay. The chimney was generally built of timber and plastered inside and out with a mortar of sand and clay. Furniture and utensils were homemade. Bedsteads commonly were built into the corners of the cabin, and were of the most simple construction.[12]

Breaking the sod was a long and arduous task for the early settler. The sod was strong and heavy, the plows were weak and clumsy, and his stock was generally in none too good condition. The earliest practice consisted in hitching six to ten yoke of oxen to a plow that cut a furrow two to three feet wide.[13] To the plow was attached a heavy plow beam, framed into an axle and supported by clumsy wheels cut from oak logs. These unwieldy plows fortunately soon were supplanted by the light highly polished shear plow, which slipped through the heavy sod like a knife.[14] The improved plows turned up a strip of turf 18 to 24 inches wide, required only three yoke of oxen, and effected a considerable saving of time.[15]

Wild prairie grasses furnished food for the livestock until the first crop was raised. They tided many a farmer over the period while he was breaking the ground and growing his first crop and was without other food for his work animals. The wild grasses made excellent hay, especially those which grew on low ground.[16] Patches of prairie grass were often kept for pasturage, but com-

---

[11] Samuel Augustus Mitchell, *op. cit.,* p. 68.

[12] Elmer Baldwin, *op. cit.,* p. 134, gives an animated description of the building of such a cabin.

[13] *Idem,* p. 136.

[14] Daniel S. Curtiss, *Western Portraiture and Emigrants' Guide* (New York, 1852), p. 291.

[15] Samuel Augustus Mitchell, *op. cit.,* p. 14, quoting Lewis C. Beck, A *Gazetteer of the States of Illinois and Missouri* (Albany, 1823).

[16] Elmer Baldwin, *op. cit.,* p. 171.

monly they were killed out in a few years, as they were not well adapted to grazing.

The first crop planted was almost invariably corn. The first year's yield was known as "sod corn," and made about half an average crop.[17] Methods of planting were born of the exigencies of the times; in many cases the upturned turf was gashed with an axe, and the seed corn dropped in.[18] After the first crop a harrow could be used, and the ground was put in fairly good shape for the second crop. This was often some small grain such as wheat or barley, though in many fields corn was raised exclusively for many years. On the whole, agricultural methods were crude and inefficient. As land was to be had almost for the asking, and anyone could grow enough to support himself and family, careful husbandry was not necessary. Wheat, for instance, was sown among the corn stalks of the previous summer's growth. It is said that the crops produced were on the average not more than half as large as they are today.

Agricultural machinery came into general use before 1850. Drills and harvesters were among the first to be introduced, and soon were used almost universally. By 1850 mowing machines and threshers had proved successful.[19] The use of farm machinery spread much more rapidly in this section than it did in the eastern states, for labor was difficult to secure so long as homesteads were waiting for entry; also the nearly level prairie surface made farming by machinery particularly easy and profitable.

So long as large areas of prairie grass remained, there was great danger of prairie fires. "From the first frost until spring, the settler slept with one eye open, unless the ground was covered with snow." [20] Until most of the land had been put into cultivation, it was customary to protect the farm buildings by plowing a strip about the farm yard, to save the buildings, if not the crop.

The cost of securing a homestead and improving it was not great. In many cases the only cash expended was the fee of $1.25 per acre paid to the land office. Breaking the prairie sod was estimated to cost about $2 an acre. The cost of fencing was greater than the initial cost of the land. Cabin and outhouses cost little or nothing, if timber was close at hand. It was estimated by contemporary writers that a quarter section could be bought and improved for $1000 or less.[21] The opportunities were unsurpassed for men of limited

---

[17] Samuel Augustus Mitchell, *op. cit.,* p. 14, quoting Lewis C. Beck, *op. cit.*
[18] Elmer Baldwin, *op. cit.,* p. 137.
[19] Daniel S. Curtiss, *loc. cit.*
[20] Elmer Baldwin, *op. cit.,* p. 145.
[21] Samuel Augustus Mitchell, *op. cit.,* pp. 14, 69.

means who were willing to bear hardships and could labor patiently.[22]

FARE OF THE PIONEER

For a number of years the settler was limited virtually to the produce of his farm, as markets were inaccessible, and as he had no means of disposing of his surplus. His food was simple, but sufficient. Corn meal, hominy, potatoes, and pork comprised his bill of fare; later, wheat flour was added. The first industry established in the region was grist milling. The first mill was built at Dayton in 1830, and for a short time its nearest competitor was the mill at Peoria.[23] Soon a second mill was built on Indian Creek, and in 1841 a large grist and flour mill was built at Marseilles on the Illinois River. These mills supplied the central part of the upper Illinois and the lower Fox River country. In the early thirties grain was shipped from Bureau County for grinding. In the eastern part of the region a mill was built at Channahon in 1837. In many places no grist mill was accessible, and the settler or, more often, his wife ground the meal by hand, generally by pounding corn in the mortar. Bad weather and bad roads forced many a family to live for weeks on meal prepared in this manner.

There were times when crops failed and provisions had to be shipped into the region. Transport was difficult and tedious, and famine came close to many homes at such times. Food is known to have been brought from points hundreds of miles distant. It is related that at one time two men traveled to central Illinois, a distance of almost 200 miles, to buy corn, have it ground, and bring it to the upper Illinois settlements. On another occasion a keelboat was sent down the Illinois to the settlements on the Sangamon River to buy grain for the settlers about Ottawa.

INSTITUTIONS AND SOCIAL LIFE

Unlike the settlers from the South, the Northern pioneers of this area came from a densely peopled region in which farms were small, and in which many of the people lived in villages or towns. They

[22] Anonymous, The Progress of the Northwest, The Merchants' Magazine and Commercial Review, Vol. 3, 1840, pp. 22–40. Reference to p. 35.

[23] H. F. Kett & Co., publ., Past and Present of La Salle County, Illinois (Chicago, 1887), p. 182.

had, therefore, developed social institutions to a more advanced form than their Southern neighbors. Church, government, and school were transplanted from New England to the prairie home. A number of colonies brought their minister, almost invariably Congregational, and most of them erected a house of worship almost as soon as they had built their cabins. Schools also were valued highly. In 1828 a "select" school was organized at Ottawa, and in a few years a log school house stood by the side of the log meeting house, and both were attended with equal zeal. The first courthouse and jail were built at Ottawa in 1830, three years after the first election had been held. The township government of this part of the state is also a Northern institution, imported bodily.

Pioneer days offered little opportunity for social contact. Settlers were few and scattered widely, roads were often impassable, and the task of improving the homestead required unceasing attention. Pioneering was especially hard on the women, who were kept at home almost constantly by their household duties. The isolation and monotony of pioneer life broke down many settlers, or impaired seriously their working ability. Baldwin, pioneer historian, says that homesickness was a real disease, in some cases a deadly one. "The bodies only of a great many people and not their minds" lived in the country of their adoption.[24] There could be slight progress as long as the heart of a man was still in his eastern home, and his mind turned unwillingly to the problems of his new surroundings. Naturally every opportunity to break this isolation was seized upon eagerly, and holidays were celebrated with an enthusiasm which seems strange and crude today. Log-cabin raisings, elections, political campaigns, corn-husking bees, and above all camp meetings— these were the entertainments of the pioneers. To these simple pleasures the people looked forward eagerly, and from them they drew food for later reflection and conversation.

News was scarce and traveled slowly. Stray copies of newspapers were read eagerly for news of the outside world. The first local newspaper was established at Hennepin in 1837. Two years later, a weekly sheet began publication at Peru. In 1840 the *Ottawa Free Trader* was established. It was not until 1852 that a newspaper was started in Grundy County; at this time half a dozen papers were issued in the upper valley. Because of the devious and slow means of communication and consequent lack of news, these early

---

[24] Thomas Ford, A History of Illinois, from its Commencement as a State in 1818 to 1847 (Chicago and New York, 1854), p. 230.

papers were filled largely with poetry, essays, and stories. The few local happenings were supplemented by clippings from the metropolitan papers whenever they could be secured. The early local sheets published particularly news from the St. Louis dailies brought by boat. In the forties, European news was generally five weeks old, and news from the Atlantic coast two weeks old. Harrison's death, for instance, was reported as a rumor after twelve days, and confirmed after nineteen. In the press, as in all other social institutions of the day, the isolation of the pioneer finds expression as the dominant feature of his life.

HEALTH CONDITIONS

The prairie states, notably healthful now, once were reputed very unhealthful. This early opinion was in part superstition based on a general distrust of the prairies. That sickness, however, was much more prevalent in the pioneer days than at present is well known. Among the early settlers the few physicians and consequent lack of medical attention may be assigned as one reason. Most of the settlers were ignorant of hygiene and neglected the drainage and sanitation of their premises. The nearly level prairie afforded little or no natural drainage, so that often the accumulated refuse of the farm polluted the water which the settler drank and the air which he breathed. Climatic conditions were new and strange, and it took the settler some time to adjust himself to them. Finally, the prairie itself probably bore the seeds of sickness to a greater extent than it does today. There were many stagnant pools of water, and most of the soil was ill drained. Under such conditions malaria, typhoid, and similar fevers were prevalent.

"Fever and ague" were the scourge of the pioneer and were thought generally to be caused by the breaking up of the prairie sod from which were said to issue "poisonous miasmas," especially in late summer and fall. Chills and fever broke up the Northampton colony near La Salle. The summer of 1838 was marked by an exceptional amount of sickness; in the river towns nearly all were sick and many died, and at La Salle there were said to be 300 graves in the fall on which it had never rained. A heavy spring flood followed by extreme heat in August is said to have favored the development of disease from the backwater of the river.[25] When the

---

[25] Elmer Baldwin, *op. cit.,* p. 159; O. L. Baskin & Co., publ., *op. cit.,* p. 151.

farmers learned to build away from marshes, on elevations with natural drainage, their health improved greatly.[26] As the ground became cultivated, the surface drained, and the farms supplied with well water, malarial fevers tended to disappear, and the evil reputation of the prairies gradually was forgotten.

TRANSPORTATION

During the first years, the settler found neither time nor urgent need for the construction of transportation lines. Until he had improved his homestead and won from it a living, he could not give attention to means of communication. As long as his farm yielded no surplus, the pioneer had scant need of markets in which to exchange his products. These were the days of home-made products, from food to clothing. A few primitive stores supplied tools, tobacco, drugs, and the other articles which the simple needs of the people demanded. During this period the only highways were those furnished by nature—streams and the level surface of the prairie —and for a time they were reasonably adequate.

The Illinois River was the first great highway of this part of the state, and by it the first settlers came into the region. In 1825 a man named Walker came up the Illinois in a keelboat as far as Ottawa, and for the next decade the Illinois River furnished the principal connection with the world outside. The upper river was of some importance commercially until about 1860, but after 1848 it served chiefly as a feeder to the Illinois and Michigan Canal. The earliest river traffic was carried by log canoe, keelboat, barge, and raft. These craft usually were home made, and were used only to float produce downstream, although an occasional boat, laden with provisions from the South, was towed against the current. Before 1820 steamboats had been adapted to the needs of navigation on inland rivers, but not until 1831 did the first steamboat penetrate to the upper Illinois Valley. For several years afterward only an occasional boat ventured above Peoria.[27] Ottawa was the absolute head of navigation, but except in time of flood boats could not pass the rapids above Utica. Even Utica was not a satisfactory shipping point because of the bars built into the Illinois below it by the

---

[26] Samuel Augustus Mitchell, *op. cit.,* p. 69.
[27] Henry Allen Ford, The History of Putnam and Marshall Counties (Lacon, Ill., 1860), p. 96.

Vermilion rivers. Most of the steamboats, therefore, stopped at Peru, which became the chief river town of the upper valley. It was situated where the stream washes the base of a high terrace on the northern side of the valley. The site afforded good landing and protection from floods. Depue was the other river town of this region. The Illinois River was never of such importance to the people of this section as to the people of the middle and lower valley. Little mention of steamboating or river traffic is made, either in the press of the day or in local history. The bars and rapids of the river cut off the eastern two-thirds of the region from the benefits of river transportation. In 1848 the Illinois and Michigan Canal diverted the trade of the region eastward, and thereafter a large part of the river traffic consisted of through cargoes from the South and West, shipped to New York by way of the canal.

Wagon trails across the prairie were used frequently. The earliest traces followed Indian trails, beaten paths a foot or two wide in the sod.[28] Several of the early roads were originally mail routes. In 1828 Kellogg's trail was laid out from Peoria to Galena, and along it were made the first settlements in Bureau County, namely Senachwine, Boyds Grove, and the settlements on Bureau Creek.[29] In 1832 a mail route was established from southern Illinois to Chicago via Decatur, Ottawa, and Fox River. A few years later the settlers began to haul their surplus products to Chicago, and in the middle thirties a number of roads were worn by the loaded market wagons. It was at this time that the Bloomington-Chicago road, which passed through southern Grundy County, began to be outlined by the droves of livestock going to market and the return teams hauling salt and supplies.[30] In the thirties also a road from Ottawa to Joliet and Chicago was established. Such a road, once fixed, was followed carefully, as it was easy to get lost, or at least to wander from the direct road on the featureless prairie.[31] After rains, and during the spring thaw, the roads became impassable for weeks at a time. Bridges were unknown in this part of the state, and streams were crossed at fords. At times streams in flood isolated

---

[28] O. L. Baskin & Co., publ., *op. cit.,* p. 152.

[29] H. F. Kett & Co., publ., The Voters and Tax-payers of Bureau County, Illinois (Chicago, 1877), p. 87.

[30] O. L. Baskin & Co., publ., *op. cit.,* p. 155.

[31] Elmer Baldwin, *op. cit.,* pp. 140–141, tells of misleading mirages, of pioneers who lost their lives on the prairie during the winter, and of other adventures of the prairie traveler.

whole settlements from outside communication, and even caused loss of life. It is recorded that before a bridge was built across the Big Vermilion twenty-five people were drowned while attempting to ford the stream in flood time.[32] But crude as were these trails and the conveyances that creaked upon them, they afforded the settlers a means of communication, and the pioneers of eastern La Salle and Grundy counties an outlet to the eastern market.

[32] *Ibid.*

2

The Barrens of Kentucky

IS THERE A QUALITY JUDGMENT INVOLVED
IN THE NAME "BARREN"?

It is supposed that the westward-migrating Southerners held a
strong prejudice against treeless lands, that they avoided these
lands in settlement, and left them in general to be occupied by
later settlers from the North.[1] Certain it is that they, the first-
comers in the prairie states, built their homes along the wooded
valleys. Perhaps their avoidance of the prairie, however, was due
to the fact that it presented a more serious problem to occupation
than did the timbered lands. On this subject the settlement of the
Pennyroyal sheds critical light.

The Pennyroyal was the first important body of grassland encountered in trans-Appalachian settlement. The seaboard South
contained many but minor unforested patches, which held little
difficulty for settlement. When the pioneer encountered the grassy
plains of the Pennyroyal, he promptly called them "barrens." The
same designation was given in part to the prairie areas in Missouri,
when shortly afterward the Kentuckian became the pioneer settler
in that state. The term also had some currency in Illinois. In both
of the latter states, however, it was soon replaced by the local
French term "prairie." When Kentucky was settled, the Americans
did not know the word "prairie." Did the name "barren," as commonly thought, imply adverse judgment of the grassy Pennyroyal?

[The history of settlement of the region gives a conclusively
negative answer to the question. More than a hundred thousand

Geography of the Pennyroyal (Kentucky Geological Survey, Ser. 6, Vol.
25), 1927, pp. 123–130. The opening sentences of the third paragraph are
abstracted from pp. 131–133.
[1] Carl Ortwin Sauer, Geography of the Upper Illinois Valley and History
of Development (Illinois State Geological Survey, Bulletin 27), 1916, pp.
153–156, this volume, pp. 11–14.

immigrants entered the Pennyroyal between 1790 and 1820, and at the latter date this area held 26 per cent of the population of Kentucky. The grasslands of the Pennyroyal did not delay settlement; there is no evidence that there was any odium attached to the term "barrens" applied to them.] The following citations indicate, moreover, that the term was applied because of the absence of the usual forest cover rather than because the lands in question were thought to be unproductive or infertile. We have indeed in our language no English word to designate grasslands other than such special types as "barrens," "meadows," and "glades." Although properly descriptive of very different site conditions, it appears that all three of these terms were used more or less interchangeably in Kentucky, the designation "barrens" gaining the greatest currency. The name is, therefore, to be considered as the result of a dilemma of language rather than as a judgment of fertility.

Filson's well-known map of 1784[2] has, written across the area between the Green and Salt Rivers: "Here is an extensive tract, call'd Green River Plains, which produces no Timber, and but little Water; mostly Fertile, and cover'd with excellent Grass and Herbage." This statement of luxuriance of prairie growth, fertility of soil, and lack of surface water shows a correct and far from unfavorable judgment of the area. In the printed account of the same year Filson uses the term "Green river barrens," apparently not considering it in contradiction to his map.

Gilbert Imlay, Land Commissioner in the Back Settlements, in his account, dated about 1792, gives the report of one supposedly familiar with the country as a competent judge of land. He makes the following significant observations: (1) That to the south of the Ohio in the Elizabethtown area "is a considerable extent of fine land"; (2) "but traveling a few leagues farther southward you arrive at extensive plains, which stretch upwards of one hundred and fifty miles in a southwest course, and end only when they join the mountainous country." This curious topographic note may refer to the "breaks" of the Tennessee River in the western part of the state. (3) As to the quality of the land, his judgment is confused and, in terms of topography, somewhat contradictory. In one passage he affirms that the plain country "is considered little better than barren land," but adds, in the same paragraph, "yet it is of

[2] Accompanying John Filson, The Discovery, Settlement and Present State of Kentucke (Wilmington, 1784). Facsimile in Willard Rouse Jillson, Filson's Kentucke (Filson Club Publication No. 35), 1930.

a superior quality to much of the soil in the lower parts of Virginia, the Carolinas, and Georgia." He points out the abundance of hazel, "which, it is well known, never grows kindly in a poor soil," of grapes, and of other fruit. He then affirms that the land between the Green and the Cumberland, which actually is a part of the plains referred to under (2), is generally rich. His general opinion of the areas which he seems to have known at first hand is rather favorable.[3]

The Elihu Barker map of about 1792, reproduced in Imlay's "Topographical Description," shows (1) a tract of "Barrens" between the Big and Little Barren Rivers, (2) "Barren and Naked Land" in Crittenden and Livingston Counties, (3) an area of "Glades" south of Crab Orchard, and (4) "very good land" on the grassy upland of southern Pulaski County.

Jedidiah Morse, first American geographic compiler, made the following statements in the American Gazetteer of 1797: "Between the mouth of the Green river and Salt river, a distance of nearly 200 miles, the land upon the banks of the Ohio are generally fertile and rich; but, leaving its banks, you fall into the plain country, which is considered as little better than barren land. . . . N. W. of Rolling Fork, a branch of the Salt River, is a tract of about 40 square miles, mostly barren, interspersed with plains and strips of good land, which are advantageous situations for raising cattle, as the neighboring barrens, as they are improperly styled, are covered with grass, and afford good pasturage."[4] Evidently the compiler missed the identity of barrens and plains and became wound up in considerable confusion.

In 1817 the grassy lands south of Russellville, fifteen by ninety miles in extent, were stated to be "prairies . . . rich, finely watered, and . . . sufficient to maintain an immense population."[5] Timothy Flint wrote in 1832: "Between the Rolling Fork of Salt river and Green river is a very extensive tract, called 'barrens.' The soil is generally good, though not of the first quality. Between Green and Cumberland rivers is a still larger tract of 'barrens.'"[6]

---

[3] Gilbert Imlay, A Topographical Description of the Western Territory of North America, ed. 3 (London, 1797), pp. 35–37.

[4] Jedidiah Morse, The American Gazetteer (Boston, 1797), arts. "Green" [River], "Kentucky." Note the language of Imlay reappearing in the Gazetteer.

[5] Samuel R. Brown, The Western Gazetteer or Emigrant's Directory (Auburn, N.Y., 1817), pp. 105–106.

[6] Timothy Flint, The History and Geography of the Mississippi Valley, ed. 2 (Cincinnati, 1832), p. 347.

The designation of the grasslands as "meadows" appears to have been customary principally in the Mountain Margin. Possibly this referred to a rather wet surface, as the name would imply. It is not certain that such was the case, however, as the really wet lands are "flatwoods," and probably were such at the time of settlement. Wayne County received its first settlement shortly after 1780 on the limestone piedmont at Price's Meadow, the local stream still being known as Meadow Creek.[7] The term "glade" was also used somewhat in the Mountain Margin, to designate grasslands partly enclosed by forest, smooth lands at the eastern edge of the limestone plateau. This term suggests an explanation for the "cedar glades" of today. In Kentucky and Missouri the term "glade" is now used to characterize slopes of thin soil, covered with cedar and scant grass. They are demonstrably located in numerous cases on limestone knolls and cove slopes that were originally bare of forest cover, or nearly so, according to local tradition and the evidence of the forest growth. They were parts of larger grassy glades, which were for the most part put under cultivation. The marginal areas of this soil, however, were occupied by cedar after a time, cedar being the most vigorous old-field growth, together with sassafras and persimmon, both also found on such sites, and therefore the vanguard of the forest. These grassy glades became "cedar glades." The normal use of the term "glade" for grassland has disappeared entirely in Kentucky, though it existed a century ago.

NATURE OF THE ORIGINAL VEGETATION

The smooth parts of the Pennyroyal were originally prairie, largely blue-stem grass. The grasslands "were adorned with islets or intersected by groves of timber." [8] "The country, sparsely clad with trees, is covered with grass like a prairie." [9] "Some few clumps of trees, and a grove here and there, are the only obstructions to a boundless horizon. It is pleasant to observe the deer bounding over the scraggy shrubs which cover the earth," adds Imlay, with his penchant for confusing our idea of the local scene.[10] According

---

[7] Arthur McQuiston Miller, Recent Cave Explorations in Kentucky for Animal and Human Remains (Kentucky Geological Survey, Ser. 6, Vol. 10, pp. 107–112), 1923. Reference to pp. 109–110.

[8] Samuel R. Brown, *op. cit.,* pp. 105–106, 83–84.

[9] Timothy Flint, *loc. cit.*

[10] Gilbert Imlay, *loc. cit.*

to oral accounts, groves of large trees were not uncommon, but not extensive, on the smooth upland. The valleys were forested, for the most part heavily so.

ORIGIN OF THE BARRENS

The local grasslands were surrounded by an area of most luxuriant forest growth. In few parts of the country is a more diversified hardwood forest to be found than in the lower Ohio Valley. Louisville, Cincinnati, Evansville, and Nashville were famous lumber markets in the early days, and still draw high-quality logs from their surrounding areas. Memphis is the greatest primary hardwood market in the world today. The Mississippi lowlands, the hill country of the Western Coal Basin, the Knobs, and the Mountains were covered with a splendid growth of giant trees, which completely surrounded the Barrens.

The valleys within the Pennyroyal were heavily forested. Audubon found enormous pigeon roosts in the Pennyroyal along the Green River, which betokened extensive forests.[11] The breaks of the Cumberland and of the lesser streams were covered by heavy forests of old growth. There is nothing in the distribution of forests in this part of the country to suggest that climate or the history of forest migration could explain the lack of forests in the Pennyroyal uplands. Indeed, eastern forest trees, such as the beech, are to be found beyond the western border of the Pennyroyal, and southern forest trees, such as the cypress and the cucumber tree, have pushed their way northward beyond this region. The area was not intermediate between two or more forest zones that had not yet met. It cannot, therefore, be regarded as a relic grassland, but must be considered as an area in which edaphic conditions were unsuited to tree growth, or one that had become deforested, in which the forest islands and tongues were remnants of a vanished forest, not outposts of an invading forest.

The partial correlation between grassland and cavernous limestones has suggested a causal connection between the nature of the soil and vegetation. This was expressed at an early date by David Dale Owen, who said: "It is altogether probable that there was a peculiar tendency in the soil to produce that luxuriant growth of barren grass which took possession of the soil, to the exclusion of

---

[11] John James Audubon, The Birds of America, Vol. 5 (New York and Philadelphia, 1842), pp. 28–29.

all timber, and which is described as having attained a heighth of
five to six feet." [12] He offers this, however, only as a partial explanation of the grassy condition. The smoother parts of the Greens-
burg area, underlain by the Waverly limestones, appear to have
been similarly grass-covered, and dissected parts of the cavernous
limestones were generally tree-covered. The correlation appears
to be entirely with topography, the lack of forest growth on the
cavernous limestones resulting from the smoothness of their surface.

There is popular unanimity in ascribing the barrens to fires. Fires
were set, first by Indians, later by whites, in order to improve grazing, and in part in order to drive game. Fires burn against the
slope. They spread readily over a smooth surface, but normally
will not descend a steep valley unless driven by a very favorable
wind. The smooth lands, probably containing a mature forest with
little undergrowth, were gradually cleared, by oft-repeated burning, of most of their timber. Owen reported the opinion of the
natives seventy years ago as follows:

> The old inhabitants of this part of Kentucky all declare that when the
> country was first settled it was, for the most part, an open prairie district,
> with hardly a stick of timber sufficient to make a rail, as far as the eye could
> reach, where now forests exist of trees of medium growth, obstructing en-
> tirely the view.
>
> They generally attribute this change to the wild fires which formerly used
> to sweep over the whole country, in dry seasons, being now, for the most part,
> avoided or subdued, if by accident they should break out. No timber appears
> to be capable of surviving the scorching effect of such fires, but the thick-
> barked black-jack oak, which, here and there resisting its ravages, stood soli-
> tary monuments of its hardy nature, and the blasting influence of the prairie
> fire.[13]

Much later N. S. Shaler, a native of Kentucky, made the following statement:

> While the Indians used this region as a hunting ground, the district be-
> tween Louisville and the Tennessee line, extending thence westerly along
> the southern border of Kentucky to the Cumberland River, was mostly in
> the condition of prairies. Except near the streams and on the margins of this
> so-called 'barren district,' the forests were scarred by fire. There were no
> young trees springing up to take the place of the old and thick-barked veterans
> of the wood, which from the hardness of their outer coating could resist

[12] David Dale Owen, Report of the Geological Survey of Kentucky Made
during the Years 1854 and 1855, Vol. 1 (Frankfort, 1856), p. 84.
[13] *Idem*, pp. 83–84.

flame. When these mature trees died they had no succession and so the prairie ground became gradually extended over the area originally occupied by the forest. After the Indians were driven away, about 50 years elapsed before the country was generally settled, and in this period the woods to a considerable extent recovered possession of the areas of open ground. The periodic firing of the grass having ceased, seeds were disseminated from the scattered clumps of wood, and soon made them the centers of swiftly spreading plantations. It was the opinion of the late Senator Underwood, who had seen this country in the first years of the present century and who was a most intelligent observer, that the timberless character of this district was entirely due to the habit which the aborigines had of firing the grasses in the open ground.[14]

We have here probably an illustration on a large scale of the fact that even primitive man is able to modify profoundly his environment by the aid of his most powerful tool, fire. That fires had been sweeping these lands for a long time is abundantly attested. That the Indians were in the habit of setting fires has not been disputed. What the original condition of the forest was is not known. It probably was an open, mature forest, under which grass and herbage grew at least fairly well. The area, quite unoccupied at settlement by resident Indian tribes, appears to have been at an earlier date the home of a numerous population, possibly for a very long time. Along the valley margins are extraordinarily numerous indications of aboriginal population. Burial grounds, mounds, heaps of spalls, stone implements and weapons scattered through fields and along roadsides and discoverable after every heavy rain, kitchen middens under rock shelters, the very quantity of ruins and debris left behind in this area points to an unusually important archeologic site. It is perhaps significant that the Ozarks, which present similar records of ancient and important aboriginal population, also show the same feature of deforested upland flats, though their geologic formations are very different from the Pennyroyal.[15] Perhaps in both cases we are dealing with a primitive cultural landscape in these grasslands, due to unusual length of aboriginal occupation, and to the greater ease of modification of vegetation in an area of smooth uplands than in a region of more diversified relief. Was the upper margin of the interior mesothermal climate the site of an important early, potamic culture

---

[14] Nathaniel Southgate Shaler, The Origin and Nature of Soils (U.S. Geol. Surv., 12th Ann. Rept., Part 1, pp. 213–345), 1892, pp. 324–325. See also John Hussey, Report on the Botany of Barren and Edmonson Counties (Geological Survey of Kentucky, 1884, Part B, pp. 34–58), p. 35.

[15] Carl O. Sauer, The Geography of the Ozark Highland of Missouri (Geogr. Society of Chicago, Bull. 7), 1920, pp. 53–55.

of which the barrens, like the great mounds of the Mississippi and Missouri Valleys, are witnesses? Though amateur collecting is wiping out more and more the Indian relics, it is perhaps still possible by field study to determine the extent to which the area contained an aboriginal culture antedating the homesteads of the Shawnees, who were the last Indian residents, presumably dislodged from this area at the beginning of the eighteenth century.

THE REINTRODUCTION OF FORESTS

All accounts later than the first quarter of the nineteenth century refer to the barrens as a past or passing condition. Thus Davenport, about 1830, speaks of "a few years since, a beautiful prairie . . . now covered with a young growth of various kinds of trees. These, however, do not prevent the growth of grass."[16] In 1833 it was said: "Here the hills are isolated knobs, wooded with oak, chestnut, and elm. . . . The soil is far from barren though much of the timber has a stunted appearance." The country near the Cumberland Valley "has been transformed within a few years from an extended and unbroken prairie into forests of thrifty and valuable timber."[17] In 1853 it was claimed that the upper Green River basin was still "thinly wooded, and covered in summer with grass growing amid scattered and stunted oaks."[18] Owen reported in 1855: "Since the settlement of the country this grass has become almost extinct, whereby opportunity has been afforded for timber to take root and flourish."[19] John Muir, in his foot tour of 1867 across the middle Green and Cumberland Valleys, reported black oaks, "many of which were sixty or seventy feet in height, and are said to have grown since the fires were kept off, forty years ago."[20] Hussey in 1875 still remarked upon the poverty of the forest floras in Barren County, a condition that is hardly noticeable at present.[21]

These various accounts suggest the following association of

---

[16] Bishop Davenport, A New Gazetteer, or Geographical Dictionary, of North America and the West Indies (Baltimore, 1833), p. 130.

[17] William Darby and Theodore Dwight, Jr., A New Gazetteer of the United States of America (Hartford, 1833), art. "Kentucky."

[18] Richard Swainson Fisher, A New and Complete Statistical Gazetteer of the United States of America (New York, 1853), p. 344.

[19] David Dale Owen, *loc. cit.*

[20] John Muir, A Thousand-mile Walk to the Gulf (Boston and New York, 1916), p. 6.

[21] John Hussey, *op. cit.*, p. 34.

events: the suppression of fires through settlement, the deterioration of the wild sod through grazing and its destruction by the plow, the spread of forest from valley sides and upland copses, and the gradual immigration of more numerous forest species. Today the land that is not cultivated is well covered with trees. Knolls on the plains, swampy flatwoods, worn pastures, and abandoned fields are the forest sites of the present. The rapidity of forest invasion in the past century indicates that the checks upon it previously were not those of climate or soil. For the second time man appears to have changed fundamentally the vegetational formation of the area. The Pennyroyal would be a fruitful field for careful ecologic study to determine whether the stage of forest succession has again reached equality with the forested areas round about. The local prevalence of red cedar on thin slopes appears to indicate that an early stage of forest invasion is still characteristic of parts of the area. The local tradition is that the stands of cedar are very much more extensive than they were even a half-century ago.

3

Homestead and Community
on the Middle Border

The date of the Homestead Act, 1862, marks conveniently for our recall a moment of significance in the mainstream of American history, the great westward movement of families seeking land to cultivate and own. This started from states of the Eastern seaboard, swelled to surges across the wide basin of the Mississippi-Missouri, and ebbed away in the High Plains. The Middle Border, as it has been named appropriately, was the wide, advancing wave of settlement that spread over the plains south of the Great Lakes and north of the Ohio River, making use of both waterways as approaches. Its advance made Cleveland, Toledo, and Chicago northern gateways. At the south, it gave rise to border cities on rivers, such as Cincinnati on the Ohio, St. Louis at the crossing of the Mississippi, and Kansas City on the great bend of the Missouri. The Mississippi was crossed in force in the 1830's, the Missouri River into Kansas in the border troubles before the Civil War. Although it did not begin as such, this became the peopling of the prairies, the founding and forming of the actual Midwest.

The Homestead Act came pretty late in the settlement of the interior. Land had been given free of cost to many. It had been sold at nominal prices and on easy terms by public land offices and by canal and railroad companies. The squatter who settled without title was generously protected by pre-emption rights and practices that grew stronger. Many millions of acres had been deeded as homesteads before the Act and many more continued to be acquired by other means afterwards. Land was long available in great abundance. The price in money of the wild land was the least cost of making it into a farm. Public land offices were set up to get land into private hands quickly, simply, and cheaply.

Landscape, Vol. 12, No. 1, 1962, pp. 3-7.

THE INDIAN LEGACY

The American settler acquired learning that was important for his survival and well-being from the Indian, mainly as to agricultural ways. The settler was still a European in culture who had the good sense to make use of what was serviceable to him in the knowledge of the Indians of the eastern woodlands. This learning began at Jamestown and Plymouth and was pretty well completed before the Appalachians were crossed.

Little seems to have passed from the Indians of the interior to the settlers. The Indian culture west of the Appalachians was still significantly based on cultivation, more largely so than is thought popularly to have been the case. Whether the western Indians contributed any strains of cultivated plants had little attention until we get much farther west, to the Mandans of the Upper Missouri and the Pueblo tribes of the Southwest.

Dispossessed of title to home, deprived of their economy and losing hope that there might be another start, many Indians were reduced to beggary or lived as pariahs about the white settlements. Their debauch was completed by alcohol, a thing wholly foreign to their ways, which became for them a last escape. Objects of despair to one another and of contempt and annoyance to the whites, the time was missed when the two races might have learned from each other and have lived together.

Most of the earlier American pioneers of the Mississippi Valley came by a southerly approach. They were known as Virginians and Carolinians, later as Kentuckians and Tennesseeans, and in final attenuation as Missourians. They came on foot and horseback across the Cumberlands and Alleghenies, usually to settle for a while in Kentucky or Tennessee and thence to move on by land or river and cross the Ohio and Mississippi rivers. The relocations of the Lincoln and Boone families are familiar examples.

THE FIRST WAVE

Theodore Roosevelt hailed the main contingent of pioneer settlers as Scotch-Irish, Mencken stressed their Celtic tone and temperament, Ellen Semple saw them as Anglo-Saxons of the Appalachians. Whatever their origins, and they were multiple, these were the back-

woodsmen who brought and developed the American frontier way
of life. They were woodland farmers, hunters, and raisers of livestock in combination, and skilled in the use of axe and rifle. Trees
were raw material for their log cabins and worm fences, and also
an encumbrance of the ground, to be deadened, burned, or felled.
The planting ground was enclosed by a rail fence, the livestock
ranged free in woods or prairie. When the New Englander Albert
Richardson reported life in eastern Kansas in the time of Border
Troubles (*Beyond the Mississippi*) he said he could tell the home
of a settler from Missouri by three things: the (log) house had
the chimney built on the outside and at the end of the house; the
house was situated by a spring which served for keeping food in
place of a cellar, and one was given buttermilk to drink. He might
have added that there would be corn whiskey on hand and that
if the family was really Southern the corn bread would be white.

This colonization was early and massive, beginning by 1800 and
having the new West almost to itself until into the 1830's. At the
time of the Louisiana Purchase, American settlers already held
Spanish titles to a million acres in Missouri alone, mainly along
the Mississippi and lower Missouri rivers. Their homes and fields
were confined to wooded valleys, their stock pastured on the upland
prairies. Nebraska alone of the mid-continent remained almost
wholly beyond the limits of their settlement.

Viewed ecologically, their occupation of the land was indifferent
to permanence. Trees were gotten rid of by any means, the grasslands were overgrazed, game was hunted out. They were farmers
after the Indian fashion of woods deadening, clearing, and planting, and made little and late use of plow or wagon. The impression
is that they gave more heed to animal husbandry than to the care
of their fields or to the improvement of crops. Central and northwest Missouri, for example, the best flowering of this "Southern"
frontier, developed the Missouri mule early in the Santa Fe trade,
and later bred saddle and trotting horses and beef cattle.

THE WAVE FROM THE NORTH

The great northern immigration set in in the 1830's and depended
from the beginning on improved transportation: the Erie Canal,
steamships on the Great Lakes, stout and capacious wagons. It
continued to demand "internal improvements," the term of the time
for public aid to communication, first canals and soon railroads,

only rarely constructed, and surfaced roads. Wagon transport, however, was important and a wagon-making industry sprang up in the
hardwoods south of the Great Lakes. It may be recalled that the
automobile industry later took form in the same centers and by
using the same skills and organization of distribution. Canals, most
significantly the Illinois and Michigan Canal completed in 1848,
linked the Great Lakes to rivers of the Mississippi system for shipping farm products to the East. Railroads were first projected as
feeder lines to navigable waters. The first important construction,
that of the Illinois Central, was chartered in 1850 to build a railroad from Cairo at the junction of the Ohio and Mississippi rivers
to La Salle on the Illinois and Michigan Canal and on the Illinois
River. It was given a grant by Congress of two million acres of
land.

This last great movement of land settlement was out on to the
prairies and it differed largely in manner of life and kind of people
from the settlement of the woodlands. It depended on industry and
capital for the provision of transportation. It was based from the
start on plow-farming—cast-iron or steel plows to cut and turn
the sod, plows that needed stout draft animals, either oxen or heavy
horses. By 1850 agricultural machinery had been developed for cul-
tivating corn and harvesting small grains, and was responsible for
the gradual replacement of oxen by horses as motive power.

The prairie homestead differed from that of the woodlands, in
the first instance by depending on plow, draft animals, and wagon.
It, too, grew corn as the most important crop, in part for work
stock but largely to be converted into pork and lard by new, large
breeds developed in the West that were penned and fed. Fences
were needed, not to fence stock out of the fields but to confine it.
The livestock was provided with feed and housing. The farm was
subdivided into fields, alternately planted to corn, wheat, oats,
clover, and grass, arranged in a rotation that grew the feed for
the work animals and for the stock to be marketed. A barn was
necessary for storage and stabling. This mixed economy, its cash
income from animals and wheat, spread the work time through
the seasons and maintained the fertility of the land. It was a self-
sustaining ecologic system, capable of continuing and improving
indefinitely, and it was established by the process of prairie settlement. There was no stage of extractive or exhaustive cultivation.

By the time of the Civil War—in a span of twenty years or so—
the prairie country east of the Mississippi, the eastern half of Iowa,
and northern Missouri were well settled. Some counties had reached

their highest population by then. My native Missouri county had twice its current population in 1860. More people were needed to improve the land and to build the houses and barns than it took to keep the farms going. Some of the surplus sought new lands farther West, much of it went into building up the cities. These people who settled the prairies were farmers, born and reared, out of the Northeast or from overseas, first, and in largest number, Germans and thereafter Scandinavians. They knew how to plow and work the soil to keep it in good tilth, how to care for livestock, how to arrange and fill their working time. They needed money for their houses and barns, which were not log but frame structures with board siding. The lumber was mainly white pine shipped in from the Great Lakes, long the main inbound freight. They needed money as well as their own labor to dig wells and drain fields. The price of the land, again, was the lesser part of the cost of acquiring a farm. The hard pull was to get enough capital to improve and equip the homestead, and this was done by hard labor and iron thrift. This is a sufficient explanation of the work ethic and thrift habits of the Midwest, often stressed in disparagement of its farm life. In order to have and hold the good land, it was necessary to keep to a discipline of work and to defer the satisfactions of ease and comforts. The price seemed reasonable to the first generation who had wrested a living from scant acres in New England or to those who had come from Europe where land of one's own was out of reach.

THE END OF THE VILLAGE

Dispersed living, the isolated family home, became most characteristic of the "Northern" folk on the frontier. In Europe nearly everyone had lived in a village or town; in this country the rural village disappeared or never existed. Our farmers lived in the "country" and went to "town" on business or pleasure. The word "village," like "brook," was one that poets might use; it was strange to our western language. Land was available to the individual over here in tracts of a size beyond any holdings he might ever have had overseas. The village pattern was retained almost only where religious bonds or social planning prescribed living in close congregation.

Normally the land holding was the place where the family lived, and this identification became recognized in the establishment of title. The act of living on the land occupied was part of the process of gaining possession. As time went on, prior occupation and improvement of a tract gave more and more weight to pre-emption rights; living on the land protected against eviction and gave a first right to purchase or contract for warranty of ownership. The Homestead Act was a late extension of the much earlier codes of pre-emption, by which possession by residence on the land and improvement could be used to secure full and unrestricted title.

The General Land Survey established the rectangular pattern of land description and subdivision for the public domain. Rural land holdings took the form of a square or sums of squares, in fractions or multiples of the mile-square section of land. The quarter section gradually came into greatest favor as the desired size of a farm and became the standard unit for the family farm in the Homestead Act. Thus four families per square mile, a score or so of persons, were thought to give a desirable density of rural population. The reservation of one school section out of the thirty-six in a township, for the support of primary public schools, provided an incentive for the only kind of public building contemplated in the disposal of public lands. Four homes to the square mile, and about four schools to the six-mile square township, gave the simple general pattern for the rural geography of the Midwest. The pattern was most faithfully put into effect on the smooth upland prairies. Here the roads followed section lines and therefore ran either north-south or east-west, and the farmsteads were strung at nearly equal intervals upon one or the other strand of the grid. It is curious that this monotony was so generally accepted, even a clustering of homes at the four corners where the sections met (and giving the same density) being exceptional.

Little attention has been given to the site where the house was placed or to the assemblage of the structures that belonged to the farm. The choice of location was of importance, as, for instance, in exposure to wind and sun.

The logistics of home location is an attractive and hardly investigated field of study, as is, indeed, the whole question of the rural landscape and its changes. The location of house and farm, cultural preferences of different colonizing groups, microclimatic drainage and sanitation were unrecognized, the toll paid in typhoid and "summer complaint."

Building was starkly utilitarian and unadorned. Neither the log cabin of the woodlands nor the box-shaped farm house of the prairies, nor yet the sod house of the trans-Missouri country (made

possible by the sod-cutting plow) was more than compact and economical shelter, varying but little in each form. Ready-cut houses,
of standard and simple pattern, were already offered by railroads
to buyers of their land, an early form of tract housing. Quality of
house and quality of land seem to be in no relation. The embellish-
ment of the home and the planting of the yard were left mostly
to the second generation, for country town as well as farm. The
history of the dissemination of ornamental trees and shrubs might
be revealing, perhaps to be documented through the nurseries that
sprang up from Ohio to Nebraska.

The economy, from its beginnings, was based on marketing products, but it also maintained a high measure of self-sufficiency. Smoke-
house, cellar, and pantry stored the food that was produced and
processed on the farm. The farm acquired its own potato patch,
orchard, berry and vegetable garden, diversified as to kind from
early to late maturity, for different flavors and uses, selected for
qualities other than shipping or precocious bearing. The farm
orchards now are largely gone, and the gardens are going. Many
varieties of fruits that were familiar and appreciated have been
lost. A family orchard was stocked with diverse sorts of apple trees
for early and midsummer sauce, for making apple butter and cider
in the fall, for laying down in cool bins in the cellar to be used,
one kind after another, until the russet closed out the season late in
winter. The agricultural bulletins and yearbooks of the past century invited attention to new kinds of fruits and vegetables that
might be added to the home orchard and garden, with diversification, not standardization, in view. Exhibits in the county and state
fairs similarly stressed excellence in the variety of things grown,
as well as giving a prize for the fattest hog and the largest pumpkin.

THE SELF-SUFFICIENT FAMILY

The Mason jar became a major facility by which fruit and vegetables were "put up" for home use in time of abundance against
winter or a possible season of failure in a later year. The well-
found home kept itself insured against want of food at all times
by producing its own and storing a lot of it. The family, of ample
size and age gradation, was able to provide most of the skills and
services for self-sufficiency by maintaining diversified production
and well-knit social organization. This competence and unity was

maintained long after the necessity had disappeared. As time is measured in American history, the life of this society, and its vitality, were extraordinary.

Looking back from the ease of the present, these elder days may seem to have been a time of lonely and hard isolation. It was only toward the end of the period that the telephone and rural delivery were added. The prairie lacked wet-weather roads. In the hill sections, ridge roads might be passable at most times; on the plains, winter was likely to be the season of easiest travel, spring that of immobilization by mud. The country doctor was expected to, and did, rise above any emergency of weather. Life was so arranged that one did not need to go to town at any particular time. When the weather was bad the activities of the family took place indoors or about the farmyard. In our retrospect of the family farm as it was, we may incline to overstress its isolation. The American farmstead did not have the sociability of rural villages of Europe or of Latin America, but the entire family had duties to learn and perform, and times of rest and diversion. It depended on a work morale and competence, in which all participated and in which its members found satisfaction. Perhaps it suffered fewer social tensions and disruptions than any other part of our society.

Though living dispersed, the farm families were part of a larger community, which might be a contiguous neighborhood or one of wider association. The community in some cases got started on the Boone pattern of a settlement of kith and kin. A sense of belonging together was present to begin with, or it soon developed. The start may have been as a closed community; it was likely to continue in gradual admission of others by some manner of acceptance. Consanguinity, common customs, faith, or speech were such bonds that formed and maintained viable communities through good times and bad. The Mennonite colonies are outstanding examples. The absence of such qualities of co-option is shown in the Cherokee strip, opened as a random aggregation of strangers.

The country church played a leading part in social communication, differing again according to the particular confession. Catholic and Lutheran communicants perhaps had more of their social life determined by their church than did the others. Their priests and pastors were most likely to remain in one community and to exercise and merit influence on it. Parochial schools extended the social connections. Church festivals were numerous and attractive. Sunday observance was less austere. The Methodist Church, on the other hand, shifted its ministers, usually every two years. In a half-century of service my grandfather was moved through a score of charges in five states. The high periods of the Methodist year were the winter revival meetings and the camp meetings in summer after the corn was laid by. For some, these were religious experiences; for others, especially for the young people, they were sociable times, in particular the camp meeting, held in an attractive, wooded camp ground where one lived in cabins or tents on an extended picnic. Almost everyone belonged to some church, and most found a wide range of social contacts and satisfactions thereby.

The churches also pioneered higher education, founding colleges and academies across the Middle West, from Ohio into Kansas, before the Civil War and before the Morrill Act fathered the tax-supported colleges. These church-supported small colleges, about fifty of which still exist, first afforded education in the liberal arts to the youth of the prairie states; and they did so by coeducation. Their students were drawn not only from nearby, but also from distant places by their church affiliations. In these colleges humane learning was cultivated and disseminated. Their campuses today are the Midwest's most gracious early monuments of the civilization aspired to by its pioneers.

Country and town were interdependent, of the same way of life, and mostly of the same people. By a tradition that may go back to the town markets of Europe, Saturday was the weekday for coming to town to transact business (note the pioneer implications in the term "to trade") and to visit. The town provided the services, goods, and entertainment that the farm family required. In time, it also became home for the retired farmer.

The era of the Middle Border ended with World War I. Hamlin Garland introduced the name in 1917 in his *A Son of the Middle Border,* a retrospect he made in middle age. Willa Cather, growing up on its westernmost fringe in Nebraska, drew its life in quiet appreciation in her two books written before the war, and then saw her world swept away. Some of us have lived in its Indian Summer, and almost no one was aware how soon and suddenly it was to end. A quarter section was still a good size for a family farm, and the farm was still engaged in provisioning itself as well as in shipping grain and livestock. It was still growing a good crop of lusty offspring. The place of the family in the community was not significantly determined by its income, nor had we heard of standard of living.

DECLINE OF THE MIDDLE BORDER

The outbreak of the war in 1914 brought rapidly rising demand and prices for supplies to the Allies and to American industry. Our intervention in 1917 urged the farmer to still more production: "Food Will Win the War" that was to end all wars. He made more money than ever before, he had less help, he was encouraged to buy more equipment and more land. The end of the war saw a strongly industrialized country that continued to draw labor from the rural sections. Improved roads, cars, tractors, and trucks made the horse unnecessary, and thereby the old crop rotation broke down. Farming became less a way of life and more a highly competitive business for which the agricultural colleges trained specialists as engineers, chemists, economists, to aid fewer and fewer farmers to produce more market goods, to widen their incomes against the rising cost of labor, taxes, and capital needs. This became known as "freeing people from the land," so that now we have about a tenth of our population living on farms (among the lowest ratios in the world), and these are not reproducing themselves.

The Middle Border now belongs to a lost past, a past in which different ways and ends of life went on side by side. We have since defined the common welfare in terms of a society organized for directed material progress. For the present, at the least, we control the means to produce goods at will. We have not learned how to find equivalent satisfactions in jobs well done by simple means and by independent judgment that gave competence and dignity to rural work. The family farm apprenticed youth well for life there or elsewhere, and it enriched the quality of American life. It will be missed.

PART II

The Southwest and Mexico

4

Historical Geography and the Western Frontier

THE NATURAL LANDSCAPE AS THE BASE OF THE FRONTIER

The three major questions in historical geography are: (1) What was the physical character of the country, especially as to vegetation, before the intrusion of man? (2) Where and how were the nuclei of settlement established, and what was the character of this frontier economy? (3) What successions of settlement and land utilization have taken place?

Even in the West we are dealing today largely with cultural landscapes, for the transforming hand of man is seen conspicuously in unsettled and uncultivated tracts as well as in those taken over by agriculture and town sites. In California, certainly, it would be hard to locate any body of land which has an unaltered vegetation. Grazing has been carried on in valley and coastal grasslands, on mountain meadows, and in desert ranges to such an extent that the plants now growing are very different from those in existence a century ago. The wild oats, alfilaria, bur clover, and mustard which give character to California grasslands above all other plants are all European immigrants. The margins between grass and brush lands have been largely altered. Lumbering, fire, and between-seasons pasturing are largely affecting the composition of our western forests. The western ranch industry has modified the native plant and animal life in so widespread and fundamental a manner that plant geography today is pretty well a study of plant successions that are taking place under conditions imposed by man. Even

---

James F. Willard and Colin B. Goodykoontz, edits., The Trans-Mississippi West: Papers Read at a Conference Held at the University of Colorado June 18–June 21, 1929 (Boulder, 1930), pp. 277–289.

our arid lands do not faithfully reproduce today the conditions
that were found by the first chroniclers.

The white man's culture has altered largely the natural drainage in the West, in the Southwest in particular. Where the San
Pedro of Arizona found its way across a reed- and rush-grown floor
by a series of *cienegas* a half-century ago, today a sandy wash has
been sunk fifty feet into the bottom of the valley. Much of the
cultivable land is gone, the water table is lowered, springs have
disappeared, and the maintenance of a road in the valley has been
made difficult and in places impossible. Where in 1846 Cooke's
wagon train of the Mormon Battalion moved across the easiest
trail to California, and where the Spanish-Pima fort and settlement
of Quibari stood in the eighteenth century, now is a country of
ravines that is almost impassable on horseback. Kirk Bryan in particular has called attention to the very recent origin of the sandy
and gravelly washes in New Mexico. In Lower California, in Arizona, in Sonora it has been possible for us to check this observation
that the "characteristic" arid-country arroyo is in large measure
induced by civilization. By initiation of erosion, lowering of water
table, alteration of soil profile, and change in composition of the
wild vegetation, far-reaching alterations of the physical site have
been produced in many localities, which may simulate a recent increase in aridity in the drier sections of the country.

In order to evaluate the sites that were occupied, it becomes necessary to know them as to their condition at the time of occupation.
Only thus do we get the necessary datum line to measure the amount
and character of transformations induced by culture. The means
for such reconstructions are fairly adequate. They are concerned
first of all with the first surveys, in particular with the surveys of
the General Land Office, with the observations of early visitors,
and with criteria that may still be found in direct field study. In
California, the hearings on land titles before the United States
District Court provide invaluable archival data. The facts of the
natural landscape become more difficultly legible, the longer they
are neglected. In most parts of the West there are still living pioneers who know the country as it appeared at the time of settlement. The vegetation, especially in forest country, still shows its
earlier composition. Field study can determine relict vegetation
and buried organic rests; even the soil may be diagnostic of a previous forest or grass cover. In these and other ways to determine
specifically, that is, cartographically, what the country was like
at the coming of the first frontier settlers becomes more and more

difficult as time passes. It is precisely this specific determination that
is necessary to understand how and why settlements were made.

THE INDIAN LANDSCAPE

Actually, a very important frontier, or series of frontiers, lies
behind the coming of the white man. The Indian was not the
negligible factor in modifying the country that he is commonly
considered to have been. The disregard of the Indian rests upon
several grounds: (1) The self-justification of the pioneer in dis-
possessing the ancestral occupants of the land; (2) the fact that,
especially through the West, an imperfectly understood cultural
retrogression had affected the Indian populations for some time
before the coming of Europeans; (3) an undervaluation of the
extent to which the Indians had been engaged in agriculture; and
(4) an underestimate of the length of time of Indian occupation
and probably also of the numbers of the Indian population.

It is increasingly apparent that the Indians have been on this
continent for a long time. It is perhaps not yet definitely established that man lived in the New World during the Ice Age, but
evidence in that direction is cumulative. If, then, an Indian residence of some thousands of years antedated the coming of white
men, and in particular since the Indians in most parts of the West,
away from the Pacific coast, were partly agricultural, the opportunities for the development of deforested surfaces and of modified forests were large in the aggregate.

The importance of this theme is greatest, of course, in the humid
parts of the country. There is abundant evidence that the vegetation of the East did not consist of monotonous primeval forests,
but that there was an abundance of open country that was not
climatically determined, the glades, cow pens, and prairies being
in the main deliberate or casual clearings. Fire, accidental and deliberate, has undoubtedly greatly enlarged the open spaces through
this long period. For the West, the significance of clearing is still
entirely problematic, though some of our California grasslands
and in particular the characteristic open park-like stands of ancient
oaks in grassy country, which commanded the attention of early
visitors and still form one of the characteristic features of the
Coast Ranges, are not known to be climatically determined, but
are significantly grouped about the more important sites of Indian
habitation. Here, perhaps, acorn gathering led to a customary burn-

ing that restricted more and more the range of forest and of chaparral. Neither in California nor in other parts of the West does
there appear to have been any extensive forest clearing by whites.
Many such communities were founded in open tracts that are not
steppes; that is, climatically determined grasslands. The possible
relation of such sites to Indian sites and clearings is worthy of further local inquiry.

The Spanish and American explorers reconnoitred an Indian
country, with Indian guides, between Indian settlements. Routes
of movement and places of settlement were marked out by the experience of Indians in the main. In the East the American frontier
took over crops, methods, and fields of the Indian agriculturists.
Spanish colonization was of course directly an appropriation of the
native peoples, and through them of the land. The Spanish conquest was successful where there were Indians of a number and
character to provide the needed peon class. The encomiendas were
grants of Indian settlements, often of entire political or tribal units.
The missionaries went to the places where the Indians were, ordinarily to the chief settlement of the petty tribal unit that usually
formed the rudimentary Indian state. The missions brought with
them a reduction of the number of Indian settlements and enlargement of the ones chosen as mission sites, but rarely did they mean
new foundations. Only in the mining towns—the *reales de minas*—
do we encounter as a rule new European foundations, and even here
there are frequent exceptions. Concerning the significance of Indian
centers of settlement to the West north of the Spanish frontier I
have no information, but the connections are probably of less importance than elsewhere, except through fur-trading posts.

FRONTIER FORMS AND ECONOMIES

It has been customary to speak of a frontier, supposed to develop
in the successive stages of the hunter-trader-trapper, the herdsman,
the farmer, and the final dominance of the city dweller. This genial
generalization of sociology is, in modern dress, nothing else than
the old culture-stage concept of the Romans, which can be traced at
least as far back as Varro. For the American scene it involves two
postulates: (1) a normal evolution of economy through which all
mankind passes, and (2) the "reversion" of civilized man to "primitive conditions" when he goes out to a frontier of settlement. Eduard
Hahn well discredited the presumed succession in primitive society.

Also, civilized man retains many attributes and activities of his particular civilization when he transfers himself to a frontier community. No groups coming from different civilizations and animated by different social ideals have reacted to frontier life in identical fashion. The kind of frontier that develops is determined by the kind of group that is found on it. The eternal pluralism of history asserts itself on the American frontier: there was no single type of frontier, nor was there a uniform series of stages. The nature of the cultural succession that was initiated in any frontier area was determined by the physical character of the country, by the civilization that was brought in, and by the moment of history that was involved. The frontier has been in fact a series of secondary culture hearths, of differing origin and composition, which there began their individual evolution. In some cases this evolution has been convergent, but it has not been such so much in terms of the compulsion of a physical environment or of an inherent tendency toward similar development inherent in cultures, but rather because of the will to unity that has come from a growing common political consciousness radiating from the older sections of the country.

Perhaps the major distinction in frontier communities is between those which had a self-sufficient economy and those that depended on specialized production and by their surplus established major commercial connections at the outset. The West was settled largely with commercial objectives, but there are important illustrations of the former type as well. If we are to generalize the types of frontiers, the following functional classification may be suggested: (1) scattered settlement, one-family farmsteads, organized so as to be essentially self-sufficient, the site being determined rather so as to have all things needful for living at hand than by the presence of a particularly valuable resource, such as an abundance of fertile land; (2) scattered settlement based on commercial exploitation of a local resource, illustrated by cattle ranches and grain farms; (3) group settlement primarily for group solidarity, specialization within the community being sufficient to support the group; and (4) group settlement for specific commercial objectives, involving numerous and varied personnel, such as mining and lumber camps.

The first type includes the frontier farm made familiar in the beginning of the westward movement, having its roots in the log-cabin building and clearing activities of the Delaware Swede-Finn colony, its single-farmstead form perhaps introduced by the Scotch-Irish. The technique of agriculture was, however, prevalently that of the Southeastern Indians, with their deadenings, corn-beans-squash crop system, and seed-hill cultivation. This culture, being primarily based on corn, could not be transferred indefinitely westward into the drier grasslands and the mountain meadows of high elevation. How much of it has been carried over I do not know. In the northern Coast Range valleys of California, and here and there on the margins of the Sierra Nevada, small farms, populated from the Upper South, almost unaltered as to manner of living, may be found. The deadening and stump-field system is, however, not widely applicable in the West, because of the wide prevalence of grasslands and coniferous forest, and the relative unimportance of the hardwood stands on which this Indian-Southern frontier depended.

Of much greater importance is the ranch, its prototype being the Spanish *rancho*. In the north of the Spanish territory the rural settlements were missions and ranchos. The busy pens of the missionaries have instructed us much more in the character of their activities than in those of the Spanish laity, to whom, indeed, they referred usually only when labor difficulties arose. In spite of revolution and social reforms, northern Mexico is a country of aristocratic landowners to this day, a land of great ranchos, among which lie the crowded pueblo lands that for the most part were once missions. These northern ranchos rarely appear to have been encomiendas like the more southern estancias and haciendas with their principalities of tilled lands. Indians were not granted with the land in the north, because of the priority of the missions. Labor was scarce, markets were remote, and agriculture was expensive and subject to competition from the mission pueblos. Horses, mules, and cattle were marketable and could be produced with the labor available. In Sonora and Sinaloa, at least, sheep appear to have been adjuncts only of the missions. It is still the tradition of northwestern Mexico to regard sheep and goats beneath the dignity of a man of reason and of substance. I have heard it asserted there that they are inedible. Even today the life, labors, and scenes on opposite sides of the border are remarkably alike away from the irrigated valleys. Perhaps not until the introduction of the windmill and of barbed wire do we get a significant alteration of the ranch system by Americans. The development of the western ranch out of the Spanish-American form is an important field for an institutional study.

In Mexico and in New Mexico the missions are important as conserving agencies of Indian populations, aggregated into pueblos. They have also conditioned some town foundings through the establishment of presidios. In California the missions are rather picturesque architectural remnants of secular conquest through spiritual means than directly important in the explanation of the later economic scenes. Mission agriculture, predisposed to the growing of wheat in California, Arizona, and Sonora, thus laid a foundation for a later crop system, but appears to have had little influence on the horticultural and livestock developments of the West. The moot question of the manner in which the Mormons got their irrigating technique may be answered in the New Mexico missions.

A frontier organized into communities designed to perform all the services of a cultural unit is found in the great Mormon settlement as truly as it was in the New England townships, of which perhaps the Mormon groups are derivative. Mormonism did not allow its Saints to face individually the hazards of the wilderness, but sent them out in close groups to carefully selected localities. Their "stakes" strikingly suggest an improved adaptation of New England settlement, their earlier settlers being almost exclusively New Englanders. Other religious colonies of the West, ranging from Quakers to Mennonites, give parallels in cohesion, planned development, and occupational specialization to the familiar illustrations of the Moravian Brethren in Pennsylvania and North Carolina.

These illustrations may suffice to validate a program of inquiry into the manner of land settlement and the replacement of settlements. For the Atlantic coast we know some of the more important ancestral forms of land settlement, even though the most important cultural nursery of the country, the middle colonies, has been sadly neglected. For the Far West and even the Middle West the sort of work begun in the Domesday Book of the Wisconsin Historical Society cannot be urged too strongly. Precisely, we need to reconstruct many specific early culture landscapes. We need to know what the community was in terms of the exact limits of the individual holdings, whence the settlers came who made up the group, what resources induced them to choose the site, how they laid out their fields and habitations, what they produced for their home consumption and for market, and what were their early errors in land utilization and how they corrected them. In short, we need to know what they did to the country they found and how they changed it.

Where a distinctive cultural group can be identified, the advisable procedure is to block out this group as to area, and proceed from cultural limits to an appraisal of the site that they pre-empted. In the Pacific Coast sections historical culture areas, post-Mexican, are hard to identify as to ancestral type. There were so many strains of immigrants by sea and land that a single California valley may contain as ancestral forms Mexican ranchos, New England village communities, single farms of the southern-frontier type, and Italian vineyard communities. In California the orchard industry seems to have come primarily from New York and in part from middle Europe; the vineyards have a strong north-Italian background; truck growing is derived at least from oriental, Mediterranean, and Portuguese sources; and the grain industry is both Mexican and Middle Western. Our towns are of similarly mixed antecedents, and the strain of social adjustment is still too visible in our architecture. Here a melting pot of cultures has been bubbling vigorously; fusions and new forms, in town and country, are resulting.

Mobility still strikingly dominates the scene of the West. We have areas decadent and partly depopulated, others repeatedly re-oriented. Changes in world and internal market conditions especially affect these western lands, where the people are not long rooted in the soil. A new tariff schedule, a change in immigration policy, the stoppage or creation of an economic demand in another part of the world, all are promptly reflected in our scene, which, like its physical background, has maintained in this part of the world an extraordinary measure of lability. This land of the West is not yet settled, its forms are far from cast. We may still see frontiers developing. To trace the record that man has been writing on the earth as the tenant thereof, to see the differences and agreements in his aims and results as expressed by culture areas, are objectives that may contribute to the culture history of the West and lead to an understanding of its present diversity. We do not believe that this land has been quite standardized into the dull purlieus of a monotonous Main Street, nor, knowing its richly varied background of nature and man, do we anticipate for it such an ending.

5

The Road to Cíbola

THE THEME AND ITS APPROACH

In the New World the routes of the great explorations have usually become historic highways, and thus has been forged a link connecting the distant past with the modern present. For the explorers followed main trails beaten by many generations of Indian travel. There was, in varying degree, intercommunication and exchange of goods between Indian villages or tribes. The resultant trails were as direct as the terrain, the need of food and drink en route, and reasonable security permitted, and were fixed by long experience as the best way of traversing a particular stretch of country. Explorers, being sensible men if their explorations succeeded, used Indian guides who took them over Indian roads. By and large, European colonization still found these routes useful. Men on horses had the same need of saving distance, of finding easy passes and stream crossings, and of food and drink, that directed the Indian's travels afoot. Footpaths and pack trails rarely differ. Only as the white man brought new economic interests, such as the search for mines, and mechanized transport, such as railroads, did he break away from the primitive routes of communication. Even then there has been a large measure of survival of the earlier historic and prehistoric highways.

The land passage through northwestern New Spain was mostly by one great arterial highway, which is a good illustration in point. From the densely peopled lands of central Mexico a road led by way of the coastal lowlands of the Mexican Northwest to the northern land of the Pueblo Indians, and, at the last, to California (see map). It is here called the Road to Cíbola, since the search for the legendary Seven Cities was the main reason for its opening by the Spaniards.

Initially the road was a well used series of Indian trails. Tur-

Ibero-Americana: 3, 1932.

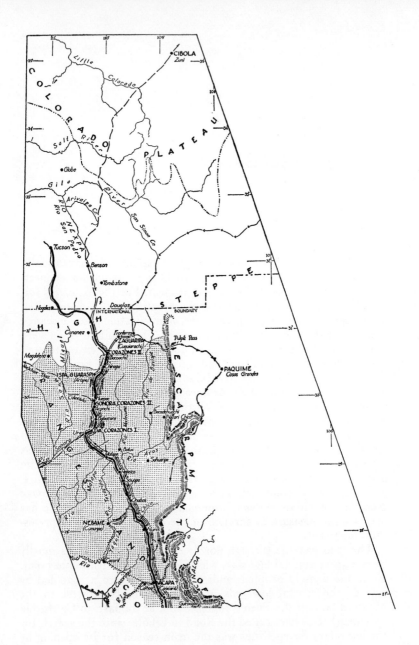

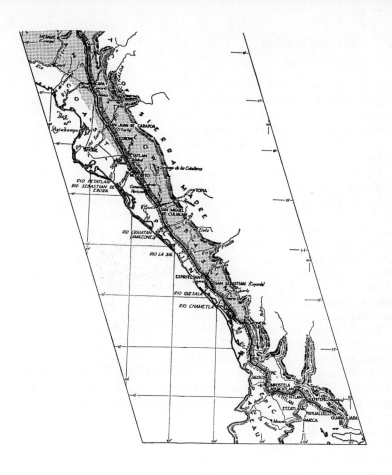

ROAD TO CIBOLA

:::::::: Ranges and Low Basins.
- - - - Approximate boundary of Colorado plateau.
━━━━ Camino real.
⊢━N━ Francisco Cortés - 1524 - 25
- - - Nuño de Guzman - 1530 - 31
•••••• Diego de Guzman - 1533 -
←━━ Cabeza de Vaca - 1535 - 36
-•-•- Fray Marcos - 1538 - 39
━━━ Coronado - 1540,
➤━━ Ibarra - 1564 - 65
Names in use in period of exploration
are in Capitals.
Modern names, Lower-case.

Scale
80   40   0   40   80   40 MILES

quoise was carried south over it; the plumage of parrots and other brightly colored birds of subtropical lowlands furnished the most important articles taken north. Buffalo skins, shells and pearls, metals, obsidian, were other trade items of more or less importance. Maize appears also to have been an item of barter when there was a local crop failure.

The successive Spanish explorations blocked out bit by bit the whole route, from the plateau of Jalisco to the Zuñi country on the Colorado Plateau. Mostly these explorations followed one continuous Indian trail. Later, the route of the explorers became the *camino real* of the frontier provinces of Sinaloa, Ostimuri, and Sonora, connecting the missions, presidios, mines, and ranchos of the northwest with Guadalajara and interior Mexico. Only during the nineteenth century did the establishment of ports on the coast and the building of railroads destroy gradually the importance of the old overland route and bring about a shift of settlement into a previously unimportant coastal zone.

The study here presented is a by-product of five field seasons spent in Arizona, Sonora, Sinaloa, Nayarit, and Colima, and was supported by grants from the Board of Research of the University of California and, in the fall of 1931, by a John Simon Guggenheim Memorial Fellowship. During field work directed to other ends, I became increasingly aware of the persistence and importance of this one great land route, which has never received the attention it deserves. Although there exists a large literature on the various explorers, the commentators have not realized the extent to which one expedition retraced the steps of the others, nor have they had, with the exception of Bandelier, the advantage of knowing the country. I had occasion to cover, by car, on horseback, and afoot, virtually all the country between the Gila River on the north and the Rio Grande de Santiago at the south. I have seen all but a very few miles of the route herein examined, and have been over a good deal of it a number of times and at different seasons of the year. In the light of this knowledge of the country a reinterpretation of the historical evidence was indicated, which differs in numerous particulars from the views previously advanced.

It does not appear necessary to state herein all the points of agreement and disagreement with other students, nor to cite more than the critical passages of the documents concerned. To do so would enlarge the presentation greatly and unnecessarily. The major documents are easily available, as are the principal comments thereon.[1]

---

[1] Sources and secondary materials are exhaustively and critically presented by Hubert Howe Bancroft (Works, Vol. 15 [San Francisco, 1886], chaps. 3

THE SEARCH BY CORTÉS FOR "THE SECRET
OF THE WESTERN COAST" [2]

Since Cortés initiated the northwestern discoveries and with better
luck probably would have carried them through to definitive results,
it is proper to begin with the mention of certain events in which he
was concerned. The capture of the Aztec capital gave control of the
Aztec state and admitted the conquerors, with little show of resistance, to all the civilized Indian principalities of the Mexican center
and south. The second stage of the conquest consisted in appropriat-
ing the rich and populous country west and north of the city of
Mexico and thereby in blocking out the western and northern limits
of the lands of high culture. This was done by a series of rapid
reconnaissances, receiving the allegiance of the native chiefs where
freely given, returning with stronger armed parties where resistance
was encountered. A distinct reconnoitering wedge was promptly
pushed westward, chiefly to get news of the trend of the seacoast,
which it was still hoped would disclose a short cut from Europe to
the Orient. The men of Cortés thus invaded the native state of
Colima in 1522, and in the following year established the Spanish
villa of Colima as a base for further operations northwestward.

An ancient Asiatic legend, that of the Amazon land, is introduced
at this juncture to reinforce the search for a strait to the north of
Mexico. According to Salazar, Cortés first heard of the Amazon

---

and 4, pp. 40–98, and Vol. 17 [San Francisco, 1889], chaps. 1 and 2, pp. 1–
48). Woodbury Lowery, The Spanish Settlements within the Present Limits
of the United States, 1513–1561 (New York and London, 1901), summarizes
contributions to 1900. Elliott Coues, On the Trail of a Spanish Pioneer: the
Diary and Itinerary of Francisco Garcés . . . , 2 vols. (New York, 1900),
has comments on the routes of Fray Marcos and of Coronado in Vol. 2, pp.
479–521. George Parker Winship, The Journey of Coronado, 1540–1542 . . .
(New York, 1904), and A. F. Bandelier's introduction to Fanny Bandelier,
The Journey of Alvar Nuñez Cabeza de Vaca and His Companions . . .
(New York, 1905) contain additions to these earlier writings. The Cabeza
de Vaca excursion was brought to a new stage by the re-examination of the
eastern part of the route on the part of a group of Texas historians (cited in
their place). The discovery of Obregón's chronicle of Ibarra's expedition resulted in a series of studies which are mentioned under the expedition. [At
this place in the text the author refers to some hitherto unpublished documents
included as an appendix in the original publication. This appendix is omitted
in the present edition.]

[2] Antonio de Herrera, Historia general de los hechos de los Castellanos
. . . , Decada V (Madrid, 1728), cap. 3, pp. 157–159.

province through the Tarascans.[3] In his Fourth Letter Cortés informed the emperor of the discovery of a very good harbor in Colima, of the existence of the Amazon province of Ciguatán at a distance of ten days from Colima, and of the visits of natives of the latter to Ciguatán, reporting the Amazon land to be very rich in pearls and gold. Cortés lost no time in following up these reports and sent Francisco Cortés de Buenaventura north by land from Colima in 1524, stating: "I am informed that on the shores below [i. e., to the north] there are many provinces well inhabited, where it is believed that there are great riches and that in a certain part thereof is an island inhabited by women . . . in the manner which in ancient histories is attributed to the Amazons."[4] The legend is involved later in the explorations of Nuño de Guzmán and perhaps in Cortés' own explorations of California.

The party of Francisco Cortés went nearly due north from Colima, ascending to the Mexican plateau by a rough but direct road which passed through Autlán, Ameca, Etzatlán, and Magdalena,[5] all important and friendly Indian towns. The party, seeking a province on the coast, climbed to the interior plateau, knowing that later they would need to descend to the coast again. Although the Spaniards made a fairly long detour, they took the only good route available, one which makes the best compromise between distance and terrain, for between that road and the sea lies a difficult land of transverse mountain ranges, deeply trenched by steep barrancas. In other words, they had expert Indian guidance and used an Indian road, passing through a chain of Indian towns and headed directly for the most feasible gap to the lower country of the north. Actually there is not a wasted league in the route followed by them.

At Magdalena (Xuchitepec) Francisco Cortés set foot upon the road from the east, which was to become later the great highway from Guadalajara to the west coast. At this place the roads from the plateau and the south converge for the crossing of the great escarpment. A few miles to the west the barrancas begin: deep, steep-sided gorges ripped into the seaward margin of the central plateau.

---

[3] Francisco Cervantes de Salazar, Crónica de la Nueva España (Madrid, The Hispanic Society of America, 1914), p. 765.

[4] [Camilo Garcia de Polavieja y del Castillo, edit.], Hernán Cortés, copias de documentos existentes . . . (Sevilla, 1889), pp. 327–328.

[5] The route of the expedition is given by Fr. Antonio Tello, Libro segundo de la crónica miscellanea . . . de la santa provincia de Xalisco . . . (Guadalajara, 1891), pp. 36–56 and Matías de la Mota Padilla, Historia de la conquista del reino de la Nueva-Galicia (México, 1870), p. 70.

In detail there are several choices of road, though the descent is in any case along steep ridges and around sharp ravines. No other northwestern gateway of the central plateau has so easy an approach to or passage of the plateau rim as this strip of country between Ixtlán and Magdalena. The margin of the plateau is unusually low here, and the escarpment less steep than elsewhere. It has always been the principal pass to the west coast, and is now utilized by the Southern Pacific Railway, which mounts to the highland by an impressive series of serpentines, tunnels, and bridges.

At the foot of the great cuesta lies a lower volcanic plateau, that of Tepic, fertile and well watered, a land of perpetual spring and fall. The expedition passed Ixtlán and Ahuacatlán in their charming valley. At Tetitlán they sustained a brush with the natives and, going around the shoulder of the volcano of Ceboruco, moved northwestward to the other important cluster of Indian towns, chief among them Jalisco and Tepic. The Tepic country marked the northern limit reached by the party as a whole. The captain contented himself with sending "ambassadors" into the hot coastal country beyond, the "Tierra Caliente," and one of these, according to Tello, visited Acaponeta. The Spaniards liked the country and the people, but they turned up nothing strange or valuable, in their eyes. They had encountered, since landing on the shores of Mexico, civilized Indians wherever they went. These west-coast Indians had, if anything, less store of precious metals than the ones of the interior.

On the return Francisco Cortés attempted to determine the character of the coastal country between Tepic and Colima, but the mountain headlands forced him to leave the coast and follow a slow, arduous, and tortuous route back. In later periods the only land entradas into this section were by occasional descent of the barrancas from the east. The return route was not of importance except in verifying the judgment of the guides who took the party out by the inland road.

The results of the expedition from Colima were important: (1) A large and docile native population, similar in culture to the native states already incorporated into New Spain, was found. The principal towns were given as encomiendas to members of the party, and missionary activity was begun. (2) Knowledge of the country was extended north to the Rio Grande de Santiago and through special messengers to the northern limits of the modern state of Nayarit. (3) The best pass from plateau to coastal lowlands of the Northwest was discovered, and thereby one of the major problems of northwestern exploration was solved at the first trial. (4)

For a distance of nearly 150 miles the route of the subsequent colonial highway into the Northwest was fixed. The railway line follows closely the route of the Cortés party from Magdalena to Acaponeta. Mountain, gorge, and marsh still restrict movement narrowly to the same passageway.

This auspicious beginning might well have been extended by Hernán Cortés into a further exploration of the northwestern lands. There was still the lure of the northern strait and of Amazon land. Colima provided good harbors, easily reached from Mexico and suitable for coasting expeditions. It was true that Colima was not suited to serve as a land base because of the necessary detour around the rugged Banderas country, but the party of Francisco Cortés had established such a base in Tepic, which could be reached directly from Michoacán through the plains of Guadalajara. The next move would have been to establish this short cut and thence proceed up the coast, but Cortés did not succeed in making the next move. The Colima party returned in 1525; Cortés is not represented on the scene again until 1532, when he sent his cousin, Diego Hurtado de Mendoza, by ship from Acapulco, to die at the hands of Indians on the Fuerte River. Colima, which might have provided the great port of the Northwest, became an obscure pocket of New Spain, and its port achieved importance only in the nineteenth century. The land route was redeveloped and extended by rivals of Cortés.

The failure of Cortés rests on misfortune, on historical accident, not on a misapprehension of the geographical problems. The ones who followed him built on his results and appropriated them to their own uses. During the Tepic venture Cortés was called south to Honduras to make good the defection of Olid. It took five years to re-establish his affairs. During this time he could give no attention to exploration; and when he returned, vindicated, as Captain General of New Spain, his principal enemy, Nuño de Guzmán, finding it prudent to leave Mexico, chose the northwestern country as the most eligible locality for creating a diversion and re-establishing an endangered name. The conquest by Guzmán of the northwestern frontier, henceforth known as New Galicia, blocked Cortés on the land route to which the latter had prior claim. As late as 1540 Cortés asserted his right to continue the conquest of the northwest, but his claims were not recognized. His other attempts were restricted to the sea and are concerned with California, not with the mainland.

ADVANCE OF THE SPANISH BASE TO CULIACÁN

The high native culture of Mexico, proceeding ultimately from Mayan Central America, reached as far northward as the valley of the Culiacán River on the west coast.[6] There is reason to surmise that the spread of this culture northward was along the Pacific coast rather than from interior Mexico to the coast. These coast people lacked the military organization of the Aztecs and Tarascans, being little accustomed to war and unfamiliar with the concerted action necessary to oppose determined invaders. The political units were small, involving rarely more than a single valley. Fertile flood plains supplied abundant crops, which were supplemented by a wealth of fish and shellfish from estuaries and streams. The Indians lived in large, compact villages, they were clever craftsmen, and seem to have been about as numerous as the modern rural population in the same section. The major settlements were strung along the great alluvial valley as far north as the Culiacán but many small villages lay in and along the margins of the interior basins, which stretch north and south, and form a sort of foothill belt to the high mountains behind.

By a single entrada, in 1530–1531, Nuño de Guzmán ruined the native scene. The conquest was cheaply won. Mostly he met no resistance, often he was received with open arms. Behind he left a trail of smoking ruins and shambles. Survivors were driven out in gangs and sold as slaves; in a few years the lowlands of Sinaloa and Nayarit became almost a wilderness.

As a part of the reconstruction of the Indian scene at the time of the conquest, I have previously traced Guzmán's route in detail.[7] The discrepancies between the route of Guzmán and the later *camino real* are shown in the map. The army followed *caminos* which were old established Indian roads through the dense *monte* or thorny bush savanna and scrub steppe that covers all the coastal region of Sinaloa. This plant formation is virtually impassable except where trails have been maintained. The Indian roads were, as many are to this day, footpaths overarched by the monte. Guzmán's army was heavily accoutred and the roads hence had to be brushed out. The In-

---

[6] Carl Sauer and Donald Brand, *Aztatlán: Prehistoric Mexican Frontier on the Pacific Coast,* Ibero-Americana: I, 1932, *passim.*

[7] *Ibid.,* Fig. 4, p. 16.

dians of Chametla, for instance, cleared (*limpiaron*) the road as far as a crossing of the Presidio River (El Recodo?), well up into the hills. The only difficulty concerning a road noted in the contemporary accounts was met in the country beyond this river: "This wide and open road led into very large montes and dry, barren grounds and thus it became desirable to go out in search of another road," which was found, "a rather wide road." [8] Since they next came to villages lying pretty well back in the hills, it appears that they left here the shorter coastal road in order to invade a series of hill villages. The advance of the army was rather mountainward of the later camino real, which fact is perhaps to be explained by the presence of a greater number of villages in the hills than out on the dry plains. The camino real follows closely the inner edge of the smooth coastal plain. There was better raiding to be had by heading for the basins in the foothills, hence the less direct course of the entrada. The camino real may well have been in existence, however, as a direct Indian trail, as was suggested in the note taken from Sámano. At any rate it was in use in the early days of the Spanish frontier settlements.

The coastal country is smooth and the interior basins are aligned north and south with numerous water gaps leading from them into the coast plain, so that the only difficulties in passing northward were the finding of roads through the dense monte and the flood hazard of the great rivers coming down from the mountains. At flood time, travel might be interrupted for weeks. The plain of northern Nayarit was especially troublesome. It is particularly low, lacks the terraces that are developed farther north, and immediately adjoins the great scarp of the central plateau, the foothill basins being absent here. This Santiago-Acaponeta section therefore was particularly hard to get through in the rainy season and was not convenient to go around. It was here that Guzmán's army was nearly wiped out by a summer flood, as it rested in camp on the Acaponeta River.

Nueva Galicia was the northwestern extremity of the civilized Indian country which had not been entered or effectively occupied by Cortés and his men. It ended north of the Culiacán River where the higher Indian culture ended. The whole of the civilized lowlands and highland margins was promptly and permanently incorporated into the Spanish colonial structure. To hold his conquest Guzmán planted four Spanish villas at approximately equal intervals: Culiacán at the northern border, Espíritu Santo on the Presidio

---

[8] Sámano, *in* Joaquín Garcia Icazbalceta, edit., Colección de documentos para la historia de México (México, 1858–1866), Vol. 2, p. 281.

River of southern Sinaloa, Compostela on the intermediate plateau of Tepic, and Guadalajara on the central plateau. These places, or their successors, are thereafter the principal way stations on the camino into the Northwest.[9] For about half a century the villa of San Miguel de Culiacán served as the starting point for all expeditions into the Northwest, as the last permanent settlement of Spain on the southern fringe of the barbarian lands. The encomiendas of Guzmán added a belt of about three hundred miles to the north of the Tepic country entered by Cortés; beyond lay the land of the Cahitas.

EXPLORATION OF THE CAHITA COUNTRY

Cortés' Amazon land of Ciguatán was found by Nuño de Guzmán's men on the modern San Lorenzo River. Because the men of the villages fled at the approach of the Spaniards, it was thought at first that here indeed were the towns of the Amazons, but soon the conquerors were undeceived. After this disappointment it was stated that Guzmán desired to follow upon the quest "of the Seven Cities of which he had notice at the time he set out from Mexico." [10] According to Castañeda, Guzmán had this information from an Indian whose father traded into the back country, exchanging fine feathers for ornaments, by a forty days' journey northward, and one that involved passage of a wilderness.[11] Castañeda says that Guzmán organized his expedition originally on the basis of this information and that for the same reason he chose the route through Tarasca to the west. Amazons and pearl shores having proved a disappointment, there remained the wealth of the Seven Cities to be prospected.

It is curious, therefore, that, being at Culiacán, about halfway on the direct road to Cíbola, Guzmán should have there altered the di-

---

[9] All of them were relocated, Culiacán perhaps four or five times. Espíritu Santo was maintained only from 1531 to 1536, at which time the new discoveries of Peru attracted so many of the settlers that it was abandoned. It was located at the foot of a sierra, perhaps at the modern site of Siqueros. Subsequently the long stretch between Culiacán and Compostela was unprovided with a way station until Ibarra founded San Sebastián (the modern Concordia). San Sebastián, like Espíritu Santo, was in the Chametla province, but farther to the east, since mines were being developed by Ibarra's men in the mountain margin about Copala.

[10] First Anonymous, *in* Icazbalceta, *op. cit.* (n. 7), Vol. 2, p. 291.

[11] Winship, *op. cit.* (n. 1), pp. 1–2.

rection of his march away from the supposed objective. At Culiacán he began a series of attempts to scale the mountain barrier to the east. Of these we can distinguish three: (1) The expedition up the Humaya Valley, the main northern affluent of the Culiacán River. It was led in two sections by Cristóbal de Oñate and Gonzalo López for a distance of forty leagues according to Pilar, or fifteen to twenty days' marches according to Sámano, before being stopped by the sierra rampart; and hence should have penetrated above Santiago de los Caballeros, about to the present western limits of Chihuahua. This route might have led to Cíbola, but it was not feasible for a party on horse. (2) Gonzalo López then tried the southern headwaters of the Culiacán, the Tamazula drainage, and got well back into the sierra country of Topia before the barrancas and cuestas, growing wilder and steeper, caused the party to give up its efforts. (3) A final attempt was made by a still more southerly route, the headwaters of the San Lorenzo, and reached at least the valley of Durango. These efforts turned the Spaniards successively farther away from Cíbola and other northern objectives. The common statement in contemporary accounts, and quoted by historians, that they turned inland because they were blocked by mountains along the coast, has no foundation in fact. These are no more than isolated hills on the coast south of the Guaymas vicinity. Guzmán simply changed the direction of his course. Why, we do not know. It may be that he had information that Cíbola lay across the Sierra Madre, but this is unlikely, since the Indians knew the proper route. Rather it would appear that he was not seriously looking for the Seven Cities, but that he had the intention of cutting across to the Gulf of Mexico to his domain of Pánuco and of establishing a frontier province from Atlantic to Pacific north of New Spain. Be that as it may, the exploring ardor of Guzmán and his men collapsed in the assaults against the Sierra of Durango, one of the most terrific mountain barriers in North America.

At the time of Guzmán's stay in the valley of Culiacán only one minor scouting party, under Samaniego, appears to have been sent northward in the coastal district.[12] It was known that some of the pueblos belonging to the Province (native state) of Culiacán lay north of the Culiacán Valley. Seemingly the expedition meant nothing more than the reduction of these last outlying settlements of the land which the Spaniards had overrun, for the party was to return

---

[12] The principal account is that of the Third Anonymous Witness, in Icazbalceta, *op. cit.* (n. 7), Vol. 2, pp. 454–456.

in a fortnight unless something of note was found. The evidence is that the expedition did not enter the last valley of the Culiacán (called the Horaba, also Tahue) Indians, which is that of Mocorito, but that their Indian guides took them by an inland route, up the dry basin in which Capirato and Comanito are situated. The expedition set out on a regular road which grew narrower and finally became a footpath, passing over stretches of rough country alternating with plains. Thus the men marched for a week through a thinly peopled country before reaching the Sinaloa River, for five days without seeing a settlement. This meant simply that in this land of high, dense monte it was easily possible for the guides to lead them around the settlements of their kinsmen, for the basin stretching northward from Culiacán past Badiraguato does and did then contain many small agricultural communities, based on *temporal* farming.

The Sinaloa River was reached six leagues above the major pueblo (the modern town of Sinaloa), the party descending here from the sierra to a very broad plain. The pueblo contained five hundred houses of a type different from those they had seen before, the walls consisting of reed mats. Thereafter the river and village were known as Petatoni or Petatlán: place of mat houses. The people, too, were strangely different, and the Spaniards "marveled to see so strange a type of house and so brutal a people, for the houses are like the covered carts of Aragon and the people are dressed in skins." Thus reads the first account of Spanish contact with the culture of the Cahita group. The modern Sinaloa River was the southern limit of a rude, vigorous population extending north to the Yaqui Valley, which alone of all the Indian populations of the Spanish north has with some degree of success resisted Europeanization to the present day. The reconnaissance did not pass the valley of the mats. The party descended the river until it was stopped by dense thickets, the seaward margin being a desert of cactus and spiny brush of the order of Mimoseae. The river was also followed for 14 leagues toward the sierra, through a settled country, but one increasingly difficult as to topography.

Two years after Nuño de Guzmán returned south he sent another party to continue northern exploration (1533). It was organized in the Culiacán Valley, then held by Guzmán's encomenderos, and was commanded by Diego de Guzmán.[13] The party set out by the road

---

[13] The journal of the expedition is preserved in the Proceso de Guzmán, published in Colección de documentos inéditos, relativos al descubrimiento, conquista y organización de los antiguos posesiones españoles . . . . Vol. 15

which the alcalde Samaniego had taken two years before, passing through the valley of Eutuacán (Pericos?), but entered Petatlán more directly from the south.[14] A reconnaissance was made five leagues down valley, and here the men heard of a greater river ahead, and one better provided with food. By a march of three days through the coast plain, an uninhabited monte of brasil wood, they came to the Fuerte River at (Te)Tamachala, below the hill country of San Blas. A side trip was made toward the coast to the pueblo of Oremy (Ahome), whence the party returned up river to the largest province, Cinaloa, the region about the modern town of El Fuerte. The principal pueblo of the Cinaloas may have occupied the very site of the modern El Fuerte, built about a small rock hill at the edge of the stream. They proceeded for a distance mountainward over a road "wide as a ball court," thus completing the reconnaissance of this great and rich valley from sea to mountains.

The continuation of the journey northward was made difficult by summer floods, which necessitated crossing the Fuerte on *balsas*. A march of three days overland brought the Spaniards to the Teocomo stream and pueblo at the place where a large arroyo, arising in the sierras, entered the Teocomo. The Teocomo was the river of the Tehuecos; the description identifies it as the Cuchuaqui, also called the Álamos, at its junction with the Guirocoba Arroyo, which carries an abundance of water from the mountains during the rainy season. Three and a half days later they came to the Mayo River in the vicinity of the modern pueblo of Camoa. The latter stage of this march was over a rocky and difficult road, lacking water from the vicinity of Álamos to the Mayo River. On the Mayo they heard of the Yaqui Valley and of a town of Nebame still beyond.

Since their next objective was the country of the Yaqui Indians, it was necessary to leave the basin they had been following and which continued northward, here drained by the Cedros River, and to take a more westerly route. Judging by the distances of march recorded and by the watering places mentioned, they took a very direct route through a hill belt to the great bend of the Yaqui River at Cócorit. It is probably possible to identify the watering places of Aquihuiquichi and Cocoraqui on the old Indian trial from Camoa to Cócorit. Only on the last day, as they began the descent to the Yaqui Valley, did they suffer serious thirst, which they slaked with water from

---

(Madrid, 1871), pp. 325 ff.; a further account is that of the Second Anonymous in Icazbalceta, *op. cit.* (n. 7), Vol. 2, pp. 296–306.

[14] The Indian name Moretia is given to the pueblo of Petatlán.

cactus. From a camp on the Yaqui, marching up-river, they reached Nebame on the third day. The place, inhabited by Indians of different character and language, had been recently laid waste by the Yaquis. This was the first contact of the Spaniards with the lower Pima Indians. The site of Nebame may be identified with Cumuripa, the lowermost Pima village on the Yaqui River. Further penetration of the Yaqui River upstream was blocked by the canyon above Cumuripa, which was impassable at that season of high water. At this point they decided to give up their search for the Seven Cities, which they had been instructed to locate. A small party, including the Second Anonymous reporter, went down the Yaqui toward the sea, and attempted to find a way around the mountains ahead of them, the later notorious Sierra Bacatete.

The return to the Mayo River was over the same route that had been followed outward. The Mayo River was reconnoitered to its mouth and for some distance toward the sierras. South of the Mayo a scouting party, which had wandered to the bay of Agiabampo, picked up the first relics of Diego Hurtado's lost party. A further search in the lower settlements of the Fuerte and on the Petatlán (Sinaloa) yielded the story of the massacre of Cortés' crew during the previous year. From Petatlán, Diego de Guzmán chose a route home by way of the Mocorito Valley, previously entered by a Portuguese encomendero of Nuño de Guzmán, Sebastian de Ébora, and for some time thereafter bearing the latter's name.

The Diego de Guzmán expedition was well timed as to season, beginning the northward march into unknown country toward the end of the summer rains. It is apparent that they had little difficulty in finding water along the way. In the height of the dry season their route from the Mayo to the Yaqui would hardly have been feasible, and some of the other parts of the journey would have involved great hardship. Although there is occasional complaint about the lack of a road, it is apparent from the diary in general and from the directness of their travel that they were well guided over direct trails connecting the several rivers on which the various branches of the Cahita people lived. The later camino real was outlined on this expedition as far north as the vicinty of Álamos, Sonora; beyond they used a trail to the Yaqui villages, which left the main northerly trail to the east. The reconnaissance covered almost the whole range of the Cahitas, previously seen only on the Sinaloa by Samaniego. It also brought the first knowledge of the Nebomes, as the lower Pimas were generally called in the early colonial period. None of the northward explorations directed by Nuño de Guzmán encountered any problems of terrain other than the skirting of the cactus desert of southern Sonora by the last expedition. The Guzmán parties extended the knowledge of the northwest for a distance of nearly six hundred miles beyond the explorations of Cortés.

RETURN OF ALVAR NUÑEZ CABEZA DE VACA
AND HIS COMPANIONS [15]

The route of Cabeza de Vaca has been critically re-examined by a group of Texas historians, who have shown convincingly that in their westward drift the party reached the confluence of the Conchos River with the Rio Grande.[16] Beyond, these authors have only suggested the route. The remainder is as readily determinable as the eastern part of the journey, and is outlined in the following paragraphs.

The permanent settlements which the party reached about the mouth of the Conchos are known to have been of the Jumano Indians. The Sumas lived farther up the Rio Grande and were inferior in culture and hostile to the Jumanos, but were reported by Cabeza de Vaca to be of the same language. The Spaniards later knew the Sumas as extending westward to the borders of the Ópata country. It may be inferred, therefore, that Cabeza de Vaca's party, between the Conchos and the maize (Ópata) country of northeastern Sonora, passed from one village or band of Sumas to another, the intrusion of the Apaches into this territory appearing to have come later by several generations. The trip up the Rio Grande from the Conchos was continued under unusual hardships because a great drought of two years' duration had made it impossible to raise maize. Maize was obtained at that time by barter from other, distant, peoples who had irrigated fields. Thus the wanderers obtained the first information about the Ópatas and the Pueblo Indians. In particular they heard of a great maize country to the west and were given instructions as to how to reach it. These directions were not to continue west (from the Conchos), but to make a great detour north following the river upstream for seventeen days, and

---

[15] Cabeza de Vaca was the metronymic of Alvar Nuñez. Since the name has passed into general usage in our literature in the shortened form, it is thus used hereafter.

[16] The final version is by Harbert Davenport and Joseph K. Wells, The First Europeans in Texas, 1528–1536, Southwestern Historical Quarterly, Vol. 22, 1919, pp. 205–259, esp. pp. 248–255.

thereafter to turn west. They were told that during this journey they would have no cultivated crops available, and that the population was subsisting chiefly on certain seeds of trees, which appear to have been mesquite. Oviedo's account also credits the party with getting information of a maize country reached by keeping the north to the right hand; that is, the Pueblo lands of the upper Rio Grande.

The progress of the journey from the Conchos is given by Cabeza de Vaca as follows:

> After two days we spent there, we determined to go in search of the maize [country] and we did not wish to follow the road of the Vacas [cows; apparently the valley of the Rio Grande; they also designated as Vacas the Indians whom we have identified as Sumas] because it leads north, and this was for us a very large detour [they did go north, however] because always we held for a certainty that going toward the setting sun we should find what we were seeking; and thus following our road [*el camino del maiz*] we crossed the entire land until we came out at the South Sea; and we did not let ourselves be hindered by the fear of the great hunger they said we should suffer (as in truth we did suffer) during the whole seventeen days' journey of which they had told us. On all these marches up the river they gave us many robes of buffaloes [*vacas*] and we did not eat of their fruit [mesquite], but our sustenance each day was a piece of deer fat about the size of a hand, which for our needs we always kept available, and thus we passed the whole seventeen days, and at their end we crossed the river and marched for another seventeen. At the setting of the sun, in some plains between some very high sierras that arise there, we found people who for the third part of the year eat only ground herbs (*paja*) ; and since it was that season [spring] when we journeyed through there we too had to eat it, until, having completed these marches, we came to the permanent houses.[17]

The account was set down from memory years after the event, and may be emended by Oviedo's relation, in the *Historia General*, secured shortly after the return of the party. Oviedo gives fifteen days as the duration of the journey up river from the Conchos. After crossing the river

> they passed to the west or toward sunset, and were more than another twenty to the land of maize, going through a somewhat hunger-stricken country, though less than before, for the people ate ground herbs and killed many hares, which they always brought to the Christians in excess of their needs. On this road they rested on several occasions, as they were accustomed to do.

The trip was made not only after a great drought of two years' duration, but also in the dry season, apparently in spring. They had

---

[17] Translated from Alvar Nuñez Cabeza de Vaca, Naufragios y comentarios (Madrid, 1922), p. 119.

to follow the Rio Grande far enough north to have water available in their swing to the west, and this probably could be done only by skirting the mountains marginal to the Colorado Plateau, chiefly the Mimbres Range. The country along the international border was out of the question, partly because of the broad belt of sand dunes and partly because of great waterless plains broken only at long intervals by small basin ranges, with uncertain water supply. The refugees may have ventured a march westward from the Mesillas Valley on the Rio Grande, but, considering the dryness of the period, it is more probable that they left the Rio Grande at Rincón and then steered across the southern ends of the Mimbres and Burro mountains. The itinerary of about fifteen days up river and of a similar distance to the west thereafter fits in well with this conjecture. There is no evidence that they crossed the Sierra Madre of Chihuahua, which would have been a most difficult trip and one that they would scarcely have failed to note. The Indians of the Rio Grande themselves apparently did not attempt a crossing of the Sierra Madre to the Ópata country, for they advised the Spaniards to make the long detour north. The only reference to relief in the accounts is to "plains situated between high sierras," and it is quite applicable to the basin and range country in which the Mimbres Mountains lie. The route here sketched involved no mountain crossing of any importance, and there were available sufficient water holes. It appears certain to my mind that Cabeza de Vaca and his companions passed both southwestern New Mexico and southeastern Arizona on their way into Sonora. To Cabeza de Vaca and his companions, not to Fray Marcos, belongs the distinction of having been the first white men to enter these southwestern states.

The maize country was of course the Opatería, its northeastern limit, the Fronteras basin of Sonora. Here we may terminate the journey across the steppe and desert country west of the Rio Grande. In the Ópata land Cabeza de Vaca found a good reception and food in plenty. The accounts contain the first precious ethnographic notes on these people but very little reference to the route followed. Oviedo places the beginning of the maize country at more than two hundred leagues from Culiacán, which estimate agrees with the location of the Fronteras basin. By slow stages the party "passed from pueblo to pueblo for a distance of more than eighty leagues," which is about the distance from Fronteras to Ures, the most densely settled part of old Sonora. For eight months, in this part of the journey, they "did not come out from among the mountains." This statement also agrees with the local relief features, for the Ópata valleys are all flanked on either side by ranges.

After passing the last of the sierras, Oviedo reports that

these four Christians arrived at three pueblos, which were joined but small, with about twenty houses similar to the ones in the country behind, and compactly built (so that there was not one house here and another there as in the land that had been pacified, which they later saw) [the reference is to the scattered rancherias of the Cahitas to the south]. And here the Christians were visited by people [Seris] from the coast, who came from a distance of twelve to fifteen leagues as they were given to understand by signs; and to this pueblo or, rather, group of pueblos the Christians gave the name of the Town of the Hearts (Corazones).[18]

This settlement of Corazones later played a conspicuous role in the Coronado expedition. The basin which is called the Valle de Sonora ends below Babiácora. Below the latter place the river breaks across the western flanking range in a gorge more than fifteen miles long, thereupon entering the Valle de Ures. Corazones was located on the Sonora River below the gorge, apparently about eight miles above Ures at the Puerto del Sol. There are a number of small ruins here at the mouth of the canyon, which can perhaps be identified with the old settlement.

Cabeza de Vaca's own statement is: "By it is the passageway to many provinces which are on the South Sea; and if those who go to seek passage should not enter through it, they will lose their way." This is hardly a cryptic remark to any one who knows this famous river pass between the coast country of Sonora and the Valley of Sonora proper. It is the most significant gateway of the state. Through this canyon passed almost all transport between the north and south of Sonora in the colonial period and for many years thereafter. To this day, although an automobile road has been constructed from Ures to the Valle de Sonora by a detour through the mountains, the pack trains and horseback travel still use the shorter road along the canyon. The Sonora Valley above is the heart of Ópata land, and later it held the principal settlements of colonial Sonora, giving its name to the entire province. The canyon also divided the Ópata country at the north from the Pima settlements to the south. Coastward, within a short distance, began the territories of several primitive tribes, then identified separately, but now

---

[18] Gonzalez Fernandez de Oviedo y Valdés, Historia general y natural de las Indias . . . , Vol. 3 (Madrid, 1853), p. 610.

usually lumped under the designation of Seris. Cabeza de Vaca properly therefore considered this place as a gateway to various native provinces.

In this part of the journey a further item concerning the Pueblo country was noted. The travelers saw many turquoises and were presented with some worked stone which they called emeralds. In this connection Cabeza de Vaca reports: "I asked them whence they had got these stones, and they said that these were brought from some very high sierras which lie to the north, obtained by barter for skins and feathers of parrots, and also said that in that country were found pueblos with many inhabitants and very large houses."[19] When the Spanish party reached the Sonora drainage it entered the old Indian trade route from the south to the Pueblo country, and became aware of the presence of trade goods brought from a distance. It is probable that the parrot plumage was brought in from more southern lands. These birds are found only sparingly in the Ópata country, and there chiefly east of the Sonora Valley. They become very abundant in southern Sonora and southward into Sinaloa, where, in addition to the common green parrots, the brilliant guacamayas, prized for their plumage, and other varieties, including parrakeets, are common.

At Corazones the Pima country began. Oviedo's statement was to the effect that the party went from Corazones thirty leagues to the river that Nuño de Guzman discovered [the Yaqui River, discovered by Diego de Guzman, operating under orders from Nuño de Guzmán]. This is approximately the distance from the Ures Valley to Soyopa on the Yaqui. The immemorial road leads directly from the granite gate of the Sonora River through the old Indian villages of Pueblo de Álamos, Mátape, and Rebeico to Soyopa. The last-named place has the only good ford on the river, shoals formed by broad reefs, which make it possible to cross the river here in safety at low water. It is still the only ford on the river for vehicles, and has been throughout the historic period the crossing of the Yaqui by the camino real of the north.

Cabeza de Vaca's statement as to the crossing of the Yaqui is not clear. It reads: "At one day's journey from it [Corazones] was another [village], in which we were overtaken by such heavy rains that because the river became greatly swollen we could not pass it, and were detained there fifteen days." If the party had gone only one day from Corazones, they must have awaited the recession

---

[19] Alvar Nuñez Cabeza de Vaca, *op. cit.* (n. 17), pp. 120–121.

of the river about at Pueblo de Álamos. The puny arroyo of that small valley could never have detained them long, and there is no good reason for thinking that they should choose to await the subsidence of a Yaqui River flood at a place situated several days' march away from that river. It is more likely that there is a slip in Cabeza de Vaca's memory as to the number of journeys to the place of their detention by the flood. This we take to have been at Soyopa. The time was Christmas, the season when winter cyclonic storms not infrequently give rise to long continued rains and thus produce the heaviest floods which that country experiences. I had occasion to spend a Christmas nearby at Sahuaripa, watching the slow passage of a cyclonic storm and the still slower subsidence of the rivers.

From the pueblo in which they awaited the recession of the flood to the one in which they had their first news of the Christians, Cabeza de Vaca places the distance as twelve leagues. The latter place would then have been Ónabas, the second station farther on, on the old camino real, downstream on the Yaqui and on the east bank thereof. Between Soyopa and Ónabas the river terraces are well developed on the east side and make for easy passage, whereas the west bank is against much-dissected slopes. Ónabas was one of the largest of the Pima settlements of the south. The information had about Spanish parties at this place argues neither for nor against the entry of some of Guzmán's men to this point. It may have referred to the entrada of Diego de Guzmán, who had been in Cumuripa, the next Pima village downstream. There may have been other, later parties that passed beyond; Oviedo for instance noting that three parties from Culiacán made entradas far into the north, probably slave-hunting expeditions. At this village the wanderers saw some Spanish trappings, and knew that they had about won through. Henceforth the pace of the journey changes. They are no longer interested in route or customs, but in reaching their own people.

The eighty or one hundred leagues, according to the two contemporary statements, still remaining between the crossing of the Yaqui and the first sight of Spanish soldiers, were traversed without comment as to route, excepting toward the end of the journey. As they continued south their excited anticipation was mingled with increasing dismay as they saw the country more and more ruined by slave raids carried out by Guzmán's men. The fields were unplanted, the villages abandoned, the Indians retired to retreats in thicket and mountain. The only locality mentioned was a pueblo located on a narrow mountain ridge, serving as a refuge to many Indians. This place was reported by Oviedo as being forty leagues from Culiacán and is to be sought therefore in the sierra overlooking the modern Sinaloa, on one of the headwaters of the stream of that name. Without information about the route and having only the knowledge that the Spaniards were moving along as fast as they could, we can only infer that from Ónabas they took the straight, main road south through the Cahita country. This would be up the Rio Chico and down the Cedros. There are only two slight suggestions supporting this shorter route. They were traveling in the rainy season, at which time it would have been especially difficult to continue down the Yaqui from Ónabas to Cumuripa through the lower canyon of the Yaqui to follow Diego de Guzmán's route south to the Mayo. Also, when the Negro Stephen, a member of their party, returned later with Fray Marcos, he left the Franciscan on the Mayo and started on ahead up the Cedros, retracing the road on which he had come with Cabeza de Vaca. Since Cabeza de Vaca's party was at Ónabas, on the Yaqui River, on the main trail south, the shortest route and the one best supplied with settlements and with least hazard of interruption by flood, there is no reason to assume that they should have undertaken a difficult detour south.

The camps of a slave-hunting party of Spaniards were traced, and the party itself, under Diego de Alcaraz, was encountered near Sinaloa or near Ocoroni.[20] (The band of Pimas who had accompanied Cabeza de Vaca down from the Corazones country remained to settle below Sinaloa in the village of Bamoa, which formed for many years a Pima colony in Cahita land.) Word was sent ahead of the coming of strange Spaniards out of the north. At a village

---

[20] The latter location is given in a manuscript fragment contained in Historia de las Misiones (Tomo 25, Misiones, of the Archivo Publico of Mexico): "De la villa de Culhuacan commençaron a hacer correrias y entradas hostilamente algunos capitanos y soldados en la tierra de Cinaloa: y a los Yndios que por fuerca o maña podian aver a las manos los ponian en miserable cautiherio y los vendian por esclavos, contra las cedulas de los monarcos catolicos y ordenes de sus governadores. . . . El que mas osadamente penetrava aquellos confines de Cinaloa, era el capitan Diego de Alcaraz, que con una compania de soldados andava haciendo esclavos de que se le seguian grandes intereses. Continuando pues Diego de Alcaraz sus invasiones en las Cinaloas, en el paraje q llamaron de los ojuelos tres leguas de Ocoroni para Carapoa reconicio una gran tropa de indios: toco alarmo a percibir los arcabusos, y como a pressa ciertos, se avanço a cautivarlos: suspendio la execucion porq atendiendo mas vio entre ellos tres hombres de estraña figura."

of pacified Indians in a valley (Pericos?) eight leagues north of the Culiacán Valley, Melchior Diaz, alcalde mayor of Culiacán and later with Coronado, came out to welcome the wanderers back to Spanish civilization.

The achievements of the involuntary expedition of Cabeza de Vaca and his companions were far-reaching: (1) Their reports of a high civilization to the north revived interest in the story of Cíbola, and led directly to the participation of the Viceroy Mendoza in northern explorations. (2) Their peregrination proved the existence of a land mass of continental proportions north of New Spain. (3) They established the existence of the trail to the north that was to become the later historic highway. The expedition of Coronado simply retraced their route as far as the headwaters of the Sonora River. (4) They made known the existence of two semicivilized Indian nations, the Pimas and the Ópatas, to the north of the Cahitas. (5) Cabeza de Vaca's flaming protest against the barbarous slave raids brought to an end the exploitation of Indians by Guzman's men, which shortly would probably have exterminated the southern Cahitas. Soon a more humane period in the treatment of the Indians begins, to find fruition in the golden age of the Jesuit missions.

FRAY MARCOS FOLLOWS THE NORTHERN TRAIL

The various missionary chronicles of the colonial period agree upon an expedition of Franciscan friars in the year 1538. Bandelier has defended the thesis that such an expedition took place, before the one by Fray Marcos, and other writers have followed his conclusions.[21] Bancroft, however, regards the expedition as apocryphal. It is my opinion that the Franciscan expedition is none other than the one of Fray Marcos:

1. The religious chroniclers all apparently drew from the same source, or copied each other successively without troubling to cite sources. The first of these accounts is that of Motolinia, of 1540.[22] Mendieta's *Historia Ecclesiástica* (Book Four) at the end of the sixteenth century used the relation of Motolinia, in part word for word. The Franciscan Salmerón repeated the story nearly verbatim

---

[21] A. F. Bandelier, Contributions to the History of the Southwestern Portion of the United States (Papers of the Archæological Institute of America, American Series, V, 1890), pp. 84–105. Examined by Coues, *loc. cit.* (n. 1).

[22] Icazbalceta, *op. cit.* (n. 7), Vol. 1, pp. 171–172.

about 1626.[23] From the same period is Torquemada's better known
relation contained in the *Monarquia Indiana,* and somewhat later
is that of the Fifth Book of Tello's Chronicle.[24] Beaumont used
Tello *in extenso* and apparently derived his restatement from that
source.

2. Motolinia's account reads as follows:

This same year [1538] the provincial, Fray Antonio Ciudad Rodrigo, sent
two friars by the shore of the South Sea, toward the north by way of Jalisco
and New Galicia, together with a captain who was going on a journey of
discovery, and having passed land already discovered and known and conquered on that coast, they found two roads well opened. The captain chose
the one to the right and followed it, which turned inland. After a very few
days of travel he encountered some mountains of such roughness that he could
not pass them. He was forced to return by the same road that he had gone. Of
the two friars the one fell sick, and the other with two interpreters took the
road to the left, which bore toward the coast, and found it always open and
direct. After a journey of a few days he entered into a land of poor Indians,
who came out to meet him, calling him messenger from heaven, and as such
they all touched him and kissed his habit. They accompanied him day by day,
3 to 400 persons and at times many more. Some of them at meal time went
hunting hares, rabbits, and deer, of which there were many and of which they
knew how to take in short time as many as they wished, and, giving first to
the friar, they divided the rest among themselves. In this manner he proceeded
more than three hundred leagues and almost on the whole road he had notice
of a land densely inhabited by clothed people, who have houses with flat roofs
and of many stories. These people they said were settled along the banks of
a large river, where there are many enclosed pueblos and at times wars are
waged between the pueblos. They say that having passed that river there are
other greater pueblos and richer ones. In the first pueblos they say are cattle
smaller than those of Spain and other animals very different from those of
Castile. They wear good clothes not only of cotton but also of wool, and there
are sheep from which this wool is taken (it is not known of what kind these
sheep are). These people wear shirts and clothing with which they cover their
bodies. They have whole shoes that cover the entire foot, a thing that has not
been found in all the land hitherto discovered. Also many turquoises are brought
from those pueblos, which, and everything else that I am stating here, were
to be seen among those poor people whom the friar had reached; not that these
things were produced in the lands of the latter, but that they brought them
from those large pueblos whither they went at times to work and to gain their

---

[23] P. Gerónimo de Zarata Salmerón, Relaciones de todas las cosas que en
el Nuevo-Mexico se han visto y sobito . . . desde el año de 1538 hasta el de
1626, *in* Documentos para la historia de Méjico, Sér. 3, T. 1, Parte 1
(México, 1856).
[24] MS in Public Library of Guadalajara.

livelihood as the day laborers do in Spain. In search of this land there had already gone out many armadas by land and sea, and God kept it hidden from all, wishing that a poor shoeless friar should discover it, to whom, when he brought the news, at the time when I am saying this, they promised that the land should not be conquered by fire and sword, as there has been conquered almost all that has been discovered in the mainland, but that there should be preached the gospel. But as this news was given, it flew shortly everywhere, and since it was a remarkable thing, many wished to go out to conquer the land. For better or worse the Viceroy of New Spain, Don Antonio de Mendoza, took the initiative, bringing to the task a holy intention and a very good will.

3. The account of Motolinia contains the essential points of what we know of the journey of Fray Marcos and omits those claims of Fray Marcos which I believe to be falsifications in the latter account: (*a*) The captain who started out with the friars was Coronado himself. Mendoza, in a letter to the King relating to events prior to the great expedition of Coronado, said that the two friars (Marcos and companion) left for Culiacán with Vazquez de Coronado, who had orders to secure information concerning a mountain province of Topira (Topia). When he [the antecedent is uncertain and may refer either to Coronado or to the friar] reached this province he came to so wall-like a mountain (*escarpado*) that he found no road to cross and was forced to return to Culiacán.[25] Another letter from Coronado at Culiacán to Mendoza reported that he was planning to leave for Topira April 10, 1539, about a month after Fray Marcos had left for the north.[26] It is apparent from these two letters, though others to which they refer are lost, that Coronado made a short trip into the mountains of Durango in 1539, after escorting Fray Marcos and his companion to Culiacán. (*b*) The companion of Fray Marcos fell sick shortly after leaving Culiacán, and was left behind. The "anonymous" Franciscan had the same experience. (*c*) The relation of Fray Marcos contains information about the poor Indians, his reception as a messenger from heaven, the accompaniment by large volunteer Indian bands, the notices of the large populations to the north all along the way, all of which feature the Motolinia account. (*d*) The discrepancy between the two accounts is that Fray Marcos in his own relation claims to have seen the civilized peoples of the north, whereas Motolinia has the friar report these

---

[25] Relation du voyage de Cibola, *in* H. Ternaux-Compans, edit., Voyages, relations et mémoires originaux pour servir à l'histoire de la découverte de l'Amérique . . . , Vol. 9 (Paris, 1838), pp. 285–290, esp. pp. 288–289.

[26] *Ibid.*, p. 352.

conditions at second hand. A subsequent discussion will attempt
to show that this is supporting rather than contradictory evidence
that Motolinia was reporting the journey of Fray Marcos. (*e*) The
Motolinia account is correct as to date. Fray Marcos was sent out
from Mexico City in 1538. He had just returned when Motolinia
wrote; apparently Coronado had not yet started on his journey to
Cíbola.

4. The gradual distortion of the Motolinia narrative is apparent, and proceeds from the fact that Motolinia mentioned the name
of neither the friar nor the captain. Mendieta, writing a half-
century later, repeated the Motolinia story, but added to it the
statement that at that time Marcos de Niza was the provincial
"who to assure himself that what the other friar had published
was true, . . . went as quickly as possible and finding true the relation and statements which the friar had given . . . returned to
Mexico and confirmed what the other had said." Apparently meantime the name of Fray Marcos had become so well known that it
did not occur to Mendieta that Motolinia was writing about the
notorious Savoyard without mentioning his name. The later chronicles follow Mendieta.

5. After the lapse of two centuries legend began to supply names
for the "unknown" Franciscan. How the names were supplied we
do not know, but since the story is still recognizably the same we
may infer that these names are only further embroidery. The
Jesuit chroniclers were influenced by Captain Mange; and Mange,
who was in military service on the northern frontier, may have
picked up local traditions in the Pimería or in the Ópata country.

Variations of Motolinia's theme appear late, during the eighteenth century, and chiefly at the hands of the Jesuit school of
chroniclers. Captain Mange's *Luz de Tierra Incógnita,* written
about 1720, has Fray Marcos seeking authority for an expedition
from his Provincial, Antonio de Ciudad Rodrigo, and, failing to
get a license for himself, getting permission to send instead one
Fray Juan de la Asunción and a lay brother, who passed six hundred
leagues to the northwest of Mexico, where they were blocked by
a river. Here they obtained notices of another greater one, ten
days to the north, settled by a numerous people, whose multitude
was expressed by heaps of sand, having houses of three stories,
walled, the inhabitants clothed and shod in buckskin and cotton
mantas.[27] Mange knew the upper Pimería at first hand and his

---

[27] Juan Mateo Mange, Luz de tierra incógnita en la América Septentrional
. . . (Publ. del Archivo General de la Nación, Vol. 10, México, 1926), pp.
282–297.

account does not distinguish sufficiently between what he knew about the country and what he extracted from an older informant. Mange's history of discovery is much less reliable than the record of his own participation in the colonization of the frontier. For instance, after this narrative, he devotes a chapter to the Coronado expedition, and then (!) has Fray Marcos make his expedition to the north in 1544. Mange is followed by Garcés in 1777 and Arricivita in 1792. Mota Padilla (1742) names the Franciscan as Juan de Olmeda. The principal deviations of Mange from the Motolinia account have been noted.

The Relation of Fray Marcos de Niza [28] gives a pretty vague itinerary, which I am quite unable to interpret as this journey has been reconstructed by the numerous students who have concerned themselves with it. Fray Marcos left San Miguel de Culiacán on the 7th of March, 1539, "finding on the way many receptions and presents of food." Three days were lost at Petatlán (Sinaloa) because of the illness of his companion, who was left behind here. The party left Petatlán, accompanied by many inhabitants of the country, with many receptions, celebrations, and triumphal arches in Indian villages along the way. "On this whole road, which may be of 25 or 30 leagues, I saw nothing worth reporting, excepting that Indians came to see me from the island where the Marquís del Valle [Cortés] had been." The friar assured himself with his own eyes that they came from an island, because he saw them pass over a strait half a league wide in balsas. Beyond lay a larger island and many smaller ones. The good friar was wrong, of course, in thinking that he was looking upon Cortés's California. The reference may be to the lagoons, sand bars, and rocky islands (Bahia San Carlos, now the site of Topolobampo) south of the debouchure of the Fuerte River, where he may also have picked up news of Hurtado's party.

From this place he passed by a waste stretch of four (?) days (across what was then desert land betweeen Topolobampo and the Fuerte River?) to another Indian settlement, presumably on the lower Mayo or Fuerte River. Here a tale was picked up of people of better understanding and living, at a distance of four to five days into the mountains. He proceeded for three more days among the same simple people, to a settlement of reasonable size, which he records as having been called Vacapa.

Vacapa was reached two days before Passion Sunday. In 1539 Easter fell on the 6th of April (Julian calendar). The arrival at

---

[28] The text used is that in Colección de documentos inéditos . . . , *op. cit.* (n. 13), Vol. 3, pp. 329–350.

Vacapa therefore was on the 21st of March, which was only two
weeks after leaving Culiacán. Three days had been lost at Petatlán
by the sickness of the other religious. Disregarding the time consumed by the festive receptions, there remains therefore a maximum
of eleven days' travel, or of nine if the father rested on Sunday.
The date of starting is given by Marcos, and checked by Coronado
in his letter to Mendoza from Culiacán. Fray Marcos describes at
some length his stay at Vacapa until Easter, and accounts for the
fortnight spent there by telling of the sending out of Indians to
the sea and of waiting for their return with Indians from the coast;
and also of the despatch of the Negro Stephen to reconnoiter the
road ahead and of the coming of a messenger from him after four
days. Fray Marcos left Vacapa the day after Easter. The calendar
therefore disposes of the varied suppositions which have sought
Vacapa on the Mátape River, in the Sonora Valley, or even on
the Arizona frontier!

It is difficult to see from the time elapsed how Vacapa can have
lain any farther north than the Fuerte River. The Indian village
of Vaca, on the upper Fuerte, and existing at the time of the conquest, at once suggests itself for the identification of Vacapa, "Vaca"
being an Indian, not a Spanish, name. In the early seventeenth century it or a similar pueblo was called Vacapa by Martínez de
Hurdaide, military commander of that section.[29] Fray Marcos
claims to have been in Vacapa at a distance of forty leagues from
the sea, which would correspond pretty well with the location of
Vaca. It does not require four days to cross from the Bay of San
Carlos to the Fuerte, and three days are inadequate to go up the
river from its delta to Vaca. There is something wrong about the
account any way it is taken. There are not enough days between
the terminal dates of Fray Marcos' calendar between Culiacán and
Vacapa to accommodate all the marches which he records.

Another possibility is that the party marched straight on from
Petatlán-Sinaloa to the mouth of the Fuerte, though it is pretty
hard to imagine the island and strait of Cortés at the mouth of
the Fuerte. In this case the march of "four days through an un-
peopled country" would have been from the Fuerte across the
desert to the Mayo River, and the village of Vacapa would have
been situated three days up the Mayo. An incident on Coronado's
expedition, which Fray Marcos accompanied, supports the latter
interpretation.[30] A brisk march might have brought the party to

[29] MS reports in Vol. 316, Historia, Archivo Nacional de México.
[30] See below, p. 87.

the Mayo in the time at their disposal, but it would have required steady and sturdy going.

The elapsed time is entirely too short to provide for a detour to the coast and a march to inland Vacapa, either on Mayo or Fuerte. I suspect strongly that the friar did not visit the sea at all, as he claimed, but that he inserted reports from the Indians who came up from the sea as included in his own observations. We can only say that Vacapa was either on the Fuerte or the Mayo. In either case his claim that the Indians had heard nothing of Christians is unintelligible, as indeed it is for any of the country he traversed later even much farther north in Sonora. This claim may have been based on policy, to bolster the rights of discovery which Mendoza was anxious to secure. Mendoza, for example, in the letter to the King with which he transmitted the Relation of Fray Marcos, makes the false claim that Nuño de Guzmán "was unable to penetrate into the interior and to learn anything new. After his first attempt, and while he was still governor of Galicia, he sent out on a number of occasions captains and horsemen who had no better success than he." [31] Fray Marcos was an advance agent for Mendoza, and it was important to make the claim of having entered unknown land.

Beyond Vacapa the itinerary of Fray Marcos is blurred still more badly. In three days he reached the people who had given the Negro Stephen the first accounts of Cíbola, and who claimed to reach Cíbola by thirty *jornadas*. He arrived at another settlement where he was well received; it appeared to him that this land was better than that which he had left behind. In this manner he went five days, finding always inhabitants and great hospitality, until he heard that after two days' journey there began an unsettled country of four days' extent. The record is not sufficiently explicit to give the total number of days elapsed. The change to a better country may indicate the drainage of the Rio Chico. The basin of Nuri is one of the finest tracts of land in the state of Sonora, and thence to the Yaqui Valley at Ónabas settlement are closely spaced along the stream courses.

The country between the Yaqui and the Sonora valleys contains a long stretch of steppe and hill country, sparsely inhabited; and here we place the second *despoblado* of four jornadas. It began at two journeys from the well peopled country (the middle Yaqui); and before entering the wilderness he came upon a cool, refresh-

---

[31] H. Ternaux-Compans, *op. cit.* (n. 25), Vol. 9, p. 286.

ing (*fresco*) pueblo, with irrigation. Mátape fits the location. It lies in a watered valley, above the level of the hot desert country, and was inhabited by Ópatas, who practiced irrigation carefully. The road to the right cuts off the entry to the Ures basin (Corazones) and swings over grassy uplands and oak-studded granite summits directly into the Sonora Valley. The failure to mention Corazones may therefore be owing to the fact that Brother Mark did not enter it. The cut-off route was later much used, as it still is.

At the end of the *despoblado* he entered into a valley that was very well settled by a people better dressed than those he had seen before. Here he found as much news of Cíbola as there is in New Spain of Mexico, and heard that the coast turns rapidly to the west. Then follows a curious statement:

> . . . and thus I went in quest thereof and saw clearly, that at 35 degrees the coast turns west, whereof I had no lesser pleasure than of the good news of the country. And thus I returned to follow my road and went along this valley for five days, it being so largely peopled by intelligent people and so well provided with food that it will suffice to sustain more than three hundred horsemen. . . . It is all under irrigation and is like a garden, the compact settlements (*barrios*) being half or a quarter of a league distant from each other.[32]

To what else can this refer than to the Sonora Valley with its closely clustered Ópata settlements? The Ópatas were superior in culture to any of the people between Culiacán and the Pueblo country. They practiced irrigated farming, lived in compact villages, and were engaged in trade with the Pueblo country. The usual interpretation that these were the upper Pimas not only does violence to Fray Marcos' previous itinerary, but to the fact that the Pimas of the San Pedro were small bands of much lower culture than the Ópatas, and lived in a very meager valley.

Arrived at the end of the settled country, Fray Marcos stated that he had come 112 leagues from the place where he had the first news of Cíbola, which is about right for the distance from the Rio Chico to the headwaters of the Sonora. The party left Vacapa on the 7th of April and reached the end of the (Ópata) settlements on May 5, which is also a reasonable schedule.

The rest of the account of Fray Marcos I consider impossible. It

---

[32] The view of the sea is apparently again an Indian report, which Fray Marcos translated into an experience of his own. It is a long and weary way to the sea and hardly possible that he might have beheld the sea from some mountain summit adjacent to the Sonora Valley.

is my belief that Fray Marcos started north into the *despoblado,* the high, grassy steppe country which begins in northern Sonora (Cananea Plain), that shortly after entering it he heard from an Indian who had been with the Negro Stephen of the latter's death among the Zuñis, and that then Fray Marcos returned precipitately southward without ever seeing the Zuñi country or climbing to the Colorado Plateau, having penetrated at most a very short distance into the modern state of Arizona:

1. Fray Marcos states that they entered the *despoblado* on May 9. It was almost the end of May when he claims to have seen Cíbola. The distance is not far 'short of two hundred leagues, the time claimed less than three weeks. This performance, though not impossible, would be extraordinary, and is entirely out of pace with the previous marches, which represent good average performance in this country for a party afoot.

2. The impossible part of the schedule is the return from the Cíbola country to Compostela in one month. We are told that he arrived at the latter place at the end of June. This would mean covering twelve hundred miles in a month, with no possibility of horse transport north of Culiacán.

3. In itself a march of forty miles a day sustained for a month is incredible, but the situation is made worse by the season. The return was made at the hottest season of the year, when this area is one of the hottest in the world, four to six hours a day being commonly at or above 100 degrees in the shade. Even the natives wisely employ a long siesta and reduce the amount of their physical activity.

4. Without special equipment and training, long marches afoot or with horses mean short daily distances. Four or five leagues a day is not bad time for a mixed party if any considerable distance is involved. There are inevitable delays for food and guides and river crossings and because of the necessity of stopping at settlements for provisions. It is necessary for ordinary people (and horses) to have periods of rest. And Fray Marcos had no record as a lean hard-bitten pedestrian, such as were many of the frontier missionaries of later days. In the Tello manuscript he is said to have been then already of advanced years.

5. Two further considerations sustain the reported arrival at Compostela at the end of June. (*a*) The rainy season begins at this time with great regularity. The lowland country is then subject to wide inundations, in particular the lowlands of northern Nayarit. Not only would each of the dozen coast-plain valleys

present after June a serious problem in crossing, but a wide and difficult detour would normally be imposed in Nayarit. It is very probable that this consideration determined the time of his reappearance in Compostela, since travel was generally adjusted in that area so as to avoid the rainy season. (*b*) Fray Marcos presented his Relation to the Viceroy in formal audience on the second day of September at Mexico City. Two months is certainly no excessive time for the preliminary report to the government at Compostela, the long ride to Mexico City, the drafting of the final report, its copying and certification, and the arrangement of the formal presentation.

6. The official Relation may well have been dressed up for official consumption. Perhaps Fray Marcos was not so bad a liar as the official account makes him out to be. It should be noted that in the contemporary Motolinia version there is no claim that the friar reached the Cíbola country, but only that he gathered circumstantial evidence from the Indians to the south of the Pueblo country. Castañeda, who shares the resentment of Coronado at the deceptions in Fray Marcos's report, states that the friar's party was in the desert 60 leagues from Cíbola when they heard the news of Stephen's death and that "they returned from here by double marches, prepared for anything, without seeing any more of the country except what the Indians told them." [33] This sounds as though the friar, when accompanying Coronado, claimed only to have entered well into the northern *despoblado,* and gave up his assertion of having seen Cíbola.

Most of the records of old exploration improve on better acquaintance with them. The sometimes impugned Cabeza de Vaca account is in fact obviously honest, and is weak only as to details in which the lapse of time would most readily dim the memory of the narrator. The same cannot be said of Brother Mark's story. (*a*) In its most significant part, the claim of having reached Cíbola, it is patently a falsehood. In several other respects the charge of dishonesty may be laid. (*b*) The two observations of the character of the coast, one in northern Sinaloa, one from the valley of Sonora, appear decidedly shady, both because of their gross inaccuracy and because they are impossible to reconcile with the time limits set by Fray Marcos himself. Having reinterpreted Indian stories into a claim of having seen Cíbola himself, why should he not similarly claim a knowledge of the coast, which also he had only at second

---

[33] Winship, *op. cit.* (n. 1), p. 8.

hand? (*c*) Again it is queer, to say the least, that he makes no mention of previous parties of whites north of Petatlán. Indeed, Brother Mark enters the explicit claim of having come early in the journey among Indians who knew nothing of Christians. Unless it be in the last days of his outward journey, the friar at no time was in territory, I think, not previously traversed by Cabeza de Vaca and his party or by some party operating under orders from Nuño de Guzmán. The suppression of this fact might be to the advantage of the patron Mendoza, but it is not to the credit of Fray Marcos. (*d*) The Relation was composed immediately upon his return, with the scenes fresh in mind. Not even a dim memory may be urged, therefore, in extenuation of the vagueness of his account. (*e*) The expedition was avowedly one of geographic exploration, not one in which the exploration was accidental, as in the case of Cabeza de Vaca, or incidental to other ends. Brother Mark was instructed to take careful observations, and appears to have been chosen for the task because of his familiarity with geographic observation. His superior, Antonio de Ciudad Rodrigo, commended his cosmographic skill, and Cortés previously had considered adding him to one of his parties because of his reputed knowledge of navigation. The paucity and confusion of data as to terrain, direction, and distances, and the one absurd determination of latitude make this easily the worst geographic document on this frontier, and indicate either that Brother Mark was an amazing dunderhead or that he indulged in deliberate obfuscation. It is difficult to see how any one could have made even half of the expedition he claims to have made, under explicit orders to report on country, people, and route, and then proceed to an official report so largely unrecognizable in these particulars. If we subscribe to the old theory that he was an arrant swindler, it is perhaps more charitable to leave him in that role, rather than have him also a fool who had no business to wander about in strange places.

The auspices of the expedition are somewhat suspicious as to the probity of the report, as was suggested earlier in citing Mendoza's letter to the King. Nuño de Guzmán and Cortés both had valid claims to the right to northern exploration. The viceroy had in his favor his official position and a lately awakened ambition to protect the Indians. It is interesting that, although Mendoza claims to have considered employing Dorantes, a companion of Cabeza de Vaca and the owner of the Negro Stephen, to head such an expedition, he himself admits that "it came to naught, he knew not why," and that thereupon he selected a man who knew nothing of the northwestern country. The good viceroy was pushing a preliminary claim to title, and it was rather up to Fray Marcos to deliver. The document that he produced certainly served the ends for which it was intended.

There remains therefore the possibility that the document transmitted to the King was edited to establish Mendoza's claim to Cíbola. Mendoza's part in the affair is not entirely above criticism, as was shown above and in Mendoza's statement to the King that Guzman had accomplished nothing. Motolinia, himself a Franciscan, omits the falsifications of the official account, and the other Franciscan chroniclers after him likewise do not claim that Fray Marcos reached Cíbola. Perhaps Fray Marcos did not make the claim for himself. On 'the other hand, Coronado and his men consider Fray Marcos an impostor. One of the statements by Coronado was "that everything the friar had said was found to be quite the reverse." [34] Castañeda reports that Fray Marcos was sent back in disgrace because it was not "safe for him to stay in Cíbola, seeing that his report had turned out to be entirely false." [35] There is also the denunciation of Cortés, which, although Cortés was an interested party, cannot be overlooked. In his memorial of 1540 concerning the injuries suffered at the hands of Mendoza, Cortés made the formal declaration that he, Cortés, had taken Fray Marcos into his confidence concerning his discoveries on the west coast and that the latter had carried the information to the viceroy, that the discoveries of Fray Marcos were only what Cortés had told him (an unjust claim on the part of Cortés); and that "having pushed himself forward in this matter the said Fray Marcos, pretending and reporting that which he neither knows nor saw, is doing nothing new to him, for on many other occasions he has done the like and is accustomed to do so, as is notorious in the provinces of Peru and Guatemala, and shall be given sufficient evidence thereof before this court if required." [36] The bias of Cortés' statement is obvious, as the whole picture of the lords of New Spain squabbling about their rights to glory in the new Northwest is unedifying, but it does cast a slight further shadow over the figure of this friar, who in any light is a most dubious fellow.[37]

---

[34] *Idem,* p. 162.

[35] *Idem,* p. 26.

[36] Colección de documentos inéditos para la historia de España, Vol. 4 (Madrid, 1844), pp. 209–211.

[37] The story of the Negro Stephen is not affected by these judgments on

CORTÉS FOLLOWS THE ROAD TO THE NORTH

The accounts of the Coronado expedition regarding the road through the inhabited country of modern Sinaloa and Sonora are very brief, perhaps because this part of the route was by that time no longer considered unknown territory. This expedition has been made the subject of more careful study than have any of the others, and in consequence there is less to be added. The following paragraphs therefore will be confined to showing that the route followed the common highway of the north and to a consideration of a few moot points, such as the location and relocation of the place of the Hearts and the position of Chichilticalli.

Mendoza ordered Melchior Diaz of Culiacán to make a reconnaissance in advance of the main party. The latter set out from Culiacán November 17, 1539, and at a distance of a hundred leagues, which distance would bring him into the Rio Chico Valley, began to experience cold weather, which became steadily more severe as the party advanced. Some of his lowland Indians died. Diaz penetrated far enough to get a very good second-hand account of the Zuñi country, strongly at variance with Fray Marcos' ro-

---

Fray Marcos. The Negro was sent ahead at Vacapa, and never seen again. His killing by the Indians of Cíbola was substantiated by Coronado's party and need not be questioned. He had orders to travel ahead. He was familiar with the route and accustomed to life in the wilderness. There was sufficient time for a small, fleet party to reach Cíbola and for Indian runners to bring back word of the killing to Fray Marcos in northern Sonora. I am therefore adding here as probably apocryphal an old note giving a different version of the fate of the Negro. It is contained in an old set of abstracts and excerpts taken from lost chronicles and contained in paragraph one of the "Punctos sacados" of Volume 25, Misiones, in the Archivo Publico of Mexico. (A brief analysis of this material is given in Herbert E. Bolton, Guide to Materials for the History of the United States in the Principal Archives of Mexico, Carnegie Inst., Publ. No. 163, 1913, p. 74.): "Estevanico llegado al Rio de Mayo preciso de la belleza y hermosura de las Yndias Mayos, sescondio o quedo alli, casose despues con 4 o cinco mugeres al uso de la tierra, tuva succession, y el ano de 22 vivio un hijo suio llamavase Aboray muy mulata adulto alto seco y mal encarado, fue capitan o casique de una parcialidad de Tesio pueblo de aquel rio. Algo desto insinua tambien Ruiz y dice q este negro avia quedado atras." In the early seventeenth century therefore, there was current a story on the Rio Mayo that the Negro had hidden out with the Mayos, raised a family, and that his descendants were still recognized among the Indian inhabitants in 1622. The basis of fact probably rests in the existence of mulatto descendants among the local Indians at the time of the first missions.

mance. The information was obtained, it appears, from the upper Pimas, living in southern Arizona. According to Castañeda this party reached Chichilticalli, on the far borders of the Pima country, either on or near the Gila River.[38] Thus the progress of exploration was pushed another step northward until there remained little more for Coronado than the ascent of the Colorado Plateau and the entry into Cíbola.

The expedition of Coronado formally assembled early in 1540 at Compostela. The first leg of the journey was to Culiacán over a "road well known and much used" (Jaramillo).[39] Coronado and a light horse party left here on April 22, the main expedition following a fortnight later. The route led through Petatlán and Cinaloa (El Fuerte). It may be noted that it took the horse party a week to reach the Fuerte River, as against Fray Marcos' calendar of nine to eleven days to get to Vacapa. Here the important question of Vacapa arises again. Jaramillo reports that while on the Cinaloa (Fuerte) River Coronado ordered a small party of horsemen

to make double marches, lightly equipped, until we reach the arroyo de los Cedros, and from there we were to enter a break in the mountains on the right of the road, and see what there was in and about this. . . . This was done, and all that we saw was a few poor Indians in some settled valleys like farms or estates, with sterile soil.[40]

The route had become sufficiently familiar so that the stream entering the Mayo from the north was then already identified as the Arroyo de los Cedros, a name it bears to this day. The valley gets its name from the unusual development of groves of the Mexican bald cypress (*Taxodium*), now usually called *sabino* along the river. There are still some excellent stands of it to be seen, as for instance at the Rancho de los Cedros. From the place where the Cedros enters the Mayo (Conicarit) the party passed by wide gaps that the Mayo River has cut transversely across the chains of hills into a meager basin above, still containing numbers of Mayo rancherias. The reason for this side trip is disclosed by Coronado:

Thirty leagues before reaching the place of which the father provincial spoke so well in his report [Winship's footnote: "The valley into which Fray Marcos did not dare enter"] I sent Melchior Diaz forward with fifteen horsemen,

---

[38] See below, p. 90.
[39] Winship, *op. cit.* (n. 1), p. 22.
[40] *Idem,* p. 223.

ordering him to make but one day's journey out of two, so that he could examine everything there before I arrived. He traveled through some very rough mountains for four days, and did not find anything to live on, nor people, nor information about anything, except that he found two or three poor villages, with twenty or thirty huts apiece. From the people here he learned that there was nothing to be found in the country beyond except the mountains, which continued very rough.[41]

Coronado was at this time on the Fuerte River. Thirty leagues ahead lay a country of which Fray Marcos had picked up wondrous tales. Brother Mark's first yarn of a rich people well supplied with gold was spun in the Vacapa country, and the golden land was said by him to lie mountainward to the east. The friar's own account favors placing Vacapa on the Fuerte, but Coronado definitely was led to believe that the country of gold was up the Mayo. Hence the scouting party sent up the Mayo from the junction of the Cedros to test the tale.

Coronado's party proceeded from the Fuerte to the Mayo at the mouth of the Cedros and north up the latter valley. From the Cedros it took about three days to the Yaqui, which is comfortable riding time from the vicinity of Tezopaco where the road leaves the Cedros to cross over the watershed to the Rio Chico Valley. Beyond the Yaqui they "reached another stream where there were some settled Indians, who had straw huts and storehouses of corn and beans and melons" according to Jaramillo.[42] These must have been the Ópatas of the Mátape Valley, later to become an important mission center. The next valley and stream was that of the Hearts, thus remembered from Cabeza de Vaca's visit. Here Coronado reported more people than they had seen before, and a large extent of tilled ground. The place lay five long days' journey from the sea. Some savage Seris from the coast were brought up for inspection by the party. A part of the group was left behind here to establish a base, and this became the first Spanish Villa, San Hierónimo de los Corazones.

The record is continued by Jaramillo: "We went on from here, passing through a sort of gateway, to another valley near this stream, which opens off from the same stream, which is called Señora." The statement has puzzled commentators, but is clear when one remembers that the basin of Ures, in which the village of the Hearts lay, ends above in a gorge, through which the Sonora

---

[41] *Idem*, p. 161.
[42] *Idem*, pp. 223–224.

River passes from the Valle de Sonora to the Valle de Ures. The term "valley" in the local usage to this day is not applied to the whole drainage-way of a stream, but to a continuous and well marked body of lowland. These valleys are in fact structural basins, and the Sonora River passes through several of them. The party simply left the basin of Ures, passing upstream by the gorge into the basin of Sonora proper. The Valle de Sonora, beautiful and fertile beyond anything else in this part of the country, beginning above Banámichi extends to a dozen miles below Babiácora. It terminates above in the gorge of Sinoquipe, a canyon a dozen miles long cut in volcanic rock. Beyond lies a third, smaller basin drained by the Sonora River, the valley of Arispe. This is readily identified as Jaramillo's Ispa. The major settlement of the Sonora Valley was called Señora by the Spaniards. From it, Castañeda reports the distance to the Valley of Suya as 40 leagues. Suya was at the northern confines of the Ópata country, and is therefore to be sought in the headwaters of the Sonora, probably about at the site of the modern Bacoachi. The march continued up the Sonora to its head, all the way through the Ópata settlements.

It was desirable to have a base in the agricultural country of the Sonora River. The first one established was at Cabeza de Vaca's Corazones. The site was soon changed to the Sonora Valley. Castañeda simply says that it was seen that San Hierónimo de los Corazones could not be kept up at its original location and that thus it was transferred to the valley of Señora. The latter valley provided a better location, being in an area of greater supplies and closer to the northern wilderness. The second location of the Spanish settlement is not certain. Apparently it was at the native town of that name, given by Arellano as ten leagues from the Hearts.[43] This would be approximately at Babiácora, toward the lower end of the Sonora Valley. The old Indian town of Sonora has always been considered as lying farther upstream, between Huepac and Aconchi, and its ruins are still pointed out locally. Diego de Alcaraz, the same one whom Cabeza de Vaca found hunting slaves in Sinaloa, was left in charge of the second San Hierónimo, which continued to bear the name of Corazones. He promptly got into difficulties with the spirited Ópatas, and lost about eighteen soldiers from the famous arrow poison of these Indians.[44] The disaster caused another relocation of the Spanish base,

---

[43] *Idem*, p. 198.
[44] Supposed to have been made from the yerba de la flecha, which grows abundantly on the dry terraces in that section.

"40 leagues toward Cíbola into the valley of Suya." [45] It was still known as San Hierónimo de los Corazones. There has been some confusion resulting from this retention of the name of Corazones by three different Spanish settlements. The case is common enough: the original Spanish Sinaloa was in the country of the Sinaloa Indians on the middle Fuerte River. It was later moved southward to the Petatlán country, and thereupon both town and river changed their name to Sinaloa, being thus known at present. Guadalajara was relocated a number of times, but retained its name. The same thing applies to Culiacán and to Compostela. The last Corazones, in the Suya Valley, on the frontier of the uninhabited steppe country of the present international border, is therefore thought to have been in the vicinity of Bacoachi, the last Ópata settlement to the north. Here, in a final Indian revolt, Diego de Alcaraz paid with his life a long overdue score, and the settlement was abandoned, no more to be established.

The party led by Coronado, after leaving the Ópata country, Jaramillo says, "went through deserted country for about four days to another river, which we heard called Nexpa, where some poor Indians came out to see the general." [46] This was undoubtedly the San Pedro River of southeastern Arizona, inhabited by the Sobaipuri branch of the upper Pimas. They followed the river downstream for two days, which took them below Benson, perhaps to the vicinity of Cascabel. An old Indian trail to the Hopi country is still remembered as leaving for the north about here,[47] swinging over and around the Galiuro Mountains to the Arivaipa basin and to the Gila above San Carlos. This trail is very direct, and is well supplied with grass and water. The next place identified on Coronado's route is Chichilticalli, the red house. This was a prehistoric ruin of some fame as a landmark at that time. Jaramillo reports that they left the (San Pedro) stream, going toward the right of the foot of the mountain chain in two days' journey, where they had notice of Chichilticalli. Then, crossing the mountains, they came to a deep and reedy river.[48] The route is clearly through the Arivaipa basin and through Eagle Pass between the Pinaleño and Santa Teresa Mountains to the Gila River. The mention of Chichilticalli suggests that it was encountered before they went through

[45] Winship, *op. cit.* (n. 1), p. 61.
[46] *Idem,* p. 225.
[47] Carl Sauer and Donald Brand, Pueblo Sites in Southeastern Arizona, Univ. Calif. Publs. Geography, Vol. 3, pp. 415–458, 1930. Reference to p. 424.
[48] Winship, *op. cit.* (n. 1), p. 225.

Eagle Pass, which evidence would place it in the Arivaipa basin. Castañeda favors a site on the Gila by the statement: "At Chichilticalli the country changes its character again and the spiky vegetation ceases," [49] and by indicating that here the ascent of the Colorado Plateau began. The Gila Valley has the last of the desert vegetation seen by the party as it went northward.

Both references are vague, and the ruins can be accommodated to either account. The area in question was occupied by a late prehistoric Pueblo people, the producers of the Middle Gila Polychrome pottery.[50] These folk built heavy compound walls about parts of their settlements, which, though now in all cases crumbled to low ridges, may have still existed as walls four hundred years ago. There are only two of these ruins that come under consideration as the site of Chichilticalli. The one is on the Haby ranch in the Arivaipa basin, perhaps the most striking Middle Gila Polychrome ruin in the entire section. It lies at the base of the ascent to Eagle Pass, on the route and at the distance indicated by Jaramillo. The other is on the Gila River bluff about a mile north of Geronimo. These and other sites are described in the paper by Sauer and Brand already cited.

At Chichilticalli began the last wilderness, the country beyond the settlements of the Pima Indians. We know that Pimas were living in the Arivaipa basin until about the middle of the eighteenth century. The situation with regard to the Indians in the upper Gila Valley is not clear. From the red house they marched 85 leagues to the settlements of Zuñi, which were the meager reality of legendary Cíbola. This last part of the route has been well determined by Bandelier, requiring the ascent of the Colorado Plateau by the White River and the passage to Zuñi by way of the Little Colorado River.

There remains to be noted only the expedition of Melchior Diaz from the town at Sonora, the second Spanish base, to the Cucopa country at the mouth of the Colorado. All that is known about the route is that it led north and west for 150 leagues. It cannot have followed the coast, as Winship has shown it, for such a route would have required an initial, long, and unnecessary detour and thereafter impossibly long stretches without water and heavy with loose sand. The route probably was the one through the Papaguería later used by missionaries and Spanish military expeditions, such as Anza's.

---

[49] *Idem,* p. 90.
[50] Sauer and Brand, *loc. cit.*

We may consider that Diaz crossed to the valley of the San Miguel, occupied by Ópatas, and thence down the Magdalena to the Altar country, where the Papaguería commenced. The desert oasis of Sonoita can hardly have been missed, as the usual gate to the lower Colorado Valley.

THE ENTRADA OF FRANCISCO DE IBARRA

Interest in the northwest frontier languished after the disappointment of the Coronado expedition. The Spanish settlement at Culiacán was maintained, but mostly the outlying encomiendas were abandoned. Meanwhile the discovery of great silver mines in Zacatecas and north thereof gave rise to a vigorous northern frontier in the interior, the province of Nueva Vizcaya. Its governor, Francisco de Ibarra, chiefly prospecting for mines, crossed the western Sierra Madre to the coast, and retraced the greater part of the route to Cíbola in 1564–1565. Henceforth the Chametla district and all territory north of it were attached to New Vizcaya. The blight upon the Sinaloa coast seems to lessen a bit with the coming of Ibarra's men. With Ibarra's death, which took place, it appears, at the end of this expedition, the plans of development were largely given up, but the coast, south of the Cahita country, was somewhat more firmly held, and became a little less forlorn a Spanish outpost. A quarter of a century later the Jesuits began the building of their churchly-worldly state, and the period of exploration and reconnaissance gave way to permanent occupation.

The principal information about Ibarra's entrada is supplied by the chronicle of Baltasar Obregón, lately rediscovered.[51] The

---

[51] It has been translated and edited by George P. Hammond and Agapito Rey as Obregón's History of 16th Century Explorations in Western America . . . (Los Angeles, 1928). The geographical notes by the editors are not very useful, nor is their reconstruction of the route satisfactory. I have not found their translation entirely dependable for my purposes. An example is their rendering of the frequently used *arcabuco* as signifying a craggy country, whereas in this section the term has always indicated the dense scrub vegetation and has no significance as to relief. Thus the translation gives the impression of passage through rough country where bushy country is indicated in the original. I have therefore followed the Spanish edition, Mariano Cuevas, edit., Historia de los descubrimientos antiguos y modernos de la Nueva España, escrita por el conquistador Baltasar de Obregón, año de 1584 (Mexico, 1924). J. Lloyd Mecham, Francisco de Ibarra and Nueva Vizcaya (Durham, 1927), attempts a reconstruction of the route in terms of place names found on the

chronicle is confused. It was written nearly twenty years after the event, apparently to present to the crown Obregón's claims for recognition. The author had a bad memory and was obviously badly muddled on many incidents. He has the very bad failing for a chronicler of letting one event suggest another which happened in another place or at another time, without indicating clearly to the reader that he is about to go off on a large tangent. The author is obsequious and verbose, anxious to impress his superiors, and thus wrote an uncommonly lurid tale, in contrast to the matter-of-fact simplicity of most of his contemporaries. Indian ethnography and language meant almost nothing to him. He was, for instance, apparently unaware of the tribal differences in the long stretch of country through which he passed. The chronicle is, however, almost the only source for a reconstruction of the expedition, and, garrulous and somewhat dim-witted though the chronicler was, the least bad parts of the chronicle are the descriptions of the country. Obregón fortunately had a fair visual memory; and his landscapes, in particular the details of their vegetation, are rather readily recognized.

Another source, hitherto unused, is the chronicle of Antonio Ruiz, who also participated in the expedition.[52]

From Durango Ibarra crossed the mountains of Topia and entered the coast country above Culiacán.[53] By this crossing Ibarra established an alternative route from Mexico to the northwest coast, a route which diverted a fair share of the traffic from the Culiacán-Guadalajara road in later years. The Topia route had the disadvantage of a difficult terrain. On the other hand, it avoided the hot and unhealthy lowlands south of Culiacán, was less subject to interruption by flood, and connected the coast settlements with the numerous and for many years highly opulent mining communities of interior New Vizcaya.

From the Culiacán Valley the party of Ibarra marched northward over the well-known road past the valley of Sebastian de Ébora (Mocorito), through very dense scrub to Petatlán (Sinaloa), and by Ocoroni to the enclosed town of Ciguini (vicinity of San Blas?)

---

map of today. The route as portrayed is in large part impossible, involving the crossing of country through which a single Indian could scarcely have traveled, much less a small army of Spaniards. In fairness to the authors it should be noted that geographic considerations are minor matters in their studies.

[52] In Vol. 316, Historia, Archivo General of Mexico. [Included in the appendix of the original edition of "The Road to Cíbola," but omitted here.]

[53] Ruiz says at Imala (Moholo viejo) on the Rio Humaya above Culiacán.

on the Fuerte River. Thence the province upstream was visited, called Cinaro by Obregón, a slightly different version of the earlier Cinaloa. At this time it appears that Tehueco was the largest settlement of the upper valley. The large and fertile valley pleased Ibarra, and shortly he decreed the erection of a frontier villa, called San Juan de Carapoa or de Sinaloa, on the southern bank of the river. The original villa may have been where the town of Fuerte now stands, or else a few miles downstream from the modern Fuerte, at Bajada del Monte. Ibarra reconnoitered the rich valley from Vaca, at the edge of the mountains, to the sea, expecting to distribute the whole country among his men.

From the Fuerte Ibarra was called south to the Province of Chametla to establish his claim to the other extremity of the modern state of Sinaloa. Thus Ibarra blocked out essentially the modern form of the state of Sinaloa, the encomiendas of Ibarra's men from the Fuerte to the Baluarte (Chametla) forming the historic basis for the detachment of this territory from New Galicia, the erstwhile principality of Nuño de Guzman. The establishment of a frontier presidio on the Fuerte was sound policy, though the death of Ibarra and subsequent Indian uprisings later caused the temporary retreat of the Spanish frontier to the Rio Petatlán, in which process the name Sinaloa was transferred to its modern position. Through Ibarra's initiative, henceforth, there was maintained an outpost farther out in the frontier than Culiacán, and this outpost retained the name of Sinaloa, no matter what its location.

The march northward was resumed at the beginning of the rainy season in the year 1565. From the Mayo the party continued for five days up the Cedros arroyo, by fine groves of cottonwood, willow, and "cedars." It appears that instead of continuing straight over the watershed to Nuri, which lies in the drainage of the Rio Chico, they turned too far to the right and thus passed from headwaters of the Cedros to headwaters of the Nuri in a pretty difficult country.[54] Obregón described graphically the difficulties of the passage, insisting that they deviated to the right; that is, toward the Sierra Madre.

The next valley which they entered was that of Oera, which can be identified with Nuri. Nuri occupies a very fine basin stretching northwest-southeast, excellently supplied with water, not only by

---

[54] The drainage and relief in this section are not shown correctly on any existing map. The arroyo of Nuri and that of Trinidad join above Movas to form the Rio Chico.

the main stream but also by many spring-fed streams from the mountains. It is now a fine, though remote, citrus-growing section. Obregón noted at some length extensive irrigation and many fields, the density of the population, and their superior well-being, including the good quality of their houses. On the route traversed, no locality between Fuerte and Ures other than Nuri meets this description. Movas and Ónabas, farther on, lack irrigable land. The Yaqui River has almost no irrigable land above the territory of the Yaqui Indians (restricted to the lower Yaqui, in the coastal plain) until the Valley of Batuc is reached. The prospect of the Nuri basin is especially pleasing after the long march through the dry slopes of the upper Cedros and across the mountain ridges between Cedros and Rio Chico. The same basin received, according to my interpretation, a favorable mention from Fray Marcos. This was the first Pima settlement entered, and it appeared to Obregón to have a distinctly higher culture than did the Indians to the south.

"From Oera the expedition descended by chains of sierras of broken terrain, by rivers, arroyos, and very dense and extremely hot thickets." [55] The march was made in early summer, when the rains were under way. The Rio Chico is not well named. Even in the dry season it carries a goodly quantity of water from the Sierra Madre of Chihuahua, and its fords are uncomfortably deep. With the rains the valley road becomes impassable, and notably rough trails must be used which wind over the spurs of the flanking mountains. Obregón failed to note the passage of the Yaqui River, though Ruiz recorded their arrival at the Yaqui soon after leaving the Mayo. At the next place where Obregón's memory served him, they were camping on top of a sierra whence they had a view of "two beautiful valleys of five and six leagues, in which there came together many flower-dotted streams and fine fertile plains occupied by sown fields." [56] According to the guides they were then at the confines of the valleys of Señora [57] and Corazones (Sonora and Ures). They may have been on the short cut from Mátape to Babiácora, which passes the granite range that hems in the Valley of Sonora at the south. This range has a rolling summit upland overlooking both the Ures and Sonora basins. The text of Obregón continues:

The next day the governor with his party entered the first settlement of the valley of Señora. . . . From here the party marched by this valley and river

---

[55] Cuevas, *op. cit.* (n. 51), p. 147.
[56] *Ibid.*
[57] Sonora was often thus named in the earlier literature.

upstream four short journeys, the greater part of the distance being inhabited by people and villages, at three and four leagues from each other and on both sides. These valleys are very hot and full of thickets, with many poison trees of which the sierras are full.[58]

Obregón says that they entered the valley of Señora, mentions it in more than a dozen places, and the descriptions of country, people, and distances fit. It is curious therefore that both Mecham and Hammond show the expedition as not having entered the Sonora Valley at all, apparently because they thought that they had to get the expedition into the modern Sahuaripa.[59] There can be no question that the expedition used the well-known highway up the Sonora or Señora Valley, a name never applied to any stretch other than the basin of the Sonora River as confined by the gorges of Ures and Sinoquipe.

The statement of Ruiz is somewhat different. According to him Ibarra "came upon the signs of walls and ruins from which it appeared that there had been in that place a Spanish settlement. Asking who had constructed them, it was understood that Captain Alcaraz had settled a villa there with 40 settlers." There follows an account of the massacre of Alcaraz and party. Ibarra's party "moved on, and always the natives subjected themselves peaceably to the crown and thus at the end of a considerable time [after leaving the Fuerte?] we reached the settlements of Corazones and the valley which they call Señora, fertile valleys and abounding in supplies of corn, beans, and squash." The ruin referred to may have been that of the second villa and the valley of Corazones may have been the place of the third Spanish villa or the Suya Valley at the north of the Ópata country.

The next parts of Obregón's narrative are badly confused. From his mention of the Sonora Valley he passes into a long digression concerning the poison tree, for which he had the most pronounced fear. This leads him to discuss the disaster that overtook the Diego de Alcaraz party of the Coronado expedition, of which they heard accounts. The narrative resumes abruptly,[60] without stating where the party was at the time:

The party marched three days through small pueblos of flat-roofed houses of one-and-a-half stories, and of mud walls, in temperate lands having clusters of small oaks and after another day's journey reached Guaraspi, a pueblo well

---

[58] Cuevas, *op. cit.* (n. 51), p. 148.
[59] Discussion of its location below, pp. 97–99.
[60] Cuevas, *op. cit.* (n. 51), p. 156.

settled by clothed people and more advanced than those seen before. It consists of six hundred houses of flat roofs, and mud walls, with regular streets, irrigation ditches for their fields . . . on the frontiers of the most valiant and courageous people of these provinces, the Querechos.

Guaraspi is to be identified with Arispe. The valley of Arispe, as has been stated, is distinct from that of Sonora, though drained by the same river. Its inhabitants were Ópatas, and it was one of the chief Ópata towns, later known for the advanced status of its population. The description of the compact, orderly pueblo can refer only to an Ópata town. The Pimas to the north lived on a much lower plane. The place moreover is identified as being on the frontiers of the plains Indians, and Arispe lies almost at the margin of the grassy steppe. The mention of oaks is significant. During the rainy season the canyon of Sinoquipe is impassable, and a trail is used along the heights, where the party must have seen at close range the scattered groves of white oaks that descend here to the lower slopes of the mountains.

The following stage of the journey was to Cumupa or Chimupa, stated by Obregón to be five days' march distant. The Valley of Cumpas is southeast of Arispe, in the next structural basin to the east, and about at this distance. There are however several difficulties in an interpretation of a swing over to the Cumpas basin: (1) This would have meant an abrupt change in direction, actually a turning back, without an indicated reason. (2) Obregón specifies that the road passed by little villages of one hundred and two hundred houses of the same sort and of the same manner of sustenance that they had been seeing. The road from Arispe to Cumpas is through a broad gap in the mountains, by gentle dry slopes covered with grass and yucca. At most they might have passed several isolated rancherias, but there is neither water nor cultivable land for a single small village on the route. (3) Cumupa is described as having a valley a league in extent. In fact the valley of Cumpas is second in size only to that of Sonora in all the north country. (4) Cumupa was said [61] to be on the frontier of the plains Indians, whereas Cumpas lies far to the south of that frontier, almost in the middle of the Ópata country. It therefore appears, rather, that the party did not alter its direction of march, but continued up the left-hand affluent of the Sonora, the Arroyo Bacoachi, passing smaller tracts of alluvial land, until they came to the more open, ample basin and larger village of Chinapa. All this is Ópata country, and here they found

[61] *Idem,* p. 173.

themselves on the actual frontier of this nation. Chinapa is easily reached in two days from Arispe. The last Ópata village on this drainage, Bacoachi, could be reached by very short marches in five days or less. Obregón is weak on Indian names, and there is always the possibility of a change of name, which has been known to occur, or of mistaking another word for the name of a town or people, which has been a very common occurrence.

Beyond this valley which I consider to have been the Bacoachi they climbed a high, rough, and hot mountain country, and on the other side came down to a place called Zaguaripa by Obregón, in a valley "surrounded by high sierras, deep gulches, crags, and large rock masses." [62] "This valley and town of Zaguaripa is on the frontier of the plains Indians . . . a defensive site, surrounded on two sides by a rough and deep barranca." [63] It was estimated as being three hundred leagues from the Rio Fuerte. There were living at this place some half-breed descendants of Diego de Alcaraz' garrison of the third Coronado base, and the local Indians, it appears, had participated in the massacre of that garrison. By the route which Ibarra followed they were two days from the beginning of the territory of the plains Indians. None of these facts fits in any way with the character of the modern Sahuaripa, with which Hammond and Mecham have identified the place:

1) The modern Sahuaripa is almost at the southern limit of the Ópata country, at the opposite end from the northern plains border of the Opatería. (2) The modern Sahuaripa is less than a hundred leagues distant from the Fuerte River, whereas Obregón says twice that this place was three hundred leagues distant, an excessive but understandable figure for the farthest margin of the Opatería. (3) The modern Sahuaripa lies in one of the smoothest basins of all the Ópata valleys. Obregón's description refers to very broken relief. Because of dissection of an ancient basin fill (the Gila conglomerate of G. K. Gilbert), some of the basins of the state of Sonora have within them gorge-fretted mesas of cemented gravel, producing a very difficult terrain. The Sahuaripa basin is notably free from such dissection. (4) Sahuaripa, being at the extreme opposite end of the Opatería, would be a most unlikely place to have held detailed news and descendants of the Suya base of the Coronado party, which at no time came anywhere near to Sahuaripa.

Moreover there is no evidence of any march to or departure from

---

[62] *Idem*, p. 159.
[63] *Idem*, p. 161.

this southern Sahuaripa on the part of Ibarra. Zaguaripa lay somewhere on the road from the valley of Sonora to that of Paquime
(Casas Grandes in Chihuahua), and Obregón gives the distance
between these two valleys as 40 leagues,[64] which is nearly correct.
The trail as we have followed it leads up the Sonora River. After
leaving Zaguaripa, we shall find the expedition very shortly in
northwestern Chihuahua. To introduce Sahuaripa into the itinerary
it would be necessary to have Ibarra swing by weeks of marching far
southward, either back-tracking over the greater part of the route
that he had come from the Fuerte or passing southeastward by the
Valley of Batuc across the Yaqui over very difficult country.
Mecham and Hammond avoid the difficulty of the back-track by
the simple and unexplained expedient of disregarding the entry into
the Sonora Valley. Having the party in the modern Sahuaripa, however, there remains for them the even greater difficulty of getting
Ibarra thence to northwest Chihuahua. The commentators achieve
this result by drawing a short line from Sahuaripa to Casas Grandes
across the Sierra Madre. The route which Mecham and Hammond
would have Ibarra take from Sahuaripa to the Casas Grandes country of Chihuahua is impossible and betrays alike a lack of knowledge of the relief and of the Indian populations. I doubt if the Sierra
Madre has ever been crossed in the section indicated by them, being
as nearly impassable a barrier as exists in North America. Moreover, to the north, northeast, and east of Sahuaripa it is far, far
more than two days to the limits of Ópata settlements. Had the
party left Sahuaripa for Chihuahua there could have been only two
routes possible. The better one—and it is difficult enough—would
have led across the Aros, up the Bacadéhuachi arroyo, down the
upper Bavispe, and across the Carretas or Pulpit passes into Chihuahua. This would have been a more arduous trip than any part of
Ibarra's journey to date, and one requiring many weeks, with Ópata
settlements extending to the farthest end of the Bavispe Valley. The
other route would have been worse, northeastward to the Chihuahua
border, about where the Papigochic joins the Aros, and thence
across the Sierra Madre. Across a part of this route I think that
Ibarra later returned from Casas Grandes, and the fearful hardships endured on that journey are graphically portrayed by Obregón.
In the latter case also there would have been Jova Ópatas to encounter for many days.

There is nothing in favor of the identification of Zaguaripa as
Sahuaripa excepting the name. There are numerous duplications of

[64] *Idem*, p. 186.

name in Indian Sonora. The name Sahuaripa in the Ópate language means "the home of the red ant people," I was told by a number of Indians. This suggests the division of the Ópatas among moieties such as have been described by Russell for the neighboring Pimas, where Buzzard and Coyote or Red and White Ant gentes were important.[65] It may therefore be that such a localized moiety may have resulted in the suppression of the other group, or that the Spaniards heard the name of one, perhaps the dominant moiety, and failed to get the true place name. The meaning of Sahuaripa is such at any rate that its repeated occurrence is strongly indicated.

If, therefore, we consider invalid the relocation of the route on the basis of a single place name and read the account of Obregón in terms of terrain and Indian tribes, we find Ibarra leaving the Cíbola road in the upper Bacoachi Valley and swinging eastward for a distance over the route by which Cabeza de Vaca entered the Opatería, the old trail from Bacoachi across the Sierra de los Ajos into the Fronteras Basin. The Ópata village of Cuquiárachi is nestled against the eastern base of the Ajos range, built on a dissected apron of the old gravel fill which gives rise to deep, narrow gulches and castellated promontories rising above an ample flood plain. The site fits the scene very well as described in Obregón's excited account of the fights sustained there with the native population, and it fits very well with the rest of the information. A short distance to the west lay the valley of Suya (Bacoachi drainage) where Diego de Alcaraz and his men were massacred, and whence the half-breed progeny originated. Immediately to the northeast lie the Terrenos de Camou, part of the high, grassy steppes that were in the range of the plains Indians, presumably Sumas at this time. Few other sites would fit the description of Obregón of the crags and pinnacles among which the fighting took place. Arispe it is true might do, but Arispe I think has been identified as lying farther back on the route, identified by Obregón as Guaraspi. Antonio Ruiz supports northern identification of the location of Zaguaripa by his mention of a scouting party there having encountered pines and suffered from cold at night, though it was only August. From Cuquiárachi-Zaguaripa the rest of Ibarra's

---

[65] Frank Russell, The Pima Indians, 26th Ann. Rept. Bur. Amer. Ethnol., (1908), pp. 1–389; ref. to p. 197. He also gives Va'af as a name for the White People. This may have a bearing on Garcés' attempt to locate Vacapa of Fray Marcos in the Papaguería (Coues, *op. cit.* [n. 1], Vol. 2, p. 487) and the occurrence apparently of a third Vacapa in the Opatería. The Pima, Ópata, and Cahita languages are so cognate that, given the same moiety organization as well, a moiety term might have been repeatedly picked up as a place name by the Spaniards.

march, according to Obregón's account, is in agreement with the terrain of northeastern Sonora.

Ibarra was nearing the end of the Ópata country. He

undertook to pursue his journey to the smooth lands and thus he proceeded, marching with great circumspection, using scouts to go through sierras of extraordinary height, passing broken and cliffy country where some of the horses gave out . . . and thus brought the party to a land of better temperature and easier passage than that which lay behind. At two days' journey we found a pueblo of two hundred houses of flat roofs [Colonia Morelos vicinity on upper Bavispe River?]. . . . Here we came to the end of the limits and lands of their friends [Ópatas] and entered into that of the Querechos.[66]

The account fits a crossing of the Fronteras basin from west to east. The margins of the basin have pretty deeply dissected gravel fills and are flanked by rugged mountains, especially at the east. By following the streams, however, there is a direct and sufficiently easy route east to the upper Bavispe basin and thus directly to the great pass route that leads over into Chihuahua.

The crossing into Chihuahua is thus described:

The expedition having marched two days from the last settlement of the provinces and confines of the valleys and dependencies of the Valle de Sonora . . . the party ascended the northern last chains of the sierra, on whose crest we beheld large and beautiful and fertile valleys composed of and adorned by the most beautiful plains, meadows, springs, rivers, and creeks of pure and clear water, and lands of agreeable temperature, better than ever I have seen. This beautiful and fertile land is adorned and accompanied by fine mountain ridges. . . . There are thick madrones, many and very high walnut trees, plums and wild grapes.[67]

Concerning the crossing of the Pulpit Pass and the descent into the cool, well watered high plains of Chihuahua, I shall quote the observations of Donald Brand, who has spent a year in this section studying the ruins which next claim Obregón's attention: [68]

The Pulpit Pass and upper Las Varas Creek, an affluent of the Carretas, fulfill the requirements of Obregón's sketch. Here is the line of easiest communication between northeast Sonora and the valley of Casas Grandes, being least circuitous, having the easiest pass, and being well provided with water, grass, and wood. The change from the rugged, narrow pass to the open llanos

---

[66] Cuevas, *op. cit.* (n. 51), pp. 172–173.

[67] *Idem*, p. 176.

[68] This statement was prepared at my request for inclusion in the present paper.

is abrupt and would be more apt to provoke Obregón's description than the gradual transition by way of the Carretas pass, farther south.

The pine-clad Sierra Hachitahueca, south of the pass, joins the Sierra del Oso, and the entire range is still noted for the bears Obregón mentions. Walnut trees in groves and as isolated trees are most common in the mountain valleys, but extend also into the plains. The madrone, a wild grape, and a wild plum are common in the mountains. The plains of Carretas are one of the finest natural pasture grounds in Chihuahua, and at present, in spite of heavy grazing, one may see deer in the foothills and antelope in the open llanos. Doves, quail, and waterfowl still abound, as described by Obregón.

Beginning with the mountain valleys of the Las Varas drainage, many prehistoric ruins are distributed along this creek, to its junction with the Carretas River, and thence quite widely over the plains. Some of the larger ruins are still of sufficient height so that they may well have had two or three stories remaining at the time of the Ibarra entrada.

The ruins of Casas Grandes proper are situated on the left bank of the river of that name in just such a location as that given by Obregón: "in some beautiful and fertile plains that surround it, with pleasant and useful hills and small ranges of mountains." The use of the phrase *el rio abajo de Paquime* signifies, I believe, that Obregón understood that the ruined town was situated on the lower course of the stream called Paquime. Cottonwoods and willows at present constitute the principal timber lining the river, but *"sabinas"* are lacking in the main valley. There are, however, two kinds of juniper in the foothills and tributary valleys. They may, being useful wood especially for charcoal, formerly have extended farther down the valley.

In view of the height of the remaining walls, and the high mounds of disintegrated adobe, his statement concerned houses of six or seven stories could be true, but probably it was an overstatement. The decomposition of the ruins has progressed so far that nothing can be hazarded regarding the nature of the superstructure, though the *torreadas* forms probably resembled the watch towers found among the Pueblos in the United States. There are at present no traces of defensive walls. A number of structures indicate the presence of "large and fine patios," but none have been exposed to a sufficient extent to prove or disprove the use of jasper-like stones as flagging. Perhaps all that Obregón saw was a quasi-paving produced by the accumulation of stones from the reduced walls. The builders often mixed stones with the mud of the walls. There remains no evidence of the pillars of heavy timber, but their former existence is almost requisite for the larger buildings. Obregón's statement that the walls were whitewashed and painted in many colors is supported by remains to be seen in the cliff dwellings of the same region. He is accurate in stating that the walls were usually of puddled adobe and that sometimes stones were mixed with the adobe. I have never noticed, however, wood used in the materials of the walls.

Obregón's mention of large and wide canals that brought water from the river to the houses is not intelligible. The only trace of an ancient acequia seen in the river plain was of one used to water the lowest fields, the ruins being on higher ground. There is evidence of a ditch carrying water from a spring to the main ruins. It is possible that farther down the river, where the ruins are dotted over the plain to varying distances from the river, irrigation canals took off from weir diversion dams and conveyed water to fields about the villages. All evidence on this score has been obliterated by centuries of erosion. Below the land at present cultivated there is only a wilderness of bunch grass, mesquite, and gullies.

The estufas in the floors of the houses may not have been kivas. None has been found to date. Perhaps the reference is simply to fireplaces. Neither is Obregón's "metal slag" intelligible. The two "patenas" of worked copper are not extraordinary; several small copper bells have been reported from the Casas Grandes region. The "rocks for grinding" were simply meal mullers. Smelting is inadmissible anywhere in the prehistoric Southwest. "Paved roads" are also out of the question, unless Obregón saw some of the many rock terraces mountainward and thought he saw a paved road winding about the mountain.

Obregón's "houses for a distance of eight leagues" down river from the first mountain ridge correspond to the distribution of ruins in the main Casas Grandes Valley from La Boquilla to the gorge below Corralitos. The fact that this stretch was explored by a separate party would indicate that Ibarra's route did not encounter the Casas Grandes River much below the site of Casas Grandes, a further implication that the main party came by way of the Pulpit Pass over the later government and missionary route. The distribution of ruins along it further indicates its prehistoric significance. We may therefore consider that the trace followed by Ibarra from the Bavispe Valley was a persistent line of travel later used in colonial days.

On the basis of Obregón's account of terrain and ruins, I think that the Rio de Paquime can be identified as that of the Casas Grandes. Obregón was trying to impress his sovereign with a colorful story, but there are no really bad misstatements in the light of what I know about that section.

The majority of the army on the return did not wish again to face the hostile Ópatas and, if we may credit Obregón, the terrors of the poison tree. It is hard to say how they made the return journey. They chose a more southerly route and had a terrible time crossing the Sierra Madre, and an equally bad time getting across a great river, whose canyon they could not follow downstream; that is, westward. The river can hardly have been any other than the Aros, and the place at which they descended to it appears to have been about where that stream enters Sonora from Chihuahua. The only other stream of important size would have been the lower Bavispe, which however is much less troublesome to cross and lacks an impassable canyon. Moreover, the Bavispe can hardly come into consideration because on it they would of necessity have encountered the Ópata settlements of the Nácori Chico Valley and of Bacadéhuachi long before coming to the river, whereas the expedition found itself in a wilderness in which the members almost starved before getting through. The only argument for a crossing of the Bavispe is that Obregón reports their coming into the settled country at Batuco, which has been identified with the modern Batuc on the lower Moctezuma. It was at Batuco that the party obtained salt for the first time. However, had they taken the trail from Nácori Chico at the base of the Sierra Madre westward to Batuco they would certainly have had salt long before. To this day the pueblo of Bacadé-huachi recovers a crude and purging salt from the red beds which are in the valley fill of that basin. I am therefore inclined to believe that the Batuco of Obregón is not the pueblo now called Batuc.

The most legible rendering of the return route in terms of the account and the terrain is that they continued from Casas Grandes through the Chuhuichupa country, passed the gorge of the Aros in the vicinity of Nátore, and continued through the southern part of the thinly peopled Sahuaripa district to the Yaqui. I should like to identify the beginning of the village country, Obregón's Batuco, with the basin of Tacupeto. At least a sort of trail leads from Chihuahua into the Sahuaripa district, although those who must cross the mountains usually prefer a more southerly detour through Maicoba. The Nátore route is bad enough for the passage of such an expedition, the mountains to the north make a crossing almost out of the question.

CAMINO REAL

Ibarra's entrada concludes the period of exploration. He followed the old Cíbola route to the American border and then left it to seek another legendary site, which turned out to be equally disappointing. A few years later the Jesuit labors commenced on the northern frontier and their missions spread rapidly northward. In this permanent expansion the ancient highway played a principal role. Along it were strung the principal administrative foundations of church and crown. The road to Cíbola became the camino real of the north-western frontier, the great artery of the entire region.

{ 6 }

The Personality of Mexico

THE GEOGRAPHIC ART

This is an excursion into the oldest tradition of geography. For, whatever the problems of the day may be that claim the attention of the specialist and which result in more precise methods of inspection and more formal systems of comparison, there remains a form of geographic curiosity that is never contained by systems. It is the art of seeing how land and life have come to differ from one part of the earth to another. This quality of understanding has interested men almost from the beginning of human time and requires restatement and re-examination for each new generation.

Many names have been given to the central and never completed theme of regional interpretation. For this essay a term is borrowed from Sir Cyril Fox's admirable study of the cultural backgrounds of the British Isles.[1] The designation "personality" applied to a particular part of the earth embraces the whole dynamic relation of life and land. It does not deal with land and life as separate things, but with a given land as lived in by a succession of peoples, who have appraised its resources for their times in terms of their capacities and needs, who have spread themselves through it as best suited their ends, and who have filled it with the works that expressed their particular way of life.

ROOTS OF MEXICO IN A LONG PAST

Mexico, like most lands of Latin America, has its main and living roots in a deep, rich past. The continuity with ages long gone is

---

Geographical Review, Vol. 31, 1941, pp. 353–364. Copyright, 1941, by the American Geographical Society.

[1] Sir Cyril Fox, The Personality of Britain: Its Influence on Inhabitant and Invader in Prehistoric and Historic Times, 3rd ed. (Cardiff, 1938).

fundamental in this country. An invasion by the modern, Western world is under way, but this conquest will remain partial, as earlier did the rude assault of the Spanish conquerors upon native ways. The American motorcar now does duty in remotest villages, but it is loaded with the immemorial goods and persons native to the land. The automobile is accepted as a better means of transport, as, centuries earlier, the pack and draft animals brought from Castile were accepted. It and the other machines, however, are being adapted to native ways and native needs; they will not dominate or replace native culture.

The two most important things to know about Mexico still are the patterns of life that existed before the coming of the white men and the changes that were introduced during the first generation or two of the Spanish period. Although a third period of transformation is under way, we may yet best delineate the basic traits of this land and its peoples from its prehistoric geography and from its geography of the sixteenth century. Our attention may be confined, therefore, to formative periods in a distant past that distinguish what are still the dominant traits of the country.

THE LINE BETWEEN NORTH AND SOUTH

For unnumbered centuries a narrow frontier has formed the parting line between the North and the South of what is today called Mexico. This is the meeting zone of the high cultures of the South and the ruder cultures of the North. In the east this line reaches the Gulf of Mexico a little north of Tampico. Immediately to the south lies the Huasteca, also called by the Spaniards the Province of Pánuco. Thence the line winds sinuously southward along the eastern escarpments of the tableland to the very margin of the Valley of Mexico. Here it turns westward and then passes more or less along the northern base of the great east-west belt of volcanoes. This northern, aggraded foot-slope of the volcanoes is often called the Bajío; it is extraordinarily fertile, perhaps the best part of Mexico agriculturally. Curiously, at the beginning of historical time the Bajío lands for the most part were held by the Northern barbarians. Near Guadalajara a sharp promontory of Southern high culture reached north-northeastward to include the Cazcán Indians, in the Mixtón or Teul country, on the borders of modern Jalisco and Zacatecas. The Cazcán land is one of high mesas and rich valleys. West of Guadalajara the dividing line turns sharply northwestward

and descends through the western sierra to the coast plain of Sinaloa, where it ends on the Gulf of California above Culiacán (see
figure).

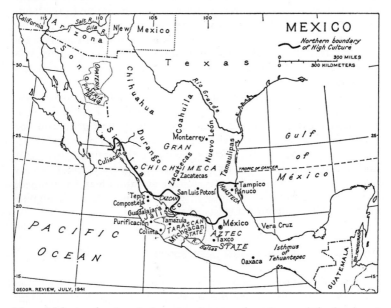

Map of Mexico showing the boundary between the cultures of the South and
the North.

The ruder cultures of the North occupied the interior tableland
as far south as the base of the central volcanic chain. The advanced
cultures held two great prongs extending northward in the coastal
lowlands and foothills. The eastern prong (Huasteca) failed to
reach the Tropic of Cancer and ended abruptly against the very
primitive cultures of Tamaulipas. On the west coast, the extension
of high culture (which I had the good fortune to discover a dozen
years ago) reached into northern Sinaloa. In the west also, "islands"
of intermediate cultures, especially the Opatería and Pimería Baja
of Sonora, formed links to the Pueblo country of our Southwest. In
general, the expansive energy of the high cultures was notably greatest in the west, next greatest on the east coast, and least in the center.

In many places the northern limit of high culture archeologically reached scores of miles beyond its historical limit. It seems therefore that the barbarian cultures had been in process of advancing southward.

THE NORTHERN AREA, THE GRAN CHICHIMECA

Climatically, the Northern country is dominantly arid or semiarid, with wide stretches of mesquite and huisache, of creosote bush, sotol, yucca, and cacti. But it contains also some of the finest and largest alluvial valleys and a great deal of good upland receiving enough rainfall for summer crops. The position of the line was determined by cultural, not environmental, reasons; and it is to be regarded as the meeting of two very different ways of aboriginal life. The Spaniards made the distinction of *Indios de policía* (polity) to the south and savages, or Chichimecs, to the north. The South was taken over at once by the Spaniards and became the *tierra de paz* (land of peace), whereas the North remained more or less unquiet, the *tierra de guerra*.

The commonest name for the whole North was Gran Chichimeca, which included a large number of very small tribes of assorted barbarians, many of whom, especially in the east, were roving hunters and gatherers (for example, in the states of Tamaulipas, Nuevo León, and Coahuila). However, more Northern tribes than have yet been recognized in anthropology were at least part-time farmers, especially on the interior plateau (in the states of Chihuahua, Durango, and Zacatecas, for example). In the northwest, farming was dominant; in the Opatería and Pimería Baja at least, agricultural skill was equal to that of the South. These and the Pueblo peoples were excepted by the Spaniards from the general designation of Chichimec.

THE SOUTHERN CULTURE HEARTH,
WITH EMPHASIS ON THE WEST

The South belonged to Indians who may, with propriety, be called civilized. Here and there, in rain forests or on excessively rugged mountains, primitive groups (mostly relicts) survived. No large, attractive site in the South, however, remained unappropriated by a population of advanced culture, whereas in the North many attractive and commodious areas were poorly, or not at all, used for agriculture.

The South and Southwest of Mexico constitute one of the great culture hearths of the world, in which was created in part, and developed largely, an economic complex that is one of the great achievements of mankind. Perhaps only in the Orient did men elaborate as ample a base for a diversified civilization. Archeology has given most attention to date to the great monumental cultures, which were mostly on the Atlantic side. Behind the named civilizations of Maya, Toltec, and Aztec lie older and more fundamental attainments in plant domestication and other inventions, of which we know only scattered bits. It is possible that greater knowledge of these more ancient beginnings will attach most importance to the Pacific side.

The Pacific slopes have been least regarded by students, yet there is evidence that they may have been the most active front of cultural origins and growth. A few indications may be submitted.

1. The basic traits of the native domesticated plants point to a source on the Pacific margin rather than the Atlantic. The Pacific areas have in general a shorter rainy season, a smaller total rainfall, and a much more sharply marked dry season. Their soils are rarely acid; most commonly they are somewhat alkaline. All the principal native crops show traits that point to an origin in the drier, western lands. Perhaps we may seek the earliest farming in western alluvial valleys, probably below an altitude of two thousand meters. All the native crops are warm-starting; that is, germinate best in well aerated, only slightly moist soils under the rising temperatures of late spring or early summer. Their vegetative growth is made when warm weather and frequent rains coincide, as is characteristic of the summer thundershower period. Short intervals of dry weather are beneficial. Although none of the crops is truly drought-resistant, they have various means, such as hairy leaf surfaces, of protecting themselves against brief dryness. Ripening takes place during the bright, dry season that follows the rains. Some of the beans need a rainy season of only a month; some of the corns may make use of nearly three months of moisture. These climatic qualities of the common crops of Mexico may indicate an origin in the lower levels of the *tierra templada* on the Pacific side.

2. On the Pacific side also, from Guatemala north to Sonora, there is an exceptionally large diversity of ecologically fixed crop types and of subspecies or varieties. Of maizes there are in the west

not only a great many kinds of the dent variety but also many flour, sugar, pop, and flint corns, which have never been collected or classified. What collecting has been done so far has been chiefly in markets of larger cities and has missed the seeds which are important to native economy but which do not enter into commerce. The result is that the economic botanist does not yet know the wealth of maize, beans, chili, squash, upland cotton, amaranth, and tomatoes that marks the hill lands behind the west coast.

3. It is also noteworthy that the wild flora of the west contains numerous close relatives of the cultivated plants (other than corn).

4. The route of dispersal of crops into the Indian agriculture of the United States also argues for the great age of west-coast culture. This route was almost certainly up the west coast into Arizona and New Mexico, and thence east from the Pueblo country to the (middle?) Mississippi Valley and the eastern seaboard of the United States. The Florida–West Indies bridge functioned only slightly, if at all; and there is no indication that any domesticated crops were carried from Mexico by way of the Gulf coast.

5. Bit by bit the work of Southwestern archeologists is producing evidence of the early operation of this western corridor in the diffusion of a variety of culture traits from Mexico into Arizona and New Mexico.

In aboriginal agriculture the lands of highest quality, of most intensive use, and of main dependability were the valley bottoms. Many of these lands are used today for a succession of crops throughout the year. During the dry season they may still hold enough moisture for cropping and are then called *tierras de humedad.* In some places water is applied artificially, though neither a main nor an early role can be ascribed to irrigation in Mexico. The valley lands were carefully tended and improved and determined the sites of many of the larger villages. However, the frequent summer showers make possible also the growing of one summer, rainy-season, or *temporal* crop on hill and mountain slopes. Growth of population soon forced expansion from the narrow valley bottoms to the far more extensive hill slopes.

To this day, southern and western Mexico is lost in a smoke haze during spring, from rubbish burning on thousands of mountain deadenings, or *coamiles,* that are being prepared for planting. Many of them are still prepared and planted without the use of a plow, by means of a digging stick (or crowbar) and hoe. The seeds are punched into the ash-covered soil and left to the rains, without further attention except weeding. As no furrows are drawn nor

regular fields laid out, the native farmer picks his planting spot
chiefly with an eye to the timber. The bigger the tree growth, the
easier the clearing, the larger the increment of wood ashes, and
perhaps also the better the cash return from charcoal. Slope matters
almost not at all, and soil very little; for the crop is grown primarily
on the fertility made available by the woody growth, the *monte*.

This untidy method of farming has given remarkable protection
against soil erosion on steep slopes. Many such mountain slopes have
gone through thousands of years of alternation of clearing (*desmon-
tar*), planting, and regrowth to monte. The process is really a long-
term rotation of crops and trees. Under this management fields and
settlements have been able to spread over terrain that plow farmers
would find impossible. Villages that have a nucleus of permanent
tierra de humedad appropriate about themselves as well a wide
fringe of hill country for their coamiles or *milpas*. Also colonization
of later generations of villages takes place in mountain terrain, without permanent (valley floor) fields, and all the subsistence is derived from such shifting mountain clearings. In both cases the village is permanent; wandering villages are absent, or at least extremely rare.

American notions of what constitutes suitable farm land, fertile
soil, and limits of rural population cannot be applied to such a land
and culture as these. These hill areas appear badly overcrowded to
us; yet the more we learn of the records of the Spanish conquest and
of the archeologic sites far earlier than that, the more it seems that
from time immemorial these western hill lands swarmed with villages as they do today. Indeed, it seems probable that in many hill
areas population was more numerous of old than it is now.

This picture of ancient population growth points to a swarming
out from the cradle lands of the rich valleys (which I should like
to postulate as being on the Pacific versant) to the mountain slopes,
gradually encountering higher and colder country. This process of
uphill migration made necessary the elimination of some of the more
exacting crop plants, occasionally a new domestication (pulque
agave) and generally the breeding of specialized forms tolerant of
less warmth. The process cannot have been rapid; the *tierra fría,*
such as the Valley of Mexico, is not part of the most anciently settled lands. The higher lands are still not very well suited to corn
(except for a few specialized types); but their agricultural utility
has increased with the coming of European crops and domestic animals.

Growth in numbers and in agricultural skills also resulted in spread of the high cultures through the tropical forests of the Atlantic slope. Least of all was the movement northward into the arid lands, except along the west coast, where great and rich valleys invited occupation, even within the desert. Here, on the American side of the international boundary, the Gila and Salt valleys provide the only known important aboriginal development of irrigation techniques in North America.

In summary, this agricultural civilization seems to have been born of a truly temperate climate with a rich equipment of wild plant materials, suitable for amelioration by breeding. As it acquired more skill in cultivation and plant breeding and more man power, this high Southern (or, as I should prefer to say, Western) culture moved up the mountains to the high central volcanic slopes and eastward across rain forest and savanna to the shores of the Gulf, but least of all northward into the fringes of the arid country. This statement must be offered as a working hypothesis, not as an established finding.

METALS IN THE SOUTHERN CULTURE

An underestimated element in aboriginal Mexico is the use of metals. In this case also, the evidence points strongly westward as well as southward. Gold was one of the most highly prized items throughout the high culture, a main tribute item and a staple of trade, a basic culture trait. The volcanic highlands of the center were barren of gold, which was found chiefly as sand in streams to the south and west in a terrain of older metamorphic and igneous rocks. These outcrop widely south of the central volcanic chain, westward to the Pacific and southward to the Isthmus of Tehuantepec, also in the "old lands" of Central America. There were two such great placer areas, one centering on Honduras, the other and larger one extending from the Isthmus of Tehuantepec northward to the Balsas graben and westward to the foot slopes of the volcano of Colima. In both these areas almost every torrent concentrated its annual increment of gold sand.

Of the other metals we know much less, but there promises to be a good deal to discover about their aboriginal use. It seems that the first Spanish vein mines previously had been Indian mines; Taxco is an example for copper and tin, and probably also for silver. In the process of looting the Aztec treasure the Spaniards soon found that the metallic wealth of the Aztecs had come mostly from non-Aztec lands and especially that the western neighbors, the Tarascans, were the great purveyors of silver, and also of copper and bronze. Archival and field studies have failed to disclose any silver mining within the territory of Tarascan stock; on the contrary, Tarascan imperialism seems to have been motivated to western conquests by the desire for these metals. Not in Michoacán, the homeland of the Tarascans, but in southern Jalisco have we found, we think, the source of the Tarascan silver and tin and of part of their copper. The trail of aboriginal mining and smelting is now partly marked from the Taxco region of the Balsas, through Tamazula of Jalisco, through the coast ranges of Purificación and the Valley of Banderas, as far north as the Culiacán River of Sinaloa.[2]

Studies indicate that in various places in the west smelting skill and alloying practices were rather advanced. We have just begun to explore this subject, which promises to change previous concepts about Indian metal arts. From present evidences we may advance the hypothesis that an Indian metallurgy was developed between Taxco and Culiacán, that it involved the reduction of sulphides as well as of oxides, that hardening, casting, and alloying of copper and silver were practiced, and that the quantity of production of copper and silver suggests the possible beginning of an age of metals, interrupted by the coming of the Spaniards.

AZTEC AND TARASCAN STATES

There were many peoples and languages in this great Southern area of high cultures, but the dominant traits of the civilizations were similar throughout. At the time of the conquest there were only two large political units, the Aztec state of México and the Tarascan state of Michoacán. In geographic design they were similar. Their main areas were at high altitudes, of modest agricultural attraction. The capital of each lay near the northern margin, close to the Chichimeca. On this exposed front both Aztecs and Tarascans were probably no more than holding their own. Both, however, showed a strong expansionist drive into the *tierra caliente,* absorbing more and more subject lands at intermediate and lower altitudes. These lands provided the master nations on the highlands with metals, cotton, cacao, varied foodstuffs, dyes, and gums. Both states de-

---

[2] A report on the Culiacán area by Isabel Kelly, in preparation at the time when this article was written, was later published: Excavations at Culiacán, Sinaloa, Ibero-Americana, 25 (1945).

pended on the subjugation of civilized but weak neighbors for the continuous enlargement of their own power and wealth. Neither ventured on the colonization of the thinly peopled but very fertile Chichimeca immediately adjacent to the north.

THE SPANIARDS FOLLOW THE AZTEC AND TARASCAN POLITICAL PATTERN

Aztec and Tarascan imperialism facilitated Spanish occupation. The Spaniards took over both states and superimposed their own tribute-collecting organization on the native system of tributes. As the Aztecs and Tarascans had been pushing southward and westward, the Spaniards also faced at first in the same directions. In twelve years (1520–1531) they had complete control of the land of high cultures. Millions of native workers exchanged Indian masters for Spanish encomenderos, Indian tribute collectors for the tax collectors of crown and church.

On the whole, the exactions were probably increased; and especially were the Indians required to give more gold. As gold had been brought mostly from the south, from the geologically older and topographically lower lands south of the volcanoes, the Spaniards elaborated a climatic thesis of the origin of gold: This yellow metal has an affinity for the sun and therefore grows in hot lands, in southern lands, in lands of low altitude. The tierra caliente of both coasts was gutted with amazing rapidity. Before 1540 the stream placers, gold sands in terraces, and even concentrations of gold in residual soil had been largely worked out from Vera Cruz to Oaxaca and Colima. Far more serious, the Indian populations of the tierra caliente had melted away to such pitiful remnants that the term "decimation" may be applied literally from Colima to Pánuco. Ten years after the fall of Mexico sober and competent men were discussing the inevitable ruin and depopulation of the country, being emptied of its native workers as it had already been emptied of its treasure.

A NEW FRONTIER FORMED IN THE WEST

Meanwhile a new economic frontier was taking form insensibly, in the western end of the lands of high culture. In 1523 Cortés quietly appropriated for himself the great Tarascan-held silver district of

Tamazula (Jalisco). Taxco became a Spanish mining camp at the same time. Nuño de Guzmán's men of the far Northwest supported themselves by locating silver properties in the mountains east of Culiacán and in the barrancas of Tepic (decade of 1530). Before 1540 the Spaniards were finding small bodies of silver ore all the way from Taxco to Culiacán. These western *encomenderos* used their civilized Indians in the service of their mines and engaged also in slave raids into the Chichimec territory beyond. The new silver-bearing West became the scene of furious rivalry among the great captains and officials of New Spain, Cortés, Mendoza, Alvarado, Nuño de Guzmán; and out of this melee grew a frontier government, New Galicia, which really saved New Spain from the fate of the Antillean islands and gave to it its later colonial greatness.

All the earlier silver discoveries were within the area of the civilized Indians. From 1523 into the 1540's a series of now largely forgotten *villas* and *reales* (formally constituted mining settlements) were founded between Taxco and Culiacán. Every one of these Spanish establishments had mining, usually of silver, as its basis. Thus was founded the first capital of Nueva Galicia, Compostela. Now drowsing around an ancient church that bears the double-headed eagles of Habsburg, it is remembered by us only because Coronado collected here the idle young gentlemen of New Spain to ride thence to the plains of Kansas.

The trail of silver led inland and upward, not down the floors of the canyons toward the sea, as the quest for gold had done. The great bodies of silver ore are associated with the lower, or earlier, volcanism of the Mesa Central. The Tertiary volcanics, enriched with metallic sulphides, overlie the older rocks, which may carry the free gold, and underlie the cones, malpais, tuff beds, and mudflows of the young volcanoes, generally barren of precious metals. The western and southwestern rim of the Mesa Central has been deeply trenched by great canyons. Here, along the upper slopes of the barrancas, the silver-bearing, lower volcanic beds were accessible to prospectors. Silver came to connote to the Spaniards high country and cold lands; they even thought of it as in some manner associated with the north, as they had related gold to southern latitudes.

Civilized tribes held the coastal districts of the West and extended inland along the warm floors of the barrancas. Barbarian tribes occupied the high mesas and reached seaward along their shredded fringes between the barrancas. The silver country, therefore, in a measure lay between civilized and barbarian habitats, in the meeting zone of the two major cultures. Thus, especially, the

barrancas behind Compostela and Guadalajara became passageways
for the Spanish prospectors, leading them back toward the central
plateau and into the Chichimeca.

By 1540 the Spanish penetration had created tensions in this frontier zone that gave rise to the most formidable Indian outbreak in
the history of New Spain: the Mixtón War. The Mixtón country
was the knobby promontory of high civilization reaching north from
Guadalajara. Here civilized Indians, mainly Cazcán, were neighbors
to barbarian tribes, such as Zacatec, Guachichil, and Huichol. The
docile Cazcáns had been badly used by their encomenderos at mining
silver in the barrancas. At the same time, slave raiding by this group
of encomenderos was irritating the nomadic tribes of the highlands.
The Mixtón rebellion was the union of desperate civilized Indians
with wild hill tribes. The outbreak was suppressed only by the use
of the whole military strength of New Spain. In the prosecution
of the campaign the Spaniards for the first time broke through this
frontier zone and began the occupation of the Chichimeca. Here
began the technique of frontier fighting, the establishment of flying
squadrons and fortified posts (presidios), that was to mark the occupation of the North for the next two and a half centuries.

To the great good fortune of Spain it so happened that immediately behind the ramparts of the Mixtón country lay the greatest
silver country in the world—the land of the Zacatec Indians. Some
of these, caught as slaves in the Mixtón War, had been sent down
to the mines of Taxco. A number succeeded in escaping and returned
home, with some knowledge of silver ores. As Spanish parties from
Guadalajara pushed closer to their homes, the Zacatec tried (1546)
to gain favor by disclosing the presence of the Veta Grande, at
Zacatecas. Soon Zacatecas became the greatest silver producer in
the world. In sustained production it has never been equaled by any
other silver district.

The Zacatecas strike was followed during the next quarter of a
century by the discovery, without parallel in history, of a series of
silver districts, first along the western fringe of the Mesa Central,
but soon also along its eastern slopes northward through San Luis
Potosí. New Galicia, previously a precariously held narrow strip in
the northwest, expanded rapidly to absorb the Chichimeca, the unlimited North. The shabby townsmen of Guadalajara and Compostela became the fabulous grandees of northern principalities
built about mines. Guadalajara was the gateway through which
miners, merchants, soldiers, ranchers, and missionaries poured
northward, carrying in their train docile Southern Indians from

Jalisco, Michoacán, and Colima to do the hard work of the new country. Guadalajara became the capital of the North as well as of the West. From this exposed march site—to use the term of Vaughan Cornish—one of the greatest breakthroughs of New World history took place, between the fateful date of 1540 and the end of the century. By that time men from the Nueva Galicia march had reached and seized Durango, Chihuahua, New Mexico, Coahuila, and Nuevo León, roughly outlining the present international border. In later years the same breed was to extend its range of operations from Texas to California. The Spanish trails of the American Southwest all lead directly back to the nuclear area of New Galicia.

This land of high steppe and pine-clad mountains has been for four centuries the primary source of the wealth of New Spain–Mexico. Its mining towns became great and architecturally distinguished. Even at the end of the colonial period they were producing, according to Humboldt's estimate, more than half the precious metal of the world. Vast stock ranches developed about the mines, to supply the great and constant demand for pack and draft animals, for meat, hides, and fat. South of the mining country, the rich Bajío lands at the foot of the volcanoes were plowed and planted to foodstuffs for the mining districts and gave rise to a large number of profitable haciendas and a class of overopulent landlords. Mexico City, center of government and trade, grew magnificent and effete, as the ultimate beneficiary of the wealth of the North.

As wealth in unheard-of amount flowed south from the silver mines of the former Chichimeca, the native populations of the North were swept out of existence, except in certain mountain retreats, such as the Tarahumara. Many natives were branded and sold south as slaves. Many more were consumed in the work of the mines. Southern Indians were brought in as free laborers in an unending stream. Thus Tlascalan, Tarascan, Otomi, Aztec, and other colonists were strewn over the North, as farming, ranching, and mining labor. The richer mines imported droves of Negro slaves. Many Spaniards of small means or none at all came north to try their hand at mining, merchandising, or transport of goods. In the course of time all these stocks except the upper-class Spanish fused into a new breed, of no one color. Thus was born the mestizo Mexico of today. Here was the frontier of New Spain, on which finally a new nationality was formed.

This design of New Spain was drawn during the sixteenth century, and has persisted to the present. Still the Northern march has dominance in part over the Southern hearth. It is still an area of immigration, receiving labor, foodstuffs, and manufactured goods from the central states for its metals, livestock, and cotton. For the most part, men of the North have made the revolutions and wielded the power, men from Sonora, Chihuahua, Coahuila, Nuevo León; men born to take risks, to the frontier habit of alternation of hard effort and complete laziness. The South still shows its aboriginal fundament of patient, steady toil done by apt craftsmen, who can create things of remarkable beauty if they have the chance. The old line between the civilized South and the Chichimeca has been blurred somewhat, but it still stands. In that antithesis, which at times means conflict and at others a complementing of qualities, lie the strength and weakness, the tension and harmony that make the personality of Mexico.

PART III

Human Uses of the Organic World

7

American Agricultural Origins:
A Consideration of Nature and Culture

On the sound descriptive principle that archeology is where you find it, the science of prehistory is being pieced together from the evidence produced by digging. It cannot, however, depend exclusively on the limited testimony provided by the enduring materials of ruins, graves, and refuse heaps, but seeks other inductive approaches by tracing culture survivals, be they words, institutions, forms of settlement, tools, crops, or other culture traits. Such data, contributed from diverse sources, may provide also new leads for the field archeologist in his explorations. Culture history, moreover, may set up working hypotheses that use partly deductive approaches, as by postulating from sufficient experience certain probable relationships between environmental advantage or disadvantage on the one hand and the origin and development of culture on the other. As in all other fields of culture history, there is permanent need of interdisciplinary synthesis and hypothesis. In these pages the probability of original development of American agriculture in certain hearths is considered in the light of certain fundamental characteristics of native crop plants and farming practices, which point to specific natural environments and hence would limit the number of eligible localities in which such cultural beginnings may have been made.

ORIGIN OF AMERICAN AGRICULTURE IN DESERT OR STEPPE?

The most widely known thesis of the origin of agriculture in America is the one formulated by Spinden, who has regarded "irrigation as an invention which accounts for the very origin of agriculture it-

Essays in Anthropology Presented to A. L. Kroeber in Celebration of his Sixtieth Birthday, June 11, 1936 (Berkeley, California, 1936), pp. 279–297.

self," and who therefore would place the beginnings of farming and sedentary village life, as well as the sites of most rapid cultural advance, in arid and semiarid parts of the New World.[1] His position is very much like the familiar "potamic" theory that Old World civilization originated in the river oases of the Near East by irrigation; a theory elaborated especially by Kropotkin and Metchnikov. The arguments which have been advanced by Spinden are in particular: (1) that the earliest records of cultivated plants, pottery, and weaving come from areas where irrigation was practised, these areas in the New World including specifically Peru and Mexico; (2) that pressure of population made itself felt early in such areas and acted as an incentive to cultural advance; (3) that "in the desert the clearing of the field is less laborious than in the jungle"; and (4) that the comparative food value of plants originating under desert conditions is perhaps higher than that of plants which belong originally in climates exacting less extreme physiologic qualities.

The archeologic evidence that agriculture originated in association with irrigation is by no means convincing, as the supporters of this thesis conclude. The case is far better for the Old World than the New, but even there it is weak. The great stratigraphic records of early culture in the Old World are in the great river oases or their margins, it is true; but what warrant is there for associating irrigation with the oldest or older of these horizons? Nor is it safe to assume, because the longest-known stratigraphic series are established in the river oases, that still earlier records will not be discovered elsewhere. The archaeologic knowledge of Mesopotamia and Egypt is enormously superior to that available for other areas because their great ruins of ancient historic civilizations first attracted scientific curiosity. We are just beginning to see attention directed to the archeology of Iran, Asia Minor, and India, any or all of which may possibly precede the rivers of the deserts in development of agriculture and sedentary life. For the New World, the assertion that agricultural beginnings in Mexico were associated with irrigation appears to be unwarranted. I am unaware of any such evidence for early Mexico or Central America, or even of the major importance of irrigation at any time in their aboriginal history. Where large populations existed on the Gulf or Caribbean

---

[1] H. J. Spinden, The Origin and Distribution of Agriculture in America, Proceedings, Nineteenth International Congress of Americanists Held at Washington, December 27–31, 1915 (Washington, 1917), pp. 269–276. I have taken exception to his views elsewhere: Carl Sauer and Donald Brand, Aztatlán: Prehistoric Mexican Frontier on the Pacific Coast, Ibero-Americana, 1, 1932, pp. 58–60.

coasts and in the interior plateaus, irrigation was generally not needed. For that part of the west coast with which I am acquainted, the evidence is that irrigation was not employed, but that farming depended on rainfall supplemented by the natural seasonal flooding of streams.

If American agriculture arose in desert or semidesert regions, whether by irrigation or by dependence on natural flooding, three areas, chiefly, would come under consideration: (1) The Sonoran desert, which lies near the Gulf of California, and the steppe lands marginal thereto. Perhaps no other area in the New World comes as close to the physical conditions of the Old World Fertile Crescent as does this one. The lower Colorado, Sonora, Yaqui, Mayo, and Fuerte river valleys are large, superbly good areas for flood farming or for irrigation, suitable for growing many crops, and in part capable of raising two major crops a season. All of them, with the exception of the Colorado River, are very favorably situated with regard to possible routes of migration between north and south. Yet, without exception, these great flood plains have yielded no evidence of important archaeology. On the contrary, the headwaters of these northwestern Mexican rivers, in more humid and mountainous country, have significant archeologic remains, though not, so far as is known, of great age. The Gila and Salt rivers, tributary to the Colorado, hold remains of the Hohokam culture, which produced the most extensive irrigation of aboriginal North America. Though the elaboration of this culture developed strikingly autochthonous characteristics, it is not doubted that the beginnings of it were introduced from the south. (2) The Pueblo culture area of our Southwest, with its major axis running from the upper San Juan River along the Rio Grande into central Chihuahua. Here, in more numerous but smaller bodies of land than those of the Hohokam, irrigation was practised. Its Basket Maker beginnings of agriculture, however, are also based on southern introductions. In neither of these arid areas of North America—and they are the only notable ones that come into consideration for this continent—is agriculture considered otherwise than as a diffusion from the south. In both, moreover, many of the small early sites depended on farming without irrigation, with or without natural flooding of the fields.[2] Perhaps for both areas the interpretation may be permitted therefore

---

[2] I have discussed the question of the natural conditions involved in agriculture in the arid Hohokam country, including the desert Papagueria, in Carl Sauer and Donald Brand, Prehistoric Settlements of Sonora, with Special Reference to Cerros de Trincheras, Univ. Calif. Publs. in Geography, Vol. 5, No. 3, pp. 67–148, 1931. Reference to pp. 119–124.

that irrigation is subsequent to the establishment of agricultural settlement and that it is especially characteristic of the period of maximum expansion and greatest vigor of the cultures. We may consider it most probable that crops and farming methods were brought in from the south, but that irrigation was a local invention. (3) There remains therefore as a likely source of agriculture under arid conditions only the coast of Peru. It has against it first of all a strongly marginal location in its relation to the higher cultures of the New World, but also increasingly the evidence that its cultivated crops are not native to that area. Like the other arid-land cultures, it appears to be a colonial area, though perhaps early, with rapid and high local elaboration under the stimulus of gregarious oasis habitation.

Against the desert thesis, the following arguments also weigh heavily: (1) The evidence of the domesticated plants of the New World overwhelmingly points not to desert or steppe but to several humid climates for their origin. With minor exceptions they have physiologic qualities that do not fit into dry-climate habitats. These qualities, critical for the consideration of culture origins, have been overlooked, and will be considered in the following sections. (2) Desert lands, unless they be forested flood plains and hence non-desert in vegetation, are not easy, but difficult to clear for cultivation. The dry areas of North America which would come under consideration abound in brush and scrub, deeply rooted, tenacious of life, and difficult to eradicate even under modern methods. The preparation even of the bare surface usually demands much labor in leveling for the effective distribution of water. The engineering problems of diversion and delayed discharge of water, in their simplest terms, are rather formidable. The irrigation works of the Hohokam of Arizona demanded a very considerable amount of engineering skill, as well as a great deal of collective labor.

SITE QUALITIES FAVORABLE TO THE ORIGIN OF CULTURE HEARTHS

Having found desert and steppe unfavorable sites for the origin of American agriculture, we may examine other situations and criteria in the search for hearth areas. Without denying the existence of irrational or "prerational" attitudes in the satisfaction of subsistence needs by primitive groups, it is nevertheless obvious that of all culture forms the business of getting food, clothing, and shelter depends most largely on rational use of the natural environment. A consideration of rational solutions of the problems that such a group may have encountered in making a living from a particular environment is therefore not to be dismissed as rationalization.

1. Ratzel has emphasized the importance of "forcing-bed" conditions in the origin of cultures. In this concept is involved the availability of a limited, valuable subsistence area which rewards intensive use by sufficiently increased returns, and which has somewhat inelastic limits, so that improved use rather than expansion of used area tends to result. A further consideration is a bounding zone which fends off easy incursions by other groups, but which is not a barrier so effective as to isolate the group from contacts with others. Under such conditions, it is argued, social advance is encouraged, and increasing pressure of population hastens the advance from gathering to planting. The view may of course be construed as favoring a multiple origin of cultivation.

2. Another stimulus to cultural advance is seen in the availability of diversified raw materials, each in moderate amount, rather than in the great abundance of one or a few staples. Each primitive group needs, as the pioneer farmers did, a varied supply of raw materials for a well-balanced economy. If it is to continue to improve or even to maintain its standards, either these resources must be maintained so as to provide a certain quota per capita or else there must be discovery or creation of at least equivalent substitutes which continue to be available in like amount to each individual. A varied sustenance basis and the possibility of maintenance or enlargement of this sustenance basis would therefore be necessary material prerequisites for cultural advance.

3. Vavilov has developed the thesis of the mountain-valley origin of agriculture: "Mountainous districts supply an optimum of conditions for the manifestation of the varietal diversity [of plants], for the differentiation of the varieties and races, for the preservation of all possible physiological types. . . . It is very probable therefore that mountainous districts, being the centres of varietal diversity, were also the home of primeval agriculture." [3] Under such varied physical conditions the best opportunities were given for the occurrence of numerous kinds and types of useful plants, the primitive plant breeder had the richest material with which to experiment

---

[3] N. Vavilov, Studies on the Origin of Cultivated Plants, Bulletin of Applied Botany and Plant-Breeding, Vol. 16, 1926, No. 2, pp. 139–248. Reference to pp. 218–219.

by selection and crossing, and hence there may be postulated the best prospect of producing new and more useful forms.

4. For primitive agriculture a soil is required that is amenable to few and weak tools and which rewards tillage by yields sufficient to encourage continued planting.

5. Similarly, the native vegetation must be such that it can be displaced by simple means and without excessive effort. The theme is developed later that forest lands yield most readily to the primitive cultivator.

6. Climatic conditions are indicated which provide a definite growing and resting season. A well-defined tapering off of the growing period into a period of vegetative rest stimulates the production of seeds and tubers, the primary objects of gathering plant food and of planting. Also, under such conditions maturity takes place *en masse* in a short period; in other words, there is a definite harvest season. The necessity of providing against a recurring period of no production places a premium on thrift and industry which is lacking in lands of weak or no seasonal contrast.

7. The early significant advances of the human race, by which the level of sedentary, agricultural life was attained, appear to have taken place in lands of genial climate. The theory that man progresses only by being continually driven by the lash of nature has been overworked, as in Spinden's statement that "theoretically, agriculture would be more likely to originate under conditions that were hard than under those that were easy." On the contrary, it appears that in the earlier stages of his cultural advance man fared better under a nature that was benign, varied, but not too opulent in any particular respect, and that offered a sufficient and ready reward to the industrious, the skillful, and the provident. How great a part of the major early advance of the human race, both before and after the development of cultivation, is to be found in the truly temperate (mesothermal) climates, away from tropical exuberance, from desert extremes, and lands of heavy winters!

INDICATED CENTERS OF AMERICAN AGRICULTURAL ORIGINS

Under these terms, then, we should seek for the cradles of higher culture in humid lands of mesothermal climate, especially such as have a marked dry season (*Cw* or *Cs* of Köppen), which were moderately forested, had loose, and preferably rich, soils, a considerable variety of raw materials such as might be provided by a sufficient range in elevation, possessed a limited but good subsistence area, and were protected by partial barriers such as coasts or mountain ranges. Vavilov has objected to the great river plains of the Near East as the cradles of Old World agriculture and has sought to place its origins in the mountain valleys of Iran, Turan, India, and Abyssinia. Similarly in the New World we would suggest that the most promising trail for discovery skirts the humid flanks of low-latitude highlands at intermediate elevations.

1. The basal flanks of the great volcanic chain that stretches across Mexico from Tepic to central Vera Cruz have highly eligible sites with plentiful summer rain and rich, friable soils. Of least promise are the central portions, which on the north open up widely to the Gran Chichimeca, the great steppe and desert country that reaches across the international border, whence raiding tribes exerted pressure against the settled lands to the south. The southern slope of the central volcanic area is also disadvantageous, for it falls off for the most part steeply into the rain-shadow basin of the Balsas or Mexcala valley. Both the eastern and western ends, however, are suitable as culture hearths. (*a*) At the west, the country west of Guadalajara is well sheltered against the north by difficult barrancas. Tepic in particular has rich land, genial climate, varied relief, a rich flora, and a well-protected location that nevertheless is sufficiently convenient for the intrusion and diffusion of cultural impulses. Of its archeology only the curious Ixtlán figurines are known. (*b*) At the east, the Valley of Mexico is a great, snug bight of most attractive land, limited in early attractiveness chiefly by its elevation and restricted flora. The basins of Puebla, mountain-rimmed and extremely well protected against the turbulent north, might be considered superior to the Valley of Mexico. They are also more diversified in relief and flora. No reconstruction of the original vegetation of these volcanic uplands has been made, but the indication is that it was a country of deciduous hardwoods, among which oaks are prominent.

2. To the south of the Mexico-Puebla area an easy corridor leads to the temperate upland of Oaxaca, a sheltered site as well as a passageway, possessing mellow soils and a highly favorable diversity of relief, climate, and flora.

3. The volcanic slopes of Central America repeat on a smaller scale the favorable conditions of the Mexican volcanic belt. Thus in a loose cluster the northern continent offers four superior areas as possible hearths.

4. The southern continent suggests only one area of equal eligi-

bility, the temperate inter-Andean structural valleys of Colombia and Venezuela.

5. However, the Brazilian Highland in its more elevated, eastern parts, and probably especially toward the south, has conditions generally favorable, except for off-side location and a terrain that is perhaps too open.

Such an inspection of the New World may be discounted as resting on the suitability of present-day climates, whereas the time here contemplated lies thousands of years in the past. There are some, and they rely especially on Ellsworth Huntington, who would argue that the distribution of climatic areas in the prehistoric past of the New World was markedly different from that of the present. Climatic change involving the progressive displacement of climatic limits requires, however, either an important alteration of relief and of the distribution of land and sea or else significant change in the general atmospheric circulation. The former operates slowly. The latter type of change did take place during the Ice Age. Then and immediately thereafter the range of paleolithic man in the Old World suffered considerable displacement. So far as we know, postglacial climates settled down to their present form in the New World before agriculture got under way. The burden of proof rests on those who think otherwise. In our present knowledge of climatology we can point to no competent postglacial disturbing force. The appeal to a climatic change in order to get around some apparently inconvenient cultural distribution is too often an easy and careless way out of a perplexing situation. It has been improperly applied to our Southwest, where the entire archaeologic distribution is fully intelligible in terms of present climates. It has been postulated for the ancient Maya because of supposed present climatic unsuitability. In both of these applications the wish is father to the thought, and more knowledge of the culture and the country makes such hypotheses entirely unnecessary.

CLIMATIC AND EDAPHIC ADAPTATIONS OF NEW WORLD CROPS

The crops of the Old World may perhaps be grouped roughly under two sets of centers of origin, one in the Near East and the other in the monsoon lands of southeastern Asia. Climatically, the former is a mosaic of dry lowlands and humid highlands, which are mesothermal with preponderance of cool-season rains and dry summers (Cs of Köppen). This climatic type recurs in detached areas as far

east as Afghanistan. The lands of lengthy winter rainy season border most of the Mediterranean, including at its eastern end Syria
and Palestine, and reappear beyond on mountain flanks eastward to
the borders of India. In these eastern mountain "islands" Vavilov
and his associates place the original home of many of the most important Old World crops. In this habitat the crops are fall-sown,
make a large part of their growth of stalk and leaf in cool weather,
and complete their maturity during the long summer days in the
season of warmest weather. These climatic adaptations made easy
the diffusion of such crops into northwestern Europe, even into latitudes where the planting shifted to spring. In the European lands
there still was the same condition of a cool, moist starting period,
though the start was shifted to spring, and maturity took place during the long days of midsummer. It is not without significance that
Europe has midsummer harvest festivals.

In the New World we encounter a strikingly different situation.
Most of the New World domesticated plants, the potato being the
principal exception, like or require a warm start, summer rains, and
a dry fall with lowered temperature. They are late in starting, and
late in maturing, and if they can be brought under one seasonal
definition they may be said to be planted at the beginning of summer
and harvested at the end of fall. This seasonal characterization is
admittedly very rough, but it does bring out a contrast with the
crops of western Asia and of Europe. The most widely spread and
most important American crop, maize, typifies the dominant climatic
adaptation of American domesticated plants. Planting is delayed
generally until the ground is well warmed and cold nights are past.
Under such conditions maize germinates well even if the soil be
only slightly moist. In north Mexico and among the Indians of our
Southwest, for instance, deep planting is practiced a month or so
before the exceptionally delayed summer rains of these sections
begin. After the corn is well sprouted, the more rain and warmth
the better the growth. The yield of the commercial corn crop in the
United States is almost directly proportionate to the rainfall and
temperature of the two months after the first leaves are formed.
The inhabitant of the Mississippi Valley calls the muggy summer
thunderstorm periods "corn weather." Then a combination of high
temperature, high humidity, warm rain, and warm nights brings
the luxuriant vegetative growth necessary for a good yield. Thereafter a tapering off of rainfall is beneficial, and maturity is aided
either by dry weather or by gradual lowering of temperature. The
most active vegetative period of New World crops tends to extend

through the period of maximum warmth and long days. Comparable conditions in the Old World are found in the summer-monsoon lands of southeastern Asia. It may be noted that the European area that has been most successful in the cultivation both of maize and of monsoon-climate crops is the Po Valley, which has a marked period of rain during the heat of midsummer. In terms of the Köppen classification of climates the optimum habitat of American cultivated plants is in the *Cw* climates, and of the more tropical varieties, such as manioc and sweet potato, the *Aw* climates. The potato and its cultural associates, however, are excluded from these generalizations because of their intolerance of hot weather.

The American crop plants are in general poorly adapted to withstand drought while making their growth, upland cotton of Mexican origin being a partial exception. The leaf surfaces of the common American crops lack the devices that even slightly xerophytic plants have for economizing transpiration. In size and abundance of leaves most American domesticated plants are far more luxuriant than the nontropical Old World crop plants. Those which are of exceptionally rapid maturity, for instance the tepari bean (*Phaseolus acutifolius*), may grow where the total rainfall is low. Even though water is needed only for a brief season, the plants require a dependable water supply while making their growth, and suffer damage quickly if water is lacking at such time. Others, such as manioc, potato, and sweet potato, make use of a short rainy season to develop tubers or rootstocks for underground storage, some of them being adapted to a double annual rainy period, others to a biennial growth period. Apparently none of these plants, however, has any provision for withstanding low, uncertain, and irregular rainfall. Although a considerable number of such native crops can get along on a short rainy season, it is hardly proper to call them drought-resistant. In the savanna climates (*Aw*) and their boreal borders, the rainy season may be shortened to two months, but during that time rainfall is quite dependable, and may come in daily thunderstorms. It has been this condition, perhaps, that has misled some observers with respect to the climatic adaptations of American crops. A climate may be dry during the greater part of the year, but it is not therefore a semiarid climate any more than is a land of long winter. Both are simply climates with long resting periods and with brief growth periods. The growth period, however, is not a time of drought at all, and the vegetation is not drought-resistant, but either matures rapidly or passes into a resting state until the next rain season. The most general remark that can be made in this connection is that American crops vary greatly in the length of rain period required, but that generally they have no provision for the conservation of moisture during their vegetative period, and that they suffer quickly if the moisture supply is seriously interrupted within the limits of this time. The Mexican cotton, which can stand drought remarkably well, is perhaps therefore especially notable among American crops. In general our New World domesticates do not have the deeply-developed root systems which are common to dry-land vegetation and to some of the Old World crops. Many are shallow feeders.

Another significant contrast to the crops of western Asiatic origin is the markedly low tolerance of American crop plants for alkaline soil conditions. Our beans are notoriously sensitive to alkali in soil. Corn fares little better. Upland cotton is rather tolerant in this respect, and one strain, the Acala, brought from Chiapas by O. F. Cook, is fairly alkali-resistant. The source of this particular variety is one of the especially dry interior areas of southern Mexico. It represents perhaps an old selection from a plant which originally favored the drier margins of a summer-rain mesothermal climate. The experience of farming practice in the United States would appear to indicate that the New World crop plants belong on the neutral border between alkaline and acid soils, cotton showing a leaning to the alkaline side, though also a large tolerance in the other direction, whereas the potato, sweet potato, peanut, and tomato are quite tolerant of fairly acid conditions, and the corn-beans-squash complex thrives best approximately on the neutral border line. These nutritive habits again point toward a moderately humid climate, with upland cotton displaced toward the dry margin and the sweet potato, peanut, and tomato toward the wetter side.

These remarks have been kept in general terms chiefly because there is little quantitative information on the optimum and limiting climatic conditions of the individual crops. Agricultural climatography has remained sadly neglected and is virtually a blank for the climates of Latin America, which are of the greatest importance for the present problem. In summary, therefore, we can only say at the present time that the cultivated plant assemblage of New World origin is dominantly mesophytic; that, with the exception of the potato complex, their growth begins with warm weather and rain and continues through the period of maximum warmth and moisture; that some require for their vegetative growth a rainy season of as little as two months, whereas others require four or five months; and that maturity takes place under a dry season following. The natural plant association most nearly representative of these conditions is to be found in summer-green forest lands of deciduous habit.

PLACE OF ORIGIN OF INDIVIDUAL CROP PLANTS

The most comprehensive evidence on place of domestication comes from the Russian Institute of Applied Botany and Plant Breeding. It is principally this material that is basic to the following discussion.[4]

The Russian Institute has added a great deal to our knowledge of native crop plants as to kind, range, habit, and kinship. For the first time the entire asemblage of American cultivated plants has been made the object of collection and study. In each area the Russian botanists have regarded the whole agricultural complex and have attempted to get specimens and data not only for each species cultivated, but also on as many varietal forms as possible. A good beginning has been made in charting geographic range of cultivated plant forms and in characterizing habitat, including elevational and phototropic limits. A generous collection of seeds and tubers made possible further study of growth habit by the planting of these materials in Russian experimental gardens, thus making possible the comparison of original habitat with new environments. Many varieties have been further subjected to genetic analysis, by chromosome counts and by an elaborate systematic determination of dominant and recessive characteristics. Thus these geneticists have undertaken a classification *de novo* of varieties and have referred these to ancestral forms. The collecting was done, it is true, by rapid but energetic sampling, mostly along main-traveled

---

[4] S. M. Bukasov, The Cultivated Plants of Mexico, Guatemala and Colombia (Russian), Bulletin of Applied Botany, of Genetics and Plant-Breeding, Suppl. 47, 1930, pp. 1–469; English summary, pp. 470–553. Includes articles by N. N. Kuleshov on maize and by F. M. Mauer on cottons. G. S. Zaitzev, A Contribution to the Classification of the Genus *Gossypium* L., Bulletin of Applied Botany, of Genetics and Plant-Breeding, Vol. 18, No. 1, 1927–1928, pp. 37–65; N. R. Ivanov, Peculiarities in the Originating of Forms of *Phaseolus* (Russian), *ibid.,* Vol. 19, No. 2, 1928, pp. 185–208, English summary, pp. 209–212; N. N. Kuleshov, The Geographical Distribution of the Varietal Diversity of Maize in the World (Russian), *ibid.,* Vol. 20, 1929, pp. 475–505, English summary, pp. 506–510; V. A. Rybin, Karyological Investigations on Some Wild Growing and Indigenous Cultivated Potatoes of America (Russian), *ibid.,* pp. 655–704, English summary, pp. 711–720.

routes and hence under somewhat unfavorable conditions for finding the more primitive plant materials preserved in the remoter
byways. Nevertheless, the collectors came out of the New World
with the most varied and remarkable body of cultivated plant materials that has ever been assembled and subjected to genetic analyses.

The Russian inquiry is not only of great interest for its facts;
further, it has used methodically the familiar procedure of culture
history in an approach to a neglected line of culture-historical evidence. In the manner in which cultivated plants have been dealt
with, these are in effect aboriginal culture traits, which are considered with respect to their geographic distribution, centers of
origin, directions of diffusion, and changes in the process of diffusion. Presence or absence of a particular plant form—that is, culture trait—has been noted throughout the area of observation. In
the determination of the identity of the form or trait the geneticist
should be able to operate with greater precision than the culture
historian can do ordinarily, since the qualities dealt with can be
classified with respect to primitiveness. If the elements of culture
in general could be arranged with reference to dominance or reces-
siveness the whole problem of cultural diffusion could perhaps be
resolved by distributional analysis. Having determined specific
identity tentatively, the Russian Institute personnel proceeds first
to establish within a species the genetic relationships of varieties
to each other and thereby to place them as differentiated from
ancestral plants; secondly, to chart the occurrence of each variety,
and thus find the area of maximum varietal diversity of a species.
If such diversity agrees also with the maximum development of
dominant traits, it is concluded that the center of origin of the
plant has been located. The procedure is obviously in close agreement with the general ethnologic method of determining origin
and diffusion of culture traits. The Russian geneticists may have
hit upon a means of recognizing relative age and manner of migration of culture that should rank next in definitiveness to the stratigraphic results of the archeologist, and that may provide knowledge that is irrecoverable by archeologic means. Here, at the least,
is an approach to culture beginnings that culture history cannot
disregard. Either it must be disproved as concealing an as yet
undiscovered error or it should be used as a major aid in the reconstruction of cultural origins.

The Russian botanists have proposed eight centers of plant
domestication for the New World, unspecified with respect to independence or interdependence. The evidence submitted does not

exclude explicitly, and perhaps not implicitly, the possibility of a primary center from which the others may have developed by supplementary and alternative domestications. Whereas the investigators have not committed themselves on the ultimate question of single or plural origin, their evidence may be interpreted in favor of multiple independent beginnings of New World agriculture.

Colombia, as in the work of DeCandolle, is moved into a major position in the history of domestication, and indeed into one where possibly it may have priority. If one may propose that the first step in domestication was the obtaining of an adequate supply of starchy food, Colombia is especially noteworthy (1) in having an important local crop in the Arracacha (*Arracacia xanthorhiza*), which the Russians consider as possibly more ancient than either maize or potato, and which occupies the altitudinal zone between manioc and potato, or roughly that of maize; (2) in having at least two primitive kinds of potato (24 chromosomes) indigenous to Colombia; and (3) in the possibility that the most ancient form of maize originated here, which is held to be flour corn (*Zea mais amylacea*). The argument for the great age of flour corn rests (1) on its distribution, by far the widest of all the maize groups, (2) on its greatest richness in morphologic and biologic diversity, and (3) on the dominant character of the starchy endosperm. Few varietal forms of this group were noted by the Russians in Colombia in spite of its abundant production in that country, and hence the reasons for considering that its origins may have been there are not apparent. For New World cotton they reduce the ancestral species to two, bringing *Gossypium peruvianum* under *G. barbadense* and making the group South American in origin. The original qualities which they have determined for this group as markedly mesophytic perennials—relative intolerance of hot weather, and marked adaptation to a short summer day—would indicate that its origin must be sought in low latitudes at moderate elevation. The intermediate humid mountain valleys of Colombia or Venezuela, where also the varietal diversity is extraordinarily high, would then be the most probable centers.

Central America, in particular Guatemala, to which may be added the adjacent Mexican state of Chiapas, yielded handsome returns to the Russian explorers. Here they found for flint corn (*Z. mais indurata*) "a varietal diversity not known in other parts of the world." Southward this group is found to continue predominant through the coast of northern Peru and eastward through the West Indies. The flint group they consider as having originated by a crossing of the more ancient starchy form with a Guatemalan *Euchlaena*. Central America is indicated also as a major center in the domestication of *Phaseolus,* the kidney bean (*P. vulgaris*) being referred either to Mexico or Central America, the ayecote (*P. multiflorus*), next widest in distribution after the kidney bean, being identified as of Central American origin, and the lima bean (*P. lunatus*) as belonging originally to moist lowlands in Guatemala and southern Mexico. They even found the tepari bean (*P. acutifolius*) important in Chiapas, in hot areas with a brief rainy period. This bean, almost unique among native crops in the shortness of its required rain period, in its tolerance of heat, and in its quickness of maturity, is widely distributed all along the west coast of Mexico as well as in the American Southwest. Its range and problem of origin are perhaps parallel to that of chia (*Salvia chia*). Both conceivably may have spread into the American Southwest from the south, out of one of the drier spots in western Mexico in which agriculture was established fairly early. This possibility gains some support from the apparent archeologic appearance of the tepari bean in the Southwest well after the introduction of the kidney bean. A careful study of the tepari bean may possibly therefore be of especial interest in reconstructing cultural diffusion between West Coast Mexico or even Central America and our Southwest.

As Central Mexico's great contribution the Russian group labels confidently dent corn (*Z. mais indentata*), which shows "no such variety of forms and types elsewhere in the globe." Popcorn of the rice-grain type is held to be a Colombian variant of flint corn. Huautli, which is a cultivated amaranth, and the mescal type of agave are other starchy foods which are more or less restricted to the areas that came under Mexican influence. "All upland cottons spread in cultivation have originated from Mexican cotton" (*G. hirsutum*), for which the Russians assert a perennial original form. Its resistance to a long dry period and to high temperature is markedly greater than that of *G. barbadense,* and it is closely related to one or more wild forms of the west coast. The indicated place of origin therefore is at low elevations in lands of markedly shortened rain period such as characterizes various areas on or near the Mexican west coast.

For South America the Russian synoptic report has not been received. The meager statements available outline a culture hearth in Brazil from which manioc and peanut originated, another in winter-rain Chile, where the investigators find the original home of the Irish potato (*Solanum tuberosum sensu stricto*), and a third in the Andes, where they assert the existence of no less than a dozen species of potatoes, none of which is ancestral to the potato of commerce. The famous old archeologic coast of Peru virtually disappears in their analysis as a center of domestication and becomes rather an area of colonization from the east and north.

Until much more material has been gathered and the genetic relationships have been made definite, the results of the Russian investigators may continue to be regarded as tentative. They are, however, a serious challenge to many customary notions of cultural origins, and they may force a large revision of American prehistory. These findings fit remarkably well with the other lines of evidence and theoretical considerations previously set forth in this essay. The rainy tropics, the semiarid steppes, and the deserts are alike strikingly missing from the picture of crop origins as presented by the Russian botanists. Mesophytism is indicated as dominant, with individual adaptations to various seasonal rhythms of rain and dryness. The limited latitudinal diffusion of many American domesticates may be connected with narrow phototropic range, maize, however, showing an extraordinary elasticity in this respect.

THE QUESTION OF COMPETITIVE OR ALTERNATIVE
DOMESTICATION AND OF THE SINGLE OR
PLURAL ORIGIN OF AGRICULTURE

One of the outstanding characteristics of native American agriculture is the large variety of plants that have been domesticated for the production of starch foods. Just as carbohydrate foods are far and away the most important element in modern agriculture, accounting for the use of much more land and labor than any other form of farm production, so we may postulate the need of a more adequate supply of starches as the most urgent and earliest objective of primitive agriculture and hence as indicating the first plants that were brought under domestication. We may consider that the most ancient plants cultivated were starch staples, unless agriculture had a noneconomic origin. In the gathering stage these were the substances normally needed in largest amount, the ones requiring the largest area for their collection, and those most likely to become depleted. Such plants therefore would first suggest the advantages of propagation and would hence be the first subject to selective improvement, the oldest members of the agricultural complexes.

What then is the meaning of the multiplicity of starch staples in the aboriginal American scene? Almost all of these crop plants as we know them are far removed from the wild ancestral forms and represent a very long process of domestication. A question to which we should like to know the answer is whether in the same area more than one such plant is likely to have been carried through the tedious business of its improvement. Would generation after generation of cultivators in one locality have given their attention to the breeding, let us say, of a grass, a nightshade, and a morning glory in order to have a multiple source of starch food? The sustained parallel effort seems far too great to be reasonable, when we consider that the end is identical. At the beginning of agriculture a variety of plants may well have been used for similar ends, but if one showed an inherent advantage over the others in productiveness, nutritiousness, or keeping quality, attention would become concentrated on its propagation and improvement and the rest would soon disappear. The competitive domestication of plants in the same area may be considered improbable.

From Old World parallels two exceptions suggest themselves, but neither appears to have much significance in New World agriculture. The one is the development of an off-season, secondary crop that can make its growth when the weather is too dry or too cold for the major staple. The American starches, however, are generally grown at the same season. The other is that some of the plants in question may have been voluntary associates, originally weeds or ruderal plants, that gradually came to be appreciated and developed. The growth habits of the several American starch plants are, however, in major part unsuited for such ecologic association, the general American practice of "hill" cultivation was not favorable thereto, and the thesis explains more readily the introduction of supplementary crops—that is, plants of different utility—than the introduction into cultivation of a competitive crop. If one successful starch food was already at hand, it is unlikely that effort would be expended on the improvement of a wild plant serving the same ends.

Such evidence as we have on the origin of the basic, or starchfood, domestications indicates that each has a center of origin distinct from the others; in other words, that there may be as many American centers of plant domestication as there are domesticated starch plants. These appear to arrange themselves in some sort of climatic series. The sweet potato points to origin under conditions of greater humidity and warmth than any other of the starches unless it be the bitter manioc. Both perhaps came from different moist margins of a savanna climate. The sweet manioc appears to belong to the dry margins of savanna conditions. Maize and arracacha belong to similar mesothermal conditions, found at intermediate elevations in low latitudes. The cultivated amaranths and the Jerusalem artichoke also come from mesothermal climates. The several Andean tubers, such as the potatoes and oca, come from high altitudes of cool to cold climates. The Chilean potato, if distinct, as determined by the Russian geneticists, is assignable to a mesothermal land which provided a winter growth period, simulating the conditions of summer growth on the Andean plateau. The basic starches thus by and large may be interpreted as alternative domestications, coming from various, climatically differentiated centers.

The cultivation side by side of two starch crops, one local, the other of wide range, suggests the priority in time of the local crop for that area. In Colombia, for instance, maize and arracacha are widely grown in the same area, and in part manioc is also cultivated in the same agricultural complex. Under such circumstances the introduced plant needs some quality of superiority over the local plant in order to invade the new area successfully. The survival of the local domesticate is aided by the inertia of habit, such as its traditional role in accustomed dishes. Qualities that are insufficient to cause the development side by side of two similar foodstuffs from different wild ancestors may be sufficient to keep one in use if a more valuable crop is brought in from another area.

The case of maize is especially significant. It is of all American starches the most widely distributed and the most useful, partly because of its ease of storage and keeping qualities, partly because it contains also fat and protein, and is a more nearly complete food than the others. Maize in the northern part of its range tends to be the exclusive starch food. In South America prevalently it is grown in areas in which other starch plants are also produced. These more localized crops, then, may have been domesticated forms available prior to the introduction of maize. Such may be the explanation of the Colombian arracacha, but also perhaps of the Mexican huautli, perhaps even for the Jerusalem artichoke of our Southeast. All these are distinctly less useful than maize and therefore difficult to explain if maize was available to these areas when the plants under discussion were taken under cultivation. The diffusion of corn, however, undoubtedly required a long time. The older forms of maize may be considered as having required a long, warm, moist season, more rapidly maturing forms developing by slow selection on the successive boreal fringes of its cultivation and in part also on the drier margins. Slow ecologic selection was demanded of all crops that diffused through a wide latitudinal and altitudinal range, the diffusive energy of such a crop being probably a complex expression of its desirability and of inherent ecologic plasticity. It is doubtful, however, whether safe inferences can be made from breadth of diffusion to comparative age of domestication of plants.

Maize is also grown as the one staple starch where there are eligible wild sources of starch that have not been taken under cultivation. An illustrative example is the excellent, hardy wild potato of Arizona and New Mexico, perhaps as good raw material as were the wild potatoes of the Andes. The fact that such a food-stuff was not domesticated in our Southwest indicates that agriculture was brought in with maize and that the forms of maize available were well enough adapted to local climatic conditions so that there was no necessity of experimenting with local wild starch foods. The availability in any area, when farming began, of an adequate set of crops is undoubtedly the reason for many unutilized possibilities in the local wild vegetation.

Having ventured thus far into a highly speculative problem, we may look at the final and most inaccessible question, that of the single or multiple origin of agriculture in America. The basic elements of native agriculture, aside from the crops, are very simple and not highly formalized. There appears, for instance, to be great irregularity from one part of the New World to another in the agricultural work as performed by each sex. The tools were similarly simple and informal for the most part, and no progressive areal variation of form has been established. The business of punching a hole and dropping a seed or tuber is an extremely rudimentary process on which to base an assertion that it must have diffused from one center to all agricultural areas of the New World. Is it reasonable to assume that agriculture spread *per se* or that it spread by the transmission of a desirable staple? Under the latter assumption, however, we are confronted by the diversity of the fundamental staples, which we consider to be the starches. Would one people, seeing that another had acquired a crop such as maize, turn to the domestication of an alternative starch or would it introduce maize when it borrowed agriculture from its neighbors?

Obviously, alternative domestication would be carried out, if agriculture spread from a common center, only if the crop could not succeed in the borrowing area. The potato complex may well have been such an alternative domestication because the cold climate of the Andean highlands barred introduction of the lowland starch crops. Perhaps there is some connection here with the veritable rash of domestication that broke out in this area, most conspicuously unsuited to the other starch plants, if the determination of the Russian Institute of Applied Botany is confirmed that at least a dozen distinct species of potatoes were domesticated in Andean lands.

Interdependence of American agriculture by alternative, imitative domestication is in general, however, by no means apparent. Though the remaining starch staples show somewhat different climatic adaptations and limitations, these are not so emphatic that they indicate original climatic restrictions by which it became easier to domesticate a new form than to introduce one already cultivated. Except for the higher altitudes the interpenetration of the native starch crops is notably free. The single origin of American agriculture in the view of such facts as we possess would appear to be a far more difficult thesis to vindicate than that of a plural origin, by which, in favorable sites, where amenable plants were available, various social groups independently of each other passed from gathering to planting and selective plant-breeding. Under this view the diffusion of the superior crops, such as maize, cotton, kidney bean, and manioc, came later but may have been more rapid because of the prior wide development of planting practices. This suggestion of the origin and spread of agriculture is made with considerable diffidence, with the hope, however, that the proponent may not be regarded as antidiffusionist because he does not see the basis for unitary origin in American agriculture.

CONDITIONS ADVERSE TO PRIMITIVE FARMING

In latitudinal and altitudinal range Indian farming was almost as widely distributed as is modern agriculture. Crops and methods from the Old World have made possible certain notable extensions however. The areal discrepancies between aboriginal and modern agriculture are principally:

1. Lands requiring drainage and irrigation. The former were excluded from agricultural penetration (an exception is the floating gardens), whereas irrigation was possible where diversion did

not involve a major problem of raising the water level. All irrigated lands, however, may be considered as late in the development of agriculture. Irrigation was of greatest extent and development on the coast of Peru and in the American Southwest, both areas rather marginal in position and probably in time to the general spread of American agriculture and both, in terms of plant conquests, indicated as areas of colonization by agriculturists rather than as areas of origin of plant domestication.

2. Areas of low rainfall, without a well-defined rainy period. The European small grains have invaded subhumid intermediate latitude areas with insufficient summer rain and in part a growing season too short for our native crops. Thus on the Great Plains and their margins climatic conditions were in large part unsuited to Indian agriculture. The Old World grains have been able to occupy additional areas in our western states and in the prairie provinces of Canada either because they can be fall-sown or because they can use winter moisture in early spring planting and get an early start that is impossible for the American plants.

3. Areas with rain during the cool season and dry weather during the warm period (*Cs* climates). The largest winter-rain region of the New World is the Pacific coast of the United States. Although the old agricultural lands of the Southwest included the lower Colorado River valley, agriculture did not establish itself farther west, on the immediately adjacent coast of California, nor to the north of it. The absence of cultivation in this large region of genial climate is sometimes referred to the adequacy of wild food supplies and to the cultural inertia of the population. Lack of contact with agricultural peoples can hardly account for the absence of agriculture on the Pacific coast of the United States. The Indians of southern California were in communication with agricultural peoples along the Colorado. It is not likely that California Indians refrained from experimenting with the crops grown on the Colorado River. The resistance to the westward diffusion of agriculture was probably environmental rather than cultural. The crops which were available had little prospect of success in winter-rain lands. Maize and squash especially were ruled out by the rain regime, but the conditions are also predominantly unfavorable for beans. The Pacific coast of the United States, as a land of Mediterranean climate, had to wait on the introduction of crops from the European Mediterranean.

The other winter-rain area, central and southern Chile, had an agricultural opportunity because it had the potato, which was not available at the north. The Russian botanists indicate that our commercial potato is a native of Chile. By the more prevalent view it has been held to be an immigrant from the cool Andean plateau, where climatic conditions during the growing period of summer simulate the temperature and moisture conditions found in Chile in winter.

4. Heavy soils could not be used by the aboriginal cultivator. Digging and planting stick, even the primitive mattock of bone or stone, are of little use except for light soils. I have no knowledge that Indian agriculture occupied anything but sandy and light loam soils. Even the early European colonist could do little with the heavier lands until he had adequate draft animals and tools. One of the reasons for the Pilgrim settlement at Plymouth was the availability of sandy Indian fields which the Pilgrims could work with their meager and weak tools. The Pilgrim chronicles leave no doubt that this quality of soil which determined the location of fields by the Indians was equally appreciated by the colonists. In northern Mexico an extension of agriculture onto heavy soils has taken place only in late years and is still continuing by reason of the introduction of American plows, farming methods, and heavier draft stock. In that area the Tarahumar and Tepehuan tribes had a territory with large bodies of rich clay and clay loam lands which were not used agriculturally by them, their settlements being restricted mainly to flood plains and to rough mountain lands which they were able to plant. A wooden stick cannot be pushed successfully into heavy soil. Soil texture, indeed, was of much more importance than productivity. Poor, sandy lands were farmed where rich, heavier lands were not, as any survey of the distribution of Indian fields in our glaciated areas will show.

California had a second drawback in soil conditions, the coastal belt being prevalently a land of very heavy soils, even in the valley floors. In availability of soil to aboriginal agriculture, the Pacific coast and large parts of the interior plains of the United States ranked especially low. Creek bottoms were most attractive to pioneer white and aborigine alike. Here the soil was likely to be mellow and productive. Outwash trains and loess areas were preferred for cultivation in and near the glaciated regions. The distribution of Mound Builder sites is closely related to loess and alluvial light loam areas. In our Southeast, there are important bodies of moderately sandy residual soils, most notably the granitic Cecil soils and their derivatives, predominant in the southern part of the Piedmont. The Carolinas and Georgia uplands for this reason and because of their long growing season were a region of superior attractiveness. The southeastern tribes, especially the Cherokees, held an especially favored country for extensive agriculture.

5. Partial or complete exclusion of agriculture from grass- and brush-lands. Perhaps most important of all was the association of Indian agriculture with forest lands. Sod was an almost impossible obstacle to such tools as they had. The white pioneer was balked for years by the grasslands. Indeed, the chief reason why the prairies were avoided by the early settlers was that they were unable to break the heavy sod until special sod-breaking plows had been developed. To grow crops in grassland the grass must be eradicated, else it will promptly choke out the crop. Planting-stick cultivation of grasslands is almost an impossibility.

The thesis may be advanced that not only in the New World, but generally, the beginnings of agriculture are to be sought in forest lands. The removal of trees from competition with the crop requires only the breaking of the cambium layer, for which no sharp tools are needed. As the trees die, full light is admitted to the forest floor, which is free from weeds and has a litter which provides food and mulch for the crop. Dead tree trunks and stumps are no handicap to planting-stick or to hoe agriculture. Under climates in which fungi and bacteria attack dead wood actively the forest deadening soon becomes an open clearing. The Indian mode of girdling trees was adopted by the American frontiersman. Our westward movement was through forest country by an advancing fringe of "deadenings."

Brushland is difficult to clear under primitive conditions. Brush cannot well be girdled and left to die but must be cut or pulled to make room for planting. Brushy growth also commonly has a tendency to sprout, and often to sprout more heavily if it is cut back. Sprout reproduction may be discouraged by vigorous burning, but the ability to burn successfully presupposes the ability to cut brush freely. Stone Age man was helpless before either grass or brush, but not so in the presence of forest. Vegetational limits may be subject to displacement for various reasons, so that it is unsafe to envision always a similar natural vegetation for prehistoric and present time. The fact that grasslands in many parts of the world extend beyond grassland (steppe) climates into adjacent (forest) climates raises the question whether this general anomaly of forest-grass limits may have been affected by early man (e. g., repeated burning), and whether areas that we know as grassy may not have been forest. Thus the North American prairies and the South American pampas cannot as yet certainly be assumed to have been grasslands *ab origine*. Whatever their origin, as grasslands they pretty well excluded the possibility of primitive agriculture except in the forest lands along the valleys.[5]

---

[5] The loess areas of central Europe, rich in neolithic sites, have been interpreted as grasslands in a forest country and hence as available to settlement by farming peoples, who did not invade the forests. The evidence for the loess areas as relict steppes rests on the existence within them of elements of a steppe flora. These occurrences, however, do not prove the original steppe character of the loess any more than would the appearance of a specialized flora along a railroad embankment. If the loess area became deforested, members of a steppe flora would readily enter and establish themselves in the artificial openings. The only question would be whether steppe plants were available sufficiently close at hand. The evidence of floristic elements is entirely insufficient for postulating original grassy conditions. We should say rather that such plants were archaeologic weeds, primordial ruderal plants about the loess areas, which escaped into those earliest of European clearings.

Loess is most unlikely material to preserve a xerophytic plant assemblage into a moister climatic period, as is implied in this thesis of steppe survival. On the contrary, a climax mesophytic forest develops more readily on loess than on almost any other soil type except, in part, alluvial lands. Absorbing moisture from rains to an extraordinary degree and providing in dry weather capillary water to roots beyond the capacity of most soils, loess is notably drought-resistant and with us (e. g., Missouri Valley) supported a luxuriant and varied forest growth where other upland soils held only a limited and scanty tree growth. Of all soils associated with continental glaciation it is the one that would be most likely to receive first the advancing forest and to lose the steppe flora that had spread north with the retreat of the ice. Were not the events, therefore, in this order? (1) Mesophytic, deciduous climax forests became established on the loess lands. (2) The variety of the forest vegetation, the ease of killing and removing the deciduous as against the ecologically less advanced conifers, and the mellowness and fertility of the loess lands continued to make these by a large margin the preferred tracts of earlier settlement. It is difficult to see why American primitives should have found forest lands preferable for farming and Old World primitive planters should have found grasslands preferable. The problem of tillage was similar. Even if the European cereals originated beyond the forest edge—that is, were of grassland origin—they would still be far more readily cultivable by digging-stick and hoe in a forest clearing than in a grassland. Leaving the breaking of sod aside, a grass association exerts a powerful pressure against weak cultivation that is wanting in a mesophytic temperate-climate forest. (3) The superiority of texture and fertility of the loess lands then retained such areas under continued agricultural occupation and thereby developed in them the longest archeologic record of central Europe.

8

Theme of Plant and Animal Destruction in Economic History

Our Zeitgeist is congenial to debate and to the planning of our future by resolution. Perhaps such a mood marks the beginning of a great era, but even though we be far better social engineers than I think we are, it is still most important to keep track of the present as to its position on the long graph of history, to see where we stand on the trend curves of social change. We have neglected dreadfully, in our impatience to get at universals, the "natural history" of man, which is also expressed as "Die Weltgeschichte ist das Weltgericht." Institutions and outlooks have their origin in time and place; they spread from one group to another; with lapse of time and shifts of place they undergo change; they meet competition and resistance. Origins, derivations, and survivals are the basic determinations of social dynamics. How much of social science have we that has meaning apart from relations of space and time? We are not metaphysicists, we know even the Logos only as a term in culture history. Today's triumph in social theory is tomorrow's footnote to culture history. The facts we dig up may find permanent place in human learning. The constructions we place upon them, if they survive, survive as data of history.

In social science interpreted as culture history, there is a dominant geographic theme which deals with the growing mastery of man over his environment. Antiphonal to this is the revenge of an outraged nature on man. It is possible to sketch the dynamics of human history in terms of this antithesis.

We have traced the beginning of our direct lineage back about 25,000 years, when *Homo sapiens* makes his appearance as an ap-

Journal of Farm Economics, Vol. 20, 1938, pp. 765–775. Presidential address given at the Eighth Social Science Research Conference of the Pacific Coast, San Francisco, March 24, 1938.

parently finished product of evolution. More than half, perhaps two-thirds, of human history has passed before we come to the tremendous achievement of plant and animal domestication. This marks the major step forward by man in his use of nature. It is carried out for a long time without any disturbance in the relation of man to his environment. Though growing steadily in cultural grace and stature, man long remains in symbiotic balance.

Perhaps as far back as Neolithic time, the first ominous discordance develops. The dry interiors of the Old World, from Cape Verde to Mongolia, are today a far more meager and more difficult human habitat than was true in early Neolithic. We know that their deterioration is much greater than can be accounted for by climatic change. Under similar physical conditions, the New World steppes and deserts bear a varied and useful cover of vegetation, whereas the Old World dry lands show tremendous wastes of shifting sands and denuded rock surface. Moisture values are not at all minimal in some of the bleakest parts of the Sahara and Arabia, for instance. There are successful drought-tolerant plants aplenty in the Old World. The inference, therefore, is that the discrepancy between vegetation and climate in the Old World is due to cultural influence. Specifically, ancient overgrazing by herding peoples is blamed for the bareness of much of the great interior of the Old World. The damage developed perhaps three or four thousand years ago. Lapse of time has brought no repair of this destruction. The dry lands of the center of the Old World are permanently and sadly diminished in their utility.

The next major destruction of habitat values is associated with the Mediterranean lands and is assigned to the latter days of Rome or to the disordered period immediately following. Here again we know that modern productivity and known condition of land at the beginning of the Christian era do not coincide. The upland landscapes of the Mediterranean are not in line with their geomorphologic situation. Bare rocks obtrude themselves on slopes where they do not belong. Normal soil profiles are wanting. The vegetation shows many characteristics of regression. Destructive exploitation has damaged seriously and permanently a great share of the lands about the Mediterranean. In spite of the lapse of many centuries, we have no evidence of significant regeneration of resource, but probably rather that of continued physical degeneration.

With these two major exceptions, we know of scarcely any record of destructive exploitation in all the span of human existence until we enter the period of modern history, when transatlantic expansion of European commerce, peoples, and governments takes place. Then begins what may well be the tragic rather than the great age of man. We have glorified this period in terms of a romantic view of colonization and of the frontier. There is a dark obverse to the picture, which we have regarded scarcely at all.

Much has been made of the disastrous impact of Spain on the New World. The polemics of Las Casas were carried on by Spain's political rivals and his theme of the Spanish destruction of the Indies lives on in popular misconceptions of the Spanish colonies. The first half-century following the discovery was indeed destructive. Then a desolation of the Indies by depopulation appeared imminent. These expectations, however, were realized only in part, partly because the severity of Old World epidemic diseases diminished and partly because of an increasingly effective governmental protection of native population and natural resources. The Spanish government developed and applied principles of conservative stewardship for which we find no parallels in other colonial countries at the time.

In the late eighteenth century the progressively and rapidly cumulative destructive effects of European exploitation become marked. They are indeed an important and integral part of the industrial and commercial revolution. In the space of a century and a half—only two full lifetimes—more damage has been done to the productive capacity of the world than in all of human history preceding. The previously characteristic manner of living within the means of an area, by use of its actual "surplus," is replaced at this time by a reckless gutting of resource for quick "profit." The early outstanding illustrations are the wearing-out of Virginia by tobacco planting and the effects of the China trade. The westward movement of Virginians was conditioned largely by the destruction of the land through tobacco. The development of the China trade via Cape Horn and the Chinese demand for furs and other animal products led quickly to a spoliation of pelagic mammals from the Falkland and South Orkney islands to Bering Sea. The opening of the nineteenth century, with the initiation of upland cotton planting, set our South definitely on its way to the permanent crisis in which it now is. In 1846 Charles Lyell described graphically the great gullies near Milledgeville, Georgia, and stated that they had not been in existence twenty years before.[1] In 1864 George Marsh,

[1] Charles Lyell, A Second Visit to North America, Vol. 2 (London, 1849), pp. 28–29.

distinguished jurist and forgotten scientist, wrote the first description and analysis of the destruction of our basis of subsistence.[2] In the early nineties the washing out of western grazing lands became notable, a decade after the last great herd of buffalo was exterminated. At the outbreak of World War I the last passenger pigeon was dead and the last important stand of the white pine of the Great Lakes was being cut. In the present decade the topsoil of the wheat fields of the Great Plains is being carried by dust storms as far as the Atlantic. These are a few notes toward a history of the modern age. The modern world has been built on a progressive using up of its real capital.

The apparent paradox results that the lands of recent settlement are the worn and worn-out parts of the world, not the lands of old civilization. The United States heads the list of exploited and dissipated land wealth. Physically, Latin America is in much better shape than our own country. The contrast in condition of surface, soil, and vegetation is apparent at the international border between the United States and Mexico. For a reconstruction of upland soil profiles and normal vegetation of California we must go to Lower California. Chihuahua shows us what New Mexico was like a generation ago. The other parts of the world that have been opened to commerce in the last century and a half show parallels to the destructive exploitation of the United States. South Africa and Australia are well aware of their serious problems of conservation. South Russia is now becoming an active field for the study of soil erosion. Increasingly troublesome dust storms are sweeping the pampas of the Argentine, which is not characteristically Latin American in its economy, whereas more primitive Uruguay still has its land capital almost undiminished.

California is still in reasonably good condition as to physical resource. On the debit side we can cite the advanced destruction of redwood stands which are not able to restock, the brief expectation of life of our oil fields, the abandonment of unnumbered hillside farms in the Coast Ranges and the Sierra, the worn soils of the old barley and wheat districts on the west side of the Great Valley, and the general heavy loss of soil through overpasturing in hill lands. An excursion through the dairy country of Marin County, for instance, will show in almost every pasture serious evidences of soil stripping. Fortunately our primary agricultural resource lies in broad, smooth valleys that can not wash away,

[2] George P. Marsh, Man and Nature; or, Physical Geography as Modified by Human Action (New York, 1864).

and the safety of the mountain forest lands is assured in large measure by the great extent of public forest land. California has sufficiently serious problems of conservation, but they are not life-and-death matters as in many states, and they can be solved without desperate expedients.

The overdraft on the young colonial lands has serious implications for the older regions of the North Atlantic. These depend on a flow of raw materials which probably cannot be maintained indefinitely. They doubled their population in this period of extractive commerce. Their own balanced agriculture is balanced only because intensive animal husbandry is made possible by the supply of overseas feedstuffs such as bran, meal, and oil cake, and of commercial fertilizer, which imply continued extraction of resources overseas. The whole occidental commercial system looks like a house of cards.

Some of the losses that the world has thus sustained are the following:

1. The extinction of species and varietal forms. The extinction of large predators and grazing animals may perhaps be checked off as failure to survive in environments altered by economic needs. This does not apply, however, to a long list of other animals. The seas and their margins have been wantonly devastated of many mammals and birds without compensating substitutions. The killing off of our sea otter, for instance, has simply removed from our coasts the most valuable of all fur-bearing animals, whose presence would not diminish in the least any fishing or other marine activity of man.

The removal of species, moreover, reduces the possible future range of utility of organic evolution. This may be illustrated by the domesticated plants. Primitive plant breeders developed a very wide range of useful plant forms from a great number of wild ancestors. Our commercial plants are only a small fraction of the primitive domesticated species and varieties. Commercial corn growing, for instance, utilizes only two subspecies of maize; and of them only a small part of the range of genes that have been fixed by primitive plant breeding. Yet the qualities on which we have standardized for present-day commercial corn growing may not be the same as will be desired a century from now.

Meanwhile, the extension of commercial agriculture is causing a rapid extinction of the primitive domestic forms. Many species and far more numerous genetically fixed varieties have been lost irrevocably in late years. Of the great varietal range of upland cotton only a very few enter into the commercial forms. The extension of cotton in the United States, Egypt, and India has resulted in its disappearance over much of its primitive area of cultivation in Mexico and Central America, where the full range of varietal forms was developed. Yet these primitive forms hold by far the greater range of plant-breeding possibilities for future, as yet unrecognized needs. Some years ago we secured from southern Mexico seeds of a type of cotton, called Acala, that made possible the current development of cotton growing in the San Joaquin Valley. Had the plant explorer missed this particular spot in the state of Chiapas or come a few years later, we might not have a successful cotton industry in California. No one knows how many domestic varieties of cotton survive or have been lost.

In most domesticated plants and animals the greatest range of genes lies in noncommercial varieties. Until the late extension of commercial production the age-long tendency of the native husbandry was to continue and expand this range. Primitive husbandry was engaged in enlarging steadily the evolutionary process. Commercial production has caused and is causing a steady and great shrinkage of forms, because suddenly restricted standards of utility are introduced. Unfortunately, immediate and prospective utility may be very different things. This applies equally in criticism of the effect of our commercial civilization on wild and on domesticated forms of life: in both cases we have drastically impoverished the results of biologic evolution.

2. The restriction of useful species. Often we have effected local rather than total extermination. There are still fur seals of one species on the Pribilov Islands, but we know no means of repopulating the many island rookeries from which they are gone. The eastern white pine is not extinct in the Great Lakes region, but it has been removed entirely from large areas where it once flourished. Its re-establishment may cause uneconomic costs of seeding or planting, or may be economically impossible because its place has been taken by inferior species that filled in the cut-over pine lands. Also ecologic associations, once seriously disturbed, may be very difficult or impossible to re-establish. Overgrazing has caused sagebrush to increase hugely in the cooler steppes of the West, and the equally unpalatable yucca and sotol on the hot steppes of the Southwest. If overgrazing were stopped at once on such lands, an indefinitely long time would still be required for the grass to replace the useless brush even if no damage to the soil has been done. Ecologic successions often are very slow; and once a de-

generative plant succession has set in, a restoration is very uncertain. Fires, for instance, may reduce for a long period of years the utility of a site, by altering the quality of the soil.

3. Soil destruction is the most widespread and most serious debit to be entered against colonial commercial exploitation. Only a brief statement is made of this dreadful problem, for which there is never an easy solution, and often none at all. Under natural conditions—given a specific climate, vegetation, relief, and rock structure—there will be a characteristic soil as to depth and profile for any position on a slope. Soil and slope are in genetic relationship. Neither is static. Both naturally are changing very slowly. In the majority of cases the slope gradually grows less, and the soil on it weathers more deeply because it forms a bit more rapidly than it is removed at the surface. Soil formation and removal are either balanced, or formation exceeds removal; or, more rarely, removal exceeds formation. Soils develop slowly by weathering. The mechanically comminuted rock flour of our glacial lands has acquired approximately optimum characteristics in the course of about 25,000 years. This does not include weathering that starts from solid rock, but from the crushed materials of the glacial mill.

The Old World peasant agriculture, by placing animal products first, has maintained a condition of the soil in which cover crops and animal manuring have kept the soil profiles reasonably intact. Parts of our Northeast show similar maintenance of natural balance by culture.

Prevalently, however, we have not provided in our cropping systems any means for maintaining an adequate absorptive cover on the soil, as has the general farming-animal husbandry of northwestern Europe and the northeastern United States. Row crops and bare fields in the off season have resulted in the diminution of absorptive organic matter in the soil. The surface had been exposed to the sluicing action of rains. Film after film is stripped by rain, diminishing steadily the depth of the topsoil, which is normally the most productive and most absorptive part of the soil, in some soils the only part that is fertile. Full soil sections are almost impossible to find in many parts of the South. The red color of southern uplands and of their streams is derived from the subsoil, which is now widely exposed at the surface. Southern farming is in large measure farming of the subsoil, made to yield crops only by liberal dosages of commercial fertilizer. The Ohio and the Mississippi are becoming yellow rivers, which indicates that the yellow subsoils of that part of the country are now widely exposed. It is in the gradual and too commonly unnoticed loss of the true soil that the greatest damage is effected. The product of uncounted centuries of weathering and soil development is removed by a few decades of farming. The much publicized destruction of land by gullying is only the final dramatic removal of the surface. The major and irreparable damage is done beforehand.

This loss of the soil horizon by rain wash is not confined to steep slopes, nor is it even most characteristic of the hillier lands. It has reduced many gentle uplands of the Piedmont and the Coast Plain to briar-grown pastures. It has destroyed, in the main, the old Black Belt of Alabama for cotton growing, with minimal slopes, many of less than one degree. It is invading the Black Prairies of Texas, and has made amazing headway in the past ten years on the smooth plains of central Oklahoma. All that is needed is a slope sufficient for muddy water to run on. Even the great Corn Belt is becoming very badly frayed about the edges. The once rich counties of northwestern Missouri have been reduced to widespread distress. Serious damage is claimed for one-fourth of the area of Iowa.

Wind erosion is not bound to slope at all; it operates best, in fact, on level land. The baring by the plow of the dry margins of our farming land has there resulted in rapidly accelerated wind transport whenever there is a marked dry spell.

These losses are in many cases irreparable. Engineering devices are in the main palliatives that reduce rate of loss, but which under extreme weather conditions may increase the risk. The saving of worn land requires more labor, more skill, and more capital than the farming of good land, and then is of uncertain results. If one could place the best farmers on the worst-used land, some headway could be made. The cycle of degeneration is very, very difficult to break, and there is no salvation by any brilliant device.

To this summary review of some of the suicidal qualities of our current commercial economy the retort may be made that these are problems of the physical rather than of the social scientist. But the causative element is economic; only the pathologic processes released or involved are physical. The interaction of physical and social processes illustrates that the social scientist cannot restrict himself to social data alone. We cannot assume, as we are prone to do, an indefinitely elastic power of mind over matter. We are too much impressed by the large achievement of applied science. It suits our thinking to rely on a continuing adequacy on the part of the technician to meet our demands for production of goods.

Our ideology is that of an indefinitely expanding universe, for we are the children of frontiersmen. We are prone to think of an ever ample world created for our benefit, by optimistic anthropocentric habits of thinking.

Let us admit for the moment that the supplying of the world with primary goods is simply a matter of the expenditure of energy, and that there is no lack of energy and no loss thereof. Even this optimistic assumption encounters the difficulty of the geography of population. The two billion inhabitants of the world have a very unequally localized distribution. It is going to be bitterly hard to arrest the declining capacity of many well-populated areas, as, for instance, our Old South. It is going to be difficult to find the means of shifting large numbers of people from crisis areas into areas of opportunity. Our Resettlement Administration has no trouble in discovering crisis areas, but it had slight success in finding areas that were ready to receive immigrants in number. The current national attitudes toward foreign immigration (witness Canada, Australia, Latin America) proceed in large part from a lately hardened conclusion that the resident populations are adequate to make use of the national opportunities. This attitude has become well-nigh world-wide. Decline in productivity is becoming characteristic of larger and larger areas. The generalization that the total productivity of the world might be maintained or raised gives no comfort to increasingly large numbers of people who are trapped in lands of fading economic resource. India may be suggested as an example, on a huge scale, of a country in which occidental political economy stimulated population growth and in which an overdraft on land resources will develop a major population crisis. What is to be done about such specific maldistributions?

Let us accept once more the view that the physical scientist will be able to make the requisite syntheses of matter to provide laboratory-made substitutes for the exhausted natural resources. There still remains the problem of the cost of distribution imposed by the geography of land and sea and climate. Freight must continue to be hauled, and costs incurred in the movement of goods. The dream of the growth of staggeringly great laboratories to give us synthetic products will require also great changes in comparative advantage of location. If we appeal to the sun for our salvation, we must build our visionary factories in deserts, along mountain fronts, and in great tidal bays, which fail to coincide with present distributions of dense and advanced populations, and which introduce additional charges in transport of power and goods.

The easy denial of our dilemma by referring it to the technologist is in large measure wishful thinking. It derives mainly from the successful, but relatively easy, experience in syntheses of hydrocarbons. We expect a lot from the laboratory technician when we ask him to supply the great range of biochemical compounds for which we are destroying the natural plant and animal laboratories, or even if we expect him to come near to meeting their cost of production from natural sources. But we demand a good deal more. Actually, we ask that chemistry become alchemy, that it achieve the transmutation of elements. The classical but far from singular illustration is the problem of the phosphates. Phosphorus is well known to be a very minor constituent of the earth's crust, too rare as a primary mineral to be recoverable in quantity. The loss of accumulated and available phosphorus from soils by destructive cropping is enormous, and forms one of our most acute problems. We are getting along by cleaning up the last of the guano deposits, which have been under exploitation for a century, and by using up the secondary mineral phosphates. The latter are highly localized fossil accumulations in certain ancient marine graveyards. These are pretty well known as to occurrence, and the reserves are not large. What then? The question, sharply asked by Cyril Hopkins, as to how civilization will survive the dissipation of this element critical to animal life, remains unanswered.

The doctrine of a passing frontier of nature replaced by a permanently and sufficiently expanding frontier of technology is a contemporary and characteristic expression of occidental culture, itself a historical-geographic product. This "frontier" attitude has the recklessness of an optimism that has become habitual, but which is residual from the brave days when north-European freebooters overran the world and put it under tribute. We have not yet learned the difference between yield and loot. We do not like to be economic realists.

9

Early Relations
of Man to Plants

Man "evolved with his food plants," forming "a biological complex in which mankind and their food plants developed *pari passu.*"
"Our staple crop plants are heliophiles, sunlovers"; from them, in
the course of time, "man developed agriculture in a sun-bathed
environment." These are basic themes of a study that deserves to
be familiar to all students of cultural origins and processes.[1] In
that long, dim period before the dawn of agriculture are to be
sought symbiotic systems and shifts of which early man was a part
and which prepared the way slowly for his advance beyond collecting and hunting. The present essay is concerned with the primordial
aspects of human time and culture as related to the vegetation with
which early man lived, long before planting was thought of.

ICE AGE: AGE OF MAN

That the Age of Early Man and the Ice Age were approximately
coincident has been well established.[2] *Homo sapiens,* i. e., physically

Geographical Review, Vol. 37, 1947, pp. 1–25. Copyright, 1947, by the
American Geographical Society.

[1] Oakes Ames, Economic Annuals and Human Cultures (Cambridge, Massachusetts, 1939); references to pp. 11, 23, and 8 respectively.

[2] See W. E. Le Gros Clark's synthesis and critique of data on fossil man:
Pithecanthropus in Peking, Antiquity, Vol. 19, 1945, pp. 1–5, and Pleistocene
Chronology in the Far East, *ibid.,* Vol. 20, 1946, pp. 9–12; and Theodosius
Dobzhansky's masterly analysis of the records of human evolution in the
light of genetics: On Species and Races of Living and Fossil Man, American
Journal of Physical Anthropology, N. S., Vol. 2, 1944, pp. 251–265. Frederick
E. Zeuner, Dating the Past: An Introduction to Geochronology (London,
1946) was seen too late to be used fully in the present paper; it is a remarkable
comparative chronology of prehistory, the value of which does not depend on
the acceptance of his absolute chronology of the Ice Age.

modern man, has been determined as having lived during the Second
Interglacial in England (Swanscombe man of the Thames basin,
and probably also Galley Hill man) and therefore antedates any
known Neanderthal man. The latter seems to have lost his status
as a separate species, and to have been only an aberrant variety
or race, which interbred on occasion with Neanthropic man, or
Homo sapiens in the narrower sense. The more primitive Peking

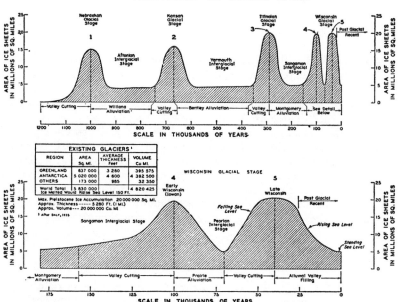

Pleistocene time. (*Reproduced by authority of the Mississippi River*
Commission.)

man is now assigned to the First Interglacial, and has been linked
closely with Java man, who seems to have been present in the First
Glacial stage. Modjokerto man, also linked to Java man, has been
placed in the lowermost Pleistocene of Java. And now Weidenreich,
who started much of this overhauling of the human family tree,
has found giant hominids that lived well before the beginning of
the Ice Age.

The curious taxonomic labels, such as Pithecanthropus and
Sinanthropus, that have been attached to different finds of fossil man

are dropped in the newer biosystematics, in which human evolution
has lost the peculiar mysteries that formerly kept *Homo sapiens*
isolated from assorted "hominids" and reserved his appearance
until almost the end of the Ice Age. The physical history of man
is thus falling into line with the rest of organic evolution. It is now
indicated that Java and Peking man (both now called *Homo
erectus*) are on the same trunk that gave rise to the men of Swanscombe and Krapina, later to those of Cro-Magnon and Grimaldi,
and finally to ourselves. An occasional branch died out without issue,
as may have been true of some of the later Neanderthal folk, but
the general phylogenetic picture now is of successive modifications
of one continuous biologic entity. Most biologists would probably
agree with Zeuner [3] that all fossil and recent men are "hardly more
than 'good subspecies.' "

Since modern man is in direct line of descent from the remoter
fossil races of man, the latter no longer have the limited interest
of collateral branches, but, and this is of greatest importance, the
cultural records of the Pleistocene represent the earliest and basic
steps in all human learning. In shedding the vestiges of special human creation, we are forced to admit that the older archeologic
artifacts mark the earlier human skills from which later developments of human art have stemmed.

That the Ice Age comprised or exceeded a million years is still
our best estimate. Lately Zeuner has given support and currency to
the astronomical-mathematical calculations of Milankovitch, which
reduce the Pleistocene epoch to little more than six hundred thousand years.[4] The Milankovitch chronology agrees closely with other
estimates of the last part of Pleistocene time (Wisconsin, Würm),
but compresses the earlier part and reduces the length of the interglacial stages.

Rather than from astronomical theory, it would seem that better
knowledge of the length of glacial time will continue to come from
more and better data of the sorts we have been accumulating by observation; namely, from the comparative study of glacial and non-
glacial deposition during the Pleistocene, from the degree of alteration of Pleistocene deposits by weathering and removal by erosion,
from their radioactivity, from the rates of growth and wastage of
ice sheets, and from the rates of origin and extinction of species of
organisms.

[3] *Op. cit.,* p. 295, footnote 1.
[4] Frederick E. Zeuner, The Pleistocene Period: Its Climate, Chronology
and Faunal Successions (London, 1945), pp. 166–171.

Knowledge of the length of the subdivisions of Pleistocene time and of the placement of human remains within them will be enlarged especially as marine terraces and stream terraces dependent on them are correlated with world-wide changes of sea level. We may learn much from terraces for which the eustatic position can be determined; that is, those that were formed by successive fall and rise of sea level due to advance and recession of continental ice sheets.[5] The latest diagram of Pleistocene time and its stages is reproduced in the figure.[6]

However fragmentary our present data, they are cumulative data and not theories of time. However inexact, the estimate that man originated more or less a million years, or almost forty thousand generations, ago is a starting point for considering what he has become and done.

INFERENCES FROM THE CULTURE OF PEKING MAN

The earliest generally accepted cultural record is that of Peking man, which is well advanced from that of a general *Urkultur*.[7] Before his appearance possibly a fourth of human time had elapsed, under the view of continuous human evolution as against that of collateral hominids. He had learned to live under a high-latitude climate of long winters, during which the requirements of food must often have exceeded the means of procuring it. Habitat and cultural remains alike show that we are not dealing with improvident half-apes but with men who were applying thought and forethought to living in a fairly exacting environment. Fire was basic to their culture.[8] They cooked food; and that fact means that experimentation was under way in making not only animal but also vegetable products palatable for human consumption. Woman was about her business of developing specialized domestic activities. The presence of hearths shows that these folk lived with some degree of permanence at particular places. The number of hearths suggests

---

[5] *Ibid.*, pp. 127–134.

[6] H. N. Fisk, Geological Investigation of the Alluvial Valley of the Lower Mississippi River (Mississippi River Commission, U.S. War Department, Corps of Engineers, 1944), Fig. 75.

[7] It must be noted, however, that the Red Crag flint "eoliths" of East Anglia, under controversy for half a century, are currently of good repute, and that they now are assigned to the First Glaciation, hence are older than the Peking record: F. E. Zeuner, Dating the Past, *op. cit.*, p. 182.

[8] As it appears also to have been for the earlier Red Crag folk.

that they may have lived in family groups, each accustomed to collect at its own place (hearth = home). There is nothing in this picture to indicate aimless wanderers, the mythical man pack or horde,
drifting freely.

If man, from such an early time, lived in family groups, which
met at the family fire, forming together a sort of primitive community that stayed put as long as seasonal changes in food supply permitted, it is also likely that each group held a more or less well-
defined territory recognized by other groups as its own.

Of plant foods the use of hackberry fruits only has been determined, but we may be sure that these people drew on all the plant
food that they knew how to prepare.

Seven-tenths of the animal remains recovered are, it is reported,
of deer. Are we to explain this dependence on deer for meat, bones,
and skins as indicating the possession of effective missiles that would
strike down this fleetest and most elusive game, or of snares or
traps that would seize and hold it? In either case a technical advance
is required that seems excessive for so early a time. Neither club,
lance, spear, nor ax is a good deer-hunting weapon, and these were
at best the arms at the disposal of primordial man. Peking men
came into bodily contact with deer only if these had been maneuvered
into positions from which they could not escape. In a desert area
they might be taken at water holes, but in North China, for which
there are no indications of aridity at that time, their habits would
hardly have provided so easy a means of capture.

The question arises therefore whether the tool that early man
managed best, namely fire, was not also the device by which he drove
this fleet and timid game to destruction at his hands. Man, who had
learned how to warm himself in cold weather and how to prepare his
food with fire, perhaps directed his curiosity to the utilization of
fire in other ways, such as hardening and pointing wooden tools and
driving game.

The glimpse into a remote past afforded by the Peking finds is
sufficient for us to ascribe to man an ancient role in the modification
of vegetation. He had habitual campsites; he wore paths out from
them that became bordered by trailside weeds that took advantage
of the added sunlight and tolerated trampling and other disturbance. Seeds and roots were dropped along the trails and at the
camps, and some of them grew and reproduced themselves. Kitchen
refuse, thrown out about the camps, enriched the soil with ashes
and nitrogenous matter, and new combinations of plants found advantage in the altered soil. Collecting grounds were disturbed by

the digging for food, from roots and grubs to rodents. Dug ground is always open to vegetation changes. If fires were set primordially, at first to facilitate collecting and then as a hunting device, a most potent aid to vegetative modification was assured. Burning clears the ground of litter and makes easier the gathering of fallen nuts, acorns, and the like; it suffocates small, slow animals. It was the best simple device for driving fleet and big game so that it could be destroyed in mass. Wherever it was used, it affected the reproduction of plants and altered the composition of the vegetation.

These are preliminary examples of ways by which ancient collectors and hunters brought about changes in vegetation. If the activity of man in any of these directions was sporadic, no permanent alteration of plant complexes might result; but if activity was maintained in the same direction, cumulative and possibly permanent effects were registered in the association and perhaps the evolution of plants.

A major question, therefore, is whether areas, when once they had been occupied, remained under continuous human occupation. A subsidiary question is whether they were subjected to increasing exploitation by larger numbers of men and developing cultures. Both questions will be considered below.

DEVELOPMENT OF OLD WORLD CULTURES

Until after the beginning of the last glaciation, somewhat more than a hundred thousand years ago, change and divergence in human arts proceeded very slowly, if one judges by archeologic remains. In Europe, the Acheulian culture extended from the early part of the Second Interglacial to the end of the Third Glacial (Riss), some three hundred thousand years. Its stone tools, such as "hand axes," were shaped from cobbles and other suitable rocks, by striking off pieces until a core of desired form and edge was fashioned. Levalloisian tools were obtained by shaping flakes struck from a previously prepared core. Levalloisian remains have been found in Europe from the beginning of the Third Glacial to the middle of the last, a span of perhaps two hundred thousand years. The two cultures were contemporaneous for about half of their duration. Each shows certain development in technique, but it is apparent in both that skills and modes of life changed very slowly over very long periods.[9]

[9] F. E. Zeuner, Dating the Past, *op. cit.,* especially pp. 282–295.

Perhaps this record of unprogressiveness is somewhat exaggerated. The meagerness of the data may be an accident of discovery or recognition. Also, an interpretation based on stone items alone is misleading; for some, or possibly many, groups may have directed their attention to working with plant and animal materials rather than with stone. It has been repeatedly suggested that cultures based mainly on wood and fiber may have been earlier than those based on stone. There are tribes still living, with a fairly rich culture, that work almost exclusively with plant and animal materials; the Bororo of Brazil are one well-known example.

Archeology perforce must deal with what it finds; for olden times the finds are almost wholly artifacts of stone or, more rarely, of bone. Archeological systems have therefore been elaborated mainly in terms of lithic industries. Stone lends itself especially well to the fashioning of arms for killing, blades for skinning and dismembering the kill, scrapers for preparing hides. Stone implements have therefore been largely interpreted as the equipment of hunters. Such gear has been preserved, the rest is lost, and thus a generalized but perhaps distorted picture of a succession of ancient hunters is construed.

On several counts it seems doubtful whether there were specialized hunting cultures in the Old World or anywhere else much before the relatively late date of the Solutrean folk, who penetrated only briefly into Europe. They were followed by the Magdalenian hunters, who seem to have come from Arctic lands. The generalized view for the farther reaches of human time should perhaps be rather that of variously differentiating cultures, depending on both collecting and hunting, some groups specializing more in plant raw materials, others showing more interest and proficiency in the chase, the direction of specialization dependent on comparative advantage of environment. The hunting peoples of historical time were strikingly limited environmentally in their distributions, in Arctic lands and on the great continental plains; and, so far as I can see, their predecessors (and possibly their ancestors) occupied in the main the same areas. There would seem therefore to be overemphasis on hunting in the interpretations of the habits of early man, and it is the purpose of this paper to take up the obscure record of his relations to his plant surroundings.

Many Paleolithic sites show evidences of sedentary occupants and long use and therefore may not be construed as campsites of folk concerned mainly with hunting. Most Paleolithic stone implements, usually described in terms of hunting use, have equal or greater utility for other purposes. The so-called hand axes would have been suicidally dangerous against any large animal and no more useful than a cobble against a small one; on the other hand, they could serve for cutting and splitting wood, for cutting bark, and in digging. The value of the ax as a weapon depends on the speed with which it can be swung and the ability to shift stance quickly; such a weapon appears after the Paleolithic in the small, polished celts. Scrapers, choppers, gravers, and various types of blades and knives served as well for the cutting and preparing of wood, bark, and bast, of roots and fruits, as for the dressing of meat and skins.

The culture of the Tasmanian aborigines is often cited in illustration of the survival into modern time of Paleolithic modes of life.[10] Their immigration, from somewhere in southern Asia, took place in the Ice Age. It is thought that they came most of the way afoot, crossing a narrow sea west of New Guinea on raft boats, and that the migration was effected mainly in a glacial stage of low sea level. They became isolated by a rise of sea level; and, being in a far corner of the world, retained in the main the Paleolithic traits that they had at the time of their loss of contact with the mainland. Sollas saw their stone culture as similar to conditions obtaining in southern Europe during the Riss-Würm interglacial, and its content does indeed indicate a separation from other peoples about then. Recently, the Keilor finds, near Melbourne, Australia, have strengthened such an inference. One of the skulls is said to have Tasmanoid qualities, and their stratigraphic position is assigned to this (Third) interglacial.[11] The interpretation is therefore that a peopling of Australia took place in the preceding (Third) glaciation, when Australia was accessible from Asia during periods of low sea level, and that these first colonists were progenitors of the Tasmanians.

The culture of the Tasmanians, then, is considered an authentic relic of the Middle Paleolithic, little changed because they remained isolated for a long time. They lived in a fairly attractive environment, and no theory of cultural losses needs to be set up. They changed little, not because they were miserable, or stupid, or slothful, but because they were cut off from contact with ideas from the outside world.

The few rude tools of the Tasmanians were used chiefly in cutting bark, scraping wood, notching tree trunks for climbing, and skinning animals. Their principal tools and weapons were of wood,

---

[10] This parallel is well drawn, for instance, by W. J. Sollas in his Ancient Hunters and their Modern Representatives (3rd ed., London, 1924), p. 107.

[11] F. E. Zeuner, Dating the Past, *op. cit.,* pp. 279–280.

such as digging sticks, spears, and clubs. Their most advanced art was the making of coiled baskets. They had no special devices for taking fish, but they did have raft boats, or balsas, made by lashing together rolls or strips of bark. As artisans they were more skillful in using plant materials than in working stone. It is of special interest that bark peeling was much practised at this primitive level; and since the stripping of bark and bast is an effective method of killing trees, we thus have evidence of the early origin of another practice that resulted in alteration of vegetation.

The Australian aborigines became isolated from the Eurasian mainland at a later time than the Tasmanians. They had, for instance, products unknown to the Tasmanians: dart thrower, bark canoe, boomerang, bull-roarer, and shield. All of these were of wood; the Australian cultures also are poor in stone artifacts.[12] The dart thrower made its appearance in Europe in the Würm glaciation, and this fact may give a clue to the age of the Australian immigration. The main colonization of Australia by post-Tasmanoid peoples may have taken place during a stage of low sea level within the last glaciation (Würm), and contacts with the outside world were largely cut off thereafter by rise of sea level as continental ice melted.

At least in the northern plains of the Eurasian continent, great hunting cultures arose during the last glaciation, principally the Solutrean and Magdalenian folk. These had projectile points of high power of penetration, finely edged blades, and a shooting weapon of precision and range, the dart thrower. In addition, the Magdalenians had harpoons made of bone, perhaps developed in a sub-Arctic habitat.[13]

Mobile hunting and warrior peoples, the Solutreans and Magdalenians, quickly ranged with their new weapons over the plains of the Old World. The place and manner of their origin is a mystery; in Europe they appear clearly as invaders out of the east.[14]

---

[12] The dog also got to Australia, but its earliest archeologic record in Eurasia is from Mesolithic time. It is known in Europe from the Maglemose (7000 B. C.?), and in Palestine from the Natufian, of somewhat older date. The question is therefore whether the dog was a later introduction into Australia, isolation from the mainland not having been completely uninterrupted.

[13] I know of no good evidence of the bow and arrow before Mesolithic time. Feathered shafts, such as are depicted in pre-Magdalenian cave drawings of wounded big game, do not prove the presence of the bow. Feathered shafts are equally characteristic of the dart thrower.

[14] Zeuner has reassembled the data on the age of Upper Paleolithic cultures. He places the Solutrean at about 70,000 years ago, the remainder of the

With the fading of the continental ice, the pace of change was greatly accelerated on the Eurasiatic continent. It was no longer a matter of slow differentiation of collecting and hunting folk, such as had occupied the preceding 90 per cent of total human time. The final periods of the Ice Age were marked by a major revolution in the coming of Great Hunters, who dominated especially the wide continental plains. After them, but not derived from them, arose the Neolithic planters. The antithesis between mobile hunters and sessile planters is extreme. I know of no evidence that the former ever turned farmers, except late, and then reluctantly, under pressure. The attention of the hunters was diverted from plants; the origins of planting must be sought in cultures with strongly sedentary qualities and major concern with the exploitation of plants.

NEW WORLD DEVELOPMENTS

On the basic early cultures of the New World, their changes, and how they are related to those of the Old World we are still mainly uninformed, in part because authority took a dogmatic position against the presence of man in the New World during the Ice Age and has maintained its censorship—even now only partly relaxed— for many years. The circumlocution "Paleo-Indian" is still used in describing the older inhabitants of the New World, and "Paleolithic" tacitly is not good usage in New World archeology.

There is no reason in what we know of the history of the Ice Age and of the evolution and spread of mankind for excluding man from the New World until the final stage of glaciation, as is the present vogue. North America was not significantly more difficult to reach from the ancestral hearths of man than Australia or transdesert Africa. Siberia and Alaska were never generally blanketed by icecaps. North America was probably inaccessible during the interglacial stages of high sea levels, but not when the levels were low during glaciations. Peking man solved at an early date the problems of survival through northern winters. It need not have taken his successors a long time to learn how to live on coasts of still higher latitudes. In view of the known expansion of man elsewhere in the Old World, it would be surprising if the margins of the Okhotsk

---

time in the last glaciation being mostly occupied by the Magdalenian. The present trend in European archeology is therefore toward making these great hunting cultures definitely Würm in time, a revision to a markedly greater age than that previously attributed to them. (Dating the Past, *op. cit.*, p. 290.)

and Bering seas should prove to have been uninhabited during the Second Interglacial, or perhaps even earlier. After the great Second Interglacial, in the Third Glaciation (Illinoian), when sea levels dropped considerably, a colonization of the New World is not at all improbable. By that time, it appears, Australia was inhabited. Farthest Africa and the British Isles were occupied long before then. Why should a feasible corridor into the New World alone have remained unused?

The fact that no skeletons more primitive than primitive forms of *Homo sapiens* have so far been recovered in our hemisphere has ceased to be an objection to man's antiquity on this side of the ocean, since Swanscombe, Galley Hill, Keilor, and other finds have established *Homo sapiens* in wide dispersal far back in the Ice Age.

Ethnologically, the case for a similarly early detachment of the Yahgan of Tierra del Fuego and the Tasmanians from a common trunk of cultural evolution has often been urged by diffusionists. The alternative to considering such very backward peoples, including primitive rests in the forests of the Guianas, of the South Pacific coasts, the collectors of the Brazilian highlands, the Guaycuru and Pericu of Lower California, the Yuki of Upper California, and the Beothuk of Newfoundland, as relics of cultures derived from the Old World well back in Paleolithic time requires alternative hypotheses of quite unlikely losses of useful skills. The cooking habits of simple tribes of the Brazilian interior,[15] who get along without any boiling, find no explanation in their environment, but rather in old cultural habits. Long in contact with pottery-making peoples, they make casual or no use of pots but restrict their cooking to roasting and baking; gourds, a late acquisition, are used for carrying water. The absence of the dog among many more primitive or archaic tribes in America, especially South America, suggests that these folk immigrated before the dog was domesticated.

Such straws of culture traits are numerous and point to ancient arrivals from the Old World of certain groups that have remained extremely conservative in the New by reason of having survived in isolated pockets. They are intelligible if acknowledged as links to the Old World Paleolithic of the later Ice Age, and it seems to me only so.

Items which impress me as having been introduced into the New World during the Ice Age (though not all at one time) and which

---

[15] Curt Nimuendajú, The Eastern Timbira, translated and edited by R. H. Lowie, University of California Publications in American Archaeology and Ethnology, Vol. 41, 1946, p. 43.

continued to be in use here and there into historical time include the following: fire (hearth, fire striking, fire drill, roasting and baking, stone boiling, hardening and pointing of tools, fire drive); bark peeling (household vessels, one-piece bark canoes, sewed bark canoes); woodworking (digging stick, lance, dart thrower, paddle, bull-roarer); fiber working and the like (cord twisting, coiled baskets, snares, nets, tied matting, balsas); boneworking (awls, drills); and stoneworking (percussion flaking, choppers, scrapers, blades, some points, grinding stones).

The older archeology of the New World is still mainly a lot of unassembled bits of knowledge. Important is the growing realization that preceramic remains stem from a very long period of time and that types of artifacts often are diagnostic of their age. The known sites are predominantly in our arid and semiarid areas, partly because there happened to be alert archeologists at work in the Southwest and partly because both preservation and inspection are aided by low rainfall. It is quite possible that a period of research and synthesis is beginning there which may make that area such a key to the American Paleolithic as France was for the Old World. The following remarks are set down in the spirit of giving aid to such hopeful inquiry.

The determination of the age of early vestiges of human occupation is broadly a geomorphologic problem.[16] Along the southern peripheries of the areas covered by the continental ice sheets direct relations of man to glacial deposition may be ascertained. Mostly, however, the sites lie, and will continue to be found, in areas untouched by glacial or fluvioglacial and loessial deposits. Equatorward displacements of storm belts resulted in pluvial periods over areas now arid. At such times rain water percolated through the roofs of caves and deep rock shelters and formed dripstone or travertine on their floors, thus sealing off the remains of earlier human occupation. In pluvial periods undrained basins held freshwater lakes and marshes, on the edges of which people lived in areas later unavailable for lasting settlement. Were the pluvial conditions, widely recorded in the southwestern United States and northern Mexico, coincident with Wisconsin glaciation?

Perhaps the greatest prospect of the discovery of early sites, however, lies in the association of human settlement with marine terraces, continued landward as stream terraces. Across Texas, and again in Sonora and Lower and Upper California, series of primi-

[16] For a comprehensive presentation of the subject see Zeuner, The Pleistocene Period, *op. cit.*, pp. 1–135, 225–252.

tive artifacts are found in characteristic positions upon and also within terrace fills. These terraces may be, in whole or in part, eustatic, and hence record the chronology of the Ice Age. If their synchronization with world stages of glaciation and deglaciation can be established, a sufficiently precise determination of the ages of their human remains is achieved. Their patterns of sedimentation, continuity of surfaces, weathering, and erosion are so persistent that their deciphering is one of the most promising tasks ahead of geomorphologic science.

In all interpretations of how men fashioned their different ways of living in the New World the length of their presence here and the number and order of their immigrations from the Old World are vexing unknown factors. The length of human presence in America is also involved in problems of our plant geography and evolution. It makes a good deal of difference whether men have been in the New World fifteen to twenty-five thousand years or much longer, say perhaps ten times as long as that, or a fourth of all human time.

The best immediate prospects for finding out are in Texas and Lower California. In Texas, it may be hoped, the interest of a number of workers in stream terraces and their relations to sea levels will give results before long that may unlock the chronology of the New World as the studies of the Somme terraces did that of the Old. We made a reconnaissance of Lower California from the University of California in the summer of 1946, and found there a promising situation to investigate. Peninsular California has persistent and consistent marine terraces in number, with an abundance of archeologic material upon, and apparently also within, them. There is good evidence that pluvial conditions, and human occupation, prevailed across the whole of the Lower California desert. Further, there are many undisturbed caves and rock shelters which were occupied by man and which have preserved plant materials and objects fashioned from them. Even our first inspection gave strong indications that human remains and their sites do not fit into the compressed time scale at present applied to man in the New World.

The assortment of available data suggests a number of ancient cultures that may have been introduced or have originated in the following order:

1. The most primitive and ancient of these may have lacked both stone points and grinding stones. I am not aware that stratigraphic or geomorphologic proof has been found, but the category seems to be necessary. These implements are lacking among numerous histori-

cal peoples in both South and North America, without environmental reason.

Seed grinding and its artifacts, for instance, are of especially restricted distribution in South America, whereas they are, or were,
widespread in southern and western North America under similar
conditions of food collecting. Away from the Caribbean coastlands
archeologic records of grinding stones in South America are few,
mainly Andean, and appear neither to be early nor to have formed
anywhere a dominant device in food preparation, except for the
quite distinct manioc graters. The inference is that many South
American peoples derived their culture from a substratum lacking
food-grinding habits and that their arts of preparing food developed
along other lines. The hafting of stone points to projectile shafts
also is a trait that numerous people never adopted, especially to the
south of the United States.

It may be expected that some of the very primitive archeologic
sites, such as have been reported from Texas and Argentina, which
yield only rudely percussion-shaped tools, without points, will prove
to be really the oldest. That the age of a complex of artifacts may be
read by the skill and specialization they exhibit is perhaps correct
where sites of minimal skill occur with more advanced ones in the
same area: folk of low skill are unlikely to displace cleverer ones.
In particular the sites of rudest art are to be regarded as the oldest
if they mark habitats physiographically and climatically least suited
to present occupation. The earliest cultures are most easily overlooked, because their products are least readily recognized as fashioned by human hands, because their sites are likely to be small and
slight, and because these sites are likely to be in places where one is
not accustomed to look for human habitation. Their search and
study have scarcely begun.

2. The ancient food grinders are known from Texas to California, and also in Sonora and Lower California. The generalized
association is the building of hearths on a bed of collected stones,
the use of a grinding or mealing slab on which a handstone (*mano*)
was rubbed back and forth or in an elliptical or circular motion, and
an assortment of rough percussion tools, mostly choppers and scrapers, which may have been made by the same technique as the Old
World Levalloisian. Rude knives are present, but projectile points
are normally wanting.

An early seed-grinding culture was first described by D. B. Rogers
as that of the Oak Grove people of Santa Barbara County in California. Their knolltop sites are recognized and characterized by
the abundance of handstones and slabs and the absence of almost

all fishing and hunting remains. Rogers' excellent pioneer work unfortunately was published before there was real recognition of the problem of early man in this country, and it has never received the attention it deserves.[17]

In the southern basin plains (Cochise) and in the Papago desert (the Ventana rock shelter) of Arizona, Haury and Sayles have found evidences of collecting and grinding cultures in the basal horizons of sites of long-continued or repeated occupation. Their work has placed the earliness of such cultures beyond all doubt in the arid Southwest. The early grinding folk lived under a pluvial climate markedly different from the present, and the important and unsolved question is how long ago a humid climate existed in our arid Southwest. In Sonora, I saw in the spring of 1946, in company with Haury, a series of sites typologically similar to early Cochise extending well south of the Mayo River, and characteristically in situations that are disadvantageous for access to water or food under contemporary conditions. In Lower California, later in the summer, a party from the University of California found many similar situations.

Early food-grinding settlements, therefore, were spread over wide areas between the Mississippi Valley and the Pacific coast. From most, if not all, of this region the mano and grinding slab subsequently disappeared, in places abruptly, and were never reintroduced, or reappeared only long after in the form of the metate, when corn growing was brought in from the south. I have seen many sites of such early grinding folk, in California, Lower California, Sonora, and Arizona. As a rule they are not properly situated now for victualing or watering a population; they do not make sense in terms of the present topography and vegetation; and this, I take it, is a good indication that they were occupied long ago.

This innovation in food preparation is not to be explained as a device for aid in cooking starchy roots, plant stalks and leaves, or fleshy fruits. These had been, and continued to be, prepared simply by roasting on coals and in ashes or by baking in pits. Even now, agave shoots, wild yams and potatoes, and other tubers and bulbs are not processed by grinding in Indian cooking. The new process made possible the utilization, or larger use, of hard seeds and small ones, such as those of grasses, of *Chenopodium* and amaranths and their relatives, of various Compositae, such as sunflowers, tarweeds, and ragweeds. It was also applicable to the preparation of bitter,

---

[17] D. B. Rogers, Prehistoric Man of the Santa Barbara Coast (Santa Barbara Museum of Natural History, Santa Barbara, California, 1929).

starchy fruits, such as acorns, and starchy roots with noxious qualities, such as various aroids, which could not be made edible by cooking the entire tuber or root. Some of these were palatable when merely cooked after the grinding; others needed the additional step of leaching. The introduction of grinding brought a long-continued series of additions to the primitive kitchen resources.

The process yielded meal, which, mixed with water, was baked in cakes, or cooked as gruel, or put into stews. Food grinding thus presupposes the presence of receptacles for holding water and of others for the ground meal and could hardly have been developed until after the possession of good, almost watertight vessels. The region of major distribution of early food grinding is poor in trees yielding suitable bark for vessels but rich in useful fiber plants. That well-woven baskets preceded the grinding slabs seems to be a proper inference. The collecting of small seeds also involved seed beaters, collecting and carrying baskets, and winnowing.

It may not be a coincidence that the general region through which the sites of early food grinders are spread is also one of the major regions of the world for the occurrence of coiled basketry, both historically and archeologically. Students of diffusion have pointed out the high antiquity of the coiling technique, by no means an obvious device for fashioning a receptacle.

The food-grinding folk were inclined to sedentary ways, and they are readily located by the quantity of remains they left behind through continued occupation of one spot. The Old World offers little that is parallel to this important development, though in simple and rather casual form it is found in Australia. In rudimentary form it may have come originally from southeast Asia, but in the major development it looks as though this mode of food preparation was an achievement of the American Southwest and its borderlands.

3. Another series of sites shows increased preoccupation with hunting and the introduction of developing series of stone projectile points. With these folk there was still permanence of habitation, shown by hearths and accumulations of artifacts, and also by the presence of seed-grinding stones.

I had the opportunity in the spring of 1946 to visit the area around Abilene, Texas, under the guidance of its acute local student, Dr. Cyrus N. Ray.[18] Although not including the earliest sites of man

---

[18] See his critical summary of archeologic-geomorphologic conditions, with stratigraphic profiles: Stream Bank Silts of the Abilene Region, Bulletin of the Texas Archeological and Paleontological Society, Vol. 16, 1944–1945, pp. 117–147.

in Texas, this area may be critical for a part of the history of Ice Age man. Ray has identified seven consecutive horizons, of wide distribution in the valley fill on the affluents of the Brazos River. All but the first horizon are deposits laid down in slack or slowly moving water. The lowest horizon (Lower Clear Fork) is of greatest interest, for the hearths and artifacts it bears *in situ,* as well as for bones of extinct large mammals. The occupants of this earliest level were both food grinders and hunters. Several kinds of primitive points have been found at this level, which impressed me as having been an old land surface probably exposed and occupied by man for a considerable length of time. This basal surface was later buried by gentle and long-continued flooding. Several of the overlying sedimentary horizons show a varying degree of soil development, with hearths and artifacts. Until adequate field and laboratory study reveals the succession of events recorded in these deposits and their weathered surfaces, the interim conjecture may be ventured that the Lower Clear Fork surface was the surface of land at the time of the last Wisconsin maximum, and that as continental deglaciation got under way and the ocean level rose, widespread silting of valleys took place. In that case the interludes during which weathering profiles developed registered halts in the process of world-wide deglaciation and need not indicate any local changes in climate. Thus the Lower Clear Fork may have been a surface of human occupation about thirty-five thousand years ago, when men were experimenting with projectile points of stone. It may even be that some of these were precursors of so specialized a development as the Folsom craft and that one need not look to an Old World derivation of the latter.

The early use of medium-sized stone points raises the question of the age of introduction of the dart or spear thrower (also called *atlatl* after Mexican usage, or *estolica* in South America). That it originated in the Old World is inferred from its use among Australian tribes that are bearers of a culture only slightly less primordial than that of the Tasmanians. This apparently oldest of all known devices for manual propulsion of projectiles is so ingenious that it is probably an invention made once and then widely and early diffused. There is growing and reasonable inclination to regard stone points of intermediate size (and it is these that appear earliest) as having been used with dart throwers.[19] The advantage of

---

[19] A. D. Krieger observes: "There is . . . a very decided chronological distinction between 'bird points' and the heavier dart points. The true arrow points with their light construction definitely appear at a relatively later time

the dart thrower over the spear and the javelin lay in its speed and precision, given by the flattened trajectory. It required a light shaft and would not bear a heavy point.

4. After a time there were mobile hunting folk, who paid no attention to food grinding. In places, as about Santa Barbara, there is an abrupt break between the two kinds of habitation, even a change in physical type, suggesting that the hunting people may have rudely displaced the earlier people. The Folsom and Yuma cultures represent high specialization in big-game hunting. Their interest in plant food and fibers was probably minimal.

5. A good while after the disappearance of continental ice sheets we get the first records of the bow and arrow, the dog, fishhooks, and polished stone. All of these, it would seem, were introduced by later comers from the Old World and appear to be the prelude to full Neolithic conditions and agriculture. They fall therefore after the times considered here.

SUMMARY OF EARLY CULTURE SEQUENCES

This sketch has attempted to outline the salient features of cultural diversification of all but the last two per cent of human time, covering nearly the whole of the Ice Age. There is no certain record of humans before they knew the use of fire. As master of fire, man had security at night from predators; he was able to move into cold climates; he had hearths, on which the life of the family centered; his women began the endless experimental chemistry of food preparation; he learned to shape tools by hardening and charring wood in fire; he learned to use its pitiless force in driving and overwhelming animals, great and small. Knowledge of the stripping of bark and bast for the fashioning of vessels and cordage taught him an easy way to kill trees and thus provide himself with a convenient supply of firewood. The fashioning of cords into nets and of fiber and withes into baskets provided early kitchen and carrying vessels. In working with stone he developed, with slowly growing skill, a series

---

in all sections of the country. In Texas, as well as to the west, south, and east, arrow points appear in the latest horizons, along with agriculture and pottery making. . . . Dart points, on the other hand, are very numerous in the cultures which precede." (Some Suggestions on Archaeological Terms, Bulletin of the Texas Archeological and Paleontological Society, Vol. 16, 1944–1945, pp. 41–51.) North of Central Mexico the dart thrower disappeared before historical time.

of simple tools that receive most of the attention of archeology because they almost alone have been preserved.

Until the final stages of the Ice Age men lived, wherever they were, by both collecting and hunting, gradually diverging into differing cultures. Toward the end of the Ice Age tempo and mood of cultural evolution (divergence) changed sharply. Especially in the New World it appears that a new age began with a basic improvement in sustenance through the introduction of food grinding. Another revolutionary impulse came with a precision weapon, the dart thrower. At the very last appeared the roving big-game hunters, owning a skill in fashioning blades and knives that has never been surpassed in stone. In terms of our present information it seems that more cultural advance and divergence took place from the middle of the last glaciation (Wisconsin, Würm) to the beginning of Recent time than in all the time between the days of Peking man and mid-Wisconsin. Also, I would suggest, the evidence is beginning to indicate that the New World may have participated equally with the Old in the cultural advances of the later Ice Age.

POPULATION GROWTH

An implication of this summary of the early human record is that successive waves of migrant peoples as well as of inventions spread outward from the ancestral hearths of man, considered as lying in southern Asia. Such pressures began early and were long continued. We need next to consider the nature of their transmission and some of their effects.

As to the manner of peopling of the earth, these main generalizations are put forth: that man has been from his primordial days a vigorous colonizer; that there have been repeated times of strong population increase; and that man's expansion over most of the world was not the result of nomadic habits.

Population growth, both for man and for other organisms, is controlled by available food. The famous sigmoid curve of population climbs rapidly to a plateau at which it levels off, when number of consumers has grown to the full use of the food supply. The history of human population is a succession of higher and higher levels, each rise to a new level being brought about by discovery of more food, either through occupation of new territory or through increase in food-producing skill. The act of expansion into new habitats also stimulated food experimentation with new sources, and frontiers of settlement therefore were likely to generate a sustained growth potential and expansiveness. A group colonizing a new terrain had at first at its disposal only those resources that were familiar from its previous habitat. It had also the opportunity or urgency to try out unfamiliar substances, some of which then became new resources through successful experimentation. Thereafter population checks became increasingly operative unless more new land was taken or new skills discovered additional resources. The term "resource" implies the determination that a thing is useful, and therefore a cultural achievement.

A new colony might increase to the limits of its sustenance in one generation; it would usually do so in several. Thereafter its population must level off, either by the gradual convergence of birth and death rates or by draining off the surplus to daughter colonies. In early human times the frontier of settlement advanced rapidly along seacoasts, where food collecting was easy and profitable and the problems of changing habitat were at the minimum. Valleys of moderate size, in diversified terrain, were also easily penetrable and rewarding. Frontier communities were always in the most advantageous position for expansion by hiving. As the edge of settlement moved farther and farther ahead of a given community, the latter had less and less opportunity to contribute to the moving frontier. Poorer opportunities may have remained in seeking out near-by tracts that were less inviting. In time there ceased to be new land to occupy, and perhaps also new modes of making use of the land, and then growth ceased. In manner any peopling of the earth at any time must have resembled the modern filling in of the frontier in America: vigorous and rapid flow into the areas of greatest attraction; slow seepage into areas of indifferent return; stagnation in more and more areas of older occupance.

Density of population of collecting and hunting peoples may not be estimated from their modern survivors, now restricted to the most meager regions of the earth, such as the interior of Australia, our Great Basin, and Arctic tundra and taiga. The areas of early occupance were areas abounding in food, where densities of one or several inhabitants to a square mile could be supported by simple skills. In such areas, such densities should have been reached within a few generations of their original settlement. Collecting man, omnivorous in habit, having the curiosity to experiment with all the plants and animals at hand and aided by fire in the preparation and preservation of food, must soon have become by far the most numerous of the larger mammals almost wherever he established himself.

Unless restrained by some belief, such as of totem, man set the limit on the number of carnivores he tolerated in his domain. The rest of creation lived in fear of him, not he of them. On his danger from fellow men we have diverse opinions, but war as a serious check on his numbers is the result of cultures advanced beyond those of early societies. Sustained and deadly warfare presupposes sustained discipline over the individual by political authority. We get perhaps the first traces of this in the big-game hunters, who were also warlike. Bad seasons brought famines, and areas subject to serious climatic variability leveled off below the densities supportable in good years. Not much significance need be attached to pestilence in primitive settlements. They consisted of small groups, not strongly intercommunicating. Epidemic diseases are bred and spread through congestion of populations; they belong to much later times of human history. Rigorous selection was operative, but its results were vigorous stocks, who enjoyed usual good health and normally lived through their reproductive years, except for the hazard of accident.

For no early time is there indication of solitary habits or nomadic mobility. As far as we know, men always preferred to form communities and were as sedentary as their food supply permitted. We may judge that when skills were minimal the community was usually small. Except for rich collecting grounds on bays and estuaries, half a dozen, or at most a dozen, families could make full use of the food supply within convenient foraging distance. We may estimate that under ample environmental conditions an area about the size of a township (thirty-six square miles) would be a full-sized unit of exploitation by such a group from a single living center. Man sensibly conserves his energy at daily and necessary tasks and does not impose on himself exhausting distances in bringing in his supplies. A radius of ten miles would be excessive for regular provisioning, since it would require most of the day en route. The center at which the habitations were placed was normally determined by water close by, by minimum effort and distance in assembling the constantly needed items of food and wood, by shelter against inclement weather, if available, and by easy convergence of trails. If the site provided all these desiderata throughout the year, it was occupied permanently; if not, camps were shifted seasonally. Man was not inclined to move about unnecessarily, and he had reason for no-

madic habits only where he depended on a nomadic staple for
sustenance, as in the hunting of herd animals, a late, not an early,
development. Over the world, hearths and middens of high antiquity attest that man's ancient custom was to fix his habitation and
not to diminish his comfort and well-being by wandering about.
Many individual shell mounds, whether or not they indicate continuous occupance, record habitation at a given spot running through
thousands of years.

If man had the sense to know a good campsite and to occupy it
as long as it was less troublesome to live there than to move, the
camp would also become the place for the storage of supplies, for
the setting up of workshops, for social and political activities, for
all the growing paraphernalia, so that increment of goods and contacts further attached people to such places.

Occasionally a new step in learning was achieved by some group,
which raised its economic potential. The invention of a better tool,
of a new food preparation, of better storage, expressed itself in
the development of a new resource, in larger inventory, and in increase in population. Such progressive cultures, by making higher
use of the land, were able to exert pressure against neighboring
groups that had failed to share in the advance. The latter, increasingly at a disadvantage, evaded pressure from the stronger group
by withdrawing into less desirable areas. Inferiority in competition
and in numbers was in time sufficient for displacement or absorption of the weaker and more backward, whether violence was involved or not. Thus a succession of colonizations could continue
with each significant advance in culture. The more progressive the
group, the larger was the number that could be supported from a
given area, the more numerous the associations possible in individual
communities, and the stronger the sedentary habits.

If this view of the nature of population growth is correct, Paleolithic time, or the Ice Age together with some thousands of subsequent years, was a period during which men spread permanently
into all parts of the world that were accessible, and this meant all
the larger land masses not blocked by ice. The rate of increase was
rapid wherever the food supply permitted. Further waves of population movement were set up outward from centers of cultural
progress. Well-being, even survival, depended on practical skill in
using the occupied habitat. Biologic population pressure was constantly building up, and was eased then, as now, by advance in territory or in art. There was no place for irrational folk (prerational
man), who failed to use their wits, who lived in illusions, who aban-

doned a good thing in their possession. There is no reason to think that primitive men drifted about through a wilderness, abandoning one home for another because of some obscure urge to wander. There is no reason to think that any area which satisfied human wants was ever depopulated or remained underpopulated. These primitives were superior, vigorous animals, gradually extending their mastery, not broken, dying remnants in confusion and despair in retreat positions such as have given rise to certain modern views of primitives. I should like these remarks on population growth and permanence of occupation to apply with equal force to the New World; whatever the time available, there was plenty to fill it to the limits of food-getting ability.

MODIFICATION OF VEGETATION

This résumé of what happened to ancient man carries implications as to what happened to vegetation during the Pleistocene. If man's spread over the earth was early and enduring, the time and manner of his intervention in the plant world were sufficient to affect plant evolution. If primitive men became significantly numerous, and especially if they were in continuous exploitation of their habitats, cumulative modifications of vegetation must have taken place. This is perhaps the most important conclusion to be drawn from the preceding pages. If men were casual habitants who drifted on, their former range left vacated until another group accidentally wandered in, the effects of human occupance would soon be erased, like the marks of a storm or other natural catastrophe. If, on the other hand, human presence characteristically was continuous, any shift, however slight, brought about by man in reproductive advantage among the local plants must result in time in important changes in the plant population. The Ice Age, regarded as the time of world-wide expansion of the human race and of its increasing domination over flora and fauna, is also the time, as Professor Ames has said, in which the evolution of man and that of a good many plants became interdependent. The natural history of the Pleistocene, then, is important in evolution not only because it was a time of extraordinary climatic and orogenic stresses but also because during this time man became more and more an agent of suppression and selection for other organisms.

For the earlier levels of human culture it is unnecessary to postulate purposeful change in vegetation at man's hands, yet he modi-

fied the plant complexes continually in directions that increased
their utility to his economy, molded the nature of his economic habits
in new directions according to new environmental opportunity, and
perhaps, as Ames suggests, thereby influenced his own physical evolution. Toward the end of the period reviewed here, I suspect, he
may have begun the first conscious steps in plant management. The
chief acts by which he intervened in the plant world I take to have
been these: (1) The campsite was the center of most intense disturbance. Here most of the vegetation was removed to make room
for the communal living. The ground was subjected to continuous
tramping and became packed. (2) Refuse accumulated about the
camp, of shell, bone, plant materials, and ashes, which formed a soil
heavily enriched in nitrogenous material, in lime, potash, and phos-
phate. (3) In forest, wood, and brushland adjacent to the community the useful woods, barks, and bast were depleted. Trees were
killed, and the resulting fall of dead branches and trunks provided
the common fuel supply. In time this process of deadening might extend to a notable distance from the permanent settlement. (4)
Trails opened up strips of trodden ground, and along them accidental scattering of seeds and roots took place, by loss in transit.
(5) Digging for edible roots and bulbs kept such harvest grounds
disturbed, mixed the soil, and gave opportunity for the multiplication of the pieces that had been missed. Root digging was, in fact,
unplanned tillage. (6) Newly immigrated groups of men often
brought along viable seeds by chance. (7) The setting of fires to aid
collecting and hunting has been stressed previously as the most effective device in the alteration of vegetation. Its effectiveness depended on recurrent use, and thus on continued occupation of area.
(8) In time the practice of protecting trees and shrubs that were
prized may have become established; living primitives are still
likely to do so, and advantageous behavior should not be denied to
early people whose existence depended on acting intelligently within
the range of their experience.

The ecologic effects included the introduction and establishment
of species from other localities, but the most important results are
to be found in the ways by which man placed certain plants under
reproductive disadvantages and increased the opportunity for others. Thus plant associations became increasingly altered or reconsti-
tuted to the extent of the elimination of species from a given flora.
Man's activities were directed especially strongly toward diminishing the shading of the ground. Every leafy tree or shrub that died
and was not replaced by a similar one made room for the coloniza-

tion of sun-loving herbs. Little by little, spaces were opened for heliophiles, and thus the first steps were taken that, as I have indicated elsewhere, may have resulted in the great grasslands of the hunting cultures.[20] Except for deserts and the permanently moist ground surface of rainy tropics, higher mountains, and higher latitudes, the vegetation of most parts of the earth bears in varying degree the impress of plant replacement by man, chiefly of fire succession. Thus plants which before man were minor and localized elements in a flora found steadily improved opportunities for increase.

Ames has pointed out the heliophile character of most of the cultivated plants. The exceptions are indeed minor, such as coffee and cacao. It is also true that the great majority of wild plants used by man as fruits or roots are sun-loving. By the gradual opening of sunlit spaces he unwittingly favored the multiplication of food for himself. Later he may have learned to do so deliberately. Whatever the climate and the terrain, even if it is marsh or pond, the plants of human food interest are usually found in the sunlit habitats of any area. Our fence rows, roadsides, old fields, and forest burns are populated by diverse berries, bush and tree fruits, and heavily seeding annuals. The wild plants that provided the Indians of the United States with their staple seeds, roots, tubers, and bulbs were harvested mainly in woods margins and on prairies, or at the edges of sunlit streams, marshes, and ponds.[21] Before the time of man such plants had more restricted habitats, especially in nonarid climates. Stream and lake margins admitted sunlight to narrow strips of ground. Windfalls opened space briefly in woods. Cliffs, slumping slopes, caving banks, and fresh alluvial surfaces made niches for plants that could pioneer in open ground. With the advent of man increasing space was provided for heliophile herbs in many climates, but especially on ground that had some seasonal

---

[20] Carl O. Sauer, A Geographic Sketch of Early Man in America, Geographical Review, Vol. 34, 1944, pp. 529–573; this volume, pp. 197–245.

[21] O. P. Medsger provides an instructive catalogue in his Edible Wild Plants (New York, 1939). From his list of edible roots and tubers I abstract the following: mainly in wet sites, arrowhead (*Sagittaria*), nut grass (*Cyperus esculentus*), calamus (*Acorus*), camass (*Quamasia, Camassia*), groundnut (*Apios tuberosa*), cattail (*Typha*), aroids (*Peltandra, Calla*); in prairies and woods margins, sego lily (*Calochortus*), bitterroot (*Lewisia rediviva*), prairie apple (*Psoralea esculenta*), hog peanut (*Amphicarpa*), cowas (*Lomatium geyeri*), yampa (*Carum gairdneri*), wild potato vine (*Ipomoea pandurata*), valerian (*Valeriana edulis*), Jerusalem artichoke (*Helianthus tuberosus*), wild potatoes (*Solanum fendleri* and *S. Jamesii*).

dryness and hence was most sensitive to effects of burning, deadening, or digging.

Additional ecologic changes should be noted: (1) Thinning of litter and leaf mold occurred, accompanied by somewhat increased runoff and reduced penetration of rainfall, and hence by some reduction in leaching, and possibly increase in pH value. A certain degree of shift from acidic to neutral soils is inferred.[22] (2) An advantage was furnished to aggressive, weedy plants, characterized by free seeding, broad tolerance in germination, and robust early growth. (3) A shift took place from long-generation to short-generation species, in particular increase in numbers of annuals, biennials, and plurennials. The Pleistocene is considered to have been the period in which very many annual species originated. It may be suggested that the disturbances produced by man may have been a major reason for the emergence of a host of new, annual species. Dug-over ground, trailsides, and village margins are still good places to encounter members of such families as the Amaranthaceae, Chenopodiaceae, Solanaceae, and Cucurbitaceae, which have played and still play a notable role in the feeding of man. Also, of course, uncounted species of grasses and Compositae are thought to have originated within the time of man. (4) That frequency of disturbance of tuber-bearing plants is likely to encourage their reproduction anyone who has dug tuberous sunflowers, yams (*Dioscorea*), *Cyperus,* or *Dahlia* can attest. (5) Whenever protection was afforded to plants (trees) of one species, man was intervening to establish the dominance of that species in a given spot (formation of groves). (6) The refuse heaps furnished a specialized habitat for plants grossly feeding on nitrogenous matter and the nutrient salts dissolved from ash, bone, and shell.

Thus, also, the processes of evolution were aided by man. Disturbances that he set up and kept up shifted survival chances in favor of an occasional variant plant. With more variants able to reproduce themselves, further diversity resulted in their offspring. (1) Gene mutations affecting the life cycle (for example, annual habit) or germination, which previously did not establish themselves under natural competition, might acquire reproductive advantage. (2) Polyploidy, especially if resulting in increase in size of seed or plant, quicker or more robust growth, might favor survival. (3) Introgressive hybridization was aided by accidental scattering of seed brought in from other localities. Unconscious human selection of

---

[22] The gradual replacement of heavy and deep-rooted trees and shrubs by fibrous-rooted herbs and grasses continued the shift.

plants was operative if any protection was given to any stand or clump because of the palatability of its fruits, seeds, or roots.

A new symbiosis between plants and men was therefore in progress. The greater the increase in human populations and the less their mobility or tendency to evacuate an area, the greater was the long-run change in the vegetation. The more seed-bearing annuals populated the lately opened spaces, the more fruit-bearing trees and shrubs encircled such openings, the more root plants were subdivided by digging, the more did plant food become available to man. A continuing cycle was thus set up. Perhaps man also harvested an increasing percentage of the plant food for himself and shared less with other mammals. As in modern agriculture, so in early collecting, a shift from animal to plant food yielded more calories per unit of surface. As man became more vegetarian in habit, he could support larger numbers of his kind. Every increase in his skill of reducing forest area, of harvesting seed, of digging roots, of cooking, of storage, raised the ceiling of population for him and, in most instances, exerted selective pressure in favor of the plants most useful to himself.

10

Man in the Ecology
of Tropical America

TROPICAL CLIMATE

For the present purpose, the Tropics are considered as the humid low latitudes, though not necessarily rainy at all seasons, or the classical Tropical Zone, if you will, flaring poleward on the eastern side of the continental masses, skewed equatorward on the western side. The concern here is not with any dispute as to where to run climatic boundary lines, those neat devices by which geographic realities are masked by the artifices of a numerical system, often compounded with an equal artifice of vegetation zones, but with the lower latitudes which have their weather determined by the equatorial low-pressure cells and their seasonal shifts for parts of the Northern Hemisphere by monsoon effects. Short days, marked diurnal temperature range and low annual temperature range are implicit. Rainfall, with rare exceptions, has seasonal quality; "the rains follow the high sun." Poleward the air is stable, and there may be a good flow of trade wind or intruding continental air from high latitudes. The rains, which come in "summer," are mainly convectional; and hence, even in the heart of the tropics, the mornings, and an occasional series of days, have bright skies. Variability of weather from year to year is low. In Recent and Pleistocene time the low latitudes have been least affected by secular changes in climate; here if anywhere we may think of climatic stability.

Year-round raininess, humid air, and wet ground are restricted to minor parts of the tropics. Such is in the New World the *ceja de la montaña* of the Andes, especially on the Amazonian side, a very long strip of cloud forest that lies well above the tropical lowlands. On the lower slopes of the montaña there is the usual daily rhythm of sunshine and rain, and there are spells of bright, dry weather.

Proceedings of the Ninth Pacific Science Congress, 1957, Vol. 20, 1958, pp. 105–110.

Over most of the Amazonian drainage there occur rather well-marked dry periods, in which there may be partial defoliation of upland trees and a sort of period of maturing of fruits. Meteorologic totals and averages may be misleading as to sequence of weather. "Humid tropics" and "rain forest" are terms subject to oversimplification and distortion by statistics.

ECOLOGIC SYSTEMS

That various organisms share the same geographic space is the concern of ecology. This sharing includes so many kinds of living things that we hardly think of a total ecology, but have been prudently inclined to reduce complexity through setting up partial systems of recognition and relation. We know, for instance, almost nothing of the synecology underground, of termites, earthworms, fungi, bacteria, and other soil organisms and their relation to life above ground. "Plant" and "animal" ecology largely have gone their separate ways. Vegetation complexes and "regions" are designated by habits of growth, abundance, and conspicuousness of constituent entities. In passing from such gross description to explanation, numbers, diversity, and variability of forms and factors confound our understanding. Numerical counts and statistical correlations, experimental eliminations and controls are employed. Beyond the reach of such quantitative inspection and experimentation, however, are the greater events and processes of natural history and earth history, of the nonrecurrent and nonreversible actuality of time.

Plant ecologists have thought to reduce the difficulties of their problems by relating vegetation directly to physical environment, the geographic limits being thought of as set by qualities of the atmosphere and of the ground. The most comprehensive thesis is that a given site is populated by groups (associations) of plants, succeeding one another as stages, until a final assemblage (climax association) is constituted which is fully adapted to the site and is therefore stable. Such climax vegetation is considered as optimally adjusted or constituted with regard to its climate. Rather elegant models are thus constructed which, however, do not take into account the flux of earth, or natural and cultural history. How organisms have come to live together in any part of the world, together with their evolutionary changes, is an historical problem of large and actual time which may not be explained by schemes of successive stages and climatic climaxes.

TROPICAL ORIGINS, DISPERSALS, AND INCREASE OF MAN

In this discussion attention is directed to the place of man in the biota of the tropical world. In our present state of knowledge there is a dispute as to whether the cradle of mankind was tropical Asia or tropical Africa. It may also be suggested that Man as our acknowledged direct ancestor may have descended from sources both African and Asiatic and that he migrated to the New World repeatedly in late Pleistocene and Recent time. In the Old World tropics, his kind has been around from the beginning. He has inhabited the New World for tens, probably for scores, of thousands of years. (The time of his entry into New Guinea and Australia is still unclear but may also have been at similar times in the Pleistocene.) Whether his earliest homes lay in the tropical rain forest is uncertain; it has been thus argued from the finds in Java. At any rate, the lower latitudes of the Old World widely have yielded the hominid forms underlying the evolution of man. We are accustomed to think of the rainy tropics as having a vegetation so exuberant that primitive man has found little to sustain him within their great forests; this is true. It is not true, however, that he has been unable to find early niches for himself there where he could live and increase in numbers and skills. I am unable to agree, therefore, with Professor P. W. Richards in his informed ecological study [1] in which he says: "Until the most recent period in its history man has had little effect on the Tropical Rain forest; large areas of it have been altogether uninhabited or inhabited only by food-gathering peoples with no more influence on the vegetation than any of the other animal inhabitants." He makes no unusual restrictions in defining the tropical rain forest; his Indo-Malayan forest reaches from southern India across Malaya and Melanesia, the African one from the middle Congo through the Guinea coast, and the American one includes the Amazon basin, the Guianas, and the Central American and Antillean rim of the Caribbean.

CONDITIONS AT THE TIME OF DISCOVERY OF THE NEW WORLD

The aboriginal presence and condition of man in the New World tropics bear little relation to rainfall and forest growth. The dis-

---

[1] The Tropical Rain Forest (1952); citation from p. 404.

coveries of Columbus, except for the pearl coast of Venezuela, were wholly in the rainier lands. The island of Haiti was praised by him in detail as an earthly paradise, with a teeming population of attractive culture. In his discovery of the Panamanian coast, Columbus spoke of the country about Porto Bello as "all like a painted garden" through which the houses were closely strewn. Eastern Panama to the Gulf of Darien and beyond to the Sinú River was well populated by agricultural folk, living in villages and larger towns. Because they possessed much worked gold, they were overrun quickly by the Spaniards from Darien, the first mainland town of Europeans in the New World. This original Spanish town was founded for convenience of access to the many Indian settlements in all directions. The native populations were soon destroyed, and the Spaniards abandoned Darien for the town of Panama on the Pacific side. The site of Spanish Darien is now midway of what is today almost trackless and uninhabited forest that runs from Porto Bello well beyond the Gulf of Darien.

The party of Orellana that made the first descent of the Amazon found numerous agricultural tribes occupying large villages; now archeology is uncovering a chain of sites along the Amazon that may link the high ceramic art of the island of Marajó at the mouth of the Amazon to Andean cultures.

Our New World humid tropics had been well prospected for native settlement long before the coming of the Europeans, and held sedentary folk numbered in the millions. Except for the cloud forest on mountain flanks, climate was not at all the limiting factor. The environmental limitations were, as they are now, edaphic: waterlogged lowlands, the deeply-leached wide interfluve terraces of the upper Amazon basin, the sandstone cappings of the interior Brazilian and Guianan massifs, the clay pans of the Llanos, lateritic and bauxitic soils, especially on igneous and metamorphic bedrock of low relief.

Our tropical lands in large part have been exposed for geologic periods to tropical weathering, in many parts are of parent materials originally poor in nutritive minerals, and in part have lacked sufficient relief to limit the accumulation of leached residuum. Such infertile tracts were also thinly peopled; not so the more fertile parts.

Modern settlement of the American tropics is largely resettlement of aboriginally occupied areas, as is going on now in Venezuela, with extensions by the addition of drainage engineering. Archeology and soil surveys are in agreement as to ancient and current attractiveness of land.

RIPARIAN HABITAT AND HABIT AT THE PRIMITIVE LEVELS

However forbidding the unbroken tropical forest was to the most primitive folk, the water breaks in the forest invited his entry by the multitude of streams that keep their sunlit way open through the forest. Lake and seashore also offer open spaces. In large measure primitive man is a riparian creature anywhere; he moved into the tropical forest along the edges of the water, lived by the water, and there gathered everything needful. It made little difference how great or tall the forest, the sunny avenues of water provided a congenial environment; widely branching, they led far inland toward the watersheds. The riparian habitat, I wish to submit, has been favorable to progress, since its environment is diversified as to plant and animal life both of land and waters. Riparian folk are likely to live sociably in groups clustered at sites advantageous for getting a living and protected from flood hazard, and affording easy communication with other groups. The economic geography of such folk is to be read from the productivity of the kinds of stretches of water and their bordering lands, from what military jargon now calls "trafficability," and from the attractions of the sites selected for habitation. Here human ecology must begin with limnology as known and used by primitive man.

There are still remnants of very primitive collectors and hunters in the farthest parts of the Amazon basin, of the Guiana highlands, and perhaps elsewhere; people without any knowledge of agriculture, in some cases even of rafts or boats. Very little is known about them. Their survival may have been by retreat into the most offside and least attractive areas. Other tribes may know only archaic water skills, such as catching fish by hand ("graveling" in the American vernacular), spearing and shooting fish with bow and arrow, and especially the use of piscicidal plants, a widespread and well-developed ancient skill. Some such tribes use balsas (rafts) but make no boats. By the addition of boats, lines, and nets, the water economy is fully elaborated. The water's edge is especially rewarding to hunting. Here turtles come out to lay their eggs; rodents such as the great capybara live, and tapirs feed; and here are the greatest diversity and number of land animals, depending on the riparian vegetation. Of animal sources for the sustenance of man, there is no lack in quantity or diversity adjacent to and in the water bodies.

Man as a ground-living creature found his place at the edge of
the tropical forest. The available and rewarding edges provided
and maintained by nature along the water courses also afforded him
an adequate plant economy. Interrupted forest canopy admits ample sunlight to ground level, where plants of lesser stature grow
successfully. Shrubby and herbaceous plants, excluded from the
forest, appear in diversity. Newly deposited alluvial materials, bars
forming and shifting within the stream banks, trees toppled into the
stream, all the accidents of rise and fall of water level maintain a
zone of disturbance attractive to plants that are able to colonize
with speed and to reproduce quickly. Such plants furnish for man not
only food—fruits, fleshy stems, and starchy rhizomes—but also raw
materials for other uses. In the New World *Guadua, Gynerium,* and
other giant grasses provide man with most of the equivalents of the
Old World bamboos. In addition to true palms, the *Carludovicas*
are used for making baskets and matting. Aroids yield tubers and
fruit (*Monstera*). Bihai (*Heliconia*) leaves supply wrapping for
things to be stored or carried in, for cooking, and plates for serving
food. These plants and many other bushes, climbers, or trees of low
habit belong to the unstable forest edge.

As to artifacts, the primitive tropical forest folk may perhaps be
said to have a wood culture, which also includes the canes and palms.
Their weapons are of wood and cane, from shaft to points. Bast
supplies cordage and clothing. The equivalent of ropes is provided
by the woody vines called *bejucos* (lianas). Rafts and fishing floats
are made from light wood such as *Ochroma*. Dugout canoes are
shaped by artful charring of tree trunks of certain species such as
Ceiba, Cedrela, and *Swietenia.* Since stone and pottery may not have
been used at all, or but little, archeologic sites may be lost, unless
recognized by an anomalous vegetation.

ALTERATION OF THE HABITAT

Not even the more primitive nonagricultural folk may be considered
as merely passive occupants of particular niches in their forest environment. By their continued presence and activity, they enlarged
such niches against the forest. In time, most of them added to fishing, hunting, and gathering agricultural occupation of their land.
(I am not implying any spontaneous, independent development of
agriculture and plant and animal domestication.) It is significant of
the extent of culture replacement in our tropics that the historic

survivals of nonagricultural peoples are so few and small and that they are found in edaphically adverse rather than climatically limiting areas, to soils too greatly leached or tough of structure to reward planting, or to swampy lands. A continued intervention of man in the ecology of the land has been the rule. The aquatic life was used, but hardly modified. Serious depletion of aquatic animals came with European arrivals; I know of none earlier. The inference is of normal predation, not of depredation of aquatic resource.

Man has been present in the continental tropics and their epicontinental islands from very remote times. Since climatic change here has been minimal, he has not been forced to abandon any part of his range other than lowlands submerged by postglacial rise of sea level. With every increment of skill that he gained, there was an increase in his numbers, for such skills were directed to the greater utilization of plants and animals. By his persistence, increase, and initiative, he has directed more and more selective pressure upon the rest of the biota. His acts have increased and perhaps introduced some organisms, and at the same time reduced and possibly eliminated others. An ecology without man, almost unchecked as he has been as to numbers and powers, is true only for an environment without man. I have grown more and more suspicious of any biogeography or ecology of the land from which man is thought of as eliminated as a factor of major importance.

SEDENTARY AND SOCIAL HABIT

Village dwelling of sorts is characteristic of water-side living. The site, if available, is chosen above high-water level. (In the New World tropics there was also an interesting habit of setting houses on high posts or piles, the distribution of which is in need of study. It may have originated where people lived in wide and flooded plains, but the style was carried into highland dwelling, as among the Chocó. Also, here and there people lived in clusters of tree houses, as in the Atrato flood plain.) The village required a landing place where boats could be beached. Stream junctions and rapids mark sites of permanent natural advantage for assembling supplies, for controlling the tributary economic area. A superior site for settlement continued to be so and normally continued to be occupied. Man is sedentary by preference, mobile by necessity; here the necessity was and is exceptional. The place that is called home acquires additional attachments, as traditions and ceremonials become rooted there. Persistence of place of habitation and cult observance is one of the major themes of cultural topography, and it extends into remote time. Nucleated and permanent settlement is the rule for most tropical habitation; the situation appears to be the same in the New World and the Old, in particular for Southeast Asia.

The village is a continuing and growing center of ecologic disturbance. Cleared spaces and refuse heaps acquire introduced plants, the two kinds of sites being edaphically in contrast. Outskirts experience the attrition common to woodlots. The knowledge that woody dicotyledons may die when the outer conductive tissue is interrupted is immemorial among woodland dwellers and perhaps common to all such people. Tropical-forest folk make little use of the ordinary fiber plants, but have many important uses for bast, both felted ("bark cloth") and twisted into lines and cords (as especially of numerous Moraceae); loss of inner bark may kill the tree. Also gums and resins are variously applied, in the tapping of which lesser damage is done to trees. The lessons of damage and destruction of the phloem were learned early. When agriculture was introduced, cutting or battering off a ring of phloem served to deaden the trees and admit the sunlight needed for planting. The dead trees provided dry wood for burning, the easiest way to meet fuel shortages as firewood grew scarce about the settlement. The "deadening" gradually becomes a "clearing" as storms break off the branches and finally topple the trunks. The mastery of the forest by man requires no axe; where tree trunks were desired as for canoes, or balsa, fire served to fell the tree, cut it to desired lengths, and to shape it to the finished craft.

DEGRADING THE FOREST BY FIRE

The most powerful tool by which man has altered his habitat and diversified his habits is fire, and this is true I think of all climes and all cultures. At the hearth fires, the processes of preparing food and the basic industrial techniques were worked out. Out of doors, man learned ways of setting fires so as to facilitate his appropriation of flora and fauna, thereby modifying both, by accident and also deliberately. It has been to his advantage to bring about what the ecologist calls secondary or deflected successions. A fully-grown forest, fully stocked with large trees, is a vegetation in its least useful condition for man. Except for lumber he has little benefit from the big trees. Together with other creatures that live on the ground his harvest is restricted to low-growing things, his interest is in a retarded or degraded "plant succession." He sets up and keeps up ecologic disturbance and drives the primary forest back. His unending attempt is to master and manage the living environment, and this he does by substituting lesser and short-lived plants for the great ones, by breaking down the forest margin into brush and herbs and widening more and more the zone of disturbance and diminution. This he has done most easily and most frequently by fire, to make easier the harvest of plants and animals and also to manage his land for greater productivity. The practices of Indian burning make clear that purpose and result were understood, be they agricultural, hunting, or collecting. Attrition and alteration in significant part have been deliberate.

The effectiveness of man as disturber of biota probably diminishes from the margins of the tropics to their equatorial regions. The domesticated plants of the New World mainly point to an origin in the outer parts of the tropics. The central tropical areas, it may be inferred, were agriculturally colonized from nearby lands of contrasted rainy and dry seasons. However, the tropical rain forests are not resistant to penetration and modification by agricultural folk. These often were its most effective attackers. "Winter" dry seasons characterize most of the Amazon and Orinoco basins, Central America, and the West Indies; at such times the surface of the ground and its litter dry out, and fires are effective and may spread until stopped by breaks in the topography. Even in the Amazonian montaña, where rainless days are few, litter is burned regularly before planting. The thin-barked and hence poorly-insulated trees of the humid tropics, particularly while young, are readily killed by burning. The continued persistence of natural vegetation unmodified by man is, I repeat, nearly limited to edaphic situations adverse to human interference, not to climate.

THE QUESTION OF THE SAVANNAS

The shrinkage of rainy seasons away from the equator to give way to a great dry season in the outer tropics is often climatically described as the change from wet tropical to savanna climates. Vegetation in the latter is made up largely of more xeric plant forms, although trees characteristic of the rain forest may still be present. An objection may be entered here against identifying savanna climate and savanna vegetation. The climatic transition from precipitation in all seasons to a long and marked dry season is delimited conventionally by convenient but noncritical precipitation data. When the Spaniards picked up the term *savanna* from the island Arawaks of Haiti and Cuba, it had no climatic meaning, nor too clearly a vegetational one. Savannas were first of all plains, largely open and grassy, but not without groves of trees, and often studded with tall palms. The rainfall in the West Indian savanna lands ranges from a hundred to a hundred and fifty centimeters a year; in parts of the savannas of Venezuela and Central America, however, it may be twice as much, in other parts less than in the West Indies. The great savannas of the Orinoco lowlands include rain-poor to very rainy areas; it may be noted that they are called the *llanos* (plains).

The inference that savannas are climatically determined tropical grasslands is not justified. They extend across very different parent materials from which different soils are derived. In part, I think in minor part, they may be edaphically based; but if so they have been greatly extended beyond primevally grassy tracts. Their one common quality is that they are plains. Another equally old vegetation term out of the West Indies is *arcabuco,* thorny thicket (largely Leguminosae) and bearing also the connotation of broken terrain. Savanna and arcabuco are contrasted first by relief and then as to plant cover.

The only explanation for the great savannas that meets all conditions is fire; fire that has run often and far over plains in dry season. Except where man has continued to burn them to the present, as in the llanos, they have lost their grassy appearance. At the north, in Cuba, Haiti, and on the mainland south into Nicaragua, woodlands of Caribbean pine and related yellow pines form rather open grass-floored stands. These may extend to low elevations and into areas of heavy rainfall (as in the Mosquito coast). Fire resistance, as by corky insulating bark, germination in mineral soil that has been exposed by soil erosion, and full exposure to the sun have given opportunity to xeric woody forms, perhaps mainly of northern origin, to extend their range. The situation resembles somewhat that of the yellow-pine forests of the southern United States coastal plain, in which controlled burning is being applied to the maintenance and reproduction of pine stands.

CHANGES BY THE EUROPEAN CONQUEST

The coming of Europeans had early and far-reaching effects. Great
native populations of sedentary farming habits were decimated or
died out in a generation or two. Mostly this collapse took place
in the coastal lowlands, Yucatán being the principal exception. The
Caribbean shores, the lowlands of Vera Cruz, and the Pacific lowlands from Panama to the northern limit of high culture in Sinaloa
were nearly and quickly depopulated. European livestock, cattle,
horses, and dogs ranged over former Indian fields, the New World
becoming largely stocked from herds built up first on Haiti and
Cuba. These animals contributed to the loss of their own range
by disseminating seeds of woody plants through their excrement.
The Spaniards complained, for example, of loss of range on Haiti
to *guayabales,* thickets of guava (*Psidium*), within a generation
of their arrival; these thickets are still extensive.

Various secondary vegetations may still help to identify prehistoric settlements. In the Mexican West I have thus noted colonies
of mesquite (*Prosopis*) in Sonora, *Pithecollobium* and *Brosimum*
farther south, and massive stands of coquito palms (*Attalea?
Orbignya*) as markers of once flourishing communities. Some of
these archeologic dominants are not known in these parts except
on old settlement sites. Chicle hunters have long been known as discoverers of Mayan archeology through the concentration of chicle
trees (*Archras zapote*) about ruins. Mahogany (*Swietenia*) and
tropical cedar (*Cedrela*), which are good colonizers, may also
have maximum stands where old fields lay. The Cecropias come
quickly into abandoned land and fade out soon, as may *Carludovica,
Heliconia,* and more slowly such trees as *Ochroma, Guazma,* and
various Malpighiaceae; but after four hundred years of abandonment of fields, certain trees (and palms) still identify the places
of human habitation. Some of these are trees that had been valued
by the natives and were introduced, as the coquito palms appear
to have been, or protected, as the chicle trees. Others, such as perhaps mahogany and tropical cedar, may be colonists that hang on.
Their persistence may underscore the extent of man's former activities. The Old World, in so far as I know, offers no parallel
to this drastic elimination of human occupance.

Steepness of slope did little to reduce the exploitation by aboriginal inhabitants; even now *conucos* and *milpas* are laid out by

preference on steep and broken terrain, not by any means only because there is shortage of land for planting, but often because of better drainage and aeration.

CONCLUSION

Lack of drainage and lack of relief, with which lack of fertility is associated, have been the main deterrents to aboriginal man in the New World. Here, and perhaps only here, may be asserted the survival of an extensive primary vegetation—of a vegetation that has been unaffected by man.

North of the American tropics we have radiocarbon dating of the presence of hunting man for more than thirty-eight thousand years (the present limit of age determination), of agricultural man for eight thousand years (Tamaulipas, by McNeish) with plants that were domesticated in the tropics at an unknown time earlier. During all his time, Man as collector, hunter, and fisherman, employed fire. As agriculturist, he was well and widely established at a time at least comparable to the western part of the Old World. As tropical planter and fisherman, his mode of life resembled that of Southeast Asia, except for lack of wet-land crops. At the time of European discovery, he was sedentary in strength in parts of the tropics that are now empty or are only now being colonized again. Under the supposed primeval forest lie the sites of quite advanced cultures. Something has been left out of the systems of synusiae and seres of ecology.

PART IV

The Farther Reaches
of Human Time

{ 11 }

A Geographic Sketch of Early Man in America

No apology is needed for scrutinizing any part of the history of man, anywhere, if insight can be gained into culture processes. Indeed, the study of human populations is regarded as having some relation in kind and in method to the general problem of organic diversity; simple and early populations may be more appropriate to study in the present state of our knowledge than late, complex, and highly derivative groups. It is neither accident nor escape that thoughtful human geographers have given much attention to primitive groups and remote time. A science of man—i.e., social science —cannot be restricted to or by the political forces and aspirations of its day.

SUBJECT AND METHOD

These notes are set down as starting from certain premises: that the natural history of man is connected with his culture history; that the culture of any human group is its organized or customary way of living, which consists of habits and skills acquired from its elders, of those learned from its neighbors, and perhaps also of inventions of its own; that, as long as a culture is viable, its complex of traits is a functionally valid and esthetically satisfying solution for living in the environment at the disposal of the group; that social science is concerned with understanding the processes of culture origins, growths, and extinctions, and with the hierarchies of social organization; and that the particular business of human geography is to examine these organizations and processes as to the manner and meaning of their localizations. In other words, the human geographer asks himself why cultures arose in a par-

Geographical Review, Vol. 34, 1944, pp. 529–573. Copyright, 1944, by the American Geographical Society.

ticular place, why they spread over certain areas, and, possibly, why they failed to maintain themselves.

A number of basic themes of anthropogeography are implicit in the discussion. For the most part they have been expressed by Ratzel, but they are here restated in terms of my own:

1. A given environment offers a determinable range of options to a given cultural group, but this range, for the same area, may be quite different for another culture. An environment, therefore, cannot be characterized properly except in the terms under which the occupant group operates. The exercise of the environmental options by a properly described population is the first concern of anthropogeography.

2. There may be external changes in the environment that alter its availability. A familiar theme of this kind is that of change in climate.

3. Men may alter the physical environment by their occupance; such changes may be ephemeral or irreversible. This theme was first explored systematically by George P. Marsh (1864), who designated it "physical geography modified by human action."

4. In the wide range of human habitation, only a small number of areas, each of no great extent, seem to have been centers of culture origin. Some have had this significance only once. Others have been recurrently centers of cultural innovation. These distinguished loci are the critical areas of history; they involve questions, still poorly understood, concerning significance of size, density, and diversity of population, the kind and diversity of local resources, and the qualities of isolation from, and communication with, other populations.

5. At the opposite extreme are areas of culture survival, predominantly static, in which peoples live on according to immemorial patterns. Such areas have markedly marginal or secluded positions.

6. The spread, or diffusion, of culture from one area (group, population) to another has been a subject of inquiry since the beginning of modern geography. Montandon has pointed out that it was anthropogeography, led by Ratzel, that combated the earlier anthropologic view of differing rates of dynamically uniform development of civilization ("evolutionistic" or mesologic concept of culture development) by insisting on comparing culture elements as to geographic distribution and thus repudiating the simple nexus of stage and environment.[1] It is of interest that anthropogeogra-

---

[1] George Montandon, L'Ologénèse culturelle: Traité d'ethnologie culturelle (Paris, 1934), p. 26.

phers, students of environment, early became skeptics regarding parallel stages of culture and frequency of parallel inventions. When sufficiently sharply defined, traits, other than those of obviously limited possibilities of alternative origin, are not likely to be of plural invention. Especially diagnostic of diffusion is the association of traits not manifestly derivative from each other. Disjunction of a culture element or series always involves the question of identity and of possible diffusion. The problem here resembles that of common genesis versus parallel variation in biology.

THE ARRIVAL OF MAN AND THE ICE AGE

Unless man originated in the New World, a thesis held almost alone by Florentino Ameghino, the first immigrations can hardly have been by any other route than Bering Strait out of northeastern Asia. The crossing from Asia into Alaska presents no problem: a small lowering of sea level or rise of land is known to have converted strait into land bridge at the beginning of Pleistocene time, and may have done so again later. Or a crossing on the frozen strait was possible to people who could live through Arctic winters. Western Alaska is an outlier of Arctic Asia. The lowlands of Alaska remained unglaciated and were available for habitation to any group of people accustomed to life in high latitudes.

If man entered the New World well after the Ice Age, there is no problem in his dispersal eastward or southward from Alaska. It is only if man came while there were still continental glaciers that there is difficulty about his passage beyond Alaska.

Folsom man contemporary with the Ice Age.—For half a century prudent people refrained from curiosity about ancient man in America. Militant authority in anthropology and, in part, in geology was against such inquiry from the eighties well into the last years. Marcellin Boule, after visiting this country in 1893, when C. C. Abbott and F. W. Putnam were supporting the case for Pleistocene man at Trenton, New Jersey, drew a parallel with the earlier "systematic and often ironic opposition" by French academicians to Paleolithic finds in France.[2] Kirk Bryan has pointed out that rejection of finds had become almost automatic, and the dogma of the recent peopling of the New World well hardened,

---

[2] Marcellin Boule, Les hommes fossiles (Paris, 1921), chapter 1; also under Trenton Man.

when the Folsom finds in northeastern New Mexico broke up this closed-mindedness.[3]

The validity of the Folsom finds was established in 1927, through the fortunate association of investigators possessed of competence, position, and courage. From chronologic correlations made largely by Kirk Bryan and his associates,[4] the original and subsequent sites of Folsom man were shown to have been in glacial or pluvial deposits. Folsom thus became the starting point of a remarkable series of discoveries and reappraisals, mostly by a new generation of students, who made untenable the older "conservative" position of the late peopling of the New World by simple, recognizable Indians.[5]

On the nature of glacial climates.—The last years therefore have made it necessary to consider the relation of the primitive American colonists to at least the final phases of continental glaciation. Thus arises the troublesome question of Ice Age climates. With due respect to everyone concerned, glacial climatology has been much neglected. Broad assumptions continue to be made of severe cold during ice advances and of marked warmth during ice retreat.

So far as I know, no American archeologist has considered the genial theory of Sir George Simpson, developed out of a lifetime of distinguished work on weather, from the Antarctic through the Indian monsoon lands to the British Meteorological Office and its directorship.[6] The essence of the theory is contained in the figure: (1) Increased solar radiation received by the earth leads to in-

---

[3] Kirk Bryan, Geology of the Folsom Deposits in New Mexico and Colorado, *in* G. G. McCurdy, edit., Early Man, as Depicted by Leading Authorities at the International Symposium, The Academy of Natural Sciences, Philadelphia, March 1937 (Philadelphia, 1937), pp. 139–152.

[4] The chief participant in and commentator on the Folsom record is Frank H. H. Roberts, Jr., of the Smithsonian Institution. See, in particular, his Developments in the Problem of the North American Paleo-Indian, *in* Essays in Historical Anthropology of North America Published in Honor of John R. Swanton, Smithsonian Misc. Collections, Vol. 100, 1940, pp. 51–116; and Evidence for a Paleo-Indian in the New World, Acta Americana, Vol. 1, 1943, pp. 171–201. The Folsom (and Yuma) record through 1938 is summarized in H. E. Fischel, Folsom and Yuma Culture Finds, American Antiquity, Vol. 4, 1938–1939, pp. 232–264. Later volumes have descriptions of subsequent finds.

[5] Since its founding in 1935, American Antiquity, under the hospitable editorship of W. C. McKern and, since 1939, Douglas S. Byers, has provided an open forum for the presentation of discoveries of ancient man.

[6] A recent, nontechnical statement: Sir George Simpson, Ice Ages, Nature, Vol. 141, 1938, pp. 591–598, reprinted in Ann. Rept., Smithsonian Institution, for 1938 (Washington, 1939), pp. 289–302; the full statement is in World Climate during the Quaternary Period, Quarterly Journal of the Royal Meteorol. Society, Vol. 60, 1934, pp. 425–478. References to biota, including

crease in the general circulation of the atmosphere, which forms a great cloud blanket and causes increased precipitation in appropriate areas. In particular, in high latitudes and altitudes there is increased snowfall, which gives rise to glaciers. (2) "As the radiation increases still further, the ice melts away and we have overcast skies and much precipitation but no ice accumulation." (3) "When the solar radiation decreases, conditions are reversed and the whole sequence is gone through in the reverse order."

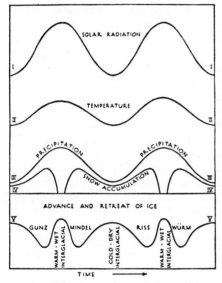

Effect of two cycles of solar radiation on glaciation. *Reproduced on a reduced scale from Sir George Simpson, "Ice Ages,"* Nature, *Vol. 141, 1938, Figure 5, p. 597.*

It will be noted that the Ice Age is interpreted by Simpson, following Penck and Brückner, as having consisted of two pairs of advances, separated by a long interval of deglaciation. In our terms these are the Nebraskan-Kansan advances and the Illinoian-Wisconsin advances, separated by the Yarmouth interglacial interval. The first of each pair of glaciations (Nebraskan and Illinoian) repre-

human associations, are in Simpson's The Climate during the Pleistocene Period, Proceedings of the Royal Society of Edinburgh, Vol. 50, 1929–1930, pp. 262–296; and Possible Causes of Change in Climate and their Limitations, Proceedings of the Linnean Society of London, Sess. 152, Part 2, 1939–1940, pp. 190–219. In 1925, C. E. Grunsky, as retiring president of the Pacific Division of the American Association for the Advancement of Science, presented a theory of glaciation through increase of warmth: A Contribution to the Climatology of the Ice Age, Proceedings of the California Academy of Science, Ser. 4, Vol. 16, 1927–1928, pp. 53–85.

sents increasing storminess and precipitation, the second (Kansan and Wisconsin) the reverse. The great (Yarmouth) interglacial, which lasted perhaps a third of all Pleistocene time, is considered to have been cold (at least in winter) and dry; the two short interglacials (pre-Kansan, or Aftonian, and pre-Wisconsin, or Sangamon) are held to have been wettest and mildest of all.

Recent time, extending to the present, may therefore well be an interglacial interval similar to the Yarmouth, with climates characterized by continental extremes; with colder winters and warmer summers, and with more widely reduced precipitation over the interior of the continent, than have existed since Yarmouth time. There is also evidence that the Coast Ranges, the Sierra Nevada, and the Rocky Mountains have experienced part of their growth in the late Pleistocene and since. Hence the barrier of the western mountains increased in effectiveness of interception of Pacific air.

The disappearance of the Wisconsin ice then is interpreted as the result of lack of nourishment under lowered cool-season temperatures. Unknown to each other, Simpson and American glaciologists dispose of the last ice by the same means, namely wastage through lack of precipitation (stagnant ice, pitted plains, and kettle moraines in New England and the land about the Great Lakes).

In earlier Wisconsin time there should still have been a great deal of melt water, discharging mainly down the Mississippi, but growing less and less toward the end of the period. The melt waters, I suggest in line with older views of glacial history (of Lyell, for example), deposited the great loess and loesslike beds of the Mississippi Valley, which were spread farther by the action of wind. So far as the beds are eolian in origin, they were not dependent on arid areas as sources of supply, but on lakes and on streams flowing from the ice front, diminished in winter and exposing dry bars. The maximum of late-Pleistocene flooding, and hence the great loess formations of later time, may thus have begun as prelude and part of the Illinoian advance, continued through the Sangamon interglacial, and decreased gradually after the Wisconsin ice maximum. In general, the main loessial deposits should have derived from glacial flood waters and should have coincided with glacial advances.

South of the ice sheets lay a belt of country along the front of the continental ice, and also between and south of the western mountains, subject to the meeting of continental (icecap) and tropical air (both Gulf and Pacific), receiving copious rains, and having its snowfall completely melted annually. These were the pluvial lands. Times of pluvial maxima should agree fairly well with those of glacial maxima and the wet interglacials. In particular, there is no reason in Simpson's climatology, or in any other, for admitting a delayed pluvial condition at, much less after, the time when the Wisconsin ice was wasting away. The pluvial lakes and marshes of the arid and semiarid southwestern United States disappeared as the glaciers faded in the north. This question is of importance, since archeologists are inclined to assign markedly postglacial and widely differing dates to extinct lakes in the American Southwest and the intermontane basins.

In higher latitudes, it would seem, the glacial sequence became simplified by the elimination of the short interglacial intervals. Here snowfall in the uplands would probably continue to exceed melting through the periods of "radiation maxima." The Nebraskan-Kansan would then merge into one glacial stage, and similarly the Illinoian-Wisconsin, leaving a single long, cold interglacial, equivalent to the Yarmouth. Taber [7] has gathered evidence showing that only two glaciations have been recognized in Alaska, the Yukon, British Columbia, and large parts of Siberia. This fact may explain the "mucks" of Alaska, for which in the unglaciated Yukon Valley and coastal lowlands Taber has established a period of deep freezing (=Yarmouth?) followed by one of deep thawing (=Illinoian-Wisconsin?). The possible correlations are offered by myself, with diffidence, as coming from one who has never seen Alaska.

Simpson has been concerned with a general mechanism that is meteorologically valid. The sequences to which he addressed himself were the major events recorded in the continental icecaps. I hope that I have not done violence to his thesis in the applications suggested. Nor do I think that it is at present more than a working hypothesis, which makes sensible use of the known mechanism of atmospheric circulation and opposes capricious and dynamically irreconcilable notions of glacial, pluvial, and interglacial conditions.

The glacial history of Europe is simpler than that of North America. In Europe one center, Scandinavia, spread its ice outward in such a fashion that the successive fronts maintained rather parallel positions, the chief difference being in length of radius of ice advance. In North America, however, very different centers of growth and directions of advance prevailed at different times. This is well illustrated by the five substages of Wisconsin advance. In the first, the Iowan, a western (Keewatin) center pushed a strong

---

[7] Stephen Taber, Perennially Frozen Ground in Alaska: Its Origin and History, Bulletin Geol. Society of America, Vol. 54, 1943, pp. 1433–1548, especially pp. 1533–1539.

lobe southward, to the west of the Mississippi River into Iowa. In the next, formerly called the Earlier Wisconsin, now Tazewell, a far-eastern (Labrador) center sent the main advance of ice southwestward into central Illinois. The third center was about Hudson Bay, the fourth mainly active from a Keewatin area. The last, the Late Mankato, expanded from a Keewatin (Great Slave Lake?) center again and advanced into the Dakotas and Montana, in general covering a more western terrain. In Europe, oceanic air fed snow to a maritime (Scandinavian) highland, and the growth and disappearance of icecaps reflected simple changes in the relation of precipitation and temperature. In North America, on the other hand, additional, undetermined forces entered, which may have included changes in sea ice in the western North Atlantic, effects of Cordilleran orogeny on storm tracks, and perhaps even shifts of the pole.

The greatest contrast between the two continents is the characteristic formation in the New World, and the absence in Europe, of successive long, southward-thrusting lobes largely independent of one another in center of origin and direction of main growth. This phenomenon is in some manner an expression of variations in continentality of interior North America, associated with important secular changes in the position of the ice-breeding storm tracks. In the substages the dynamics of glaciation in the New World depart markedly from those on the other side of the Atlantic. It is inadmissible therefore to transfer detailed climatic parallels from the glacial history of the Baltic or other parts of Europe to this continent.

The corridor from Alaska.—The corridor by which man may have come from the open lowlands of Alaska to the plains of the United States is uncertain, as are the times at which this may have been possible. The answers wait on the determination of glacial successions in western Canada. Viewed from south of the border, a late corridor through Alberta does not look promising, because of the Late Mankato drift on the northern Great Plains and the probable ice center over Great Slave Lake. We need to know in detail the drift history of the plains east of the Rockies both in Alberta and in Yukon Territory. An alternative route may be an intermontane corridor through British Columbia and the western Yukon, where rain-shadow conditions possibly facilitated deglaciation or prevented glacial spread.

Arrival of first colonists in interior North America.—The remains of Folsom and Yuma man point definitely to hunting cultures. Such people had high mobility and could follow herds of game animals through any corridor that opened between Alaska and the United States, provided that nutritious vegetation speedily reoccupied ice-free surfaces. In the case of Folsom man, the associations of sites with glacial and pluvial deposits have made acute, since the first discovery, the question of the earliest moment at which a gap opened in the Wisconsin ice of Canada through which immigrants might have squeezed.

If we knew nothing of European archeology, an estimate of these folk as going back at least twenty or twenty-five thousand years, such as was made by Kirk Bryan for the Lindenmeier site in Colorado, would meet with no opposition. The alarm at these figures is due partly to the ingrained habit of setting up short calendars for the New World and partly to the high stoneworking skill of these ancient hunters, who in Old World terms would be called advanced Mesolithic. Archeologists are not ready to face the disquieting thought that any skill may have been introduced (or developed?) in the New World as early as in Europe, or the even more disturbing one that the New World may have had priority in any part of culture history over western Europe.

Yuma man lived well into postglacial time, and his arrival has been thought to present no difficult time problems.[8] However, recent studies in Nebraska are indicating a greater age for the culture of the Yuma hunters than has hitherto been accepted:[9]

1. In the White River drainage basin in northwestern Nebraska deeply buried fire hearths, charcoal layers, and artifacts have been found that antedate the deposition of varved clays. The clays are interpreted tentatively as having been formed in a lake dammed by a late-Wisconsin ice lobe along the Missouri River near the mouth of the White River. If this is correct, these lake beds have since been unwarped by more than two thousand feet at their western end near the foot of the Rocky Mountains, an indication of an unsuspectedly late and large uplift of the Great Plains and the Rocky Mountains, which may have contributed appreciably to the continentality of climate in the interior

---

[8] To nonarcheologists the name Yuma is confusing. It is derived from a Great Plains county in Colorado, and has nothing to do with the Yuma Indians or river.

[9] Later publications are: A. L. Lugn, The Pleistocene Geology of Nebraska, Nebraska Geol. Survey, Bulletin, Ser. 2, No. 10, 1935, especially pp. 142–145 and 183; E. H. Barbour and C. B. Schultz, Palaentologic and Geologic Considerations of Early Man in Nebraska, Nebraska State Museum, Bulletin, Vol. 1, No. 45, 1936; and Paul MacClintock, E. H. Barbour, C. B. Schultz, and A. L. Lugn, A Pleistocene Lake in the White River Valley, American Naturalist, Vol. 70, 1936, pp. 346–360.

plains and thus to the ending of glaciation. Fire pits and other evidences of human occupation predate significantly the formation of this White River lake. At the time of the latest published account, typical Yuma artifacts had not been definitely established beneath the varved clays. It is possible, therefore, that the oldest human layers apply to a pre-Yuman people.

2. In blowouts in the Sand Hills of western Nebraska, many Yuma (and some Folsom) points have been found at depth in an old soil. They carry an extinct fauna that may be the equivalent of that of the *Citellus* faunal zone of the loess areas (Peorian?). The time scale of the ancient sand dunes is difficult to decipher, but the Nebraskan investigations seem to be gradually delineating the outlines of a late-glacial history.

3. The Scottsbluff Bison Quarry has produced artifacts, in part Yuman, in association with vertebrate and invertebrate remains identified as late-glacial.

The Nebraska investigators agree in considering the Yuma hunters to have been plainsmen contemporary with the Folsom people of the Rocky Mountain border. There is little doubt that the Yuman culture survived well after the Folsom one had disappeared. The evidence, however, is becoming formidable that Yuman goes back as far as Folsom. The Yuman people fashioned the fine leaf blades that have so often been compared with the Solutrean blades of Europe, but in their art the New World craftsmen clearly surpassed those of the Old. On the record as it stands, Yuman predates Solutrean by an uncomfortable margin. The origin of Yuman culture is thus most perplexing.

Pre-Folsom hunters must also be considered:

1. One such record, underlying a Folsom horizon, is from the basal level of Sandia Cave, in the Sandia Mountains east of Albuquerque, New Mexico.[10]

2. Projectile points from the shores of vanished pluvial lakes (Mohave and Pinto basins) in the desert of southern California are less advanced in development than the Folsom type and are held by some to be pre-Folsom. Antevs has characterized well the great change in climate that has taken place since these lakes existed and has stated that "they [the artifacts] may be at least 15,000 years old." [11] At the time this seemed a daring claim for antiquity of man. Now, however, it seems inadequate; for this estimate implies a long delay in pluvial conditions in California, for which no climatologic basis is known.

3. West-central Texas has at notable depths the remains of a hunting cul-

---

[10] F. C. Hibben, Evidences of Early Occupation in Sandia Cave, New Mexico, and Other Sites in the Sandia-Manzano Region, Smithsonian Misc. Colls., Vol. 99, No. 23, 1941.

[11] E. W. Campbell, Archaeological Problems in the Southern California Deserts, American Antiquity, Vol. 1, 1935–1936, pp. 295–300; Ernst Antevs, Climate and Early Man in North America, *in* G. G. MacCurdy, edit., *op. cit.,* pp. 125–132, reference to p. 128.

ture, said to be more primitive than the Folsom, which Sayles has called the Abilene type. These are in silt beds (Elm Creek) formed under more humid conditions than the present and possibly referable to late-Wisconsin time.[12]

These early hunting remains are found in localities that at present are semiarid to arid but at the time of occupation were humid. The sedimentary and biotic evidence indicates that they belong to a well developed pluvial period, and I know of no climatologic basis for postulating a postglacial pluvial period. Except Sandia, they have not been determined stratigraphically as pre-Folsom, but they are old and the points are cruder than, and suggestive of, Folsom. Nothing resembling the fluting of the Folsom points appears in European archeology, and it has been thought therefore that this may be a New World invention developed out of more generalized points of an earlier, also western, hunting culture.[13]

The problem of antiquity is raised by yet other finds of early man. Gladwin has pointed out the position of ancient non-projectile and non-blade-making cultures to the south and east of the main range of the ancient hunters and has suggested justly that their position farther inside the New World indicates that they preceded the hunters.[14] Such material lacks the sharply diagnostic qualities of Folsom and Yuma, is decidedly more primitive, and belonged to peoples that were gatherers rather than hunters. It is difficult to see how such apparently unwarlike folk could have forced their way through a wide deployment of tough hunting peoples and taken their stations beyond them within the continent.

1. The best known of these early gathering cultures is the Sulphur Spring (Cochise I) culture of semiarid southeastern Arizona, developed under well marked pluvial conditions (a lake border with hickory trees),[15] and perhaps the oldest human record of the Southwest.

2. At the base of the Texas Abilene series are crude percussion tools, to-

[12] E. B. Sayles, An Archaeological Survey of Texas, Medallion Papers, No. 17, 1935; M. M. Leighton, Geological Aspects of the Findings of Primitive Man near Abilene, Texas (Preliminary Report), *ibid.*, No. 24, 1936.

[13] However, the recent discovery by Frank Hibben of Folsom culture in Alaska, including its southwestern part, is a very strong indication that Folsom was a direct immigration from an unknown Asiatic area: Frank C. Hibben, Our Search for the Earliest Americans, Harper's Magazine, Vol. 189, 1944, pp. 139–147.

[14] H. S. Gladwin, The Significance of Early Cultures in Texas and Southeastern Arizona, *in* G. G. MacCurdy, edit., *op. cit.*, pp. 133–138.

[15] E. B. Sayles and Ernst Antevs, The Cochise Culture, Medallion Papers, No. 29, 1941.

gether with used flakes and charcoal, found on the surface of and within buried, deeply weathered Pleistocene (Durst) silts, much older than the overlying (Elm Creek) silts of the normal Abilene hunting series. Leighton, on reasonable evidence, is disposed to place the older silts well within the Pleistocene, possibly as far back as the latter part of the Sangamon (pre-Wisconsin) interglacial stage. In terms of our present knowledge of man in America, this may be too great an estimate.

3. Greenman of Michigan has reported very primitive (Levallois-like) artifacts on an old beach of glacial Lake Algonquin near Killarney, Ontario, 297 feet above the present lake level.[16] The fact that these tools are water-worn suggests that they are somewhat older than the beach on which they lie, though Greenman uses this quality as evidence that they are contemporaneous with the beach. At any rate, their occurrence is intelligible only as connected with lakeside habitation not later than the time of glacial Lake Algonquin.[17]

To this bystander it seems that the fight, first joined at Trenton in New Jersey in the eighties, has been won at last, and that Abbott and Putnam are vindicated. Pleistocene man can no longer be denied; it is only a question as to how far back his title extends in America, and that will not be settled by European records. What does it matter that a skull of Cochise I or of Minnesota man can be brought within "the range of the modern American Indian"? That range has been stretched and stretched until it will accommodate the bones of any New World *Homo sapiens*. Of this, more in its place later.

EXTINCTION OF PLEISTOCENE MAMMALS

At the beginning of Pleistocene time our western plains held a diversified mammalian fauna of large forms, including ground

[16] E. F. Greenman, An Early Industry on a Raised Beach near Killarney, Ontario, American Antiquity, Vol. 8, 1942–1943, pp. 260–265.

[17] Minnesota man cannot be assigned to either a hunting or a gathering culture. The skeleton was found with only a knife and a shell pendant that came from the Gulf coast. The determination was that it was *in situ*, and hence predated glacial Lake Agassiz. When the report on Minnesota man was attacked, the authors invited the leading glaciologists to make their own examination of the site. Kay and Leighton made a joint inspection; Bryan and MacClintock also visited the scene together, but not in the company of the other two. The separate reports of the two pairs of judges, George F. Kay and Morris M. Leighton, Glacial Notes on the Occurrence of "Minnesota Man," Journal of Geology, Vol. 46, 1938, pp. 268–278, and Kirk Bryan and Paul MacClintock, What is Implied by "Disturbance" at the Site of Minnesota Man?, *ibid.*, pp. 179–192, are models of dispassionate and competent summing-up. Both reports completely sustain the good faith of the discoverers and the validity of the find and its interpretation.

sloth, giant beaver, mastodon, horse, tapir, camel, and wolf; and in California, deer also. By Kansan time a great invasion of Old World immigrants had reached the middle of the continent, represented principally by species of the elephant, bovine, and cervine families. It was then that mammoth, giant bison, musk ox, and giant elk (moose) began to range the interior of North America. The bears seem to have moved in more slowly, perhaps not becoming established until the Yarmouth interglacial.[18]

By mid-Pleistocene the great countermigration between Asia and North America had been effected and our plains and valleys were well populated with the most diverse big-game fauna in their history. On the whole, these animals were larger, some of them much larger, than their modern representatives. The western mountains, in the meantime, had been occupied by mountain sheep and goats, also of Old World origin.

This great new assemblage of higher mammalian life established itself easily and harmoniously; enrichment, not extinction or displacement, marked the Pleistocene in America. Only minor, normal evolutionary changes subsequently altered this picture of the large fauna until we get into the period of Man. All these animals withstood the changes in temperature and precipitation that marked the later succession of Pleistocene time. In general, they seem to have done very well and to have increased in numbers and kinds.

Remains of extinct mammals in sites of early man.—The camps of the early American hunters are yielding an impressively growing record of association of man with the great Pleistocene mammals, all of which are now extinct. Their slaughtered remains are found in mass, as at the Lipscomb Bison Quarry.[19] Cracked and charred bones bear witness to the manner of consumption, and projectile points have been found in animal skeletons. Commonest are the remains of extinct bison (no association of modern bison with the early hunters has yet been proved); next, perhaps, those of mammoth. Ground sloth, giant beaver, mastodont, camel, horse, tapir, cave bear, and musk ox are all documented at human sites, especially Folsom, but including also Yuman and the possibly pre-Folsom hunting cultures.

The ancient hunters and the ancient game mammals seem to have left the scene together. The animals, we know, became extinct; the

---

[18] E. H. Barbour and C. B. Schultz, Pleistocene and Post-Glacial Mammals of Nebraska, *in* G. G. MacCurdy, edit., *op. cit.,* pp. 185–192.

[19] C. B. Schultz, Some Artifact Sites of Early Man in the Great Plains and Adjacent Areas, American Antiquity, Vol. 8, 1942–1943, pp. 242–429; reference to pp. 244–248.

hunters may have drifted out of the plains of North America and blended into other populations and cultures elsewhere in the New World. We can hardly make a surmise at the present time. The plains have been pictured as empty of human occupation for a long time thereafter. That long emptiness is perhaps an illusion, but we do know that when the old game animals were gone the record of the old hunters stopped. It may be that their disappearance was due to the disappearance of their accustomed game.

Disease or climatic change as cause of extinction?—The cause of the extinction of the great Pleistocene mammals has been sought in disease, in change of climate, and at the hand of man, or in the guess that somehow their allotted span of time was up. Elimination by disease is most improbable; for this would have required some epizootic unequaled in malignity, because it must have struck across many families and even orders of mammals, and incredible in manner of attack, because it singled out for destruction apparently only the big species, whatever the family. Nor is the most malignant epidemic successful, except in crowded populations; recovery is the rule, not extinction.

That these animals died out during a period of climatic change is likely. According to Simpson's thesis and from the evidence of Pleistocene orogeny, this took place at a time of decreasing precipitation over the interior and intermontane plains, and during increasing contrast between winter and summer. That parts of the intermontane basins of the West and also parts of the Southwest finally became too arid for these animals is admitted. The losses, however, must have been offset by the deglaciation that was uncovering the plains of the North. Also, the decrease in precipitation and in the melting of the ice reduced the areas of flood inundation and of waterlogged flats in the Mississippi Valley. On the whole, one should expect a substantial net gain in habitable territory to result from the ending of an ice age. At any rate, the change was slow, not cataclysmic, and provided ample time for accommodation by migration, unless the beasts refused to shift. Even in that case only the more southern and western groups should have experienced a crisis of climate; the rest would have benefited from increase in range. It must also be remembered that these animals had passed through at least equally great climatic changes before without harm, some of which changes (i.e., ice advances) certainly had brought marked contractions of habitable area.

Hunting weapons of early man.—Only two items in the problem stand out clearly. It was the big and clumsy animals that disappeared, and the new element added was hunting man. These Old Hunters of the New World were predators, as their remains well show, and they were the only known addition to the fauna at this time. Their tools were the tools of killing, or of the preparation of the kill. Nevertheless, it will be objected, and properly, that men were too few and too weak to have destroyed this great fauna with the tools the archeologists have recovered. And it has also been objected, with some justice, that the disappearance of the great mammals was not a matter of slow attrition, ended only recently.[20] Yet the rapidity of their disappearance must not be overemphasized; thousands of years seem to have been involved.

The artifacts of the Old Hunters are distinguished by their projectile points and blades; Folsom and Yuma man attained an astonishing perfection of lithic technique. Rarely have as fine leaf blades or as adequately designed points been made out of stone. Yet it seems that these superior instruments were suited rather to the finishing off of the kill and its dismemberment than to the main business of securing the large game animals. The Yuman blades, for instance, are considered by some to have been knife or dagger blades rather than projectiles. It is thought that these hunters did not use bow or dog. Nor can appeal be made to the use of bolas, which may possibly have been employed, but if so were suited to smaller game. Opinion seems to be somewhat divided as to the spear thrower. None has been found, and the points are rather heavy for such use. Also, since the spear thrower is not documented from Europe until the Magdalenian, a prior appearance on this side is looked on askance. The atlatl, as I know it, is properly a dart thrower. As such it is effective in the accelerated propulsion of a light shaft (cane) tipped with a sharp, fine dart, and is a weapon of rather high precision in the stalking of small game. Among the Tarascans it is used especially for the still-hunting of waterfowl. The points that have been described for the Old Hunters would seem to be rather those of javelins, hurled with the force of the entire body, or of lances used mainly for jabbing. In any case, the ability of atlatls to bring down woolly bisons more massive than the modern species or thick-hided mammoths would seem pretty inadequate. The weapons, therefore, do not explain the mode of hunting. Lacking superior weapons of the chase, the hunters nevertheless attacked successfully animals extraordinarily well protected by their size, hide, and fur.

---

[20] L. C. Eiseley, Archaeological Observations on the Problem of Post-Glacial Extinction, American Antiquity, Vol. 8, 1942–1943, pp. 209–217.

Hunting in organized bands.—We are forced to rely, therefore, on an explanation apart from the archeologic record, and to appeal to the use of organization and stratagem. There should be no objection to considering the hunters as operating in organized bands, under leaders of the hunt, perhaps chiefs. This is so familiar a quality in the ethnology of hunting peoples, especially where gregarious big game is the object of the hunt, that it has become a commonplace and is incorporated into basic classifications of social organization, as in systems of patrilocal or patriarchal society. The hunt is thought of, not as the pursuit of an individual animal by an individual hunter on his own initiative, but as an undertaking by the band under a prearranged plan of strategy, with assigned tasks and tactical direction. The stratagems of hunters were directed toward taking animals in traps, such as pits, or toward driving them to exhaustion, self-destruction, or demoralization of the herd. Of deadfalls and other contrivances such as are known in Europe from the Aurignacian on there is no trace. Driving game such as giant bison or mammoth by beaters could not have been very successful.

Stratagem by fire.—There was one terrible weapon available, able to frighten, injure, and demoralize the strongest: fire. In fire drives we find the principal method of hunting big game where powerful weapons and attack on horseback are lacking. It is ineffective only where vegetation is scanty, as in deserts, or where the ground is permanently moist. It is basic to hunting practices of modern Indians. Where physical conditions permitted and hunters were present, it was customarily and methodically employed in the New World. That it was first brought in by the earliest hunters of big game is a reasonable assumption. Archeologic proof is difficult to establish, but I know of nothing else that would explain the high frequency in these campsites of the bones of the large, powerful, and protected mammals. By the use of fire alone, it would seem, could such animals be caught, crippled, and made ready for destruction in number. Their mass placed them at a disadvantage; they could not run fast enough or far enough to escape an advancing line of fire directed against them.

The interior plains of North America are ideal for the employment of fire drives. The Great Plains in particular, chief habitats of the great mammals, have now, and undoubtedly had then, a dry season in the spring and a lesser one in the fall, and dry spells may occur at any time. The inflammability of the ground cover is repeatedly high throughout the year. Dry weather is likely to be accompanied by dry, fairly strong winds that blow steadily and with little change of direction for days. In the primitive condition of such plains a fire, once started, travels with the wind and may sweep the great, smooth interfluves until it meets a balk in the broken ground along the streams. A herd of lumbering animals, feeding on the plains, could be cut off by a line of fire before they gained the shelter of a valley. Or, panic-stricken, they could be driven toward a valley in such a fashion that they piled up in the ravines at its edge or tumbled over the rimrock that hems many plains valleys. In either case the fire hunters had only to dispatch maimed and injured animals. That such kills sometimes far exceeded the needs of the hunters is indicated by the piling up in one spot of numerous complete animal skeletons. The conditions at the Lipscomb Bison Quarry are especially illustrative.

Major indirect results of fire drives.—The fire drive provides an apparently adequate explanation of the extinction of the large mammals in post-Pleistocene time, well before the appearance of the assuredly Indian peoples. (1) Such drives destroyed considerably larger numbers of animals than were used by the hunters. (2) The device was selective against the larger kinds of animals, for which lower initial population densities and lower reproduction rates would apply than for the smaller mammals. (3) It was used especially against animals of gregarious habit and must have resulted in breaking down the social organization of the herd. This is a problem in animal sociology, and perhaps an important one. (4) It must have produced unbalanced sex ratios, since females carrying or nursing young, together with the young calves, suffered the highest losses. The cumulative effects of a continued unbalance of sexes are large. (5) The burning off of the feed range of a herd forced the herd to trespass on the range of another colony, to the injury of both. (6) Repeated burning of a surface alters the plant assemblage and may reduce its carrying capacity for animals adjusted to a given set of plants. (7) The great herbivores became weakened in relation to other animals. Predators, such as wolves, should have increased in response to the increased number of injured herd animals. Disturbance of vegetation and surface has been observed to increase the rodent population greatly, which then competes with large herbivores on more advantageous terms.

Destruction of a symbiotic balance and maintenance of disturbance are probably sufficient to eliminate a faunal group. This is precisely what seems to have happened in our interior plains, in which the ancient hunters maintained deliberate pressure against certain elements in the fauna, over a considerable period of time.

The more the great fauna was weakened, the more certainly did it approach its extinction. The final collapse may have been relatively rapid, but the period of attrition was prolonged. Yuma man was present at the finish, but the start may have been made by pre-Folsom people. That the entire span could have been thousands of years may seem exaggerated, in view of the small number of chronologically placed sites. However, the time from pre-Folsom man to the end of the Yuma folk seems to be impressively large. Much of the typologically primitive projectile material found at the surface in many parts of the United States may actually be old: the great majority of occupied sites did not leave an unequivocal record.

What happened on the plains of Europe and Asia was similar, and the time was not greatly different. Solutrean hunters, thought to have come from inner Asia, played a principal role in big-game extinction in Europe.[21] The resemblances between Solutrean and Yuman blades are striking, and form the basis of not a little conjecture. The bulkiest and clumsiest animals in Eurasia went first, such as mammoth and rhinoceros. Elephants, various cattle, horses, and camels were eliminated from most of their range, especially from the open plains that had annual dry periods. Marginal survival areas are more characteristic of the Old World than of the New; namely, moist forests of low and high latitudes, deserts, and remote corners that seem not to have been penetrated by hunting peoples.

How far the Pleistocene mammalian immigration from the Old World spread in the New and how much evolutionary development it experienced here are not well known. Both the bison and the mammoths ranged pretty well across the continent but made their principal domain the plains east of the Rocky Mountains. It was here that they favored a concentration of the hunting people, and it was here that they awaited their doom. The shrinking herds stayed put in their accustomed habitats. Whatever the reasons of biotic balance and herd psychology that had located the major populations and forms in the plains at the period of colonization, the time of decline set up no migratory impulse. Perhaps dying species do not migrate.[22]

[21] J. G. D. Clark, New World Origins, Antiquity, Vol. 14, 1940, pp. 117–137. Clark, commenting on the susceptibility of large fauna to human activities, gives a late instance, citing E. W. Bovill on the influence of the games at Rome on the pluvial fauna of North Africa.

[22] L. C. Eiseley, Did the Folsom Bison Survive in Canada?, Scientific

THE EXPANSION OF GRASSLANDS

There are so many different kinds of grasslands as regards ecology and composition that we can summarize them only as areas in which woody vegetation has been supplanted by herbaceous growth, especially by grasses. The elimination of the woody element perhaps is the general key to the question of the origin of grasslands.

The mechanism of this suppression is commonly thought to be climatic. Arid regions are not grasslands, nor are very humid ones, except for marshes and wet meadows. In areas intermediate between the extremes of moisture lie the extensive grasslands. Here we distinguish between humid and semiarid, tropical and extratropical grasslands. We are accustomed to speak of steppe and savanna climates and thus to imply that reduction of rainfall beyond the limits of humid climates and, also, the occurrence of a strongly marked dry season are the causes of grassy conditions. In the case of humid grasslands, where there is no strong contrast of dry and rainy seasons, as in our Midwestern prairies and in the Pampas of the Argentine, emphasis has been put on occasional droughts or the intervals between rains: apparently a forced construction. In general, periods of dryness are thought of as favoring the establishment of grasslands.

The climatologic description of grasslands is not at all satisfactory. It proceeds from the existence of a grassland, for which a roughly limiting set of climatic values is sought. It thus happens characteristically that, when rainfall and temperature values have been selected for a "savanna climate," they are found to apply also to areas covered with shrub. The same thing is true in "steppe climates." We confess thereby that the selected combination of climatic values is not reproduced everywhere by the same conditions of vegetation, and this admission places the causal relation

Monthly, Vol. 56, 1943, pp. 468–472. Here Eiseley calls attention to qualities of the Canadian woodland bison as it was known to the early naturalists that show closer affinities to the bison of Folsom man than our American prairie bison does. This suggests that bison became established in the Canadian North, perhaps soon after the disappearance of the ice, and that the lately surviving northern variety may have been related to the older plains bison. Our modern plains bison may have been a small, southern variant form, place of origin unknown, that moved in intermediate prehistoric time into the plains vacated by his vanished relatives. It may be added that the species recognized in Pleistocene and modern mammals are taxonomic, and may not be genetically valid.

in doubt. The premise of the climatic grasslands assumes that grasses have become dominant to the exclusion of non-herbaceous vegetation because of climatic factors that differ in different areas. This premise needs re-examination.

Evolution of grasses: supposed Tertiary prairies.—The great diversity of forms and vast geographic extent of the grasses are a late development in earth history.[23] Originating supposedly in moist, warm woods, probably in the tropics, they are considered to have invaded drier and colder lands in Tertiary time, which was largely a period of increasing continentality of climates. New plant forms then arose, specialized to succeed in sun-drenched and rain-poor habitats. The earliest nonprimitive, nonhygrophilous grasses known are from the Tertiary of our Great Plains. Here Elias has found a remarkable lot of Tertiary grasses, with hulls preserved. These belong to one species in the Lower Miocene, but form a notably branching phylogenetic series in the Upper Miocene and especially in the Ogalalla formation (Pliocene). The fossil forms are mainly *Stipeae;* their modern relatives are commonly known as needle or spear grasses. In the Pliocene there appeared also some species of millets (*Panicum*). In late Pliocene time the Stipas gradually disappeared from the High Plains.[24] The studies by Elias indicate an earlier (Upper Tertiary) evolution of at least one grass tribe, and an earlier migration of grasses into an ecologic situation involving notable climatic extremes, than had been known before. I am unable to see, however, that these paleobotanical determinations demonstrate the existence of wide Tertiary grassland in the Great Plains.[25]

The Great Plains were built in Tertiary time by streams that spread eastward the waste of the Rocky Mountains. The coarser materials remained lodged in the stream channels. The finer ones were spread broadly in flood stages over the aggrading plains. Widely braided patterns of drainage prevailed, and stream channels shifted frequently. By overflow and rain, temporary pools formed on the low interfluves. The time was dominantly one of aggradation; valley trenching was exceptional. Volcanic ash fell

---

[23] J. W. Bews, The World's Grasses (London and New York, 1929).

[24] M. K. Elias, Tertiary Prairie Grasses and Other Herbs from the High Plains, Geol. Society of America, Special Papers No. 41, 1942.

[25] See, for example, R. W. Chaney and M. K. Elias, Late Tertiary Floras from the High Plains, *in* Contributions to Palaeontology: Miocene and Pliocene Floras of Western North America, Carnegie Institution, Publ. No. 476, 1938, pp. 1–46.

in places; here and there dune sand was blown out from stream bars. For a modern parallel we should not look to the Great Plains as they are today, but rather to such an area as the Gran Chaco, where the drainways are unstable, on top of the surface, not let down into it, and where there is neither upland nor valley. The ancient Great Plains probably not only absorbed most of the precipitation that fell on them, but were in addition widely irrigated in summer by melt waters and rain waters from the mountains to the west. Today the mountain waters are sluiced across the Great Plains in valleys well sunk beneath the upland level; in the Tertiary there was no such demarcation between upland plain and valley lowland. The general plains surface was at that time a vast piedmont fan, subject to inundations that spread flood materials, flats of silt, patches of sand, and strips of gravel, each soon to be buried by another deposit.

A surface in such a condition of active fan building does not have the stability for the development of a climax vegetation or for the formation of a deep soil. It is wide open to all plants that are able to pioneer, plants that find an advantage in disturbed and changing conditions. The late-Pliocene aggrading surfaces played an important role in the evolution of a herbaceous heliophile flora. The Stipas are in general good pioneers, with deep roots and the habit of forming strong clumps, and their awns stick to the coats of passing animals. As is true of their modern representatives in North and South America, they may be thought of as taking hold on exposed surfaces, lately formed silt flats, sand bars, and gravel banks. They accompany other aggressive plants, both herbaceous and woody. The seeds of hackberry (*Celtis*) are more abundant in the Tertiary beds of the Great Plains than the hulls of grasses. Both kinds of remains are especially well suited to preservation in fossil form. No ecologic inferences can be made from the occurrence of either, except that both were abundant and that both were good pioneer forms.

The attempt to assign the woody vegetation to flood plains and to construe the grasses as covering interfluves seems a gratuitous transfer of present conditions into a different past. Certain Tertiary trees, such as the cottonwood poplars, willows, sycamore (*Platanus*), ash, and box elder (*Acer negundo* group) are properly associated with watercourses. But in addition to the hackberries a goodly number of shrubs and small trees were present that today are characteristic forms of Texas brush country and north-Mexican *monte:* yucca, spiny *Bumelia* and *Gymnocladus, Diospyros,*

Sapindus, Arctostaphylos, palms, and (scrub) oaks.[26] These are not mesophytic elements that need sheltered alluvial valleys, but shrubs able to take care of themselves with an irregular and uncertain supply of moisture under disturbed surface conditions and without developed soils.

The Tertiary plant record of the Great Plains, like the geomorphology, suggests a condition like that of the Gran Chaco or the brush country of Texas and Durango, a land where lines of gallery forest followed the stream courses but where for the most part a mingled vegetation of scrub, bunch grass, and quickly maturing herbs prevailed.

Nor may one assume that the development in the Tertiary Great Plains of new forms of horses, with teeth suited to the grinding of hard vegetation, demonstrates the replacement of bush mingled with grass by bushless steppe. At most it shows a specialization of one part of the fauna to make use of an increasingly abundant group of herbaceous plants; for no one denies the vigorous evolution of grasses and other herbs in Tertiary time. Many older forms of animals, not thus specialized and hardly capable of living on grass, continued to make up a large part of the fauna; among these was the older line of nonhypsodont horses.

Neither the known nature of the land surface nor the fossil vegetation and fauna sustain the case of the supposed Tertiary prairies.

Pleistocene vegetation of the interior plains.—The Pleistocene record of the Great Plains tells little of plant remains. By that time the plains had ceased to be the piedmont of aggradation for the Rockies. Instead they were being trenched by streams that flowed across them to form a series of Pleistocene and Recent stream terraces. Aggradation gave way to erosion in the northern Great Plains, while the Texas plains were still accumulating deposits. (The Blancan beds have been placed in the Pleistocene, perhaps as late as the Aftonian.[27])

For the most part, Pleistocene deposition was restricted to materials washed or blown out from ice tongues and to morainal deposits. A faunal record is available, however, and it is especially good for a significantly located area, western Nebraska.[28] The mammalian fauna from the earliest Pleistocene (pre-Kansan) includes ground sloths, mastodonts, large horses, giant camels and

---

[26] The last three according to oral information from Herbert L. Mason.

[27] P. O. McGrew, Early Pleistocene (Blancan) Fauna from Nebraska, Chicago Natural History Museum, Geol. Series, Vol. 9, No. 2, 1944.

[28] E. H. Barbour and C. B. Schultz, *op. cit.*

Camelops, giant beaver, muskrat, and cottontail rabbit; an assemblage better assigned to a woodland than to a prairie environment. The Kansan ice advance was accompanied by a great influx of Asiatic immigrants: half a dozen forms of mammoths, several giant bison, giant elk, musk ox; on the whole, members of a woodland society. In the Yarmouth interval (previously suggested as a period of increased continentality of climate) several ground sloths, giant bear, peccaries, saber-toothed tiger, and numerous rodents were notable. The post-Sangamon (i.e., Wisconsin) *Citellus* beds yield ground squirrels, pocket gophers, three mammoths, peccaries, *Camelops,* and *Bison antiquus.* From none of these animal assemblages can dependence on grasslands be inferred. Browsing, rather than grazing, habits are implied for the larger forms.

The modern plains flora denotes an energetic evolution of herbs, especially of annual species, during the Pleistocene. Whether the climatic tensions and freshly formed surfaces of successive stages of the Ice Age placed woody plants at a disadvantage in this evolution, in comparison with annuals and plurennials, is unknown. Continued disturbances of surface may be attributed to the mammalian inhabitants. The large herbivores, by trampling, bedding, and wallowing, undoubtedly exerted pressure against the vegetation in such a manner as to favor in many spots the development of ruderal plants. Rooting and burrowing animals may have reinforced such pressure. An increasing state of tension for the long-generation perennials may be postulated as part of a slow symbiotic shift, but the evidence that great grasslands replaced shrub-grass and woodland complexes is wanting for the whole of the Pleistocene. The geologic and paleontologic data give little support to a thesis of wide grasslands before Recent time.

Late replacement of mixed vegetation by grasslands.—According to the present state of our knowledge of earth history, the great grasslands seem to have formed extraordinarily late; to fall, indeed, well within human time. May we look for an explanation to a very late spurt in the evolution of the grasses themselves, which created forms that constituted a new and exclusive plant society, the grassland, able to take over and to hold areas previously morphologically and physiologically of more diverse vegetational composition?

I am not clear how a climax vegetation develops with reduction of floristic diversity, unless it is by heavy intensification of shade. I know of no satisfactory explanation, therefore, of the process by which grasses could have wrested large territories from an older, more diversified vegetation. The stoloniferous grasses are most aggressive, yet such forms do not dominate in natural grasslands. Sod-forming grasses are often able to prevent the establishment of other plants within the sod, but their protection is destroyed by any injury to the sod, and such injuries happen often. The sod cover is, apparently, a late development within established grasslands. It requires in all likelihood fairly heavy grazing, by means of which a selection takes place of those grasses that withstand cropping and treading (i.e., question of buffalo-grass sod). If we concede the aid of herbivores and rodents in the dissemination of grass seeds and in the alteration of surface to favor ruderal vegetation, we still do not account for grasslands, and especially for their great size.

The human element.—It seems, therefore, that the added ecologic element, man, must be taken into account. "Natural vegetation" over the greater part of the earth's surface has long been subject to constant deformation by man, and his hand has been directed steadily against the great plants, as it has against the great animals. In Recent time the human geographic agency has been wanting only in outlying shreds of the land masses; in the Old World it carries back pretty well through the Pleistocene. For our hemisphere, man's presence before the end of the Pleistocene is indicated; that is, for at least twenty or twenty-five thousand years. It is now permissible to think of a possible span of forty or sixty thousand years if evidence such as has been coming out of Texas and elsewhere in the Southwest is confirmed. (Reference is here made to the pre-Folsom gatherers and the time of a pre-post-Wisconsin corridor from Alaska to the interior.)

All the early people used fire, the gatherers rather casually, the big-game hunters, I have suggested, as a major and formidable hunting device. I return, therefore, to the old view, held by the American pioneers of the West, that prairies are caused by fires. Time, motive, opportunity, and weapon are all accounted for; is there a better explanation?

Grasslands occupy plains.—The most general description of the localization of grasslands is that they occupy plains areas which are neither truly arid nor continually moist. Where these conditions are met, it is the rule to find grasslands. Where rough slopes lie beneath the level of the plains, the grass limit is usually sharply set off from the broken terrain below, the latter being occupied by brush, trees, and herbaceous growth. The sharper the break between upland plain and valleys cut therein, the narrower is the transition in vegetation. The valley floors offer a more mesophytic habitat than the upland plains, but not the slopes marginal to the valleys; yet these flanks, even on unstable or fresh surfaces and on xeric southern exposures, are likely to support woody as well as herbaceous plants. Where hill belts rise above plains, the upper margin of the grass assemblage is usually an irregular fringe extending part way up the hill slopes, the depth of penetration up-slope decreasing as intricacy of dissection of slope increases. The grasslands coincide in general with broad, smooth surfaces.[29]

Fire as ecologic agent on plains.—The formation of grasslands requires a process that operates against long-lived perennials. These plants, as compared with grasses and many other herbs, have reduced ability to reproduce or to persist with recurrent damage to their above-ground parts. Such elimination or suppression of woody plants is characteristic of plains surfaces but is ineffective on surfaces of irregular relief. The one widespread agency certainly known to act in this direction is recurrent burning.

Ecologists concede a place to fire in the establishment of certain grasslands and in extending their borders, but they also postulate grassland climaxes and grassland stages in ecologic successions. Thus Bews says:[30]

Relatively [morphologically] primitive types of grassland as, for instance, the high grass savanna of the tropics and much of the temperate meadow type have largely replaced forest. The action of fire in maintaining the supremacy of the grasses, especially in tropical regions, is rather important. The natural plant succession in such cases is from grassland to forest. In more [morphologically] advanced types of grassland the climatic conditions are such as do not permit of the development of close forest, but over wide areas in the sub-tropics scattered patches of woodland are found dispersed over the grassland regions, growing in relatively favourable situations, or over still wider areas the grassland has scattered trees or small clumps of trees forming a parkland type of scenery. This type in turn gives way to great areas of pure grassland without trees, or with the trees confined to stream and river banks. So far as the grasses themselves are concerned it is not necessary to distinguish between types with trees and those without, since the composition is largely identical in both cases.

The perplexed geographer finds climate incompetent for the segregation of areas of herbaceous plants from those of woody plants. He observes that such separation coincides with changes

---

[29] C. O. Sauer, Geography of the Pennyroyal, Kentucky Geol. Survey, Ser. 6, Vol. 25, 1927, p. 128; this volume, p. 28.

[30] *Op. cit.*, p. 292.

in the terrain. The same grasses that occupy smooth steppes or grass savannas are at home on adjacent hill lands of scrub, *monte,* or chaparral. The grasses of humid prairies and meadows are also those of their neighboring woodlands. Why, then, should one humid grassland be designated by the ecologist as a stage on the way to forest, and another as having replaced forest? In both cases the hill lands may have the same herbaceous flora as their contiguous plains, but in addition a variety of forest trees and shrubs. In both cases the soil and moisture conditions on the plains are more conducive to a diversity of mesophytic plants than on the greater part of the hill surface. Again, why are semiarid grasslands usually regarded as climax formations by ecologists when the same herbaceous elements enter into more complex biotic assemblages where plains give way to hills?

The development of climax vegetation is usually in the direction of increased mutual tolerance and accommodation and hence of maximum floristic and habit diversity, including maximum range in growth permissible for the given climate. How, then, are the supposed climaxes explained that are characterized by impoverishment of flora and intolerance of diverse growth habits? Are parklands ecologically stable, or are they remnants of forest lands in retreat? Are the great grasslands of the world of recent development, and may they have been formed in the main by the action of fire, selective against the long-lived woody perennials through frequent and sufficiently long-continued recurrence? The ecologic systems that have been set up do not account for the characteristic association of an exclusively herbaceous assemblage with minimal relief, given long or short periods of dryness of the ground surface.

Natural fires versus burning by man.—The common occurrence of fires in nature has often been assumed. For almost a century there has been discussion of the *tierra cocida* of the Argentine pampas. This consists of lumps or spots of baked and even fused earth occurring at various levels in the pampean beds. By most students this material is thought to have resulted from the burning of the local earth. One group considers the *tierra cocida* to have been caused by man; another appeals to natural fires.[31] Bailey

---

[31] Bailey Willis, Tierra Cocida; Scoriae [with notes by Aleš Hrdlička], *in* Aleš Hrdlička and others, Early Man in South America, Bureau of American Ethnology, Bulletin 52, 1912, pp. 45–53, with a bibliography. See also Oscar Schmieder, The Pampa—A Natural or Culturally Induced Grassland?, Univ. of California Publs. in Geography, Vol. 2, No. 8, 1927.

Willis dismissed it with the statement that "any fire whatever, whether originating in spontaneous combustion, in lightning, or in other natural conditions, independent of man, would have the effect of burning the earth under favorable conditions" and referred to "the hills of Dakota and Montana . . . banded by red clays burnt to the consistency of tile by the combustion of lignite beds, without the agency of man." [32] The natural origin of fires is not to be disposed of thus easily. If spontaneous combustion occurs in nature, it is a very rare and highly localized phenomenon, dependent on accumulations of volatile hydrocarbons. The actual happenings need to be recorded as to place and time, not postulated ex cathedra.

Except in areas of active volcanoes, lightning is undoubtedly the chief cause of natural fires. Such fires are not uncommon in summer in the Sierra Nevada of California. The United States Forest Service reports an annual average of about four thousand lightning-caused fires (usually small) in the Western states. Such fires are phenomena of the mountains; they may be the result of dry thunderstorms, or of a thunderstorm that brings little rain and comes after times of dry weather. They are likely to get started in heavy accumulations of dry material, especially in snags of dead conifers standing on a surface covered with dry duff. A smoldering dead tree may then ignite the duff, which soon dries after a light summer storm. The fire-causing storm is especially characteristic of summer in interior mountainous areas of intermediate latitudes. Yet in these areas, peculiarly liable to such fires, lightning fires are not known to alter the ecology in any permanent direction. It is doubtful whether they have eliminated any of the species of inflammable conifers or effect more than very local and ephemeral deforestation. Forest and brush dominate in the parts of the country that have the greatest number of natural fires.

For the plains I know of no documentation of lightning-set fires. The meteorologic mechanism is less favorable than in the Western mountains; the tinder of dead resinous softwoods so important in nursing a fire until the ground dries off is and was wanting. There is no known evidence that fire-setting lightning strikes any plains often enough and at the right times to result in the burning out of the woody elements.

In conclusion, too little is known about the great grasslands, and for too short a span of scientific observation, for us to be dogmatic about their origin. The items of evidence assembled herein suggest that they are late features of plant geography, that they may have

---

[32] *Op. cit.,* pp. 48 and 49. Information is desired on this reported situation.

developed within the time of human occupation, that they may
have been formed primarily by fire, and that the cause of the fires
may have been man. Plant ecology has taken too little account of
the directional modification of vegetation of which man is capable.
The capacities of preagricultural man, in particular, may be underestimated in this respect, partly because the time of his presence
has been underestimated, but especially because the fundamental
importance to him of fire as a hunting device has been little noticed.

ROUTES OF DISPERSAL OF MAN

During the Ice Age the Alaskan lowlands seem to have been continuously habitable for sub-Arctic plants and animals. As the continental icecap disappeared and the modern outlines of Arctic
America took form, both plants and animals from Alaska colonized
eastward along the margin of the polar sea. This, it seems, was also
the route followed by the ancestral Eskimo, who spread eastward
from Bering Sea to Greenland and southward along the Hudson
and Labrador coasts, there possibly fusing in part with an Indian
culture that was moving north.[33] The advanced, sea-hunting character of the proto-Eskimo cultures makes doubtful a remote occupation of the far North by man.

Northwest coast unavailable at an early date.—The southward
drift of immigrant peoples at an early date cannot have been by
way of the Pacific coast. This route was available only to skilled
navigators. Snow fields and glaciers, a heavy forest poor in food
and extending to the water's edge, and a coast of intricately inter-
laced fiords and mountains eliminated the possibility of land travel
along or near the shore. The coastlands of southern Alaska and
of British Columbia could support only a people that knew how
to move about, fish, and hunt on the sea. It is inferred that this
was the last important part of the New World to be occupied by
man, except as routes out of the interior may have led migrants to
the coast.

We do not know yet whether the earliest corridor connecting
Alaska with the interior United States lay along the eastern foot
of the Rocky Mountains or was an intermontane passage between
the Rockies and the Coast Ranges. If such a way was open south

---

[33] Diamond Jenness, The Problem of the Eskimo, *in* Diamond Jenness, edit.,
The American Aborigines, published for presentation at the Fifth Pacific Science Congress, Canada, 1933 (Toronto, 1933), pp. 371–396.

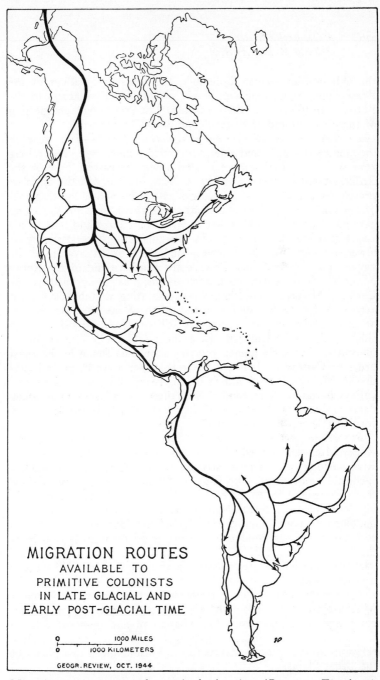

MIGRATION ROUTES
AVAILABLE TO
PRIMITIVE COLONISTS
IN LATE GLACIAL AND
EARLY POST-GLACIAL TIME

0	1000 MILES
0	1000 KILOMETERS

GEOGR. REVIEW, OCT. 1944

Migration routes open to early man in the Americas. (*Drawn on The American Geographical Society's "Outline Map of the Americas," 1:50,000,000, as a base.*)

through interior British Columbia, the transverse valleys of the
Fraser and the Columbia probably provided earlier access to the
Pacific than to more northern reaches. The archeologic prospecting
of these valleys and of Puget Sound is still to be done.

Dispersal south along Rocky Mountain front.—The work in
the nineteen-twenties and nineteen-thirties demonstrated that a long
zone of early colonization extended along the eastern base of the
Rockies from southern Canada to New Mexico. On the basis of
present evidence this is the central axis from which the dispersal
of early man took place. There are indications that the Wyoming
gap may have been used to get to Great Salt Lake and thus to the
Las Vegas area of Arizona. (In this connection the possibility of
lower elevation of the Rockies, suggested by the White River
varves, may be recalled.) Toward the southern end of the Rocky
Mountain front a western branch of dispersal is outlined by the
Cochise, Mohave, and Pinto sites, indicating that bands drifted
across to the Pacific not far to the north of the Mexican border,
at a time when pluvial conditions still made the desert on both
sides of the lower Colorado River hospitable. The implication is,
of course, that early human remains should be found in the coast
areas of California. It is not likely that men were living in basins
in the Mojave Desert and failed to reach the coast ranges and
valleys beyond, where food was available at all seasons in abundance and variety. A revision of the short and simple annals of California archeology seems overdue.

Spread to the Atlantic coast.—The eastward drainage of the
Rocky Mountains traced a long series of avenues to the Mississippi
River. Along each of these streams food, water, fuel, and shelter
facilitated movement. The finds in Minnesota and Ontario show
that man spread far to the east, following closely upon the retreating Wisconsin ice front. Neither bare land nor tundra need be
imagined as having lain at the edge of the continental ice. Whatever plants of our mid-latitudes were good pioneers moved in as
the ice front retreated. We may even estimate that a vigorous and
varied vegetation covered the debris of earth that mantled the rot-
ting ice blocks.

Minnesota man shows a trade connection between the upper
Mississippi and the Gulf of Mexico. That the early big-game hunters found their way down the Mississippi and passed freely up
the Ohio Valley and into the deep South is inferred from the close
relationship of eastern artifacts to the Folsom and Yuma points of
the Great Plains.

From earliest time the drainageways converging on the St. Louis area must have operated to make this an aboriginal crossroads. Here was also an extraordinary diversity of resources useful to primitive man. On the lower Missouri primitive man first found the rich flora and fauna of the mesothermal woodlands: groves of nut trees on flood plain and loess-covered uplands, including walnut, hickory, and pecan; stands of oak of many kinds, some with sweet acorns; grape, black cherry, persimmon, and pawpaw; Virginia deer, opossum, turkey, quail, woodcock. Here the flights of migrant waterfowl converged in the fall, and from here they scattered in the spring to their northern breeding grounds. River bluffs and Ozark hills held a limitless supply of superb chert, suitable for tools, and salt licks marked the outcropping of shale beds. Creek and river bluffs, cut into Paleozoic beds of varying resistance, formed snug coves and rock shelters that gave protection from the sweep of winter winds. An extension of the record of primitive man in Missouri is to be expected.

Routes south from the Great Plains.—For the southern Rockies and Great Plains, Clovis and Sandia are known early centers. Terrace sites on Texas rivers, such as that at Abilene, indicate diffusion toward or to the Gulf coast. Here habitat conditions were sufficiently attractive so that the spread of man through the lower river valleys to the coastal lagoons will probably be demonstrated by future archeologic work. Whether dispersal southward along the Gulf took place is unknown. South of the United States, we have still only that tantalizing bit of knowledge from the vicinity of Managua in Nicaragua, where a deeply buried ash bed holds the track of barefoot men and large bison.[34]

At the time when pluvial conditions prevailed north of the Mexican border (and in northwestern Chihuahua), the belt of steppe and desert climate was displaced somewhat to the south. Possibly, also, it was of more extreme aridity than at present. Whether the east and west coasts of Mexico were suitable for passage and subsistence or not, a comfortable corridor did lead southward along the eastern flank of the so-called Sierra Madre Occidental. Here the familiar vegetation included mesquite and its associates at lower altitudes, oaks and piñon at higher altitudes. In this southward movement man became gradually accustomed to the exploitation of a new and tropical flora, which occupied both coasts and reached

---

[34] Reports on the work of F. B. Richardson, Carnegie Institution Year Book No. 40, 1940–1941 (Washington, 1941), pp. 300–302, and *ibid.*, No. 41, 1941–1942 (1942), pp. 269–271.

inland in numerous hot barrancas. No serious obstacle or major reorganization of life was met until man reached the tropical rain forest along the Caribbean.

The entry into South America.—Where, or whether, the rain forest of the tropics blocked his southward path, we do not know. If man did not enter South America until the modern pattern of climates was set, then, of course, he had to pass a most formidable rain forest east and south of the Gulf of Panama. For a land crossing the minimal width of this forest is at least two hundred miles, and in the middle of it lies the multiple barrier of the streams, swamps, and lagoons of the Atrato Valley. Those who would have man come late to South America, and have him come almost bare-handed and unskilled in the use of boats, have proposed no solution as to how he crossed these hazards of water and forest and made his living while groping his way through. The Indians whom we know historically as living in the Chocó, and even in higher degree those on the Gulfs of Darien and San Miguel, were excellent boat-men and wise in tropical woodcraft. No one imagines that such skills were owned by the first colonists of South America; indeed, there are numerous tribes now living in South America who would not know how to pass such a barrier.

On the other hand, if we are permitted to contemplate a first peopling of the southern continent while glacial and pluvial conditions still prevailed in the mid-latitudes, a different climatic situation may have existed about the Gulf of Darien. A very slight equatorward shift of the Atlantic horse-latitude high-pressure belt would also shift the savanna climate somewhat southward and westward. A southwestward displacement of 2° of the present borders of savanna climate in northern Colombia would clear the route easily. This is more than wishful thinking, though I know of no observations on Recent and late-Pleistocene sediments and fauna in that area: (1) the mechanism is reasonable, and (2) we know that numerous plants and some animals which could not cross a tropical forest migrated between North and South America in the Pleistocene. Numerous species of grasses, shrubs, and herbaceous annuals that range from the semiarid Southwest of the United States to the Argentine and Chile required a corridor with low rainfall at some time, and some of them late, in the Pleistocene. A similar condition applies to a number of mammals. The true horse and deer passed into South America, it would seem, later than the early Pleistocene. Edentates and ground sloths came north from South America, pre-

sumably in the late Pleistocene.[35] Although many, if not all, of these
migrations were effected before the time in which man is thought
to have penetrated, they do argue for a corridor of less rainy climate
available in latter Pleistocene time. If this corridor was opened by
an increased circulation of air between tropics and high latitudes, it
should have existed through Wisconsin glaciation, but not into later
time. The argument, therefore, is against the recent penetration of
primitive man through the Darien-Chocó area.

Routes through South America.—Beginning with the Cauca Valley, a hospitable and diversified country awaited the immigrants.
One set of routes led eastward, flanking the Venezuelan Andes and
diverging into the llanos of the Orinoco. Some of these early trails
should have extended into the northern Guayana highland, which
lies apart from the rain forest.

Southward from the Cauca Valley, the passageway lay within
the Andes, I should judge, well into Bolivia. This long, intra-Andean
passageway is postulated from the repellent character of the outer
Andean flanks. Very primitive man could perhaps not make use of
the Peruvian desert. (It may not be coincidence that the most primitive and probably the oldest known remains of the desert are from
the vicinity of Taltal, near its southern end.) The eastern flank of
the Andes was a more formidable barrier. It is inhospitable nearly
to the southern end of Amazonian drainage, by reason of the
tangled cloud forest at higher altitudes and the tropical forest in
the lower montaña. However, about Santa Cruz de la Sierra attractive valleys with open mesothermal vegetation lead from interior
Bolivia to plains at the east. Thence the whole of Brazil south of
the Amazonian forest is freely accessible. Southward lie also the
hunting and seed-gathering grounds of the Gran Chaco, which merge
into the pampas of the Argentine. The southern *punas* of Bolivia
descend into the *chañar* and *algarrobo* steppes of the western Argentine, and further routes lead across the western Andes to the
coast of Chile, south of the Atacama Desert. Bolivia, therefore, is
thought of as a center of dispersal for migrants from the north for
all of southern South America and for a large part of Brazil.

There is no way yet of estimating the time of the first peopling of
South America. Highly subjective guesses have been made that man
advanced slowly southward from the interior United States and
reached Patagonia only several thousand years ago. We know only

---

[35] P. O. McGrew, *op. cit.,* p. 43.

that he was present at the extinction of a variety of great herbivores in South America as well as in the north, and that some of the archeologic sites, such as those in the lake country of Minas Gerais, antedate important and probably long physiographic changes. The climatologic problem of the Darien area also weighs against his late arrival. I see, therefore, no reason for pleading that the passage of man into South America must have been greatly delayed.

Contrast between Atlantic and Pacific coasts.—The main trails of the early migration led southward from Alaska, ultimately to Tierra del Fuego, through the interior of both continents. The Atlantic coast almost everywhere was hospitable and accessible, but it was reached by long side routes out of the west and formed a series of separate termini of dispersal. Such terminal branches, tending to express themselves as conservative ethnic peninsulas, are Labrador and Newfoundland, Acadia, Florida, the Guayana, and northeastern Brazil. The Pacific coast, on the other hand, was in considerable part inaccessible and inhospitable to the people of the simplest and earliest cultures. Its high latitudes are occupied by fiorded coasts and unattractive rain forests; the world's longest desert coast lies in Peru and Chile, its lesser Northern Hemisphere equivalent about the Gulf of California; between the Isthmus of Panama and the coast of Ecuador is a tropical rain forest of extreme development. Areas of early attraction along the Pacific, therefore, were few. Above all, the west-coast lands between northern Mexico and Panama must have been colonized vigorously, and this section may be expected to yield primitive remains. Coastal California (with Oregon) and Chile were the other attractive early habitats along the Pacific. Since they were also fairly accessible to early migrants, their primordial records are not likely to remain blanks.

AGE INFERENCES FROM DISTRIBUTIONS OF TRAITS

The doctrine of the recent peopling of the New World has been joined to that of the Mongoloid origin of the settlers, in which the Indians are held to be a somewhat rufous lot of transplanted northeastern Asiatics, occupying the New World south of the Eskimo. Time is essential for this view. The further back the immigration took place, the less proper is it to speak of Mongoloids, or of Indians. Since the Folsom finds, ten, or at most fifteen, thousand years have been admitted by assuming that the association of New World man with glacial and pluvial deposits might be held to such a span.

We are thus given as revised version "an essentially modern type of Indian arriving in the New World approximately 15,000 years ago." [36] The "modern Indian" is thereby made into an incongruously old race; for at so remote a date modern "races" elsewhere are only suggested here and there by prototypes such as Cro-Magnon and Chancelade in Europe.

Indian racial characteristics.—The doctrine of the essential unity of the American aborigines preceded the modern evidence on time of settlement of the New World and also on diversity of physical types (to be discussed below). Its retention has made of it a Procrustean bed into which any aboriginal body or skeleton is fitted by the device of character averages, from which there are indefinitely large individual departures. Thus Hrdlička has described the smallest brain capacity known among normal archeologic Indians skulls as matching Pithecanthropus, and the largest as exceeding the most voluminous normal skulls thus far reported from the rest of the world. Crania range from round to very long, with low to high vaulting; faces are round or long and narrow, features flattened to aquiline; stature ranges from small to very tall; and even skin color has a wide range.[37] What the nature or basis of this high "variability" is remains unclear genetically and seems not to be considered important.

The archeologic skeletal material points increasingly to one generalization: the ancient people were long-headed, in contrast with the great majority of modern Indian peoples. The Lagoa Santa skulls from Minas Gerais, found a hundred years ago, are the beginning of this trail of discovery. The data for North America have been well summarized by T. D. Stewart.[38] The only older group that he identifies as round-headed are the Red Ocher people, who followed the Black Sands people in Illinois. With this exception, the long period from pluvial Cochise I and glacial Minnesota man to the Hopewell and Basket Maker folk is a record of long heads. These seem to consist of a number of racial strains: (1) a short-

[36] Frank H. H. Roberts, Developments in the Problem of the North American Paleo-Indian, *op. cit.,* p. 107; F. M. Setzler, Archaeological Exploration of the United States, 1930–1942, Acta Americana, Vol. 1, 1943, pp. 206–220, reference to pp. 211–212. It must be stated that this is a view originating in the United States; note the references to De Quatrefages and Deniker in later paragraphs.

[37] Aleš Hrdlička, Normal Micro- and Macrocephaly, Amer. Journal of Physical Anthropology, Vol. 25, 1939, pp. 1–91, reference to p. 82.

[38] Some Historical Implications of Physical Anthropology in North America, *in* Essays . . . in Honor of John R. Swanton, *op. cit.,* pp. 15–50.

statured type with low-domed skull, represented by Minnesota man, the Wyoming Cave material, and the Oak Grove (California) skulls; (2) a small, gracile people with high-vaulted skulls (the so-called Basket Maker type), most widely spread; and, I may perhaps add, (3) a long-limbed tall people, such as are known from the early horizon (moderately old) in the Sacramento Valley near Lodi, California. Skeletal remains of the Folsom and Yuma hunters have not been established. In South America dolichocranic finds of notable antiquity have been made at Confins in Minas Gerais (in addition to the Lagoa Santa ones), at Punin in Ecuador, in Peru, and in the Argentine pampas and Patagonia. If head form has the hereditary persistence it is thought to show, we are confronted here by a riddle in the absence of round-headed people in the remains of New World occupance, supposedly until Christian time is reached.

De Quatrefages erected a separate race on the basis of the Lagoa Santa people, and Deniker thought their descendants survived sufficiently strongly to differentiate the modern Indians into four subraces, each of which was distinguished by characteristic head form and each having a geographic center. He called these major subdivisions North, Central, and South American, and Patagonian. Deniker's subdivisions are still apparent in the latest somatic classifications by European and Latin-American scholars, who in general attach major importance to differences in geographic distribution of morphologic traits among living natives.

The epochal world map of cephalic indices designed by W. Z. Ripley called attention, at the same time as Deniker, to specific areas of long-headedness in eastern Brazil, about the Gulf of California, in upper California, and in northeastern North America, and to an increase in brachycephaly away from these centers.

In 1919 Griffith Taylor, also using the cephalic index, made an adventurous design of the evolution of races and inferred that the long-headed peoples, situated on the outskirts of the land masses, were the more ancient races, which had been pushed into far corners by the later roundheads.[39] In 1923 Roland B. Dixon published his much discussed "The Racial History of Man," the main thesis of which agreed with Taylor's, and stated that "a series of drifts or waves of differing physical types . . . have on the whole arranged themselves in such fashion that the dolichocephalic and presumably

[39] Climatic Cycles and Evolution, Geographical Review, Vol. 8, 1919, pp. 289–328. Two years later Taylor presented a still more elaborate plan of successive waves of migration: The Evolution and Distribution of Race, Culture, and Language, *ibid.,* Vol. 11, 1921, pp. 54–119.

older peoples are found distributed mainly along the margins of the continent." [40] If Dixon had said instead, "found at the far ends of available early routes of dispersal," he would have escaped such errors as that on the origin of the Eskimo and would have applied a familiar principle of dispersal in biogeography. Dixon's races are determined not only by cranial form but also by degree of vaulting of the skull and by facial features, especially as characterized by the nose.

These studies, which won the interest of a wide circle of readers to the historical implications of contemporary distributions, were made by students who were concerned with the world-wide problem of race. More recently, Hooton, Oetteking, Von Eickstedt, and Imbelloni have stressed geographic positions of physical traits in America as implying diverse origins.

The traits selected differ somewhat according to the investigator or availability, but through all of them runs a recognizable pattern of marginal elder stocks about a core of later comers. The general principle is that the distributions of contemporary and near-contemporary populations, identified and classified as to their morphologic configuration, should indicate by geographic position the succession of migrations. Objections have been raised against the subjective selection of traits to compose the physical type, and similarly against the interpretation of the geographic patterns. In plant and animal phylogeny, it may be said, morphologic traits are found and used in precisely this qualitative manner wherever the precision tools of genetics cannot be, or have not been, employed.

Imbelloni's map of the distribution of races in the Americas is reproduced in the figure as a late revision of qualitative morphology.[41] As a tentative phyletic picture it may be examined briefly to illustrate what the older and more primitive components in the aboriginal population seem to be.

1. The Fuegids are so named from the Yahgan (Yamana) of the south end of Tierra del Fuego.[42] This type Imbelloni also recognizes as extending

---

[40] P. 404.

[41] Accompanying José Imbelloni, Tabla clasificatoria de los Indios: Regiones biológicas y grupos raciales humanos de América, Physis, Vol. 12, 1936–1938, pp. 229–249. A current statement of his views is given in his essay The Peopling of America, Acta Americana, Vol. 1, 1943, pp. 309–330.

[42] O. Menghin, Weltgeschichte der Steinzeit (Wien, 1931), pp. 578, 594. Menghin would see in them the remnant of one of the "protomorphic" races of man; he erects them into one of the three ancestral races of the world, the Yamanoids, from which he derives the great Eurasian series of people. This

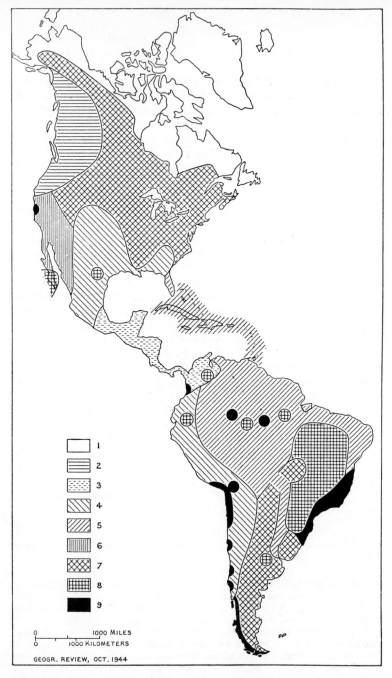

Map of distribution of races in the Americas according to Imbelloni.[41] Key:
1, Subarctids; 2, Columbids; 3, Isthmids; 4, Pueblo-Andids; 5, Amazonids;
6, Sonorids; 7, Planids in north and Pampids in south; 8, Laguids; 9, Fuegids.

through western Patagonia (for example, Chono), in the Chango of the Atacama coast, and among the Ura in the Bolivian highland. On the east coast he notes it for the living Botocudo and the extinct people of the coastal shell mounds (*sambaquis*); in the north among the Motilón, Goajira, and other tribes of the sierras of Perijá and Santa Marta. This is held to be the most primitive and oldest racial element of the New World; small in stature, moderately long-headed, with low skull and often with heavy supraorbital ridges. It is thought to have been thrust bit by bit into the farthest and least hospitable corners of South America. Possibly, I suggest, it has an ancient expression in North America in Minnesota man, and in the Wyoming Cave and Oak Grove people.

2. Next in time of arrival and primitiveness are the Laguids, named after the remains of Lagoa Santa. These are the small, slight people with long heads and skulls. Surviving elements are considered to be found especially among Tapuyan tribes of Brazil. Archeologically, the long-headed people of the southern extremity of the peninsula of Lower California are classed with this group. One may guess that the Basket Maker type of the United States should also be accommodated here.

3. The other longish-headed stocks are the Pampid, Planid, and Sonorid. These are all well above medium stature and in Patagonia reach the extreme proportions that gave rise to the early stories of a race of giants. Massive heads with high cheekbones are common.

4. In part the Amazonids, of medium to small stature, conserve dolichoid traits and may be a blurred lot of descendants of earlier immigrants to the New World.

A generalized morphologic thesis, built on geographic distribution and probable archeologic sequence, would then read as follows: (1) A primordial small race occupied the New World (pre-Folsom?), was driven gradually to posts of last defense in South America, in Tierra del Fuego, Amazonian refuges, and the Goajira cul-de-sac, and is now nearly extinct. (2) A second drift, of well proportioned, slight folk with long, high skulls (also pre-Folsom?), has left its remains in Lower California, widely in the southwestern and south-central United States, and through the Brazilian highland and the pampas. Its survivors are found in Brazilian highland tribes and possibly in California (Yuki?). (3) Thereafter began the inflow of tall, powerful longheads, probably of several strains. The pampas Indians and numerous of their neighbors, the Cahita and other tribes about the Gulf of California, the Great Plains Indians, and those of the Eastern Woodlands bear the marks of such an-

---

refers, of course, to a supposed ancestral location in Asia and an early migration of one branch to the New World, a small shred of which survived in the far end of South America.

cestry. Their habitats are not refuge locations, and their hunting prowess is notable. These tribes include most of the aborigines who fiercely resisted subjugation by whites.

These morphologic traits and their geographic arrangement, if valid, outline a succession of pre-Mongoloid, pre-Indian settlement of the New World. I do not see that understanding is helped by speaking of Paleo-Indians, any more than it would clear our thinking to speak of all prehistoric remains in China as Paleo-Chinese. The Indian race, if it must be thought of as such, is suggested as something that has been in process of forming through gradual mixing of stocks and lengthening separation from the Old World. The process of Indianization, not the defense of an original "Indian race," needs attention. Anthropometry and qualitative morphology, therefore, need to be associated in many more field observations, to study populations as defined in the genetic sense.[43]

Blood groups.—Physical anthropology had an elaborate descriptive apparatus before the concepts of genetics were developed. The manner of heredity of the physical traits that have been compiled from many measurements is unknown; they may involve some adaptive selection, and supposedly identical forms may be parallel variations. The quantitative systems of human races are open to the criticisms of Dobzhansky: [44]

The concept of race as a system of character averages logically implies a theory of continuous, rather than particulate germ plasm. Such a concept is obviously outmoded and incapable of producing much insight into the causative factors at work in human populations. Although the genic basis of relatively few human traits is known, it seems that following up the distribution of these few traits could tell us more about the "races" than a great abundance of measurements. Furthermore the concealed genic variability can no longer be disregarded. . . . In so far as this variability consists of recessive genes, only a part of it, often only a very small part, is manifested in the phenotype.

The geography of the genes, not of the average phenotypes, must be studied. In illustration thereof Dobzhansky commends the work

---

[43] An area of critical importance, for instance, is Sonora, for which there are well known anthropometric data. These, in my experience, are almost meaningless except for the Seri. There are striking physical differences from village to village and valley to valley within each former tribal or linguistic group. No Pima or Yaqui averages, for instance, have meaning; a detailed cartographic representation, by population units, of physical traits and morphologic types may well have.

[44] T. G. Dobzhansky, Genetics and the Origin of Species, ed. 2 (New York, 1941), pp. 358–361 and 79 respectively.

of Dr. William C. Boyd, on which the following paragraphs are based in the main.[45]

Blood group O is so strongly represented among American Indians that an erroneous view has gained currency, which holds that pure Indians belong only to this group. A score of tribal lots have been examined in the New World that exceed in percentage of group O individuals anything known from the Old World. These range from the Loucheux of the lower Mackenzie Valley to the Ona of Tierra del Fuego, strung along the whole length of the primordial migration axis. A large number of Indians in North and South America belong exclusively to group O, except for late white or Negro admixture. No such condition seems to hold for the Eskimo, or for any part of the Old World. The highest Old World groups on record are some desert Bedouins and Copts. Northern and eastern Asia, alleged cradle of the Indian, is not high in O; in fact, minimal values are found in Korea, Tibet, and Shantung, and among the Ainu.

Populations entirely lacking blood group A are known only in the New World, and here only in some South American Indian populations, especially in the Argentine, Paraguay, and Peru. On the other hand, little attention has been given to the discovery that the highest known percentages of A in the world are among the Blood, Blackfoot, and Piegan. Values far too high to be explained by white admixture are found among the Beaver, Slave, and Stoney Indians of Canada, the Flathead of Montana, the Shoshone of Wyoming, and the Navaho of the Southwest. It is also unlikely that

---

[45] W. C. Boyd has been the most active investigator and exponent of blood groups as genetic mechanisms in the phylogeny of human, especially American, stocks. The following papers constitute a series of major importance for orientation regarding the bearing of genetics on the question of race: L. C. Wyman and W. C. Boyd, Human Blood Groups and Anthropology, American Anthropologist, Vol. 37 (N.S.), 1935, pp. 181–200; *idem,* Blood Group Determinations of Prehistoric American Indians, *ibid.,* Vol. 39 (N.S.), 1937, pp. 583–592; W. C. Boyd and L. G. Boyd, Blood Grouping Tests on 300 Mummies, Journal of Immunology, Vol. 32, 1937, pp. 307–319; W. C. Boyd, Blood Groups, Tabulae Biologicae, Vol. 17, 1939, pp. 113–240 (includes tables of blood-group determinations for the world as known to 1938); *idem,* Blood Groups of American Indians, American Journal of Physical Anthropology, Vol. 25, 1939, pp. 215–235 (a later table for the American Indians than in the preceding reference); *idem,* Critique of Methods of Classifying Mankind, *ibid.,* Vol. 27, 1940, pp. 333–364 (the latest and best article for general orientation, with bibliography to 1940); A. S. Wiener, Evolution of the Human Blood Group Factors, American Naturalist, Vol. 77, 1943, pp. 199–204 (brings the status of investigation to date).

white crossbreeding accounts for Cree, Dogrib, and Tsimshian groups in the north, Hopi and numerous Rio Grande Pueblos in the Southwest, and Sac, Fox, and Micmac, together with others in the Eastern Woodlands. (Boyd has also determined three A individuals among twenty Southwestern Basket Maker mummies.) There is outlined in these data, which were recently obtained, an impressive, old North American center of group A along and behind the front of the Rockies, as far south as the Navaho and Pueblo, but reaching also in the Eastern Woodlands to the Atlantic coast and westward to the Pacific coast about and above Puget Sound. In South America an excess of A above probable crossbreeding is suggested for some northern Argentine tribes.

Blood group B is absent or extremely low in most Indian records; the values present are probably accounted for by modern crossbreeding. However, there are three areas in South America that cannot thus be regarded:

1. The area from central Chile to Tierra del Fuego needs careful study, not only as to Indians, but as to mixed-blood *Chilenos*. (*a*) As of latest knowledge, the Yahgan are by a large margin the purest B group in the world. (*b*) The distribution of blood groups known for the Araucanians is somewhat high for Spanish admixture, especially considering the importance of Basque blood in Chile. The Araucanians overran older populations in their migration across the Andes into Chile, and it would probably be from an older, submerged stock that the B was derived. (*c*) The one report available for mixed Chilenos has frequencies of B out of all reason for any Spanish or other European ancestry. If correct, an Indian strain of extraordinarily high B values must be preserved.

2. In mixed populations in highland Peru notable excess of B over possible Spanish ancestry appears. Moreover, Boyd found six Peruvian mummies belonging to group B and two to AB.

3. The third highest value of B known in the world is for the Carayá of interior Brazil, a very primitive tribe, and the only one in Brazil for which blood tests are reported.

Few observations have been made among Indians of blood types M and N. These are, however, consistently extremely high in M, whereas Old World populations have high N values. A single Old World group of Rwala Bedouins of Syria is known to have a blood-type distribution like those reported for Indians.

Blood groups and migrations.—These gene-controlled biochemical differences are the fundamental things known about human heredity. Their geographic distributions, scanty as the observations still are, are sufficient to show that in the aboriginal populations of the New World there has been very much less mixing of blood than all over the great continents of the Old World. The pure, or strongly preponderant, O populations are exclusively in the New World. The highest known values of A and B and of blood type M are also found in New World populations. Nor, except for the absence of B in numerous Australian and Oceanian populations, are minimal values present in the Old World such as are characteristic of the New. Single-group and dual-group populations prevail in the New World; all groups occur in most Eurasian and African populations.

It is possible that the basic peopling of the New World (with the exception of the Eskimo) may have taken place out of primary Old World hearths before the primordial blood streams of man became mingled; certainly separation has been maintained between stocks in the New World more largely than on the Old World continents. The New World as a whole seems to express long isolation from the Old World and within itself. And therefore it would seem as though the American aborigines might be basically very old racial stocks. Here, more than in any other part of the world, one may speak of pure-blooded groups. How, then, may they be derived from a Mongoloid race, known only as being made up of all blood groups well scrambled?

The distribution of the blood groups in the Americas may resolve itself into a sequence of immigrations. The position of B in remoter parts of South America is remarkable, and the suggestion is offered that the carriers of B were the earliest immigrants down the long trail from Bering Sea and were pushed into the most extreme position in the world for land migration. (As cradle of the B group Southeast Asia is possible; relatively high B values are characteristic from Indochina as far east as the Strait of Macassar, the probable rim of the continent in the Pleistocene. Northeastward the Ainu are also notably high.) There are also some indications favoring the A carriers as immigrants ahead of the O people: (1) The excess of A over Spanish infusion in parts of the northern Argentine may mean that some of the early hunters of the South American plains were of this stock. (2) There is an appearance of antiquity to the wide area of A in North America, as shown by its strength in Algonkin tribes and among remote Canadian forest and western intermountain peoples, and also as suggested by a trail of O people, splitting through the mass of the A folk, beginning with the hundred-per-cent O-group Loucheux on the Mackenzie, through the high O tribes of the Great Plains, to the Gulf of Mexico.

But such speculations may wait; what are needed are many more

investigations such as have been made recently in Canada. Most of
the Pacific coast of the United States is unknown, including California, with its great diversity of tribes. Between the Pueblo Indians of the Southwest and those of the Argentine the samples are
too few to say anything except that there are large bodies of O
people.

The determination of the actual "population" in the genetic
sense has usually been lacking. Records of bodies of conscripts, fel-
ons, pupils of Indian schools, and people assembled at markets may
be very misleading. The "population" of the geneticist and the
"community" of the social scientist are closely related terms, and it
is for as many such as is possible that the blood census needs to be
taken for the critical cartography that remains to be drawn. It is
not important to get large aggregates of numbers (the old fallacy
of the average and the range) but to get as detailed a geographic
distribution as possible of as many stable interbreeding populations
as possible. The historical background of the community must also
be regarded. The forcible settlement and mixing of peoples were
engaged in by the Inca state (*mitimaes* and *yanaconas*), by Spain
(*congregación* and *reducción*), and by Portugal (*Paulista* raids).
The historical documentation can often be obtained and misinter-
pretation avoided. Boyd has given an analysis of the possibilities of
detecting miscegenation from blood percentages. In addition, he
and P. B. Candela have made a promising start in the testing of
mummified tissues and of bones. The tale of human genes is unfolding; perhaps it will also disclose in time some pattern of external manifestations of race.[46]

The roots of aboriginal cultures.—The growth of culture in the
New World is still commonly interpreted in evolutionistic and en-
vironmentalistic terms. For example, N. C. Nelson has said that
"so complete was the adjustment between the aborigines and their
widely differing types of environment . . . that it had produced
no less than twenty-three distinguishable archaeological culture centers, some of them of such complexity and strength that they are
still functioning." [47] The prevailing mode of inquiry is not as to
whether different cultural goods and attitudes were brought into the
New World by various colonists, but as to differences in direction

[46] P. B. Candela, The Introduction of Blood-Group B into Europe, Human Biology, Vol. 14, 1942, pp. 413–443. Proposes the thesis that brachyce-
phalic Mongoloids carried the B group into Europe during the Middle Ages.

[47] The Antiquity of Man in the Light of Archaeology, *in* Diamond Jenness,
edit., *op. cit.,* pp. 85–130; reference to p. 96.

and degree of cultural evolution estimated to have taken place subsequent to an original colonization. Parallel to the doctrine of one
original race runs that of one original, meager but basic culture, the
only clear exceptions being the Eskimo and perhaps some people of
the Northwest coast.

The thesis has obvious weaknesses. If the growth has been from a
common stock and a basic original culture, it must explain the great
cultural diversities, achieved, it is held by the devotees of a short
American calendar, in less time than in the Old World. The original
stock must have separated into very progressive peoples and into
others that learned and invented almost nothing. This might be accounted for by environmental advantages and handicaps. Yet there
are many glaring discrepancies between environment and culture.
Northeastern Mexico and lower Texas are excellently suited in resources and position to cultural advance, but here good and poor
country alike was occupied by various rude folk called collectively
Chichimecs by the Spaniards. Highland Brazil and its coast invited
cultural advance in many areas but remained primitive except as
overrun in late time by Tupi peoples. There were, moreover, sharp
cultural disconformities in markedly contrasting neighboring peoples. These are not to be explained simply by the late extension of
one group at the expense of a weaker one. In the Southwest, California, and northwestern Mexico differences in cultural form and
level cannot be referred adequately to lateness of contact or comparative advantage of environment. The culture configurations were
different; to refer this difference to stage of cultural development
explains nothing. The thesis must fall back on unexplained parallel
inventions to which some peoples were disposed, while others were
too thickheaded to make or borrow them. Finally, it does not give
heed to the intricate geographic pattern of cultures in the New
World, with the primitives in the marginal locations.

There seem to be many millenniums available for the coming of
successive waves of colonists to the New World. On this side no
barrier is in evidence until perhaps the time when the Eskimo became established across Alaska. Blood groups and physical types
suggest that the colonists had very different ancestry and that they
probably came originally out of very different parts of Asia, possibly all the way from the southeast to the southwest. A diversity of
primordial culture complexes should therefore also have been carried into the New World, which in some measure should still be
traceable, however much altered by later borrowings of culture elements and loss of early ones. In this field of comparative ethnology

there are innumerable gaps in data, discrepancies in presentation, and disagreements in interpretation. The most promising key lies in those abstract (and hence largely nonadaptive) manifestations of culture that are expressed in social organization, religious beliefs, natural philosophy, and language, for each of which there probably is a significant geography or chart of diffusion.

Language distributions.—Any language, for example, depends on isolation for its origin and development and tends to operate as a cultural cement for those who speak it; and, except as the group expands over weaker neighbors, as an isolating mechanism to preserve particularism. It is of interest not only that connections between American non-Eskimo and Old World languages have not been established, but also that, in contrast with the Old World continents, there are very many apparently unrelated languages.[48] Considerable effort has been expended on the study of Indian languages without much success in reducing the number of New World stocks. It is certain that more connections will be found, but it is also apparent that Indian languages have great diversity. These are, of course, arguments for the antiquity of separation not only of New World populations from those of the Old but also within the New World. The entire mosaic of the language map of the New World weighs against the view of the evolution of a general, originally unitary New World culture. It sustains rather the idea of a long series of waves, which left the languages as deposits.

South America, which is regarded as the far peninsula of the *oikoumene,* has especially interesting language distributions. In the southern continent primitive tribes (here considered as older immigrants) are linguistically isolated from their more progressive neighbors. In the end-of-the-line positions that we have used as criterion of priority are, at the south, the Yahgan and neighboring western Patagonian languages, in eastern Brazil the Gês and the independent Carayan and Bororoan languages, on the Atacama coast the Chango, and in the northeastern corridor that ended north of the Amazon possibly the Carib. From Tierra del Fuego north to the Gran Chaco extends a series of language groups that may mark successive shore lines of early intrusive waves of hunters: Ona and Tehuelche, Puelche and Querendi, "Araucanian," Charrua, and Guaycuru. Farther north lie an indefinitely large number of small language stocks, to be considered as in secondary locations; that is,

---

[48] The Instituto Panamericano de Geografía y Historia (Mexico City) published in 1937 a reproduction of Krickeberg's language map of South America and one by Jiménez Moreno for North America.

as remnants of early peoples, driven by later comers into refuge areas and fastnesses of tropical forest, swamp, cloud forest, and *puna.* Here belong such peoples as the Uru, Choo, various tribes of the Gran Chaco, and a considerable number of the unclassified groups of the middle and upper Amazon and Orinoco basins that form secluded enclaves in the wide territory appropriated by Arawak and Carib.

In North America language has no such connotation of cultural affiliation or level. The Mísquito belong to the Chibcha languages; the Lacandon speak Maya. Within the Uto-Aztecan language group, culture ranges from most primitive to most advanced. Even in the Nahua division of this family the range probably includes the wandering Zacatec and the urban Aztec. The most extreme condition is that of the Pima, where within a single, almost undifferentiated language there was one fraction scarcely familiar with agriculture and another, the Pima Bajo, living in complex pueblo culture. The discussion of this problem is beyond the purposes of the present paper.

The Pacific coast, from central California north through Oregon, is a mosaic of languages like the Caucasus, the two small families restricted to this area being construed as earliest: Yuki most isolated and eldest, and later the Penutian group. The California-Oregon coast is apparently an illustration of the end-of-the-line position, repeatedly used by immigrant drifts. Another may be the Tunica-Atacapa-Chitimacha family about the delta of the Mississippi. Finally, the great Algonkin family may well be in nearly original possession of the northeastern part of the continent. The extreme headland location in this part of the New World, and hence the claim of earliest penetration, of course belongs to the mysterious Beothukan family.

Material culture.—As to material culture, the map repeats the general pattern of distribution previously traced. South America harbors more primitiveness than North America. In both continents the simplest and most archaic conditions are found in the end zones of the migration routes (primary position) and in unattractive intermediate areas (secondary position).[49] The former cultural situation is shown again by the Yahgan and their western Patagonian

---

[49] The two positions are called "externally marginal" and "internally marginal" by Father John M. Cooper: Temporal Sequence and the Marginal Cultures, The Catholic University of America, Anthropological Series No. 10, 1941. My attention was called to this learned and wise study after the manuscript of the present article was completed.

neighbors, the tribes of the Brazilian highland, the Pericu and Guaycuru of Lower California, the Yuki and Penutian peoples of California, and the Beothuk of Newfoundland. These are classical areas for the study of paleocultures, and protagonists of diffusion have drawn many parallels between them and with the most primitive peoples of the Old World. In higher or lower degree all these inferentially primordial groups picked up certain skills that were more advanced than their general cultural configurations, but on the whole they remained highly conservative and primitive in their arts as well as in their languages and mores. Although it is doubtful whether they can all be referred back to one *Urkultur,* they got their livelihood mainly by simple routines of collecting, possessing only indifferent hunting skill that depended more on stealth and patience than on prowess, organization, or weapon. Skill and design in stoneworking are uniformly rudimentary. Weapons were simple: clubs, spears, throwing sticks, perhaps slings, and later, in part, a simple bow, a borrowing with which they showed no great expertness. Some of these tribes had no means of water transport; others knew how to tie rushes and reeds into balsas; and the Yahgans and their western neighbors made one-piece bark canoes (a borrowing?). Containers were made of bark and skins, but skill in basketry is present, and represents their highest manual art. (Yahgans and the people in and adjacent to California made baskets by coiling, as the Tasmanians did in the Old World.) Dress was informal or lacking. Shelters were lean-tos or round huts of brush, some on frames of bent poles. (Araucanians, who are pieced together from a number of cultures, in part primitive, make round huts of this type, called *rucas,* to the present day.) It is not an unreasonable surmise that we have in these modern primitives the descendants of the first immigrants; that is, of people who came before the Folsom hunters.

The plains of South America beyond the tropics were filled with hunting tribes, about whom there is little information before they got horses. A hint of a far southern reappearance of kinsmen of the early hunters of the Great Plains is given by the superb prehistoric leaf blades (of Yuman type?) in north-central Chile. It may also be of significance that the Algonkin type of moccasin is reported to the south from Patagonian tribes only. The hunters of the pampas and Patagonia were not simply such by reason of environment. They had valley soils suited to farming, and they had northern neighbors who were excellent farmers. They were hunters by force of their immemorial habits, which may indicate the earliness of their arrival. Markedly more advanced than the primitive collectors and less so than the Andean and Amazonian farmers, they occupied that part of the continent where we should expect to find intermediate waves of immigrants deposited.

In the United States the disappearance of the Folsom and Yuma people, together with the great mammals, has been given dramatic emphasis, and thereafter more or less of a gap has been thought to exist until the Basket Maker and Hopewell folk and their like began to plant the soil. Between the early hunters and the early farmers, however, many culture items either were brought into the New World or were invented. Possibly the early hunters did not have the dart thrower; there is no evidence that they had dogs; certainly they did not have the bow and arrow, or the tomahawk. The whole assemblage of polished stone tools is later than they, and so are probably canoes of all descriptions and permanent houses. There is an impressive development of culture to be accounted for between early hunters and early farmers, and a good deal of time is needed. The diagnostic items of the Early Hunters are the great blades and the fluted points. These would have become obsolete when bow and arrow and celts became known. Why should not the Folsom and Yuma folk merely have merged into later hunters who brought in these new instruments and dogs, or have taken over the new and better methods of the chase?

The far corners of the New World are jumbled but real museums of the remote antiquity of man. Here, in the contemporary populations, common primordial traits, physical and cultural, are preserved by which waves of colonization may be traced that spread southward from the Alaskan gateway and began within the Ice Age.

{ 12 }

Environment and Culture
during the Last Deglaciation

PERIOD OF DEGLACIATION VERSUS POSTGLACIAL TIME

In the prehistory of man, we are accustomed to divide glacial from postglacial time as though we were using a common point of reference. Actually we bring on ourselves no little confusion, since the end of glaciation differs greatly from place to place; there is also no agreement by different students on the terminal event selected. An event of local significance serves as a datum line satisfactory for the local history, but is incompetent for any general chronology. In Scandinavia, De Geer proposed a date nine thousand years before the present as the beginning of postglacial time, and this date has been used widely, and far away from that peninsula. Yet the date, if correct, marks only the detachment of the icecap on the Scandinavian highland into two separate masses: the so-called bifurcation. It may be a convenient marker in dating the Scandinavian past, but even there other workers have preferred other, earlier events for the beginning of postglacial time; nor is the bifurcation a critical turning point in the physical history of Scandinavia. Someone's good local date unfortunately may become someone else's wrong date elsewhere by unawareness of the locally limited validity of the datum.[1]

There are indicated, however, two late moments of earth history

Proceedings of the American Philosophical Society, Vol. 92, 1948, pp. 65–77.
[1] Richard Foster Flint, Glacial Geology and the Pleistocene Epoch (New York, 1947), pp. 205–208, gives a good discussion of the boundary between the Pleistocene and the Recent. This informed and judicious volume, together with Frederick E. Zeuner, The Pleistocene Period (London, 1945), *idem,* Dating the Past (London, 1947), and Carl Troll, edit., Diluvial-Geologie und Klima, Geologische Rundschau, Vol. 34, 1944, Klimaheft, pp. 305–776, summarize present knowledge of the Ice Age and its aftermath.

as sufficiently brief, significant, and general to serve as critical mark- ers of time. The first is the beginning of the great deglaciation fol- lowing the last major ice advance;[2] the second, its ending. The former is here taken as dating about 35,000 years back; the latter around 7,000 years ago. Both of these estimates will be examined later.

During this time there was a general glacial deficit; we know of no widespread readvance of the ice. There were halts in its reces- sion, probably brief, perhaps local, and an occasional local advance; but nothing that contradicts the general record of continuing and world-wide failure of the ice masses in intermediate latitudes and altitudes, a loss that continued until the ice margins had retreated to positions in high latitudes and altitudes not greatly different from the present. The beginning, course, and end of this deglaciation are parts of one process, connected with general climatic change.

The present essay is limited to events thought to belong after the last ice culmination and before the end of the major glacial retreat, and the period included is here estimated to be somewhat in excess of 25,000 years. In this period falls the cultural revolution known as Mesolithic; the coincidences of great environmental and cultural changes are thought to be connected.

THE ISOSTATIC REGISTER OF DEGLACIATION

Both in North America and in Europe the maximum extension of the Fourth Glaciation (Wisconsin of North America) was early in that stage: in Europe the Warthe and Weichsel-Brandenburg (?) substages, in eastern North America the Iowan and Tazewell, and in the western mountains probably the Tahoe. Later there was a major readvance, in northern Europe both Frankfurt-Posen and Pomeranian, around the Great Lakes the Cary, and in our West the Tioga.[3] Time equivalence of the substages around the north- ern hemisphere is conjectural, but the general deployment of the Fourth Glaciation was of sufficiently similar pattern in all three areas to indicate that a correlation exists.

Subsequent events appear to belong to the time of deglaciation:

---

[2] R. J. Russell, Quaternary Geology of Louisiana, Bulletin of the Geological Society of America, Vol. 51, 1940, pp. 1199–1234; reference to p. 1201.

[3] I am departing from the usual interpretation in suggesting that the west- ern Tioga may be bracketed with eastern Cary rather than with Mankato. My reason is explained later in this article.

1. The latest glacial substage in the eastern United States is now called the Mankato, to which an estimated age of 25,000 years is assigned. As at present interpreted, east from Minneapolis to Lake Ontario it is mainly recessional, like the Scandinavian moraines. Westward, however, in the long and narrow Des Moines lobe, there was a curiously belated outburst of ice, which is one of the most puzzling features of glacial history. The explanation of the Des Moines salient, jutting far south from the continental ice margin of its time, remains to be found.[4] The Cary substage, most familiar in the Valparaiso moraine festooned about the southern end of Lake Michigan, is held to be the last ice culmination, the Mankato to belong to the time of deglaciation. The chronology used here is shown graphically in the figure.

The existence of the Des Moines salient is hardly sufficient reason to assign the late (Tioga) mountain glaciers of the West to that moment of time, as has been done. Two probable Wisconsin substages have been recognized widely in the western mountains, as far south as the San Francisco Mountains of Arizona.[5] Differences in their weathering establishes the Tahoe as significantly older than the Tioga stage. The very widespread occurrence of both stages suggests that both belong to times of general extension of glacial conditions, and hence that the later one may correlate with the Cary of eastern North America rather than with the Mankato substage.

2. A safer guide to the waning of glaciation is to be found in the isostatic upwarping of the earth's crust in areas formerly covered by continental ice. The forming of continental icecaps depressed the underlying bedrock; shrinkage of icecap was followed by re-

---

[4] More knowledge is needed of the Late Mankato glaciation, especially for the Dakotas and the Canadian prairie provinces. Their climatic conditions can hardly be reconstructed from the data we have. If I understand the situation for Late Mankato time rightly, the great ice mass of the Northeast, from the Great Lakes to the Atlantic seaboard, was being thinned and driven back strongly, but over the northwestern plains a comparatively thin and short ice margin was briefly re-energized. An accumulation of snow pack over Alberta, Saskatchewan, and Minnesota resulted from vigorous passage of winter "fronts" across them, with deep penetration of moist, relatively warm Atlantic air. Both profile and outline of the Des Moines and Grantsburg morainic lobes suggest such inflows out of the east. The atmospheric circulation pattern involved in the final Mankato glaciation seems to me to involve the operation of air cells and oceanic circulation over the Atlantic as beginning to approximate contemporary conditions and not those that initiated the great deglaciation and the end of Pluvial conditions in the Southwest.

[5] R. P. Sharp, Multiple Pleistocene Glaciation on San Francisco Mountain, Arizona, Journal of Geology, Vol. 50, 1942, pp. 481–503.

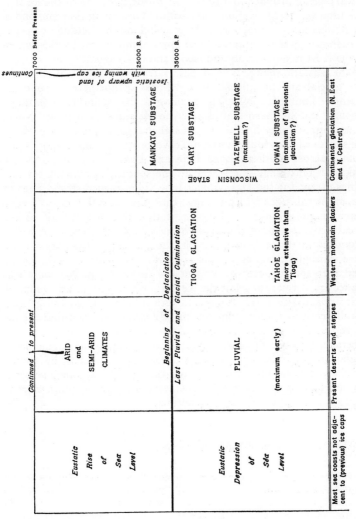

Schematic Representation of Late Pleistocene Time for the United States

7000 Before Present			
Eustatic Rise of Sea Level	ARID and SEMI-ARID CLIMATES	Continued ↓ to present	Continues → *Isostatic upward of land with waning ice cap*
	Beginning of Deglaciation Last Pluvial and Glacial Culmination		25000 B.P.
Eustatic Depression of Sea Level	PLUVIAL (maximum early)	TIOGA GLACIATION TÁHOÈ GLACIATION (more extensive than Tioga)	MANKATO SUBSTAGE CARY SUBSTAGE TAZEWELL SUBSTAGE (maximum ?) IOWAN SUBSTAGE (maximum of Wisconsin glaciation ?) WISCONSIN STAGE 35000 B.P.
Most sea coasts not adjacent to (previous) ice caps	Present deserts and steppes	Western mountain glaciers	Continental glaciation (N. East and N. Central)

elevation of the land that had been ice-buried, the amount of crustal upwarp being proportional to the weight or thickness of the ice that was removed. Deglaciation and isostatic upwarping thus go hand in hand, the crustal compensation lagging behind the melting of the ice, as is shown by the continuation of upward movement to the present of the crust in northern Scandinavia and in Canada.

The isostatic change is read mainly from the deformation of the late glacial and postglacial strand lines. In northern Europe the southern limit of upwarping is along a line from Lake Ladoga through the southern Baltic and the Bristol Channel. In North America the "hinge line" of no crustal change has been traced from the shores of Newfoundland and Nova Scotia through Long Island Sound, across southern Lake Erie and Lake Michigan to North Dakota.[6] This hinge line is well to the south of the post-Cary moraines except for the Des Moines lobe. The warped strand lines of the ancestral Great Lakes show that the crustal upwarp began "early in the Mankato substage. At that time nearly half of the Great Lakes region had already been relieved of its load of ice." [7] From glacial Lake Whittlesey on, the succeeding ice-margin lakes were warped during, as well as after, the Mankato period, and record therefore progressive and major deglaciation. Not only was the ice front retreating but the ice mass was being greatly reduced. It is apparent therefore that the continental icecap was in general in full process of destruction during Mankato time, and that the decisive turn of events in glacial history came before, not after, this substage. It is for this reason that I am assigning the beginning of deglaciation to about 35,000 years before the present, by adding ten thousand years for the span from Cary to Mankato, a guess that may be wide of the mark. The isostatic history of northern Europe appears to parallel that of our continent.

LATE GLACIAL AND PLUVIAL CLIMATES

The general circulation of the atmosphere, a heat engine maintained by solar radiation and earth rotation, forms a more or less permanent latitudinal pattern of climates, which can shift only within limits set by the limits of variability of the general circulation. The most serious alterations recognized in this circulation are those of glacial times. The displacement of climates at such times,

[6] Richard Foster Flint, *op. cit.,* pp. 418–421.
[7] *Ibid.,* p. 423.

however, does not involve the substitution of a different mechanism, nor has it been thought to necessitate the elimination of any of the zonally distributed cells of air masses.[8]

It is not in place here to consider the causes of glaciation, but only conditions before and at the beginning of the late deglaciation. The growing continental ice sheets are thought of as distorting the normal climatic pattern by crowding extratropical storm tracks equatorward. A belt of unstable air is thus construed as marginal to the continental ice fronts; here masses of cold and warm air jostled and mingled, producing frequent precipitation and much cloudiness. Along and behind the ice front the disturbed air brought increased snowfall; before it there was also increased precipitation and overcast. The ice front continued to push its storm belt ahead of it and thus to advance until a latitude was reached in which ice melt balanced snow accumulation.

Such an effect is not adequate to explain pluvial climates at a great distance from the ice fronts and in a geographical position normally unfavorable for rainfall. An ice front situated in Minnesota and Saskatchewan, or even Iowa, can hardly be the primary cause for the former pluvial climates that prevailed over the intermontane basins of the West and across the Southwest to and beyond the Mexican boundary.

The evidences of a time of markedly higher moisture are found throughout our arid and semiarid West, Southwest, and adjacent Mexico; and it is to this time that the term "Pluvial" is applied. The Mohave and Arizona deserts of the Southwest have numerous dry lake beds that then held fresh-water lakes and marshes, evidences of perennial streams where water now rarely runs, caves now dry that have at depth dripstone under which are remains of extinct fauna. For instance, the Ventana Cave in the middle of the Papago Desert of southwestern Arizona has yielded from depth remains of ground sloth, bison, horse, tapir, and man. Where now there are severe desert conditions, then browsed large herbivorous mammals of species now extinct and dependent on a vegetation unlike the present. These were hunted by man, who made his camps by vanished lakes, springs, and streams.[9]

---

[8] Sir George Simpson, Possible Causes of Change in Climate and their Limitations, Proceedings of the Linnean Society of London, 152nd Session, 1939–1940, pp. 190–219. Contains a strong criticism of the Milankovitch thesis of thermal change, currently in vogue in European glacial geology and among archeologists interested in an "absolute" chronology.

[9] Late summary by F. H. H. Roberts, Jr., The New World Paleo-Indian, Annual Report, Smithsonian Institution, 1944, pp. 403–433.

The discovery of man in our Pluvial record has given rise to reduced estimates of the time involved. The Pluvial conditions are
still conceded to have been far-flung effects of glaciation, but it is
now the mode to say that this Pluvial time must have lasted well
into "postglacial times." Thus the sites of Pluvial man are most
likely to have assigned to them an age of about ten thousand years
or a little more. This revision of the Pluvial dating is due solely to
the discovery of the presence of man. It would seem more proper to
revise opinion as to the age of man in the Southwest than to reinter-
pret its physical history to suit preconceptions of the antiquity of
man in the New World. The supposed lag of Pluvial conditions remains unsupported by evidence, unexplained in principle; and is a
solution in dilemma only in order to accommodate traditional views
of American prehistory.

Additional light is shed on the Pluvial problem by the neglected
situation in lower latitudes, in Mexico. The basins of northwestern
Chihuahua held a series of extensive and deep fresh-water lakes,
possibly comparable in size and history to Lake Lahontan, though
without any contributing glaciers. In the heart of the formidable
desert of Lower California a number of small dry lake beds have
been found, at elevations above two thousand feet, and unsupplied
by mountain drainage. Their physical and cultural features parallel
closely the history of the dry lakes in the Mohave Desert. Thus Dry
Lake Chapala, at latitude 29°20′, is in the most desolate part of the
peninsula, now lacking water and food or feed for minimal human
needs. It is surrounded by beach lines and benches at two or more
levels, and formerly had an outlet. We have had opportunity thus
far only for reconnaissances, but we know that there was human occupation in force, at both lower and higher lake levels, the cultures
differing by level. The human remains in and behind the old strands
are fairly abundant and indicate campsites of respectable size and
duration. The occupants were hunters and food grinders, and the
later cultural horizon is identified provisionally with the Pinto-
Gypsum culture of the Mohave Desert.[10]

The desert of Lower California is an effect of the subtropical
high that lies adjacent over the Pacific. If circulation of the atmosphere during glaciation involved a narrowing of pressure cells, as
is held by some, the desert would still have been in the middle of
Lower California, then as now. If glaciation involved a major
equatorward displacement of the descending air, we are in fresh
difficulties to explain the Pluvial lake basins of Durango and the
Valley of Mexico.

[10] Tentative determination by William Massey.

It would seem that these subtropical highs went out of business during Pluvial time, at least in so far as the land mass of North America was concerned. The air that brought marked increase of humidity to northern Mexico, the Southwest, and the intermountain Great Basin must have come mainly from tropical oceans, especially from the Pacific; and this freer penetration out of the south would seem to require greatly weakened horse-latitude cells. The problem of the Pluvial is far greater than any by-effect of continental ice sheets. Glacial and Pluvial climates are locationally distinct expressions of a former general circulation, with a critical difference as against the present in the behavior of that mechanism at the tropical margins.

Change in mountain barriers is negligible at this late time. The probable existence of a land barrier across Bering Strait would bar cold Arctic water from discharge into the northern Pacific and affect to some extent sea temperatures, but this alone would seem inadequate to reduce greatly the subtropical highs.

Modern climates begin with the present position and dimensions of the subtropical highs; desiccation in the west and south and deglaciation in the north and the high mountains resulted. Deglaciation required a long time for the removal of the continental ice; desiccation followed quickly on the change in circulation. If we are correct in thinking that the turn of climatic dynamics came with the end of the Cary substage of glaciation, we may suggest that the deserts and steppes of most of the West and of Mexico were established then. Instead of a "lag" in climatic change in the south, the change should have come earliest there. The whole record of Pluvial time has been placed far too late in American archeology. It should be antecedent to deglaciation, and it may well fill the whole of Wisconsin time from Iowan to Cary.

EUSTATIC RISE OF SEA LEVEL

Deglaciation restored water to the sea in sufficient volume to cause a notable rise in sea level. This late transgression of the sea, sometimes called Flandrian, is world-wide because the seas are connected. Locally it may be canceled out by vulcanism or diastrophism, or more widely where the isostatic upwarp of formerly ice-weighted land has exceeded the rise of the ocean. Observational data indicate that the rise of sea level is at least 250 feet.[11] A late study made for

[11] R. F. Flint, *op. cit.,* pp. 444–448; F. E. Zeuner, *Dating the Past, op. cit.,* pp. 128–129.

the Mississippi River Commission indicates a rise of the Gulf of Mexico by 400 to 450 feet.[12]

This transgression reduced the width of coast plains, made shallow seas of some of them, such as the North Sea and the South China and Java seas, and made islands of continental peninsulas such as Great Britain, Sumatra, Java, and Borneo. Away from the former icecaps, the 50-fathom line gives in rough outline the position of the coast line at the start of deglaciation. The greatest loss of land to the sea thus would have been between southeastern Asia and Australia, on the Atlantic coast of North America from the Banks of Newfoundland to the Mosquito Bank off Nicaragua, and in the South Atlantic from Rio de Janeiro to Patagonia. Lower courses of streams were drowned to form estuaries and bays, and smooth coast lines replaced by increasingly irregular ones.

The process of transgression, though neither uniform nor quite continuous, dominated from the beginning of deglaciation, it would seem, until about seven thousand years ago. Then, in the Atlantic phase of the Blytt and Sernander chronology, modern sea levels were approximated in northwestern Europe.[13] Since then there have been brief and local fluctuations, but no over-all trend is recognized. By inference the general retreat of glaciers ceased at that time, and the remnant icecaps had been reduced mainly to Antarctica and Greenland and northeast Canada, as now. From this time of near stabilization of sea level dates the beginning of the present detailed physiognomy of seacoasts, the cutting of present sea cliffs, building of spits across lagoons, modern beaches and bars, and the formation of our salt marshes.

CLIMATIC AND VEGETATIVE CHANGES

The thesis has been advanced above that a major climatic change initiated and thus preceded glaciation. During the earlier part of the deglaciation (Dryas time), cold periglacial conditions prevailed in northern Europe, as shown by solifluction earths and tundra vegetation and fauna. However, these latitudes are subarctic or nearly so. In North America no such periglacial effects have been found, possibly because of incomplete study, but perhaps because glaciation extended into lower latitudes than in Europe. Several human sites

[12] H. N. Fisk, Geological Investigation of the Alluvial Valley of the Lower Mississippi River (Mississippi River Commission, U.S. War Department, Corps of Engineers, 1944), p. 68.

[13] F. E. Zeuner, Dating the Past, *op. cit.,* pp. 92–98, 340.

of Mankato age around the Great Lakes indicate that men were living close to the ice margin, as on the Algonquin beach near Killarney, Ontario, and at Brown's Valley and Pelican Rapids in western Minnesota.[14] Apparently they experienced no climatic or provisioning difficulties in moving up as the ice receded. It may also be significant that neither in North America nor in Europe were loess deposits associated with the deglaciation, or with the final phases of the last glaciation.

The climate of the period is read mostly from the changes in peat beds, as by analysis of pollen. For north Europe, consistent trends in plant succession have been established; our postglacial climatology is less advanced as yet by parallel studies.[15] The existence of the so-called "Climatic Optimum" seems established, a time when certain plants reached higher latitudes and altitudes than at present. In Europe a dozen or more species are involved, including oak and hazel. The conclusion is that more warmth was then available, perhaps warmer summers or a somewhat earlier spring, or both. The time of this optimal condition has been estimated variously, ranging from 8000 B. C. for southern Germany to 4500 B. C. for southern Sweden and as late as 1000 B. C. for Denmark and New England.[16] Some of the differences in time, especially the contradiction in the Danish and Swedish dates, suggest observational error.

The peat studies are in the main of bogs on surfaces uncovered by the last deglaciation and colonized by successive waves of plant immigrants. It would be incorrect to associate each ecologic change with climatic change; most of the record can be accounted for as one of normal plant succession appropriate to the local situation. Birch and willow are superior pioneers in the higher latitudes; conifers follow and are gradually replaced by mixed hardwoods. The more fertile mineral soils developed most rapidly an enriched and enlarged soil-biotic complex; sands and wet surfaces retained longer less exacting plant species. Progressive drainage gradually improved aeration and humus development. The plant successions that have been preserved in peat pollens may therefore chiefly reflect differences in edaphic alteration, in competition between species, and in their mutual accommodation.

---

[14] C. O. Sauer, A Geographic Sketch of Early Man in America, Geographical Review, Vol. 34, 1944, pp. 529–573; reference to p. 539; this volume, pp. 197–245, reference to p. 208.

[15] Latest contribution by H. P. Hanson, Postglacial Forest Succession, Climate, and Chronology in the Pacific Northwest, Transactions of the American Philosophical Society, Vol. 37, 1947, pp. 1–130.

[16] F. E. Zeuner, Dating the Past, *op. cit.*, pp. 67–68.

The botanical record supports a "xerothermal" period during deglaciation, with "continental" characteristics for those latitudes, in reduced cloudiness and humidity, and with moderate summer warmth. There is no certain evidence of any general climatic change within the period of deglaciation, the whole of which may have had the meteorologic structure that initiated the deglaciation. The Climatic Optimum may record merely the edaphically and synecologically delayed attainment of climax vegetation, attained only towards the end of deglaciation. It may, however, register a modest increase in growing season and warmth in high intermediate latitudes.

Later, and perhaps after the time with which we are concerned, a certain deterioration of growing conditions occurred in northwestern Europe and in northeastern and northwestern America. There was less summer warmth, possibly owing to more "marine" conditions. A connection with the dying out of the process of deglaciation and freer entry of Arctic water into both Atlantic and Pacific seas, of course, may be suggested. The time of these occurrences, however, is later than the period under discussion.

In summary, during the great deglaciation no continuing or general readjustment of climates needs to be inferred. The meteorologic shift that terminated the last glacial culmination may be adequate to account for the subsequent climatic conditions until the end of the Climatic Optimum, although a minor positive thermal change cannot be ruled out.

ENVIRONMENTAL CHANGES

For man the time of waning ice sheets brought great and rapid alteration of environment throughout the world, for the most part offering increased opportunities, but in some areas reducing the possibilities of living:

1. According to the view here presented, the deserts and steppe lands of the present were in existence in the beginning of deglaciation. Except on alluvial lands, mesophytic plants had given way to xerophytes. Most of the big game had disappeared from the more arid parts, and with them the hunting folk. Primitive collecting people of unspecialized habits held on, their habitation sites restricted because water could be secured at fewer places. These sites were in general those at which water is found now. Cultural regression may have taken place, but more likely there was cultural and racial substitution by less exacting folk.

2. The recession of ice sheets uncovered millions of square miles of land in higher latitudes, which became available promptly for human colonization. No unvegetated interval is known, nor have tundra conditions been found within the United States. Morainic and ice-scoured surfaces held very many lakes, ponds, and marshes, rapidly stocked with aquatic and semiaquatic life. The world population of migrant waterfowl increased hugely with the addition of the great northern breeding and summer-feeding grounds. Such increase was reflected in lower latitudes by improved hunting and trapping opportunities along flight routes and in wintering grounds. Northern woodlands, wet prairies, and marshes became major big-game ranges (bison, deer, elk, moose, musk ox), compensating for loss of range in arid lands.

3. The transgression of the sea on shallow continental margins crowded back the inhabitants of coast plains. For primitive man the loss of area was perhaps more than made good by the improved attractions of seashores. The more the sea rose, the more sinuous did the shore line become and the more diversified. Increased length of coast line made it possible for more people to live as strand collectors. Drowning of valleys increased the tidal range and thus the vertical zone between high and low tide, which is most valuable for food collecting. Encroachment of sea on land of moderate or even slight relief gave added diversity of bottom and strand; rocky shelves, gravel, sand, and mud flats all acquired distinctive useful faunas. The forming of quiet, landlocked bodies of water gave a favorable setting for early trials in navigation.

4. Alluvial valleys grew in length and breadth, burying flanks and spurs of the older erosional valleys, as has been fully documented for the Mississippi and its lower tributaries. This was a time of major growth of flood plains wherever streams discharged into the ocean, and thus of growing meanders and relict oxbow lakes, gradually to be filled with sediment and organic matter, of natural levees and backwater swamps. Levee and higher land adjacent to flood plains afforded habitation sites, relocated from time to time as alluviation proceeded.

Marshy parts of the flood plains were colonized by plants, many of them of high usefulness to man: the great perennial grasses that yield canes and reeds and palatable shoots and seeds; rushes and sedges, among the latter some, such as species of *Cyperus* and *Eleocharis,* that form edible tubers; various species of the Arum, Iris, Canna, and Water Lily families, with succulent roots, stalks, or seeds. In southern Asia in fresh-water marsh margins sago and rattan palms are of importance. The well-drained alluvial lands are optimal sites for plant growth, and here useful mesophytic species are found in maximum diversity, including in warm lands species of yams (*Dioscorea*), *Manihot, Maranta,* and *Ipomoea,* that store starch in underground stems and tubers.

A new world took form, developing the physical geography that we know. The period was one of maximum opportunity for progressive and adventurous man. The higher latitudes were open to his colonization. In mild lands river valleys invited his ingenuity. It was above all a rarely favorable time for man to test out the possibilities of water-side life, and especially of living along fresh water.

MAN IN THE NEW WORLD DURING DEGLACIATION

The time and order of events, as presented, disagree with the views of American archeology, which has held to the premise that the entry of man into the New World is "postglacial," and is inclined to place any early site in time between ten and fifteen thousand years ago, at about the earliest time at which a recessional corridor might have opened in the Canadian Northwest to admit immigrants from Asia. Against such a view is the evidence for a true Paleolithic position of the Pluvial human sites, which preceded deglaciation and some of which may belong to an early Wisconsin stage. These Pluvial finds are the greater part of the known human record in North America; they are here excluded as anterior to the time under consideration.

The sites of Mankato age, related to recessional lakes from Minnesota to Ontario, are within the time of deglaciation, but too early for postglacial landwise immigration out of Asia. They are here considered as of epigonous Paleolithic folk whose ancestors were living elsewhere in North America during the last glaciation. The Abilene, Texas, material of the Elm Creek–Nugent horizons probably also is a belated continuation of American Paleolithic. The view that the Wisconsin ice in its retreat opened a land corridor for Asiatic pedestrian immigrants not more than fifteen thousand years ago I find quite acceptable, but not the opinion that such immigration was of extraordinarily delayed archaic cultures.

After the corridor opened, some of the great cultural changes, known as Mesolithic, that had been sweeping the Old World, found their way into the New. Both new culture elements in the archeology and their stratigraphic position suggest that we may have such

Mesolithic in the Early Culture of the Central Valley of California,[17] and in the San Pedro stage, possibly even the Chiricahua stage, of the Cochise culture in Arizona.[18] If there were available immigrants possessed of boating skills, they could have used the Northwest Coast route at any time.

THE MESOLITHIC ARCHEOLOGIC RECORD

In Europe the last glacial age saw successively the rise and waning of Aurignacian, Solutrean, and Magdalenian cultures. With the onset of deglaciation, the Magdalenian faded and new modes came in from North Africa and the Near East, heralds of Mesolithic life. The Upper Paleolithic hunters of big game, masters of stone-blade making, and probably strongly masculine societies, left some legacies to Mesolithic habits, but mainly the latter originated elsewhere, and had a very different cultural configuration.

We need not look to the old hunting folk as distinct forebears of later planters; we do turn to the Mesolithic record for the earliest background of agriculture. It is still held, but without evidence, that hunters, by increase in their numbers and decrease of game, became farmers. One line of evidence from the Upper Paleolithic is, at first sight, persuasive, the Venus statuettes. These have been interpreted as fertility idols, called Earth Mother figures, and thought of as a sort of proto-Demeter. The lush exaggeration of feminine contours that characterizes them may be only the play of male eroticism or at most the nuptial counterpart of the animal figures and cave drawings, which are thought to have given magical aid in the capture of the object desired.

(In the New World the Pluvial food-grinding folk may be a link to later high cultures. Possibly the metate of Mexican corn grinding is a lineal derivative from the grinding stones found in the oldest sites from Oklahoma to California. The age, content, and meaning of our old grinding cultures still await serious comparative study. Little is known in the Old World comparable to them.)

---

[17] Jeremiah B. Lillard, R. F. Heizer, and Franklin Fenenga, An Introduction to the Archeology of Central California, Sacramento Junior College, Anthropological Bulletin 2, 1939.

[18] E. B. Sayles and Ernst Antevs, The Cochise Culture, Medallion Papers, No. 29, 1941; E. B. Sayles, The San Simon Branch, Excavations at Cave Creek and in the San Simon Valley, I. Material Culture, *ibid.*, No. 34, 1945. The two authors differ widely in their interpretation.

The existence of Mesolithic was not recognized until long after Paleolithic and Neolithic were established concepts. Gradually the so-called "hiatus" between Paleolithic and Neolithic has been partly filled, mostly in Europe and its borders, but the Mesolithic record is still meager compared with anterior and subsequent time. The scantiness of Mesolithic data, it may be suggested, is connected with the fact that Mesolithic culture falls wholly within the time of the deglaciation.

1. Throughout the Mesolithic, sea level was rising. Coastal lowlands which these folk inhabited are now beneath the sea; human record is recovered from them only by such rare chance as the dredging up of Maglemose artifacts from the Dogger Bank of the North Sea. The greater part of our knowledge of the European Mesolithic significantly comes from parts of northern Europe in which isostatic upwarp of the land outdistanced rise of sea level. With rising sea level were associated increased alluviation of river valleys and continued burial of lowland living sites. The situation is reversed from prior times, for which terrace sites are most revealing. The recognition of Mesolithic sites is in general difficult: they are buried out of sight in lowlands; they cannot normally occur on terraces, unless isostatic; they postdate most deposits of glacial origin; and where they occur as upland sites they are likely to be overlooked because they are physiographically nondescript.

2. The desiccation of the Pluvial areas and attendant loss of game and seed and root harvest greatly reduced occupation in the dry interiors and on the western sides of continents in low intermediate and subtropical latitudes. Widely dispersed occupation was replaced by a few settlements along the margins of permanent or seasonal water.

3. Skill at stone flaking reached its highest development in Upper Paleolithic and gave rise to readily recognized forms. The arts of the Mesolithic people were directed otherwise; their stone work was less in amount, poorer in execution, and less diagnostic. The kill of big game became incidental; heavy projectiles, great knives, and daggers were used less; instead the Mesolithic people worked with perishable plant materials.

Mesolithic sites are chronologically well determined in north Europe where isostasy has provided a clock; elsewhere, as about the Mediterranean, the absolute and even relative positions of the individual cultures are uncertain. The north-European sites are late; and in their inclement situations are obviously marginal and partial extensions of the main stream of Mesolithic cultural developments, with parts of the older northern (Magdalenian) culture adhering. There is likelihood that the European Mesolithic is adventive in the main and that the new ideas, and perhaps people, came from the south and southeast. A general derivation out of the Near East is likely, and the ultimate hearth may have lain farther east. We have as yet hardly more than a record of a far colonial fringe, in which the environment was not favorable to the entry of the full cultural complex.

Notable innovations in the Old World Mesolithic are: (1) Reduction in size of most stone artifacts, especially the so-called microliths; (2) general use of the bow and arrow, perhaps originating before this, but at this time becoming very widespread, and perhaps linked to the microliths; (3) varied fishing gear, including advanced development of the harpoon, introduction of fishhooks, sinkers, and floats; (4) use of boats; (5) a new axe, the tranchet, probably a woodworking tool; (6) the appearance of grinding slabs in the Sebilian of the Near East, probably early; (7) deliberate fashioning of stone by grinding, as in the doughnuts or perforated "mace heads" (a term showing the preoccupation of archeologists with notions of warfare) and cylindrical celts with ground edge; (8) the domesticated dog, found in Mesolithic sites from the Near East and the Crimea to Portugal and the Baltic; and (9) late, the making of pottery.

AS TO A MESOLITHIC CULTURE COMPLEX

The Mesolithic is not yet seen clearly enough to be delineated as are the times before and after. It still has the qualities of an interval, later than certain great culture complexes in the prehistory of man, and earlier than another great record. With continuing archeologic study, the interval is getting greater length assigned to it at the far end. Archeologic evidence does not yet warrant making the Mesolithic equal to the whole period of deglaciation. Nor do I wish to argue that a great change of environment must make a great change in culture. It requires, however, no forcing of the imagination to see in this period the trial arrangements and finally the full prelude to the Neolithic. These developments took a very long time unless invention suddenly became very different in kind and pace from what it had been. It might help our inspection of the Mesolithic past if we concede the possibility that it may have comprised most or all of the time of the deglaciation. This consciousness of need of a good deal of time, it may be admitted, is based mainly on the changes in plants and animals effected at the hand of man by the time when the Neolithic record begins.[19]

The meagerness of the Mesolithic record may be a permanently characteristic feature. The peculiar turn of events in earth history noted may well conceal from us forever more of man's history than for contiguous periods. We know from the subsequent period that a great deal must have been accomplished by man during the Mesolithic, and it is not inappropriate to make the most of the clues we have.

Upper Paleolithic traditions of hunting life penetrate to some extent into the Mesolithic cultures, as in Magdalenian influence on Azilio-Tardenoisian, but the roots of Mesolithic culture are rather to be sought further back in the Paleolithic core or hand-axe cultures, known in the western Old World as Acheulean and Micoquian. These are usually interpreted as fashioned by woodland folk, who favored humid and mild climates. They may have originated in monsoon Asia. They directed themselves strongly to the exploitation of plant resources for food, fiber, bark, and wood. A great deal of practical plant lore may be ascribed to them, and a trend toward as much sedentary living as skill and environment permitted.[20] In Europe the older woodland folk were pretty much overwhelmed by the Upper Paleolithic hunting folk, but in lower latitudes their descendants were not thus disturbed.

Accepting the peripheral nature of the European Mesolithic, which is most of the record that we have, and its connection with earlier hand-axe cultures out of mild climates, then the known dominant traits, namely microliths, bow and arrow, fishing gear, boats, adze and axe, grinding slabs, pottery, and the domesticated dog are sufficient parts of a mosaic to venture a preliminary hypothesis as to the nature of Mesolithic culture, its general place of origin, and its age. These particular traits are not discrete, but complementary; they do make sense together and in context with the newly formed environment.

It may be that, when we have more varied knowledge of Upper

---

[19] Oakes Ames, Economic Annuals and Human Cultures (Cambridge, Massachusetts, 1939), *passim,* especially the final chapter, pp. 119–143.

[20] C. O. Sauer, Early Relations of Man to Plants, Geographical Review, Vol. 37, 1947, pp. 1–25; in this volume, pp. 155–181.

Paleolithic time than the European record affords, with its dominance by hunters of plain and cave, the roots of Mesolithic origins will appear more clearly to come from a farther antiquity:

1. The domesticated dog is almost the index fossil to Mesolithic sites, yet it may have originated before then. The Australian dingo may be part of a Paleolithic culture that has survived in isolation; certainly the animal was carried there by man. The doubtful reports of dogs in late Pleistocene deposits may be resolved by new finds or restudy. It appears reasonably sure to me that the dog does not belong originally to mobile hunting folk, and probable that its domestication was not a casual event, but a difficult step carried out only once. I think it was possible only to quite sedentary people.

2. Those who venture to reconstruct the historical branching of cultural complexes from living peoples—and the effort is worth the risks—assign the *balsa* or raft boat to a culture of mid-Paleolithic aspect. The bark canoe is a later invention, but perhaps still Paleolithic, if the Australian culture complex is properly interpreted as a late Paleolithic relic.

3. The trait of fish poisoning may be of similarly high age, being found in many parts of the world among tribes of simplest and most archaic culture. It again is widely present in Australia, was practised by the more primitive tribes of California rather than by the more advanced, and was the only means of taking fish known to the Ssabela of the upper Amazon, a people of extraordinarily archaic character.[21] The techniques of fish poisoning are in need of study with respect to their culture-historical significance. The discovery may have been the result of processing fiber. A general procedure is the macerating of some part of a plant, usually root or stalk, and scattering the mash into the fishing pool. To a considerable degree the plants thus used are also used for fiber, and a number of them serve for toughening cords and nets: for southeast Asia, for instance, species of *Derris, Albizzia, Diospyros, Daphne,* and *Barringtonia.*[22] Such may have been the original uses, and in preparing a certain fiber the observation was made that fish were made unconscious. Trial showed that these fish were safe for human consumption; then the trait of fish poisoning became adopted and the learning was passed on to others. These are some of the traces of possibly more ancient roots of the Mesolithic advance.

---

[21] Günther Tessmann, Die Indianer nordost-Perus (Hamburg, 1930), p. 300.

[22] I. H. Burkill, Dictionary of the Economic Products of the Malay Peninsula, 2 vols. (London, 1935), under the names of the respective genera.

HYPOTHESIS OF THE PROGRESSIVE FISHING PEOPLE

The archeologic content and sites of the Mesolithic show attraction to the water side which is in contrast to the prior period. Attention shifts from land hunting to fishing and other riparian and aquatic economy. The water's edge sustained human groups as far back as we can trace man, but they had been quite conservative collectors, and are pretty well lost sight of during the Last Glaciation. With deglaciation and its attendant drowning of coasts and flooding of valleys a new environment was resolved into new opportunities by a series of cultural inventions, improvements, and recombinations. The cultural revolution of the Mesolithic was pioneered, by this view, by progressive fishing people who also initiated the basic steps in plant and animal domestication.

The harpoon was much improved and diversified during this period and the fishhook added, and so we know also that strong water-resistant cordage must have been made. Netting also has been recovered on the Baltic, also bark floats and stone sinkers. Boat making was carried on. The simple bow and arrow, widely diffused during this period, is a precision weapon at short range, well suited for still hunting of waterfowl and small water mammals as well as for shooting fish in shallow pools. It was not of much account for big game or for combat. The older "hand-axe" during this time was developed into wedge, adze, and axe, the last toward the end acquiring a ground edge. Weight, shape, and size of these instruments indicate use for digging and hewing rather than for combat. The so-called stone maces or doughnuts may have been slipped over digging sticks, as was done in historic times in central Chile. They would therefore be anticipations of the spade. In line with our martial traditions, there has been inclination to interpret many things as fighting weapons; the cultural additions of this time were more apt for peaceful arts.

The habitat in which the new culture had its origin is thought of as having been at the edge of bay, lake, and stream, and the elaboration of the culture as progressive domination not only of the waterside but the adjacent land side. Land plants were as important as water life; cultural progress depended on the increasing domination over both kinds of resources. Seaside habitat was less favorable to cultural development than was fresh water. The most backward culture of the European Mesolithic was that of the Asturian strandloopers, as Gordon Childe calls them. Some of the Brazilian sambaquis should also belong to this period. We still have in various parts of the world primitive peoples who are beachcombers, living on coasts rich in shellfish and perhaps fish, and almost mid-Paleolithic in their cultural configuration. The open coasts offer a modest competence, but seem always to have discouraged primitive ingenuity. Moreover, nonalluvial coastal lands are below average in diversity of economic plants, and few from such areas have been made into domesticated plants. On the other hand, fresh-water and alluvial soils do give the requisite background for the cultural advances that were realized by the beginning of Neolithic time.

The most probable hearth of the great Mesolithic developments is to be sought in monsoon Asia, somewhere from India to southern China. The preference for a southeast Asiatic center of cultural origins is based on (1) its earlier role as cradle of human races and cultures; (2) the habitat requirements that have been postulated are well met by various parts of India, Indo-China, and southern China; (3) interior mountain barriers gave protection against raiding nomad hunters; (4) the position of the area is most favorable for culture dispersals involving water preferences; (5) a great number and diversity of old domesticated plants and perhaps the oldest domesticated animals derive from here. If domestication of dog and pig can be assigned to southeastern Asia, the case becomes very strong.

The most nearly comparable area as to early advantages are the lands about the Caribbean and the Gulf of Mexico; but the time involved seems too early to initiate a great culture center in the New World. Southwestern Asia is ruled out of consideration as a hearth in the critical period of beginnings, largely because I do not see that the things it contributed, such as small grains and other economic annuals and the larger domesticated animals, belong to the earlier stages of the sequence that led to agriculture. Since contemporary climates were already in force, its dryness is incompatible with the present hypothesis of the basic culture complex.

In southeastern Asia, both more primitive hill peoples and higher cultures share in institutions that may be derivative from the ancient fishing-culture complex. From this area traits of social organization and ritual have been cited by numerous adherents of cultural diffusion as showing an early cultural nexus that became widely spread over the world, on the economic side some special aptitude in fishing, boating, and planting being recognized.

Southeastern Asia has a combination of plant-using traits that link fishing and farming and which seem to have originated in common and ancient procedure that may antedate even Mesolithic time, namely the crushing or macerating of plant parts and their washing. The beginning may well have been in the breaking and retting of fibers for bowstrings and net cords, with the discovery of fish poisons incidental thereto, as stated earlier. This is also the major center for making bark cloth and for dart poisons, for both of which the processes have much in common with fiber and fish poison preparation. In no other part of the world is there such familiarity with and variety in the use of poisons, chiefly from stem or root of plants; and numerous of these are important for fiber. The fearsome upas tree (*Antiaris toxicaria*), most potent component of dart poisons, has also been one of the main sources of bark cloth. The genus of breadfruits (*Artocarpus*) is "invaluable to the jungle tribes for the manufacture of bark cloth"; [23] it also supplies fibers for fish nets and lines, and some species enter into the making of dart poison. Species of *Gnetum* furnish food from their seeds, strong and pliable fiber, and fish and dart poisons.

Various aroids are acrid or actively poisonous as to tuber or stem but have become important sources of starch food. They require rasping or grinding, with repeated washing before cooking. The *Alocasias*, especially *A. macrorhiza,* are and formerly were more used and cultivated for their starchy stems. The *Colocasias,* or taros, in their wild and less ameliorated forms, are highly irritant unless grated and washed before cooking, and this quality may have been originally responsible for the preparation of taro as poi paste. The tuber-bearing poisonous aroids that have yielded cultivated races of importance are *Amorphophallus campanulatus* and *A. konjac.* The treatment of yams (*Dioscorea*) was probably the same, and one kind still much used to the present (*D. hispida*) is very poisonous. Two of the cultivated gingers (*Zingiber cassumunar* and *Z. zerumet*) are on record as arrow poisons.

The more humid part of monsoon Asia is the home of various nonpoisonous esculent tubers important in the history of man, and often ground to meal before cooking. Some of them are aquatic or grow at the water's edge, such as the water "taro" (*Ottelia arismoides*), the arrowhead (*Sagittaria sagittata*), sweet flag (*Acorus calamus*), the tuber-forming sedges (*Cyperus esculentus-tuberosus rotundus* complex), and water lilies (*Nelumbium nelumbo* and perhaps *Nymphaea lotus*). All of these are or have been culti-

---

[23] *Ibid.,* Vol. I, p. 248.

vated, the rest of the world offering few hydrophytes that have been brought under cultivation as foodstuffs.

Finally, we have the securing of starch food from stems through shredding or pounding and thereafter separating the starch by washing. This making of sago is mostly limited to monsoon Asia and is a trait of high antiquity. Certain cycads and palms are thus exploited, either in the wild or brought into the village planting, namely *Cycas circinalis* and *revoluta, Arenga pinnata, Phoenix farinifera* and *rupicola, Coelococcus* spp., and *Metroxylon laeve, rumphii,* and *sagu.* The fermentation of toddy from these and other sugary palm trunks is probably an associated trait.

The practice of shredding, pounding, washing, and decanting runs through plant uses throughout southeastern Asia, and seems to tie fiber making and toughening, poison preparation for fishing, hunting, and medicine, and food preparation, including the coagulation of sago, into one culture complex. The origin of this interrelated set of skills was favored by the presence of suitable plants, but it would appear to be derivative from the direction that intellectual curiosity took among a particular group of fresh-water fishermen.

PERMANENCE OF HOUSES AND VILLAGES

The process of domestication will not be explored further in this essay. I hold it to have been carried out, whether uniquely as to origin or not, by the culture which has been sketched, and mainly to have taken place during the period of deglaciation. The progressive fresh-water fisher folk, it is suggested, became in course of time the Earliest Planters (the *Altpflanzer* of the *Kulturkreis* systems).

The life of such people was fully sedentary; they had no necessity to move about, for a good fishing site was such throughout the year. The water harvest was continuous, though the product might change with the season. The land also yielded its fruits proper to their seasons. Neither on water nor on land was there the sort of seasonal disparity that enforces migrant food searching. Houses were permanent and they were framed with wood or cane, and covered with cane or bark, by people who were also boat builders, men using adze and axe familiarly and who were applying their thinking to the fashioning of wood and cane. The "culture area" proponents are probably right in assigning the origin of the rectangular, framed, and gabled house to such a culture, and in emphasizing the spaciousness of such houses, which were combined living quarters, storehouse, and tool shed. Boat transport made easy the carriage of supplies from a distance and their assembly at a permanent base. Living was made better and more comfortable by the accumulation of goods. Since there was no moving day ahead, there was no restraint on the getting and keeping of goods. Personal property could be added indefinitely so long as it added to the comforts of home.

Having the ability to range easily by water, it became advantageous to live together in villages, as at river junction or rapids, at lake end or narrows. The community had opportunity for diversified skills and for exchange of ideas. Association meant diffusion of ideas or learning; an innovation could become a group practice. By boat other settlements could be visited and ideas spread readily as far as there was intercommunication. Given leisure to experiment and to learn in an advantageous environment, such communities needed only sustained curiosity in a given direction to make the advance from fishing to farming. Since their interests were directed strongly toward plant processing, as has been outlined, increase in population and in experience made the understanding and use of plant resources more and more rewarding.

Planters, I think, must be fully sedentary folk; and I cannot accept the widespread view that wandering people might plant a crop, wander on, and later return for its harvest. In the first place, I do not think that a definite season of crop harvest enters into the early steps towards agriculture, but that attention was first given to having certain plant items, not necessarily foodstuffs, conveniently at hand at all times. Our conventional views of proto-agriculture are still based on our own past as grain farmers of sown fields, which was not the way by which man took the first steps towards farming by such evidence as we have. Also, it is well known that primitive folk as we know them do not and dare not leave their plantings unwatched. The planted crop, in fact, must be watched over incessantly lest the creatures that fly, walk, crawl, and burrow move against the plantation to begin its destruction almost from the day it is made. There is partial protection by growing plants that are poisonous, but man's poison may be an animal's food. The predilection for dealing with poisonous plants as sources of food may, however, not be unrelated to their unpalatability to plant predators. Only plants quite unpalatable to all the local fauna, however, have much chance of survival if left untended. The menfolk may get away for fishing and hunting trips, but the women and children must stay to guard the plantings. This watching over the clearings against the wildlife is indeed one of the first impressions that a civilized visitor gets from seeing a primitive agricultural or horticultural community unless it be in far oceanic islands. The increased food supply for man is equally an increased attraction to a diversity of animals that compete for food with man, as every farmer knows. The myth of casual, untended sowing is part of the myth of the hungry mobile hunter who decides to add to his food by sowing seeds and capturing a herd of wild animals for their increase.

CONCLUSION

The general premise of this reconstruction is that there is no general succession of cultural stages. Nor was there a general evolutionary transition of fisher folk to farmers. However, only in sedentary fresh-water fishing communities do I find the seminal qualities out of which came the Neolithic modes of life. The transformation of culture perhaps was pioneered only in one area, which most probably lay in southeastern Asia. The change in mode of living by developing interrelated skills was one of the greatest in the history of man and required uninterrupted and long-continued intellectual activity in one direction. Cultural diffusion is favored, therefore, against independent parallel invention. Neither the invitation of a favorable nor the lash of a harsh environment in itself brings cultural advance. Time by itself works no social evolution of large proportion. There are certain parallels between biologic evolution and culture growth: high isolation stops progress early, too great accessibility leaves an area open to be swept by every invading force and without the chance to develop variant and novel forms. The hearths of human learning needed to be somewhat sheltered from the world at large, but also to have the option of outside communication. They also needed ample and varied resources in their environment, so that thoughtful people could work with them, with leisure to experiment and reflect. The milestones of human learning have been set here and there at opportune times by a few exceptional groups in exceptional locations for discovery and transmission of ideas.

The time of the great deglaciation lies on the steeply ascending part of the curve of cultural innovation. We know now that our own kind, probably with our own intelligence, was in existence as far back as mid-Pleistocene, and that very slow increments of learning had been added here and there over hundreds of thousands of years. The last glaciation or Upper Paleolithic saw a notable acceleration of learning. The rate of innovation increased quite rapidly during the Mesolithic, the bright days of cultural youth for the most progressive branch of mankind. Where and how this progress was achieved is still veiled, but the clues point to a great intermediary culture between older collectors and later farmers, of fairly low latitude habitat in wooded stream sides.

{ 13 }

The End of the Ice Age
and Its Witnesses

Currently there is increased interest in the past that extends back into the Ice Age. Physical science has developed new and more exact means of inspecting the deposits of Man and of Nature, including tests to determine their age. Geophysicists and oceanographers especially have begun to examine and compare events on sea floor and land surface over a span of some tens of thousands of years, using as principal measure the loss of radioactivity in the contained carbon.[1] Thus we are getting a revised and more orderly view as to the time and manner of the last waning of the continental icecaps and of their connection with the circulation of air and ocean waters in the northern hemisphere.[2] Some facts of the presence and condition of the human witnesses of this interesting moment in geologic time are now well located in the new chronology and invite attention to synchronous events of human prehistory in the northern hemisphere.

TIME: 12,000 TO 10,000 YEARS BEFORE THE PRESENT

We are accustomed to distinguish Pleistocene time, or the Ice Age, from Recent time by the disappearance of the great icecaps from intermediate latitudes. For the United States the Ice Age is considered to have ended with the melting off of the last ice sheet

---

Geographical Review, Vol. 47, 1957, pp. 29–43.
[1] W. F. Libby, Radiocarbon Dating (2nd edit., Chicago, 1955). Science and American Antiquity report additional dates as these are recovered and interpreted.
[2] Maurice Ewing and W. L. Donn, A Theory of Ice Ages, Science, Vol. 123, 1956, pp. 1061–1066. This article contains a bibliography of recent investigations on sea-floor and oceanic circulation.

within our borders (the Mankato substage), during which our present Great Lakes were formed.[3] It now appears possible to reconstruct in broad outline the physical geography of the United States at that time, dated as comprising the span from 12,000 to 10,000 years ago. Comparable data are available for the same period for northern Europe. Enough has been learned about both continents at that time to invite the interim and partial commentary implied in the imprecise title of this article. Although there is good reason to think that we are living today in an interglacial stage,[4] we continue to speak of the present as part of "postglacial time" and of the last advance of the continental icecaps as the "last glacial time."

The time band of 12,000 to 10,000 years ago was first indicated to be of critical importance by the now famous date of 11,500 years ± before the present from Two Creeks in northeastern Wisconsin. Here a forest was flooded by a rising glacial lake and then overriden by the advancing Mankato ice.[5] A steadily growing series of radiocarbon dates in the United States and Europe supports and amplifies the physical and cultural record of this time. The more such determinations are made, the more do they show that this was the time of the last major changes in physical geography. The terrestrial data are newly reinforced by those gained from the ocean floors. From the shore of the Baltic, across the Atlantic Ocean, along the margins of our Mankato drift, from the base of the Rocky Mountains to the Great Basin, we have a new and significant illumination of this segment of the past.

PHYSICAL GEOGRAPHY OF THE END PHASE

The physical geography of this "end" phase of the Ice Age may be sketched as follows:

1. The last ice advance over the interior of North America occurred much later than we have thought. As against a supposed age of some 25,000 years or more, we must now accept one about 11,000. The Mankato ice advanced farthest south in a long tongue that pushed across south-central Minnesota and northern Iowa to the vicinity of Des Moines. Another tongue lapped about Green

---

[3] R. F. Flint: Glacial Geology and the Pleistocene Epoch (New York, 1947, 4th printing, 1953), and continuing reports in scientific journals.
[4] Ewing and Donn, *op. cit.*
[5] Flint, *op. cit.,* pp. 251 and 255.

Bay and the north end of the Lower Peninsula of Michigan. A third extended across the Dakotas toward the Missouri River at Yankton. The ice margin to the west and north of Yankton paralleled the course of the Missouri River, at some distance from the river valley. By means of the Altamont moraine and its continuation, this ice front has been traced into Canada beyond and to the east of Edmonton, Alta.[6] This is an astonishingly deep, as well as late, penetration of interior North America, about 10° lower in latitude than the maximum extent of the icecap in Europe, which was reached much earlier. The Mankato advance, as at present understood, was brief. There are reasons for thinking that the ice was not very thick and that it followed the preceding substage (Cary) without significant intervening deglaciation, but as a somewhat more westerly displacement of ice advance.

2. The Great Basin and, inferentially in higher degree, its rimming mountain ranges experienced increased winter precipitation and less summer evaporation during Mankato time. Radiocarbon dates from rock shelters formed by wave cutting in late stages of glacial Lakes Lahontan and Bonneville fall into the same period and record a human occupation. It is thought that the shelters were occupied by man shortly after the lake levels had dropped below the levels at which the rock niches were cut. Two from the Lahontan Basin of Nevada are the Fishbone Cave above dry Winnemucca Lake and the Leonard Rockshelter near Lovelock. In the Bonneville Basin the Stansbury lake level is at the base of human occupation in Danger Cave, near Wendover, Utah. The Fishbone Cave dates are 10,900 and 11,555 before the present, and the Leonard date is about 12,000;[7] those at the base of Danger Cave are between 11,150 and 11,450.[8] These dates definitely establish for the first time that a moderate, late-Pluvial condition in the Great Basin and glaciation in the adjacent mountains coincided with the Mankato glaciation of the interior plains.

3. It has been thought that our Mankato glaciation agreed in time with the last European ice advance, which built the Pomeranian moraines south of the Baltic Sea. Instead, it is now identified as of

---

[6] "Glacial Map of North America," 2 sheets, 1: 4,555,000, Geol. Soc. of America Special Papers No. 60, Part 1. The western limits of Mankato ice are from Flint.

[7] Phil Orr, Pleistocene Man in Fishbone Cave, Nevada State Museum Dept. of Anthropol. Bull. 2, 1956.

[8] J. D. Jennings, Danger Cave: A Progress Summary, El Palacio, Vol. 60, 1953, pp. 179–213.

a later time, that of the recessional halts of the ice front north of the Baltic Sea. These are marked by the Scanian moraines of Sweden and the Salpausselkä of Finland, and by the Baltic Ice Lake that formed southeast and south of Scandinavia. This was the time of the two cold-climate Dryas floras, separated by the warmer Allerød interval. This period has been long and well studied as to ice position, water-laid sediments, and bog pollen. The European radiocarbon dates agree with the independent and numerous findings of glaciologists and botanists. The final European advance of the Pomeranian substage cannot, therefore, have been later than our pre-Mankato Cary advance.

4. Cores taken from the floor of the Atlantic Ocean were at first interpreted as recording a steady rise of ocean temperatures, beginning 16,500 years ago, interrupted by a minor cooling from 12,000 to 10,000 years ago before the warming was resumed.[9] However, Ewing and Donn,[10] more recently and using in part unpublished data, conclude from cores taken from both the Atlantic and the Gulf of Mexico that in the Gulf "the sediments give no evidence of any climatic change except that 11,000 years ago." In general, they "regard 11,000 years ago as the date of the most recent significant temperature change in the Atlantic Ocean, and also as marking the end of the Wisconsin glacial stage." [11]

5. Shepard and Suess [12] estimate that 11,000 years ago sea level stood about a hundred feet lower than at present and that, except for a possible temporary halt some 7000 or 8000 years ago, sea level has continued to rise, though of late at a slower rate, without "any indication of a postglacial sea level higher than that of the present."

6. Our ideas of climate in the last glacial time must be revised. The Mankato advance was not in phase with the last major European advance. The Mankato "effect" was somewhat extreme over the northwestern part of our interior plains, which normally have low precipitation and humidity. Toward its end there began a rise in ocean temperatures, succeeding a long time of steadily low sea temperatures. Thus a different pattern of atmospheric circulation

[9] Cesare Emiliani, Notes on Absolute Chronology of Human Evolution, Science, Vol. 123, 1956, pp. 924–926.

[10] Ewing and Donn, op. cit., p. 1062.

[11] Latest data on Atlantic Ocean cores supporting the critical rise in ocean temperatures beginning about 11,000 years ago are given by D. B. Ericson and others, Late-Pleistocene Climates and Deep-Sea Sediments, Science, Vol. 121, 1956, pp. 385–389.

[12] F. P. Shepard and H. E. Suess, Rate of Postglacial Rise of Sea Level, Science, Vol. 123, 1956, pp. 1082–1083.

must have prevailed, which, at the end of Mankato time, appears to have been rather abruptly replaced by the one under which we live. What movement of air masses could have freighted in moist oceanic air to the Far North and to the heart of the continent so as to feed snow to the icecap and western mountains and to reduce evaporation over the Great Plains and the Great Basin?

Ewing and Donn [13] have proposed an attractive new theory of Ice Ages, which dispenses with changes in solar radiation and with other extraterrestrial causes. It proposes for the beginning of the Ice Age a migration of the North Pole from the North Pacific into the Arctic Ocean, into "positions very favorable for the development of glacial climates," from which resulted the stages of the Ice Age by "alternations of ice-covered and ice-free states of the surface of the Arctic Ocean." The major deployment of continental icecaps throughout the Pleistocene was adjacent to the North Atlantic Ocean. Significant sea-temperature changes in the Pleistocene are thought by the authors to have been limited mainly to the Atlantic and Arctic Oceans. They conclude that the "temperature of the surface layer of the ocean, rather than external conditions, regulated the climate of the land," and that there occurred "fairly abrupt alternations between warm and cold conditions of the upper layer of the Atlantic and Arctic oceans." "When the Arctic Ocean is ice-covered, surface temperatures in the Atlantic increase and continental glaciers decline; when the Arctic is open, surface temperatures in the Atlantic decrease, and continental glaciers develop." The theory rests on evidence supplied by the cores taken from deep ocean floors, and also on the effects of sea-level changes caused by glaciation and deglaciation on the interchange of Arctic and Atlantic surface water. The atmospheric circulation during a glacial stage is inferred as having a major low-pressure area centered over an open Arctic Ocean. An old theory newly revised is built on newly available data and deserves most careful attention. The geophysicists and oceanographers are likely for some time to continue to make the major contributions to our understanding of these past conditions.

PALEOLITHIC MAN AND CULTURE

What do we know of the human witnesses to this critical turn in earth history? What of the people who lived near the edge of the icecap, by the lakes ponded by the ice front and filled with

---

[13] Ewing and Donn, *op. cit.,* Quotation on pp. 1062 and 1066.

meltwaters, along the streams swollen with summer floods from the glaciers, using the vegetation cover as it then existed, and hunting game animals that have since disappeared? In cultural terms the time is the last part of the Upper Paleolithic, the last of the Old Stone Age. We shall use the conventional terms, since nothing else is current, though both ways and people are set off strongly from those of earlier Paleolithic time. Both in Europe and in North America the Upper Paleolithic was a time of hunters of big game. The hunters are known to us mainly by the cleverly worked weapons and implements with which they took and prepared their kill. These were blades and points of "flint," and also of bone and antler. Physically, the people were in an unambiguous sense modern men, *Homo sapiens* without any qualification.

The term "Paleolithic" is of European origin and is freely applied throughout the Old World. It denotes certain kinds and levels of culture that have a known position in time, after which they were replaced by, or changed into, other ways and skills. As yet "Upper Paleolithic" is hardly admitted to good usage in the New World, though we have long known that our admittedly older archeology has consisted, in its nonperishable remains, of artifacts of Paleolithic aspect. The exclusion of the term from the New World is due to the old doctrine that anything human turned up in this hemisphere must be markedly postglacial and hence later than Paleolithic time.

THE DOCTRINE OF POSTGLACIAL PEOPLING OF THE NEW WORLD

The doctrine of the postglacial entry of man into the New World arose more than half a century ago and had its origin in the then prevailing views as to the age of true man, alias *Homo sapiens,* or Neanthropic man, and of his relation to the Ice Age. In those days it was thought that true man first appeared on the scene with Cro-Magnon man and his contemporaries in Europe, that is, with the bearers of Aurignacian and other cultures that replaced the Mousterian arts of Neanderthal man (the statement is not distorted by its simplification). It was then thought that this first appearance of true man took place very near the end of the last glaciation (final phase of Fourth or Würm stage). Since man had to migrate from the Old World to the New, it seemed to make sense that he could not have appeared here until postglacial time.

Moreover, no Neanderthal man, then considered the predecessor of *sapiens* man, was (or is) known over here. Therefore there could be no claim for human antiquity in the New World beyond a safely postglacial time. Thus I was taught as a young student, by no less than Professors Chamberlin and Salisbury, who got their anthropologic views from Hrdlička and W. H. Holmes.

However, by subsequent study the appearance in Europe of Cro-Magnon folk, their associates, and the Aurignacian and Chatelperronian cultures has been moved far back in time and is now referred to the early part of the Fourth Glaciation (to the time between Würm I and II, which by our insecure reckoning might be the Peorian interval between the Iowan and Tazewell glaciations). However uncertain we still are of any absolute chronology beyond the present reach of radiocarbon tests, the time span of post-Neanderthal man in Europe is a sizable multiple of postglacial time. The first objection, therefore, has fallen.

Moreover, the classic thesis that *sapiens* man came later than Neanderthal man means little today, since such *sapiens*-type remains as Fontechevade and Swanscombe have been found and are earlier than any known real Neanderthal remains. As has the succession, so has the evolution of *sapiens* man out of Neanderthal ancestry lost probability. We are not further concerned here with such matters beyond the notation that all original bases for a much-delayed entry of man into the New World have become invalid. The reasons having failed, prejudice alone may continue to object to comparison of common elements and sources of Old and New World prehistory.

Thus I think also that it is time to stop speaking of our earlier colonists as "Paleoindians." This is another derivative of the invalid doctrine that is maintained only by thoughtless use of the word "Indian." Our primordial folk are no more to be identified in terms of living races than are those of Europe or Africa.

We shall not deal here with the time of original human settlement of the New World. This is far older than the Mankato and Dryas time of 12,000 to 10,000 years ago, for which alone a cultural comparison is attempted here.[14] Since Europe at that time still held a Paleolithic culture, it is appropriate as to both time and content to speak of contemporary culture in America, or the New World, as "Paleolithic."

---

[14] Prompt and adequate reports of these developments have appeared in American Antiquity.

THE EUROPEAN UPPER PALEOLITHIC

In Europe the time of the Dryas-Baltic Ice Lake was the final period of Upper Paleolithic cultures. Over much of Europe the people were the late Magdalenian hunters, less expert than their predecessors in shaping fine cutting blades and points of stone, but working artfully in many forms with bone and antler, as in harpoons. In southwestern Europe they used rock shelters to some extent, but they lived mainly and widely in the open, ranging over the plains in pursuit of herds of big game. Lately another hunting culture has become known about the North Sea lowlands, which is named after Hamburg. The Hamburg people, after the milder Allerød interval, were followed by a similar lot, the Ahrensburg folk of Younger Dryas time. Both were highly mobile hunters, moving with the seasons. Both are thought to have depended on reindeer as almost their sole game, following the animals that grazed on the tundralike vegetation of the North Sea and Baltic plains. It is now known that all three groups used the bow and arrow along with the older weapons and that they dwelt in roomy tents. The Hamburg and Ahrensburg folk "appear from nowhere" [15] and are thought to have come out of the East. They are the last of the Paleolithic men and habits. After Younger Dryas time the spread of Mesolithic ways began; the great game animals were no longer the staple about which economy and living ways were organized.

THE NORTH AMERICAN UPPER PALEOLITHIC

Our knowledge of this period in North America would be greater were it not for the long dominance of the doctrine of the postglacial entry of man into the New World. When a discovery of ancient man was announced, there was always an adverse opinion from someone who knew that it couldn't be so. Year after year newly found evidence was rejected as incompetent or insufficient. Much of what was found in the early years is no longer available for re-examination, but some of the sites can be restudied. The change in

---

[15] A. Rust, Die jüngere Altsteinzeit, *in* Historia Mundi, Vol. 1 (Bern, 1952), pp. 288–317. A synoptic chronologic table appears at the end of the volume.

attitude began with the discovery at Folsom, New Mexico, in 1926, of an extinct form of bison, hunted by man. The Denver Museum people who worked the site took every step necessary to validate the association. Later, Kirk Bryan established the late-glacial age of a Folsom-culture site at Lindenmeier, Colorado. Year by year the rate of discovery of early man has increased. From the beginning at Folsom to the present it has been mainly persons attached to museums in the trans-Missouri West and the Southwest who have advanced the recovery of early man and his cultures.[16]

It is apparent that a notable series of cultural differences existed in North America by the end of the Wisconsin glacial stage. The diversity increases steadily as inquiry continues. I wish to suggest that we can now recognize three principal cultures, each ecologically based. I am not suggesting that these originated in, or were introduced into, America at this time, or that they disappeared with the end of the period, but only that they were contemporaries of the Mankato glaciation, and hence are our latest Paleolithic inhabitants.

THE OLD BISON HUNTERS

The best-known and probably the largest and most widely distributed lot were specialized hunters of big game. Sellards happily has named them the "Bison Hunters," as distinguished from his earlier "Elephant Hunters." The bison, of large, extinct species, was almost as dominantly the staple of life as was the reindeer for the late Upper Paleolithic people of northern Europe. Other now extinct forms of big game were taken here and there, but never as a basic resource. The known range of the Old Bison Hunters is chiefly the Great Plains, where the bison seem to have gathered in herds as the Plains buffalo did in historic time. The hunters mainly camped in the open and shifted camp as the game moved, like the historic hunting tribes of the Great Plains. There was no tundra or tundralike condition. Grass and browse were available throughout the year, though reduced in winter, as now, by snow and cold.

---

[16] An able summary of the growth of knowledge to 1949 is given by H. M. Wormington, Ancient Man in North America, Denver Museum of Nat. Hist. Popular Ser. No. 4, 3rd edit., 1949. Miss Wormington is curator of archeology in the Denver Museum. See also E. H. Sellards: Early Man in America (Texas Memorial Museum, Austin, 1952). Dr. Sellards, who has worked in this field longest, and with admirable persistence, stresses the sites he has investigated as geologist and paleontologist.

The best-delineated culture is known as the "Folsom complex," recognized by the fluted, elegantly shaped, and sharply edged Folsom points and blades. Somewhat different techniques of making blades and points, resulting in other forms (such as "laurel leaf"), were used by other groups of the Old Bison Hunters. These latter artifacts are now called technically Parallel Flaked Points, with a number of specifically named types,[17] but they are still known collectively to the nonprofessional as "Yuma" (from a Colorado locality). An especially notable site of Yuman character was excavated by Sellards [18] and associates at Plainview, Texas, in the headwaters of the Brazos River, where the remains of about a hundred of the extinct bison were found with dart and spear (?) points and hide (?) scrapers. The several bison-hunting groups attained a skill in shaping points and blades that is not surpassed by stone tools anywhere else in the world; the finishing is characterized by special techniques of pressure flaking.

Folsom and Yuma points and blades have been found in many parts of the United States, as well as in Mexico, Canada, and Alaska, mostly without determination of their age, though similar age may be inferred and similar culture. These, for the most part, may be of any time when the Old Bison Hunters flourished. It is unlikely that hunters of this sort failed to range through the eastern woodlands at the same time that they occupied the High Plains. South from the Great Lakes to the Gulf of Mexico the land at that time provided good feed for herbivorous creatures great and small, including the earlier bison. If there was less grass than to the west, there was more browse and no lack of water. Though water holes did not attract congregations of animals as in the drier lands (and thereby fix campsites), salt licks did so, and some of these, as in Kentucky, were noted early by pioneers as flanked by bone beds, since destroyed. The bits of knowledge about early man in the East have not yet been fitted into a chronologic pattern, but it is hardly thinkable that at whatever times he lived in the West he was not equally at home in the East, as far north as the glacial border.

OLD BASKETMAKER CULTURE

A different culture complex, known from the Great Basin, awaits naming and proper description. For the time here considered the

---

[17] Wormington, *op. cit.*

[18] *Op. cit.* [see footnote 16], pp. 60–68.

story begins with Mark Harrington's excavations in Gypsum Cave, Nevada, near Las Vegas.[19] The cave was occupied by man when the ground sloth, camel, and horse were living in the locality. Distinctive dart points and their painted shafts were recovered. Of special interest is a piece of basketry under a seal of stalagmite. Its position has been questioned because it appeared at the time of discovery to be too early for such technique. The available radiocarbon dates, from sloth dung within the time of human occupation, are 10,075 and 10,092 years.

In southeastern Oregon, Luther Cressman located sandals, basketry, and parts of a fire drill and of a dart thrower beneath volcanic ash in Fort Rock Cave. The radiocarbon dates are 9188 and 8916.[20] In excavating Danger Cave, near Wendover, Utah, Jennings found four fireplaces used when the cave was just above the Stansbury level of Lake Bonneville.[21] A date of about 11,300 years has been given for the lowest cultural layer. At the base of the next-higher cultural horizon (dated 9300 years) two twined baskets were found.

The newest discovery is by Phil Orr[22] in Fishbone Cave, above dry Winnemucca Lake in western Nevada. This wave-worn recess has dates of 11,555 and 10,900 for material out of the early culture stratum. Wood of juniper in quantity and bones of woodchuck, both now absent from the region, give evidence of cooler, moister conditions at the time, as does the former lake. By good fortune, fires by later occupants failed to destroy the organic materials in one part of the lower occupation bed to which the dates above apply. Here Orr found two-strand cordage, a burial with pelican skin and a piece of fine netting made by square knots, fragments of wicker basketry, some finely woven twined-basketry fragments, and matting with weft twining. These articles are illustrated in the report and show notably good technical skill. Orr says: "Had Fishbone Cave been an open site without perishables we would have found several 'crude scrapers,' some split and burned camel and horse bones, and we would probably have described a 'simple culture.'"

These Great Basin shelters have given us the world's earliest records of cordage, matting, basketry, and fiber sandals, products of arts previously thought to be later inventions, of Mesolithic time. Desert caves, it is true, provide exceptional conditions for preserva-

[19] Summarized by both Wormington and Sellards.
[20] Summarized by both Wormington and Sellards.
[21] Jennings, *op. cit.*
[22] Orr, *op. cit.*

tion of perishable materials, but such an inventory is hardly appropriate to mobile hunters of big game. The Basin people sought out rock shelters for habitation, in part at the side of now-vanished lakes. Their ingenuity was directed toward working with plant fibers rather than with rawhide and the dressing of skins. Netting and various waterfowl remains suggest that aquatic birds were netted; it seems probable that fish would also have been taken. The first outlines of a markedly different culture are here indicated, perhaps foreshadowing ways of sedentary living based on the utilization of plant materials and water resources. Provisionally, we may call this complex the "Old Basketmaker culture."

ANCIENT MILLER CULTURE

A third major culture, it would seem, was present in the United States in late Pleistocene time, characterized by milling, or mealing, stones. On a portable slab of rock food was ground by rubbing and crushing with a handstone (*mano*), a process known in the Old World only well within Mesolithic time. We may term the people the "Ancient Millers."

The first recognition of the notable antiquity of such a culture was by David Rogers [23] of the Santa Barbara Museum of Natural History. Rogers called these early inhabitants of the Santa Barbara coast the "Oak Grove People." He located village sites in number, always in the open air, on hilltops and terraces, and usually marked by oak groves. Each village was "composed of from five to twenty semisubterranean dirt-bank huts—circular—from thirteen to fifteen feet in diameter," with "a hard, firmly packed floor of ash and clay with a fireplace occupying the center." The induration of the floors of these sites is indeed marked: a *caliche* or "hardpan" has been formed by long weathering. The milling bases and handstones are partly, and a few are greatly, disintegrated by weathering. Rogers' work did not receive the attention it deserved, perhaps because it was done before the presence of early man was taken seriously in California. It remains a notable pioneer study, which could not be fully repeated today because of the destruction of sites by suburban development. Rogers was able to estimate age by surface and weathering changes only. Orr, his successor in the museum, and the person most competent in the natural history of the Santa Bar-

---

[23] D. B. Rogers, Prehistoric Man of the Santa Barbara Coast (Santa Barbara Museum of Natural History, Santa Barbara, California, 1929).

bara Channel, has recently said: "Contrary to the literature, there is excellent reason to think that the Mainland Oak Grove extends back into the Wisconsin period." [24]

Jennings found grinding stones at Danger Cave also and has wondered, "Could the flat milling stone and a subsistence upon seeds be originally an American invention of 10,000 years ago?" [25] Here milling and basketmaking may occur together.

The earliest (Sulphur Springs) archeologic horizon of the Cochise basin in southeastern Arizona is characterized by large milling stones and small handstones and is thought to have been basically a plant-food-gathering economy. It is true that the radiocarbon dates here are only 7756 and 6210 years, but these I hold suspect. The accompanying fauna is diverse and markedly Pleistocene, including, according to Chester Stock, the imperial elephant (*Archidiskodon*).[26] The plant remains also record a cooler and more humid climate; for example, the presence of hickory. I do not understand how a fauna and flora of a Pleistocene Pluvial climate could have lingered in a low basin in southern Arizona, now arid and hot, long after such a condition had ended to the north and east. The site lies in the lower part of a wide, occasionally flooded basin. The possibility of contamination with younger Carbon must therefore be considered.

Crude milling stones and manos occur widely in the older archeologic sites from the valley of California to Venezuela and usually are absent from later ones. There is no doubt of a widely distributed mealing and milling culture early in our archeologic series; that it reaches back into Mankato time and beyond is probable.

CULTURAL LIKENESS AND CONTRAST
BETWEEN OLD WORLD AND NEW

The cultural likenesses between Old World and New at this time were few, the contrasts strong. In Europe the bow and arrow had

---

[24] Phil C. Orr, Radiocarbon Dates from Santa Rosa Island, I, Santa Barbara Museum of Nat. Hist. Dept. of Anthropol. Bull. No. 2, 1956, p. 1.

[25] Jennings, *op. cit.*, p. 205. See also J. D. Jennings and Edward Norbeck, Great Basin Prehistory: A Review, Amer. Antiquity, Vol. 21, 1955–1956, pp. 1–11.

[26] E. B. Sayles and Ernst Antevs, The Cochise Culture, Medallion Papers No. 29, Globe, Arizona, 1941, p. 64.

become the principal weapon, employed by tent-dwelling reindeer hunters of the northern plains. In the southwest, around the Pyrenees, the astonishing genius of Magdalenian cave art still lived. Nothing of the sort is known or probable on this side of the ocean. Here the spear, dart thrower, and cutting blade, of a workmanship rarely equaled, continued an older European tradition of weapons. The use of the bow and arrow appears to have been unknown here until some later time; their introduction into the New World is thought to have been relatively late, possibly associated with people who brought the dog. Nor is there any early record of tents. But by the end of Mankato time there were in America folk who were adept at ropemaking, netting, and basketmaking—arts not reported from Europe until later. Also, it is probable that we had a milling culture at the same time, processing acorns, small seeds, and perhaps nuts. This seems to mean that women had learned to bake starch foods.

For the Old Bison Hunters and their kind we have long native antecedents in what Sellards calls the "Elephant Hunters." These earlier hunters lived upon other extinct big game of more remote time. It appears that their weapons and tools may well have furnished the models from which Folsom and Yuma points and blades were derived. The resemblances between the Solutrean and Gravettian blade cultures of Europe and ours have often been noted, but the time disparity has been considered too great. However, the European cultures are now dated as having existed within twenty thousand years, later than dates now ascribed to our Sandia and Clovis cultures, either of which may have been ancestral to Folsom and Yuma. These several blade types of similar techniques may well stem from a common ancestry. For Europe, Rust [27] has said that "somewhere and at some time the Upper Paleolithic must have developed out of older forms of a flaking industry that was leading to blade forms. To which we can say that this did not take place in the hitherto studied parts of Europe, the Near East, or Africa." Did such a common hearth lie in some unglaciated part of inner or northern Asia and send offshoots into western Europe and interior North America? That it did not do so by continuous dispersal is apparent. The near coincidence of time in both worlds reduces the probability that each invented independently such parallel techniques and forms.

The background of our primordial cordmakers and basketmakers

---

[27] Rust, *op. cit.*, p. 292.

and of the millers is still completely enigmatic and may remain so until we know more about other, probably still earlier, lithic sites of crude stoneworking that lack projectile points.

SOURCE OF NEW WORLD CULTURES

The suggestion in the preceding remarks is that Mankato time and the time immediately preceding and following were inauspicious for the entry of immigrants from Asia into the interior of our continents. For instance, the late appearance of the bow and arrow (and of the dog) in the New World suggests a long interruption of communication out of Asia.

The Mankato ice spread far over the western plains toward the Canadian Rockies. There is no indication that it was preceded by any significant deglaciation. Formerly, Late Wisconsin glaciation was held to include both the Mankato and the Cary advances. There is still reason to consider that they are phases of one substage. Both are known almost only from their southern margins, which tell us only that the maximum Cary advance was deployed about the Great Lakes and was followed shortly by a more westerly thrust of the Mankato phase toward the Missouri River. No major recession is known to have intervened; the few available radiocarbon dates do not attribute more than a few thousand years to the Cary advance. An ice-free corridor along the eastern base of the Canadian Rockies is more probable earlier than in Late Wisconsin time. Whenever in Wisconsin time such a passageway existed, if it did, it would have been available only to folk able to live under the extreme cold of continental Arctic weather, as in the never-glaciated Yukon Basin and in the plains of western Canada.

The problem of ingress of man into the New World thus remains difficult. Alaska was accessible at most times from the Siberian Arctic lowlands if there were hunters who could provide for themselves through the Arctic winters. The great lowlands of Alaska, and even much of the high country of the upper Yukon drainage basin, remained unglaciated during all glacial stages because of low winter temperatures and light snowfall. A recent study of wildlife in Alaska [28] shows that winter survival of the larger game, especially caribou, depends on reindeer lichens, which do not grow in

---

[28] A. S. Leopold and F. F. Darling, Wildlife in Alaska: An Ecological Reconnaissance (New York, 1953).

muskeg or wet tundra, but mainly in the dry tundra of ridges and in the margins of spruce forests. For moose, winter browse of willow, aspen, and birch is of major importance. If we project these range conditions backward in time, it would appear that, irrespective of the kind of big game, the critical winter range still lay above the plains, in the foothills where drainage was better or else in dissected and drained plains when sea level was significantly lower. The Alaska climate well back into glacial time probably made demands on human inhabitants as exacting as it does at present.

Men could have skirted the glacial barriers of Canada by moving south along the Pacific shore if they had sufficient boating and fishing skills. The shores of Alaska that face the open Pacific were probably out of the question by reason of their stormy seas and thick weather. However, provident and winter-hardy fishermen might have followed the great runs of salmon and other anadromous fish up the Yukon well into Canadian territory. If they got so far, an occasionally ice-free pass, such as the Whitehorse, might have provided a crossing southward to the fiords and channels of the Inland Passage of British Columbia. We have no knowledge, however, that the necessary skills were present.

A hyperborean thesis is now revived, that people may have lived "beyond the north wind" on Arctic shores. It was suggested to Ewing and Donn by the Arctic studies of Giddings.[29] According to this hypothesis, the Arctic Ocean was open during glacial stages, and its margins would have been habitable for man during glacial stages. The occasional Alaskan finds of Yuma oblique and Folsom points might then have real significance. Bits of evidence may possibly be found to add up to an ancient story of Ice Age man distributed all along the shores of the Arctic Ocean. The inquiry will face many difficulties; the occupation sites have been churned by solifluction and ground-ice formation; shore lines have changed by both isostatic and eustatic displacements. We may admit, however, the possibility that the shores of the Arctic Ocean harbored Ice Age people. In that case, dwellers on the Arctic coast may have found early routes into the United States by following eastward to the Atlantic. This is indeed drawing a long bow, but all shots into this target are long.

The old, simple belief that man waited at the threshold of the New World until the last ice sheet was gone has been proved wrong. The late growth of knowledge of his remains and of the nature of

[29] J. L. Giddings, Jr., Early Man in the Arctic, Scientific American, Vol. 190, 1954, pp. 82–88.

the Ice Age has not yet disclosed how or when or how often he entered from the Old World. But the last phase of the Ice Age is only an intermediate chapter to be taken into account in the peopling of the New World.

14

Fire and Early Man

THE ANTIQUITY OF MAN

Pleistocene Period, Ice Age, and Age of Man have been used as loosely interchangeable terms for latest geologic time, a time that extends to the present if we are still living in an interglacial stage, as has been suggested. The beginning of this period, it was thought, was marked by the onset of glaciation in high mountains and out of high latitudes, for which the first stage, the Alpine term Günz, came into use in Europe; in North America Nebraskan was applied to what was considered its equivalent in time. The convenient marker of such a "first glacial stage" has become less and less satisfactory as more has been learned of preceding events. The chart of geologic time thus coming under new scrutiny, the entry of man is also claiming further attention. Two questions need to be considered, the revision of the geologic time scale and the evidences of the antiquity of man.

A time of Plio-Pleistocene transition has been accepted rather widely, but in 1948 the International Geological Congress resolved to assign this span to the Pleistocene period. Thus the Villafranchian-Calabrian series, previously classed as the latest phases of Pliocene, became the Lower Pleistocene and the old-style Lower Pleistocene became the Middle Pleistocene. If dividing lines are to be preferred to transition zones, the revision of the geologic chart is justifiable. The more important changes of fauna, both terrestrial and marine, took place well before, not at the conventional beginning of the Pleistocene and its "first Glaciation." These changes of life forms are held to be connected with an alteration of climatic conditions in the direction of the Pleistocene pattern. Also there was glaciation, probably repeatedly, in the Alps before the Günz stage; and the same appears to have been true in the

Paideuma: Mitteilungen zur Kulturkunde, Vol. 7, 1961, pp. 399–407.

Rocky Mountains. Marine terraces that mark the high-sea stages of interglacial times and which were thus first identified and named along Mediterranean shores are preceded by similar terraces at higher levels that cannot be ascribed to the Pleistocene sequence of the older definition. There were good reasons therefore for wanting to put the start of the last geologic period farther back in geologic time, actually about doubling the duration of the Pleistocene. Unfortunately we now have two systems in use, some following the new system, others adhering to the older usage, neither perhaps saying which calendar is being used.

An estimate of a million years from the beginning of the Günz or Nebraskan glaciation to the present has long been current. It is an educated guess that rests mainly on the differential weathering and erosion of glacial materials and surfaces in their sequence or origin, as best shown perhaps in the areas covered by the successive continental ice caps in North America. The classical study of the recurrent cutting (glacial) and alluviation (interglacial) of the lower Mississippi Valley by Harold Fisk, concurred in by R. J. Russell, arrived at a similar chronology. The attempt by Milankovitch to compute the length of stages of the Pleistocene (from Günz on) reduced the elapsed time to about six hundred thousand years; this astronomy-based system has had and still has wide acceptance, especially among archeologists. It has not been well received by climatologists. There have been still later proposals of further reduction of the time span.

Geophysical measures are now being applied to determine absolute age. The most advanced of these for the time in question is by determining rate of conversion of a potassium isotope into its argon one, developed in the Department of Geology of the University of California at Berkeley under the direction of J. F. Evernden and G. H. Curtis.[1] They have thus sampled the volcanic tuffs of Olduvai Gorge in Tanganyika and found an age of 1.75 million years for its recently archeologically famous Bed I, known as carrying a Villafranchian fauna. This is by a very wide margin the earliest date attached to hominid remains (Zinjanthropus) and culture (Olduwan).[2]

---

[1] Principle and method are described in Garniss H. Curtis, A Clock for the Ages: Potassium-Argon, National Geographic Magazine, Vol. 120, 1961, pp. 590–592.

[2] Announced in L. S. B. Leakey, J. F. Evernden, and G. H. Curtis, Age of Bed I, Olduvai Gorge, Tanganyika, Nature, Vol. 191, 1961, pp. 478–479. L. S. B. Leakey, Exploring 1,750,000 Years into Man's Past, National Geographic Magazine, Vol. 120, 1961, pp. 564–589, is a popular account.

Other Pleistocene dates by K/A determination that are of major interest are these: *a*. Volcanic tuff covering morainic deposits of the Sierra Nevada in the area of Bishop, California, ranges in age from 0.9 to 1.2 million years. Whether this is a mountain equivalent of the continental Nebraskan cannot be said. *b*. Samples provided from the Trinil beds of Java (Java Man) give an age around .5 million years. *c*. The Chellean level of Torre at Pietra in Italy has an age of 0.42 to 0.44 million years.[3]

The potassium-argon procedure is competent, and the results are consistent for an impressive series of analyses, such as for the whole of Tertiary time in western North America. Corrections are to be expected by resampling to eliminate sources of contamination and distortion.

This new physical measurement of time tends to confirm the views that the Ice Age (as of the old-style terminology) covered a million years and that it is doubled in length by the inclusion of the Villafranchian. It has established a high age of the human remains and culture in East Africa and thereby emphasizes the exceeding slowness of early cultural development. The age of Java Man, if validly sampled, would then seem to be about the same as that of the more highly evolved and advanced Swanscombe Man of the Thames Basin, for which a position in the Mindel-Riss interglacial is assured.

The short chronology of the Ice Age and of early man appears to have become untenable, by mounting evidence. Archeology is faced with a large revision of the calendar of early human events.

ACQUAINTANCE WITH VOLCANIC FIRE

That Africa is the cradle of our kind is hardly under controversy any longer. Even before Dr. Leakey uncovered Zinjanthropus or described an Olduwan culture, East Africa was getting preferential attention for human origins. Spade and pick are documenting on the archeologic record the superior location of East Africa as suitable diversified environment for the primate groundling who was becoming man and as center from which he began to disperse into far parts of the three joined continents.

---

[3] Quoted by the kind permission of Dr. Curtis from paper presented by Evernden and Curtis, Present Status of Potassium-Argon Dating, International Association for Quaternary Research, 6th Conference, Warsaw, 1961.

Olduvai Gorge, from which we are supplied with the earliest dated human habitat, lies in the high volcanic country of Tanganyika. The fact that the dating was possible is due to the cover of volcanic tuff that was spread massively over the occupied sites. The inhabitants of Olduvai lived in the immediate presence of active vulcanism, an outbreak of which marked securely their presence and activity in a primordial Pompeii.

East Africa, still a land of volcanoes, was much more so at the time when the human record begins. The faults along which the rift valleys have sunk were active, with frequent vulcanism accompanying crustal movement. Lakes were in process of forming on the sinking crustal blocks and by damming of drainage through volcanic flows and detritus. The longest depression riven through the ancient table land runs from Lake Nyasa north to the Red Sea in Eritrea; another holds the lakes Tanganyika and Albert and extends to the Nile. Land forms and water bodies were being made, changed, or destroyed. Relief was increased by faulting and the building up of volcanic cones. The mature soils and surfaces of the older plateau were covered to a considerable extent by beds of ash, cinders, or lava. Old lines of drainage were stopped and new ones formed. An intricately variant lot of land forms, great and small, replaced an earlier simplicity.

Such areas of young vulcanism have diversity of micro-environments, edaphically and climatically. A *malpais* of broken lava or volcanic bombs is of minutely textured ecologic pattern. Cinder and ash beds differ a lot in their capacities of storing and yielding water. Hot and cold springs and their mineral content and deposits about pools diversify the hydrologic environment. The large assemblage of physical forms and qualities provides attractive habitats for an unusual range of plants and animals. The primitive collector, lacking special skills, could pick, dig, turn over rocks, and find food in variety and quantity.

A volcanic outbreak may wipe out life over an area, but also open it to fresh stocking by a pioneer vegetation, the fire succession of freely-seeding, rapidly-growing annuals and perennials that thrive on sunlight and the quick fertilizing by plant ashes. The new vegetation in turn attracts the entry and increase of a new fauna profiting by the abundance of seed, leaf, and shoot. Insects, lizards, birds, small mammals, and even ruminants may thus benefit. In California, for example, the rapid increase of rodent and deer populations after heavy burning is well known. Such temporary fire gardens and feed lots may be inferred to have added to the foraging success of the early human inhabitants who were at hand.

Volcanic outbreaks kill by heat and by smothering. The smaller and slower creatures may seek safety by hiding underground, the larger and fleeter ones by flight. After the fire the burned tract provides carcasses to be picked up and dug up, perhaps tubers and roots that were roasted in the ground. Such opportunity for mass harvest provided also the earliest experience of the taste of roast flesh and skin and of cooked plant starches and proteins. The omnivorous human digestive tract, like the unspecialized hand man retained, are basic to the direction (and success) of hominid evolution. Rejection of nourishing food has no place in primitive economy and society, even in historic time. Primitive foraging is also scavenging, with little concern as to the state of the flesh. Animals fleeing in panic from such natural fires could be clubbed down, especially the young and infirm or disabled ones.

The African record shows that very early man lived in the presence of fire that broke out or rained down about him. The catastrophes that occasionally overtook him were compensated by the livelihood to be gained. That there might be sudden and common danger perhaps served to stimulate his wits, sharpen his attentiveness, and perhaps even to select the breed. The hazards at any rate did not turn him away from living in such places. Through the ages volcanic lands have attracted occupation by man.

RIPARIAN ORIGINS?

The ecologic niche in which a ground-living and -feeding primate could develop into the human kind has been construed variously. A current stereotype is of such emergent or early human as wandering about freely on tropical savannas, usually thought of as plains, in search mainly of flesh, and thus characterized as of carnivorous habits. The bias therefore is toward mobility, organization into bands, provision of food largely dependent on male participation and prowess, and leadership by a dominating male. In this manner the model of late hunting societies living in special habitats is referred back in time to the rudimentary beginning of human society. I have taken exception to such a construction of primordial society, proposing instead a basis of maternal provision, the family, sedentary trend, and the selection of living sites where potable water and continuous and sufficient food were available close by, adding up to a riparian habitat as providing the original ecologic niche for mankind.[4]

If we accept, in terms of our present knowledge, the East African cradle of the human kind, there are two attractive options, the shores of the adjacent Indian Ocean and the lakes of the interior high country. Bed I in Olduvai Gorge was a living site by the side of water, as is shown by its remains of fish and frogs. Lakes like those of the present and also lesser ones were to be found in the rift valleys and beyond in the highland. The ocean shores to the east I should judge to have been more favorable to human evolution and the beginning of culture. The sea offered plenty of food, in diversity, daily and in all seasons and the choice of permanent places to live. The seashore had pebbles and cobbles, shells, and seasoned wood at hand for immediate use and for fashioning into tools. The seashore regulated activity by the daily and monthly rhythm of the tides. Observing the phases of the moon as connected with the tides, mankind should first have learned awareness of the ordered passage of time beyond the monotonous tropical succession of day and night. I should think that the tropical seaside provided the optimal location for the origin of man and his culture and that thence the road of some of the early descendants led to the lake sides of the high interior where they found somewhat similar but more limited means of living. In the interior they met up with seasons of rain and of drought, of which they were scarcely aware by the sea. Also they experienced to some extent the discomforts of nightly cold at the higher elevations.

THE ACQUISITION OF FIRE

The old view that the use of fire was developed very early, following upon that of tools and speech, lately has been sharply challenged by the archeologic record. It is objected that the early sites, such as those in Olduvai Gorge, show no evidence of the employment of fire. The earliest generally admitted site of fire-using man is that of Choukoutien inhabited by Peking Man, the age being uncertain but perhaps of the Second (Mindel-Riss) Interglacial. Thereafter, it has been inferred, followed a long interval without use of fire, its continuing and regular employment beginning

[4] Carl O. Sauer, Seashore—Primitive Home of Man?, Proceedings of the American Philosophical Society, Vol. 106, 1962, pp. 41–47; this volume, pp. 300–312.

only with the Neanderthal and Fontechevade people at or prior to the onset of the Würm Glaciation. Thus Carleton Coon argues vigorously that fire was first employed to keep warm in cold climates, such as by Peking Man, and only much later for cooking.[5] If we try to put this into time elapsed, there would be fire-lacking Zinjanthropus and his fashioned stones of 1.75 million years (as change of potassium to argon has been measured), Peking Man as pioneer of housewarming a half million years ago more or less, and the beginning of cooking only about a hundred and fifty thousand years ago.

The archeologic sampling is far too small and localized to accept one or a few sites as marking a *terminus a quo.* There are still very, very few sites known older than Mousterian, and these are presences but not beginnings; nor may absence of perishable things be construed, from absence in the record. Charcoal and ashes are lost from open-air sites. Rock shelters waste away. The few really old sites of human habitation that are known owe their preservation to some uncommon protection. The occasional ancient site that has been discovered is likely to be a remnant of the original one.

There are disputed cases of early use of fire: *Australopithecus prometheus,* also called the fire ape, lived in limestone shelters of South Africa which bear some evidence of fire. In the Red Crag of the East Anglian coast the controversy has not been about the presence of fire, which is admitted, but whether these are true eoliths or whether the stones were fashioned by natural forces. In the years when Reid Moir advanced his findings of humans in Britain as at and even before the onset of the first glaciation of the island, the weight of opinion was against such possibilities. It may be time to reopen the "eolith question." The presence of fire has been explained away too easily and in too many instances as the accidental sweeping-over of a site by a natural fire, usually thought of as caused by lightning. This dismissal of the problem is done without regard to the climatic position of the locality as to such probability and without knowledge of what a lightning strike does or does not do to stone or earth. Lack of evidence of fire has been construed as meaning that the people did not know its use; presence of fire has been explained away as due to natural origin.

In Tanganyika there is no doubt that primordial man was well acquainted with volcanic fire. It may be inferred that the same was true for the long stretch of volcanic lands of East Africa. When man moved northward into the eastern Mediterranean and east-

---

[5] Carleton S. Coon, The Story of Man (1954), pp. 60–63.

ward into Southeast Asia he lived again in an environment of vigorous vulcanism. Widely and early he was accustomed to living with and making use of the peculiar qualities and demands of such habitat. He patrolled warily the fringe of fire to knock over fleeing creatures; he searched over the burned area to harvest its casualties; he watched the restocking of an old burn with new life. The step from watching the effects of fire to using fire was bound to be taken. The awareness of fire was strong; attention became inquiry and this led to experiment. It may have taken time, perhaps a long time, before someone picked up a brand, carried it, and set a fire. It may have taken some more time before someone carried fire back home and fed it there. However it was done, curiosity was rewarded with success. Trial was followed by imitation, act led to desired effect, a new way of living was started. Man had broken the limitations of environment that had previously confined him. Henceforth he could make warmth where it was cold; he could scare away predators and drive creatures to their destruction; he could prepare food. We speak of mankind as masculine collectively, but the great innovation and its elaboration was mainly done by woman, keeper of the hearth and provider of food. The early capture of fire was from the hot insides of the earth; Prometheus came late, too late to be anything but a romantic myth.

ENTRY INTO COLD LANDS

We should not overestimate the differences between present climates and those of the Pleistocene past. We are living in a time of strongly contrasted climatic regions, the contrasts perhaps being more extreme than they were during a good deal of the time that we call Pleistocene. Perhaps we are still in a Pleistocene climatic regimen; and if so the present is an interglacial stage. The concern in the present context is with heat and cold rather than with wet or dry.

The complexities and uncertainties of climatic changes in the Ice Age need not concern us here, except to say that these are not resolved by saying that the glacial stages were cold and the interglacial ones warm. The continents were about as they are now, in latitudinal position, in extent, in relief, and in elevation. The last statement needs qualification: Before there were ice caps and during interglacial stages sea level stood high. The latitudes beyond the tropics experienced the seasonal cold of long nights and low sun. The interior of the Asiatic continent, chilled in winter and heated in summer, probably maintained a monsoonal circulation over the northern part of the Indian Ocean. The lands where winter never came were not greatly different in location or extent from the present.

Man, the only naked primate, can hardly have migrated beyond the genial climate of his origins without acquiring protection against cold. Huddling together under a natural shelter may have sufficed against the chill of night in low latitudes; in many parts tropical nights do get chilly. To enter lands having seasons of cold man needed the warmth of clothes or of fire. Fire he knew from his native home, and he could carry it with him. To cover his body with animal skins can hardly have been a first or decisive step in poleward or mountainward migration. Skins must be supple to be worn, and this requires their proper dressing by more than rudimentary skills. The skins of small animals, mainly the ones available to him, needed to be pieced together to serve, and this required other skills, such as sewing, braiding, or knotting. It would seem more likely that man learned, earlier than by clothing, how to protect his body against heat loss by rubbing himself with animal fat. This, however, again requires the use of heat.

The colonization of Europe beyond the mild Mediterranean shores I think improbable except by people who possessed fire. The inhabitants of the caves behind Peking lived through hard and long winters, the climate perhaps no less severe than at present. They could hardly have gotten that far except by bringing fire along as they moved northward. The dispersal of man into far places of Africa, Europe, and Asia took place when his cultural remains consisted of a small range of rudely-worked tools. That he passed barriers of cold thus early and widely points to the early possession of fire. The discoveries of ways of making fire came much later. The fire he took with him is considered to have been derived from the volcanic fires of his early home.

SUMMARY

The concern of the human geographer is to identify where human events take place and to make sense out of their localization. To this question of location (*Standort*) is attached that of migration, dispersal of persons, spread of ideas which include skills. Hettner called it the "Gang der Kultur über die Erde."

This occupation of the earth by man and his works may lead

us to look back toward his beginnings as far as we may see into the dim past. It appears increasingly that the cradle of our kind lay in Africa: the living and fossil primates point to such a place of origin, as do the oldest known hominid remains. The environmental range required for human emergence (*Menschwerdung*) was narrow, narrower than for many primates: ground habitat, low exposure to cold, high transpiration and frequent drinking, and low mobility through long maternal dependence of the young. Finally a geographic location was required from which suitable avenues led outward into different parts of the Old World continent. In all respects East Africa holds the superior location, lately supported by the Olduvai record.

In the origin of mankind a riparian habitat is inferred, peculiarly suited to his biologic evolution and to cultural beginnings. This special ecologic niche is not known to have been occupied by any other primate stock. Two kinds of riparian habitation were available in East Africa, the shores of the Indian Ocean and the lake country of the interior plateau. I have considered the former in the article cited, "Seashore: Primitive Home of Man?"; the interior lake country in the present one. The seashore may have offered superior advantages in food, materials for tools, and stimulation of social life. The lake country near-by is of the earliest known occupation, and gave its inhabitants the earliest familiarity with fire, of volcanic origin. It also served as corridor to the Congo river system and so to the South Atlantic and to the Nile and Mediterranean shores.

Instead of the currently popular model of earliest men as freely wandering bands dominated by a male leader, living in a nascent hunting society, the reconstruction here proposed is of primordial collecting ways in riparian habitats, the chief providers being the women, and the trend of human society directed toward sedentary and familial living from the beginning.

The first use of fire is attributed to the borrowing of fire that was set by vulcanism, the place the volcanic highlands of East Africa. The older view that fire entered very early into the making of man's culture is thus reaffirmed, whatever the order in which it came to be employed for protection, heating, harvesting, cooking, and the fashioning of tools. By taking it with him man could undertake to colonize lands climatically beyond his ecologic range. The archeologic record of his presence in lands of seasonal cold is interpreted as meaning that he had fire. By the possession of fire he was able to enter new environments and was securely started on his way towards dominating and modifying the world, the world of nature to become that of culture.

ADDENDUM: LIGHTNING FIRE

This has been written on the inference that volcanic fire is competent to account for the use of fire by man. The only other assured source of natural fire is lightning. Spontaneous combustion, sometimes cited as another source, is hardly of moment. I am not aware that organic matter accumulating in nature may build up the necessary heat in its decay or that the weathering of minerals, oxidation of pyrites having been that proposed, does so.

"The thunderstorm represents a violent and spectacular form of atmospheric convection. In its method of development it appears to be a cumulus cloud gone wild. Lightning and thunder, usually gusty winds, heavy rain, and occasionally hail, accompany it." [6] The point of interest here is the electrical discharge from cloud to earth, the lightning strike, which in most areas is accompanied by downpour of rain, and hence no firing of vegetation. In the eastern United States lightning scars can be seen on many living trees and also the lightning-riven trunks of dead ones. Not many areas equal it in the severity and frequency of thunder storms, without fire following.

Without violent convection thunderstorms do not form; and thus cold lands and those subjected to the inflow of stable maritime air lack them. Such are the extratropical western coasts of the continents in the main. Lightning strikes are much increased in frequency in mountainous terrain. Certain mountain areas are known for dry thunderstorms that create fire hazard. Such are of common warm-season occurrence in the mountains of the western interior United States that rise above arid and semi-arid land. Here strong differences in heating of ground and air and strong contrasts in relief and exposure set up local wildly turbulent convection that may trigger lightning strikes into dry ground cover, accompanied by little or no rain. It is not known that such areas commonly subject to lightning fires were accessible to primitive man.

The popular association of lightning with fire is mainly derived and dramatized from occasional happenings that are the result of civilization. Civilized man stores dry fuel in various ways, under

[6] H. R. Byers and R. R. Branham, The Thunderstorm: Report of the Thunderstorm Project (Washington, 1949), p. 17.

the roofs of houses, sheds, barns, in stacks of hay and grain, in piles of wood and lumber. He provides attractive points and prominences to attract and conduct the discharge by building towers, steeples, poles, gabled roofs, even by trees standing in open ground. And latterly he has strung wires for various purposes. The reports on fires caused by lightning do not distinguish between those that are culturally induced and those that are really natural.

We cannot assert that primitive man never saw a lightning fire anywhere. If he did so it was under most exceptional circumstances which did not encourage him to stay around and see what he could do with it. Nor may we invoke an unknown and unlikely past difference in the geography and nature of thunderstorms that would account for a Promethean capture of fire. We do know that the earliest known culture existed in familiar experience of volcanic fire. It is proposed that thus man learned the management of fire and that thence he took it with him in his dispersals.

15

Seashore—Primitive
Home of Man?

ANTIQUITY OF MAN

Since Professor Dart discovered the first Australopithecine remains in 1925, Africa has been central to the search for human
origins. The prescience of Charles Darwin that Africa was the
center of primate evolution and might be "the birthplace of man"
was noted in the recent Darwin centennials at the American Philosophical Society and at the University of Chicago. To the growing number and kind of South African finds there have been added
others from Kenya and Tanganyika in East Africa, mainly owing
to Dr. L. S. B. Leakey. At Olduvai Gorge in Tanganyika very early
and primitive human occupation, called Olduwan, was found in association with a Villafranchian fauna. In the summer of 1959 the
Leakeys found in an Olduwan camp site the skull and tibia of one
of its occupants, to be named *Zinjanthropus boisei* and recognized
as a major link in the lineage of man.

On the occasion of the Darwin Centennial of the American Philosophical Society Sir Wilfrid LeGros Clark was asked to give the
account of human evolution.[1] How well he succeeded is shown by
the fact that the shortly subsequent announcement of *Zinjanthropus*
confirmed and extended the presentation at Philadelphia. At the
Darwin Centennial of the University of Chicago the year following
Leakey gave his accordant version of *The Origin of the Genus Homo*
which placed *Zinjanthropus* and the Olduwan culture into general
context.[2]

Proceedings of the American Philosophical Society, Vol. 106, 1962, pp.
41–47.
    [1] Wilfrid E. LeGros Clark, The Crucial Evidence for Human Evolution,
Proceedings of the American Philosophical Society, Vol. 103, 1959, pp. 159–
172.
    [2] L. S. B. Leakey, The Origin of the Genus *Homo*, *in* Sol Tax (edit.),
Evolution after Darwin, Vol. 2 (Chicago, 1960), pp. 17–32.

A newly developed method of absolute dating of geologic time has made it possible to determine the age of *Zinjanthropus* and Olduwan culture. This has been by the Potassium-Argon method of J. F. Evernden and G. H. Curtis of the Department of Geology at the University of California in Berkeley. Beds of volcanic tuff, associated with Olduwan sites in the Olduvai Gorge, provided the requisite materials. The first results, published in *Nature* of July 29, 1961, based on seven samples from three hominid sites, gave an age ranging from 1.57 to 1.89 million years. "The conclusion is inescapable that Olduwan culture and Villafranchian fauna are synchronous in time and that both are approximately 1.75 million years old." [3] An objective and absolute measure of time, independent of faunal association, has thus been applied for the first time to remote human antiquity.

A word is to be said about conflicting usage of Pleistocene time terms. Pleistocene time (or the Ice Age) has long been considered as beginning with a "first glacial stage" (Günz in Europe, Nebraskan with us), though it has been well known that lesser glacial stages preceded this so-called "first," and that climate, fauna, and vegetation had been changing for some time earlier in the direction of Pleistocene regimen. Paleontologists in particular were dissatisfied with placing this preceding time (Villafranchian for land fauna, Calabrian for marine life) into Upper Pliocene. The International Geological Congress at London accepted a resolution that Villafranchian time should be considered as Lower Pleistocene. The newer definition of Pleistocene time thus includes at least twice as long a span as does the older one. Leakey, following the revised usage, classes *Zinjanthropus* and Olduwan as Lower Pleistocene. In terms of the older classification, of those who have not heard of the London resolution, and of those who do not accept it, the Olduwan is Upper Pliocene. Since there are two different current usages as to Lower, Middle, and Upper Pleistocene, which mean quite different things to different persons, the more specific stage terms still need to be given.

The African evidence has supported earlier inferences from comparative anatomy as to the lineage of man and that of the great apes, that they are and have been distinct. *Zinjanthropus* has not been challenged as a hominid and the Australopithecines finally have passed the qualifying tests. [4] The human hand, remaining unspecial-

---

[3] L. S. B. Leakey, J. F. Evernden, and G. H. Curtis, Age of Bed I, Olduvai Gorge, Tanganyika, Nature, Vol. 191, 1961, pp. 478–479.

[4] LeGros Clark is leading referee and participant in studies of human evo-

ized in man in contrast to the hands of apes and monkeys, is credited with a major role in the evolution of man as "competent to erect a world proper to him alone: the world of culture" (Kälin). Man alone walks erect on long straight legs, his fore-limbs shortened as arms that were freed of the task of locomotion and support. This divergence from primate ancestry to become a plantigrade biped is considered to have been effected early. Less importance is now attached to the size of the brain as marking a threshold for the beginnings of humanity. The faculty of speech is having attention from the anatomical side as well as by cultural remains. Sequences of bodily change and of habits are becoming legible markers of a long passage by which our kind moved from the world of creature into that of culture.

EARLY ENVIRONMENT

It is now apparent that not only the whole of the conventional Ice Age but an additional and probably longer span of earlier time (the expanded Pleistocene that includes Villafranchian time) is involved in cultural origins. The physical environment of such past times is largely obscure as to climates, land and sea vegetation, and somewhat less as to animal forms.

The African continent as an ancient and rigid land mass was less affected than most of the world by late crustal deformations except for the rift valleys of East Africa and the vulcanism along their margins. This geologically young region is now shown to have been an early, perhaps the original, center of man; it continued to be especially attractive to him. The greater part of Africa is old as to surfaces, soils, and drainage, its Tertiary map much like the present. Except along the Mediterranean Sea, the position and character of the coasts also have not changed greatly.

Climatically, Africa has remained tropical and subtropical by location. The general circulation of the atmosphere probably operated then as now, with an equatorial girdle of rising air and with descending air on both poleward sides. Dislocations of climatic regions have been considerable, somehow related to the succession of glacial

---

lution. See, for example, his Fossil Evidence for Human Evolution (Chicago, 1955) and Antecedents of Man (Chicago, 1960). Joseph Kälin, Die ältesten Menschenrechte und ihre stammesgeschichtliche Deutung, Historia Mundi, Vol. 1, 1952, pp. 33–98, stresses the significance of evolution as a whole of the human organism, emphasizing studies done in continental Europe.

and interglacial stages of higher latitudes. How local pluvial and dry phases of the past fit into the glacial and interglacial pattern of higher latitudes needs much further study.

It may be doubted that either the rainy tropics or their dry margins were eliminated at any time of human existence. The qualities of rain forest, savanna, and desert are deeply inscribed in many forms of the living African flora and fauna. A long selective adaptation to seasonal or general aridity is indicated, for example, in the great diversity of xerophytic African kinds of Euphorbiaceae and Crassulaceae, of mimosaceous and liliaceous plants.

Two million years ago the march of the African seasons, it is inferred, was fairly much as it is now, the rains coming at the same time though they might be more or less in a particular area, the temperatures at low latitudes not greatly differing from the present. The plant cover perhaps was greater and more varied, the xerophytic forms less conspicuous, partly because the soils were less old and less leached and compacted and in part because the cumulative pressures by man had not begun to take effect. I accept the conclusions of African ecologists that the grassy savannas are secondary, derived from woodland savannas of more varied composition, and that they are largely due to deforestation by man.

ECOLOGIC NICHE

The various kinds of primates can be described as to their proper habitats; for early man there is no such agreement and the most familiar assignment of him to living in savanna plains is perhaps the least likely. He was not specialized for predation; he was inept at flight or concealment; he was neither very strong nor fast. His daytime vision was good but he avoided moving about at night. He was not a forest creature; he lacked a protective pelt against cold, or thorns; he sweated most profusely on exertion and in dry air and so could not live far from water. He seems to have rejected no nourishing food, the range of his digestion being greater than that of most creatures. The restrictions on his mobility will be considered below.

A riparian location is indicated for his earliest living. Here there was water to drink and he needed to drink often. Here also was found the greatest concentration and diversity of plant and animal life, on land, at the water's edge, and in the water. Habitat by the waterside is the most general term proposed for the primitive ecology of mankind, be it along stream, lake, or seashore. Such lakeside and streamside sites were available in interior East Africa, the famous camp of Olduvai being an example. Another riparian beginning was available on seashores. Sir Alister Hardy has proposed lately that the evolution of man may be accounted for by a more aquatic past, as by seeking food in tropical waters. Ranging from beach into shoal water, from wading to swimming and diving are steps that Professor Hardy has invoked to explain certain characteristics of the human body, such as the symmetry of his body, the erect and graceful carriage, the loss of body hair and development of hair on the head, the distribution of subcutaneous fat, the streamlined hair tracts.[5]

It is a curious fact that no other primates appear to have taken to living on seashores, though certan Asiatic macaques do come to them for crabs and other shellfish, and are able to swim. Most primates seem not to forage in water, and some do not swim at all.

May it be that by seaside living our physiologic system established its particular needs of iodine and salt, its apparent benefits from unsaturated fats, and its inclination to high protein intake?

Whether the human lineage won through on freshwater shores and moved thence to occupy seacoasts, or whether the direction was reversed is undetermined. The interior Olduwan sites are not far removed from the Indian Ocean. Olduvai Gorge holds the earliest dated and perhaps the oldest known site of human occupation, but it is in Leakey's words "a well-established Stone Age culture" and may have originated elsewhere.

EARLY COASTAL SITES

Pleistocene events are recorded on ocean coasts by a series of eustatic terraces, each named after some Mediterranean type locality. The oldest and highest of these, the Sicilian, nominally said to lie about three hundred feet above present sea level, was formed during a long high stand of the world ocean that preceded the "First" or Günz glacial stage. It corresponded therefore roughly to Villafranchian in age. Such a high and old marine surface is found widely about the more stable oceanic margins of the continents, usually from three to four hundred feet above the present sea. It has been subjected to more weathering and erosion than have the younger and lower terraces, but since it was formed during a long, high sea

---

[5] Alister Hardy, Was Man More Aquatic in the Past?, New Scientist, Vol. 7, 1960, pp. 642–645. Ensuing correspondence on p. 889 of the same volume.

level it was unusually wide and continuous and its remains are to be found on many coasts.

The old Sicilian surfaces have been subjected to undercutting and trimming by later wave erosion, to dissection by ravines, and to sluicing by surface wash, all of which have reduced greatly the chances that sites occupied by man have been preserved. Nor have these terraces been the object of close study except at a few places. Nevertheless, there is record of seaside living in Sicilian time, mainly from Africa, with an extension into southern Portugal.[6]

Near Casablanca in Morocco a strand of Sicilian age has yielded worked cobbles and a few crude hand axes (Abbevillian bifaces) that had been worn subsequently by the Sicilian sea. Behind and immediately above the strand is an extensive "workshop and place of habitation with hundreds of artifacts" (designated as Clacto-Abbevillian).[7] At Magoito in Portugal a strongly iron-cemented Sicilian strand contains primitively-worked cobbles in abundance and an occasional hand axe. From the vicinity of Stellenbosch at the Cape of Good Hope Breuil reported to the 1947 Panafrican Congress the finding of heavy, roughly-made tools at about four hundred feet above the sea, and stated that these had been worn by waves.

The tools of Sicilian seashores were made from wave-fashioned cobbles or pebbles of size and shape suitable to be held in the hand. They were dressed at one end by somewhat practiced blows to form a cutting edge. There was enough difference in the designed forms so that some are called choppers, others hand axes by inference of the manner of their use. Flakes that had been struck from cobbles were also fashioned into cutting tools. The assemblage of worked stone has been called a "pebble culture," although the artifacts are not of small size. The sites contain also quantities of spalls, the waste of workshops of these early toolmakers; they were places of habitation, as Breuil says, not casual camps.

PRIMORDIAL ECONOMY

Primitive economy depends on collecting whatever is edible or otherwise usable. However, it does not follow that such a primitive level

[6] H. Breuil and R. Lantier, Les Hommes de la Pierre Ancienne (Paris, 1959), pp. 130–131. H. E. P. Breuil, Raised Marine Beaches Round the African Continent and Their Relation to Stone Age Cultures, *in* L. S. B. Leakey, edit., Proceedings of the Panafrican Congress on Prehistory, 1947 (1952), pp. 91–93. A. Ruhlmann, Prehistoric Morocco, *ibid.,* pp. 140–146.

[7] Casablanca discoveries of Neuville and Ruhlmann, summarized in Breuil and Lantier, *loc. cit.*

of food gathering was one of free wandering habits, such as are being postulated in certain current models of prehistory.[8] The archeologic evidence is to the contrary, as is the logic of supplies. From the beginning, there was the need to minimize cost of assemblage, to have what was needed with the least expenditure of effort and to have it continuously. Access to potable water was, as it still is, the first consideration in determining the place to live; adequate food came next. In modern time, the collectors are found mainly in arid areas of scant and uncertain food and water where they survive by intimate knowledge of where and when to find both. The Australian aboriginals stay put as much as possible. The California natives, also of collecting economy, included quite sedentary tribes with permanently occupied villages where there was food and water available the year around; others shifted with the harvest of the seasons, making the rounds of their particular living places. The direction of progress for early humanity was not into diffuse and uncertain dispersal but by locating areas of superior advantage, tracts of highest and most continuous yield, where it was possible to settle and increase. Mobility is not a primitive trait, but the result either of a specialized economic mode such as big-game hunters or cattle nomads or of giving way before pressure from a stronger group.

With the exception of man the food habits of the primates are mainly or even wholly vegetarian. It has been somehow inferred that man developed early and strongly carnivorous habits. The ancient camp site at Olduvai contains the bones of rats, mice, frogs, lizards, birds, fish, snake, tortoise, and of juvenile pig, antelope, and ostrich,[9] all creatures that could be taken by hand or clubbed down. Primitive collectors took, as they have continued to do, small animals by hand, club, digging, and larger ones by scavenging carcasses and knocking over sick, injured, and juvenile game. Such rudimentary predation still is to be considered as part of omnivorous foraging and does not imply that mankind had started a way of life toward hunting, or that this would become in general the next stage of human society. Some collectors did in the course of time become hunters, others never did, but remained basically dependent on collecting or turned to quite other cultural directions. Primitive man lacked the social organization, artifices, effective weapons, even the special environment for training himself into the discipline of a

[8] See R. J. Braidwood, Levels in Prehistory: a Model for the Consideration of the Evidence, *in* Sol Tax, edit., Evolution after Darwin, *op. cit.* (n. 2), pp. 146–148.

[9] Leakey, *loc. cit.* (n. 2).

hunting life. Before Mousterian time the artifacts are too unspecialized to be designated as hunting weapons. By then, as it now appears, a good nine-tenths of the span of human time had elapsed. That there were implements earlier than the Upper Paleolithic points and blades which could serve, among other uses, also for dismembering, skinning, or killing of game does not establish earlier hunting societies.

A BASIC SOCIETY?

Expressed or implicit, there is widespread assumption that from a general collecting stage humanity passed into a general hunting stage. Hunting is almost exclusively a masculine activity. A society organized on a base of hunting will normally be one of male dominance and has developed in the direction of greater mobility. In support of a hunting stage some have sought to introduce a simian model in which the protohumans are thought of as living in troops or bands under the leadership of a dominant male. The simian model is defective and irrelevant in terms of known human evolution. The archeologic evidence does not support an early or general succession into a hunting stage. The simpler and more archaic societies that survive or of which we have historical knowledge do not fit such a general pattern. May the ethology of our lineage indicate that there was one original direction by which human society took form?

The primate social modes show different kinds and degrees of male dominance, but none of male responsibility for providing food. Male attachment and attention to the young and the mother are not monkey traits; food snatching is. Among the great apes such family ties as exist hardly extend to paternal food-getting or care of the young. Primate behavior fails to indicate that males were the founders of human society. The new direction taken by the human branch arose rather from the relation of mother to child.

In the course of its evolution our lineage took off into a new experiment of reproduction. The period of gestation has remained about the same among the higher primates, but the human infant at birth is less advanced in its development. It remains wholly dependent on maternal care far longer than any other young, and it develops the ability to fend for itself most slowly. The baby must be carried in the mother's arms, for it does not know how to cling; its getting about, by crawling and walking, is unmatched in slowness of learning. The human nursing time is longest; it may be two to three years among modern primitives. The weaned child still requires to be given food.

As long as the mother bore children, and also beyond such time, she had the feeding and care of the young to look after. In her daily foraging she carried or was accompanied by her brood, the older ones learning from her what was good and how to secure it. She discovered the first hard rule of economic geography, the cost of distance. Hers was the greater necessity to learn the use of tools, digging stick, handstone, and club.

The while the women and children combed the area at close range, the males might roam afar, unconcerned about dependents. Stirred by some sentiment of affinity one might return with an offering, as has been recorded for apes. The adult human male was last to become attached to (his) family, by the joint attraction of bed and board, the most persuasive influence (his) woman could use. Accepting paternity, the male came to share in family responsibilities. Humanity is thus thought of as beginning with the maternal family which became bilateral, not out of a roving promiscuous troop dominated by the strongest, most virile, and most aggressive male.

The enduring family, maternally based as I think, sets our kind apart from the ethology of all other primates. Though one cannot say that affinity and affection are to be explained wholly by biology, there is such basis to the continuity of family ties. The juvenile period was longest and probably grew longer in the time of emerging humanness. Throughout the years of childhood the bonds between mother and children were maintained and developed, and in time such attachment became true of both parents and their siblings. The uniquely retarded puberty and mating also favored the forming of extended family groups through continuing coexistence. Family ties were expanded and elaborated, to be relaxed but not broken in the matings of the younger generation. Mankind alone lived in continued awareness of blood ties and thereby entered upon a social course of its own. Recognition of kinship is persistent through all we know of human society and is inferred as basic to its origins. Kinship systems, it may be noted, are most elaborate in the more primitive societies, and bespeak the ancient bond of consanguinity, real or imagined.

Like other groundlings that produce immobile young (and the human case is extreme), the mother was concerned with choosing a good site to deposit and shelter the offspring. The rock shelter is most suited to serve as the earliest home, providing protection from rain, the chill of night, and the heat of day. A roof is almost a prerequisite of human habitation. A superior shelter also served as a lookout against surprise and for observing the movement of other creatures on the ground and in the air in search of food. A good living site required drinking water close at hand and good foraging near by. Materfamilias roamed no farther than was necessary. The best locations had easy access to abundant and diverse provisions, enjoyed least seasonal contrast in their availability, and experienced natural replenishment. The more these advantages were present, the more sedentary the life, the larger the number that could live together, the greater the margin of leisure, the better the prospect of social advance.

THE SEASHORE AS OPTIMUM HABITAT

It may be, as has been thought, that our kind had its origins and earliest home in an interior land. However, the discovery of the sea, whenever it happened, afforded a living beyond that at any inland location.

The hypothesis thus is that the path of our evolution turned aside from the common primate course by going to the sea. No other setting is as attractive for the beginnings of humanity. The sea, in particular the tidal shore, presented the best opportunity to eat, settle, increase, and learn. It afforded diversity and abundance of provisions, continuous and inexhaustible. It invited the development of manual skills. It gave the congenial ecologic niche in which animal ethology could become human culture.

To primitive collector and modern naturalist alike, the borders of the sea are richly rewarding. Between high and low tide a wide assemblage of life forms useful to man is to be had for the taking. These differ from place to place according to the bottom, whether it is sand, silt, or rock, according to the qualities and motions of the water, and by the extent of daily exposure above the water. Marine mammals and fish are stranded on occasion. In warm oceans sea turtles visit sandy beaches to deposit their eggs. From back beach to sea cliff a different and varied fauna and flora yield edible shoots, fruits, eggs, and nestlings. The shallow sea holds yet another living assemblage.

The inhabitants of the seashore thus had their attention directed along the strand, back onto the land, but also out into the sea. However primitive the people who live by warm or temperate water, they are generally excellent swimmers and divers. European seamen who

visited Tasmania in early days were impressed by the ability of the
aborigines to swim and dive, especially to bring up shellfish from
the sea floor. The natives who lived about the Gulf of California
were among the most primitive inhabitants of North America; they
included the Seri of the mainland and, on the peninsula of Lower
California, the Pericu, Guaicura, and Cochimi. All were very adept
at swimming and diving. Some came to be thus employed by the
Spaniards to dive for pearl oysters (of the genus *Pinctada*), in diving for which they weighted themselves with stones. The Pericu also
were able to spear fish while diving. Large and deep middens of
unknown age stretch along the Gulf of California and contain in
quantity numerous shells of species that could be secured only by
diving.

There is no privilege or preference of sex in swimming and diving.
The sexes are of equal ability, endurance, and performance in the
water, and they could participate equally in the work of collecting
and in water sport. The Spaniards, newly come to the tropical New
World, looked on the amphibious native habits of both sexes and
all ages with astonishment and some disapproval. It may be suggested that a merging of recreation and economic activity attracted
the primordial males to join in provision from the sea long before
they amounted to anything as hunters on the land, and also that
such participation helped to establish the bilateral family. Under
such ways there is least difference by sex in the training of the young
and most joint participation in the procuring of food.

The strand, and especially the tropical strand, offers the greatest
variety of things to be picked up, toyed with, and tried out as to use.
There are shells already shaped to serve as containers, as scoops, to
use for cutting, chopping, and punching, or to don as adornment.
The carapaces of turtles, tough strands of beach vines and kelp,
driftwood that has been seasoned in salt water are usable as found.

The strand is stocked with items that await manipulation, tools
prepared by nature before there were artifacts of man. To choose
one shell or cobble as against another was to make a decision as to
its fitness for a purpose in mind. To dress it so that it might better
serve a particular function was to make it into an artifact, contrived
for greater utility. As improved forms were kept and copied (accepted patterns), the first step into technics had been taken.

The child at play on the beach today selects and rejects this piece
and that, thinking what it can do with them, putting its faculty of
visual image to work. We still like to go beachcombing, returning
for the moment to primitive act and mood. When all the lands will

be filled with people and machines, perhaps the last need and observance of man still will be, as it was at his beginning, to come down to experience the sea.

The cobbles and pebbles of the seashore are stone in the forms best suited for human use. Streams do but a rough and intermittent job of shaping and sorting stones; the waves, currents, and tides of the sea are constantly rolling and shaping, shifting and sorting them, the stones becoming rounded and smoothed as they rarely are in streams. The hardest and toughest stones that have best resisted abrasion and pounding persist and accumulate on beaches. Strands lying between cliffed headlands provide the readiest source of stone preselected for use, convenient as to size, round or oblong in shape, durable by texture and hardness. The earliest artifacts are known as pebble cultures, directly or indirectly of coastal origin, as noted above.

The invitation to primordial occupation was greatest on high coasts, where headlands alternate with low re-entrant strands. Here a succession of cliffs and beaches grade from cobbles through pebbles to sand and silt, giving most diversity of surface and material, both above and below sea level. Here there is the greatest range of plant and animal kinds and habitats. Along such differentiated coasts rock shelters are available, in process of forming and destruction by sea and weather. The Indian Ocean, likeliest sea of earliest human occupation, exhibits to a large extent such inviting articulation of shore line, from Africa to the Sunda Islands.

There was choice of good living sites by the sea, where all things needful were at hand and were to be had throughout the year. There was no need to move because of seasonal shortage or depletion. Sedentary living was possible, with leisure. Families could cluster about an attractive site in mutual assistance and continuing communication. Human sociality could begin here by common interest, not by the dominance of an aggressive leader. A pacific basis of human society is inferred rather than one by organization and exercise of power.

The dispersal of early man took place most readily by following along the seashore. The coasts ahead presented familiar foods and habitats. The life of sea and strands is least dependent on local climate. Desert shores are not impoverished as is the adjacent land. If there were desert coasts, and it is most likely that there were such, potable water could still be found. Ground water, however slow and slight its movement by gravity, seeps out in places at the shore, at least at low tide. (The desert coast of the Gulf of California was and is thus habitable.) Coastwise there was scarcely a barrier to the spread of early man through tropical and subtropical latitudes, nor was he much affected by the secular changes of climate and biota inland. Even when the zone of winter cold was reached, the supply of food was less altered or seasonally restricted than was that of the land.

In later time the inhabitants of the coasts became cultural laggards. Their ways, it may be thought, had early become adequate to their needs; the ample early invitation of the sea became a later restraint. The invention of fishing gear and techniques and of boats, for example, can hardly have taken place on coasts open to the sea. For the long early time, however, the sea gave the best advantages for the beginnings of technics and society. The riparian origin of mankind is most probable whether by the side of fresh or salt water. The discovery of the warm tidal ocean gave to emergent humanity an opportunity to learn, increase, and spread coastwise and inland. The seashore offered the best route of dispersal from continent to continent.

PART V

The Pursuit of Learning

{ 16 }

The Morphology of Landscape

Diverse opinions regarding the nature of geography are still common. The label geography, as that of history, is no trustworthy indication as to the matter contained. As long as geographers disagree as to their subject it will be necessary, through repeated definition, to seek common ground upon which a general position may be established. In this country a fairly coherent series of viewpoints has been advanced, especially through presidential addresses before the Association of American Geographers, which may be accepted as mirror and mould of geographic opinion in America. They are sufficiently clear and well known that they need not be restated.[1] In European geography a somewhat different orientation appears to be developing. In various quarters significant activity is being displayed, probably in some measure influenced by anti-intellectualist currents. At any rate a shaking up of some vigor is under way. It may therefore be appropriate to re-examine the field of geography, keeping current views abroad especially in mind, in order to attempt a working hypothesis that may serve to illuminate in some degree both the nature of the objective and the problem of systematic method.

THE FIELD OF GEOGRAPHY

The phenomenologic view of science.—All science may be regarded as phenomenology,[2] the term "science" being used in the sense of or-

University of California Publications in Geography, Vol. 2, No. 2, pp. 19–54, 1925 (Reprinted 1938).

[1] In particular, the following addresses are notable expressions of leading opinion: W. M. Davis, An Inductive Study of the Content of Geography, Bull. Amer. Geogr. Soc., Vol. 38, 1906, pp. 67–84; N. M. Fenneman, The Circumference of Geography, Annals Assoc. Amer. Geographers, Vol. 9, 1919, pp. 3–12; H. H. Barrows, Geography as Human Ecology, *ibid.*, Vol. 13, 1923, pp. 1–14.

[2] Hermann Graf Keyserling, Prolegomena zur Naturphilosophie (München, 1910), p. 11.

ganized process of acquiring knowledge rather than in the common restricted meaning of a unified body of physical law. Every field of knowledge is characterized by its declared preoccupation with a certain group of phenomena, which it undertakes to identify and order according to their relations. These facts are assembled with increasing knowledge of their connection; the attention to their connection denotes scientific approach. "A fact is first determined when it is recognized as to limits and qualities, and it is understood when it is viewed in its relations. Out of this follows the necessity of predetermined modes of inquiry and of the creation of a system that makes clear the relation of the phenomena. . . . Every individual science is naïve as a special discipline, in so far as it accepts the section of reality that is its field *tel quel* and does not question its position in the general scene of nature; within these limits, however, it proceeds critically, since it undertakes to determine the connection of the phenomena and their order." [3] According to such definition of the grounds of knowledge, the first concern is with the phenomena that constitute the "section of reality" which is occupied by geography, the next with the method of determining their connection.

Geography as a "naïvely given section of reality."—Disagreement as to the content of geography is so great that three distinct fields of inquiry are usually designated as geography: (1) The study of the earth as the medium of physical processes, or the geophysical part of cosmologic science; (2) the study of life forms as subject to their physical environment, or a part of biophysics dealing with tropisms; and (3) the study of the areal or habitat differentiation of the earth, or chorology. In these three fields there is partial accordance of phenomena, but little of relation. One may choose among the three; they may hardly be consolidated into one discipline.

The great fields of knowledge exist because they are universally recognized as being concerned with great categories of phenomena. The experience of mankind, not the inquiry of the specialist, has made the primary subdivisions of knowledge. Botany is the study of plants, and geology that of rocks, because these categories of fact are evident to all intelligence that has concerned itself with the observation of nature. In the same sense, area or landscape is the field of geography, because it is a naïvely given, important section of reality, not a sophisticated thesis. Geography assumes the responsibility for the study of areas because there exists a common curiosity about that subject. The fact that every school child knows that geography

---

[3] *Ibid.*, pp. 8, 11.

provides information about different countries is enough to establish the validity of such a definition.

No other subject has pre-empted the study of area. Others, such as historians and geologists, may concern themselves with areal phenomena, but in that case they are avowedly using geographic facts for their own ends. If one were to establish a different discipline under the name of geography, the interest in the study of areas would not be destroyed thereby. The subject existed long before the name was coined. The literature of geography in the sense of chorology begins with parts of the earliest sagas and myths, vivid as they are with the sense of place and of man's contest with nature. The most precise expression of geographic knowledge is found in the map, an immemorial symbol. The Greeks wrote geographic accounts under such designations as periplus, periodos, and periegesis long before the name geography was used. Yet even the present name is more than two thousand years old. Geographic treatises appear in numbers among the earliest printed books. Explorations have been the dramatic reconnaissances of geography. The great geographic societies justly have accorded a place of honor to explorers. "Hic et ubique" is the device under which geography has stood always. The universality and persistence of the chorologic interest and the priority of claim that geography has to this field are the evidences on which the case for the popular definition may rest.

We may therefore be content with the simple connotation of the Greek word which the subject uses as its name, and which means most properly areal knowledge. The Germans have translated it as *Landschaftskunde* or *Länderkunde,* the knowledge of landscape or of lands. Their other term, *Erdkunde,* the science of the earth in general, is falling rapidly into disuse.

The thought of a general earth science is impossible of realization; geography can be an independent science only as chorology; that is, as knowledge of the varying expression of the different parts of the earth's surface. It is, in the first place, the study of lands; general geography is not general earth science; rather, it presupposes the general properties and processes of the earth, or accepts them from other sciences; for its own part it is oriented about their varying areal expression.[4]

With this preference of synthetic areal knowledge to general earth science the entire tradition of geography is an agreement.

The interdependence of areal phenomena.—Probably not even the adherents of other, recent schools of geography would deny

---

[4] Alfred Hettner, Methodische Zeit- und Streitfragen, Geogr. Ztschr., Vol. 29, 1923, pp. 37–59. Reference to p. 37.

place for such a view of the subject, but they deem this naïvely given body of facts inadequate to establish a science, or at most would consider it an auxiliary discipline which compiles fragmentary evidence, to find its place ultimately in a general geophysical or biophysical system. The argument then is shifted from the phenomenal content to the nature of the connection of the phenomena. We assert the place for a science that finds its entire field in the landscape on the basis of the significant reality of chorologic relation. The phenomena that make up an area are not simply assorted but are associated, or interdependent. To discover this areal "connection of the phenomena and their order" is a scientific task, according to our position the only one to which geography should devote its energies. The position falls only if the nonreality of area be shown. The competence to arrive at orderly conclusions is not affected in this case by the question of coherence or incoherence of the data, for their characteristic association, as we find them in the area, is an expression of coherence. The element of time is admittedly present in the association of geographic facts, which are thereby in large part nonrecurrent. This temporal quality, however, places them beyond the reach of scientific inquiry only in a very narrow sense, for time as a factor has a well-recognized place in many scientific fields, where time is not simply a term for some identifiable causal relation.

Historical development of chorologic relation into scientific system.—The older geography was troubled but little by critique. It was casually, even trivially, descriptive rather than critical. Yet though it is idle to seek in most of this literature a "system which makes clear the relation of the phenomena," we cannot dispose of all of it as accidental or haphazard in content. In some measure the notion of areal interdependence of phenomena as giving rise to areal reality was present, as any reader of Herodotus or Polybius knows. The *historia* of the Greeks, with its blurred feeling for time relations, had a somewhat superior appreciation of areal relations and represented a far from contemptible start in geography.[5] However much it may have been embroidered by geophysical, geodetic, and geologic notes, classical geography in general, not cosmology subsequently interpreted by some as geography, gave primary emphasis to areal description, with frequent observations on the interrelation

---

[5] Alexander von Humboldt, Kosmos, Vol. 1 (Stuttgart & Tübingen, 1845), pp. 64–65: "In classical antiquity the earliest historians made little attempt to separate the description of lands from the narration of events the scene of which was in the areas described. For a long time physical geography and history appear attractively intermingled."

of areal facts. The culminating school, of which Strabo was chief, was by no means entirely naïve, and rejected vigorously other definition of geography than as chorology, with express exclusion of cosmologic philosophy.

During the period of great discoveries a bona fide but uncritical geography attained its greatest development in the numerous travel relations and especially in the cosmographies of that time. An ever-increasing body of facts about countries was at that time being brought before the Western world, which took keen interest in the rapidly widening horizon. With such a deluge of newly acquired facts about parts of the world, attempts at systematic ordering were numerous, but often grotesque rather than successful. It is not surprising that dynamic systems of geography should have emerged only as the furor of exploration became spent. Yet it is perhaps even more difficult for us to judge the thought of this period than that of classical antiquity. Yule has helped us to better appreciation of the geographic acumen of some of the men of this period. Of the cosmographers, at least Varenius has been accorded a higher rank than that of a compiler. One very great step in synthesis certainly took place at this time, that of the development of cartography into a real chorologic discipline. Only through a large amount of classification and generalization of geographic data was it possible to consolidate the scattered and voluminous data of exploration into the geographically adequate maps that characterize the latter part of the period. To this day many of the maps of the seventeenth and eighteenth centuries are in some respects monumental. However much may have been added since in precision of measurement, in many ways we have retained the chorologic content as formulated in the maps of this period beginning the "Age of Surveys." [6] "Every map which reproduces the form of the earth's surface is a kind of morphologic representation." [7] Not only for physical morphology, but also for the cultural expression of landscape, these maps represented a highly successful series of solutions that are still used. Without such a preliminary synthesis of the facts of geography the work of the next period would have been impossible.

In the nineteenth century the contest between the cosmologic and the chorologic views became acute and the situation of geography was much in doubt. Rationalism and positivism dominated the work

[6] Oscar Peschel's *Zeitalter der Messungen:* Geschichte der Erdkunde bis auf A. v. Humboldt und Carl Ritter (München, 1865), pp. 404–694.

[7] Albrecht Penck, Morphologie der Erdoberfläche, Vol. 1 (Stuttgart, 1894), p. 2.

of geographers. The milieu became a leading doctrine and thus continued through the century. Divine law was transposed into natural law, and for geography Montesquieu and Buckle were prophets of major importance. Since natural law was omnipotent the slow marshaling of the phenomena of area became too tedious a task for eager adherents of the faith of causation. The areal complex was simplified by selecting certain qualities, such as climate, relief, or drainage, and examining them as cause or effect. Viewed as end products, each of these classes of facts could be referred back fairly well to the laws of physics. Viewed as agents, the physical properties of the earth, such as climate in particular with Montesquieu, became adequate principles for explaining the nature and distribution of organic life. The complex reality of areal association was sacrificed in either case to a rigorous dogma of materialistic cosmology, most notably in American physiography and anthropogeography. About twenty years ago the most distinguished American geographer took the position "that neither the inorganic nor the organic elements which enter into geographical relations are by themselves of a completely geographic quality; they gain that quality only when two or more of them are coupled in a relation of cause and effect, at least one element in the chain of causation being organic and one inorganic. . . . Any statement is of geographical quality if it contains a reasonable relation between some inorganic element of the earth, acting as a control, and some element of organic existence . . . serving as a response." Indeed in this causal relation was, he said, "the most definite, if not the only unifying principle that I can find in geography." [8] Cause was a confident and alluring word, and causal geography had its day. The *Zeitgeist* was distinctly unfavorable to those geographers who thought that the subject was in no wise committed to a rigidly deterministic formula.

Latterly, Vidal de la Blache in France, Hettner, Passarge, and Krebs in Germany, and others have been reasserting more and more the classical tradition of geography as chorologic relation. It may be said that, after a period in which special, essentially physical disciplines were most in vogue, we are in process of returning to our permanent task and that this readjustment is responsible for the current activity of inquiry as to content of our field.

Summary of the objective of geography.—The task of geography is conceived as the establishment of a critical system which embraces the phenomenology of landscape, in order to grasp in all of its meaning and color the varied terrestrial scene. Indirectly Vidal de la

[8] W. M. Davis, *op. cit.*, pp. 73, 71.

Blache has stated this position by cautioning against considering "the earth as 'the scene on which the activity of man unfolds itself,' without reflecting that this scene is itself living." [9] It includes the works of man as an integral expression of the scene. This position is derived from Herodotus rather than from Thales. Modern geography is the modern expression of the most ancient geography.

The objects which exist together in the landscape exist in interrelation. We assert that they constitute a reality as a whole that is not expressed by a consideration of the constituent parts separately, that area has form, structure, and function, and hence position in a system, and that it is subject to development, change, and completion. Without this view of areal reality and relation, there exist only special disciplines, not geography as generally understood. The situation is analogous to that of history, which may be divided among economics, government, sociology, and so on; but when this is done the result is not history.

THE CONTENT OF LANDSCAPE

Definition of landscape.—The term "landscape" is proposed to denote the unit concept of geography, to characterize the peculiarly geographic association of facts. Equivalent terms in a sense are "area" and "region." Area is of course a general term, not distinctively geographic. Region has come to imply, to some geographers at least, an order of magnitude. Landscape is the English equivalent of the term German geographers are using largely, and strictly has the same meaning: a land shape, in which the process of shaping is by no means thought of as simply physical. It may be defined, therefore, as an area made up of a distinct association of forms, both physical and cultural.[10]

The facts of geography are place facts; their association gives rise to the concept of landscape. Similarly, the facts of history are time facts; their association gives rise to the concept of period. By definition the landscape has identity that is based on recognizable constitution, limits, and generic relation to other landscapes, which constitute a general system. Its structure and function are deter-

[9] P. Vidal de la Blache, Principes de géographie humaine (Paris, 1922), p. 6.

[10] J. Sölch, Die Auffassung der "natürlichen Grenzen" in der wissenschaftlichen Geographie (Innsbruck, 1924), has proposed the term "Chore" to designate the same idea.

mined by integrant, dependent forms. The landscape is considered, therefore, in a sense as having an organic quality. We may follow Bluntschli in saying that one has not fully understood the nature of an area until one "has learned to see it as an organic unit, to comprehend land and life in terms of each other." [11] It has seemed desirable to introduce this point prior to its elaboration because it is very different from the unit concept of physical process of the physiographer or of environmental influence of the anthropogeographer of the school of Ratzel. The mechanics of glacial erosion, the climatic correlation of energy, and the form content of an areal habitat are three different things.

Landscape has generic meaning.—In the sense here used, landscape is not simply an actual scene viewed by an observer. The geographic landscape is a generalization derived from the observation of individual scenes. Croce's remark that "the geographer who is describing a landscape has the same task as a landscape painter" [12] has therefore only limited validity. The geographer may describe the individual landscape as a type or possibly as a variant from type, but always he has in mind the generic, and proceeds by comparison.

An ordered presentation of the landscapes of the earth is a formidable undertaking. Beginning with infinite diversity, salient and related features are selected in order to establish the character of the landscape and to place it in a system. Yet generic quality is nonexistent in the sense of the biologic world. Every landscape has individuality as well as relation to other landscapes, and the same is true of the forms that make it up. No valley is quite like any other valley; no city the exact replica of some other city. In so far as these qualities remain completely unrelated they are beyond the reach of systematic treatment, beyond that organized knowledge that we call science. "No science can rest at the level of mere perception. . . . The so-called descriptive natural sciences, zoology and botany, do not remain content to regard the singular, they raise themselves to concepts of species, genus, family, order, class, type." [13] "There is no idiographic science, that is, one that described the individual merely as such. Geography was formerly idiographic; it has long since attempted to become nomothetic, and no geographer

---

[11] Hans Bluntschli, *Die Amazonasniederung als harmonischer Organismus,* Geogr. Ztsch., Vol. 27, 1921, pp. 49–68.

[12] Quoted by Paul Barth, *Die Philosophie der Geschichte als Soziologie,* 2nd ed., Part 1 (Leipzig, 1915), p. 10.

[13] *Ibid.,* p. 11.

would hold it at its previous level." [14] Whatever opinion one may hold about natural law, or nomothetic, general, or causal relation, a definition of landscape as singular, unorganized, or unrelated has no scientific value.

Element of personal judgment in the selection of content.—It is true that in the selection of the generic characteristics of landscape the geographer is guided only by his own judgment that they are characteristic, that is, repeating; that they are arranged into a pattern, or have structural quality, and that the landscape accurately belongs to a specific group in the general series of landscapes. Croce objects to a science of history on the ground that history is without logical criteria: "The criterion is the choice itself, conditioned, like every economic art, by knowledge of the actual situation. This selection is certainly conducted with intelligence, but not with the application of a philosophic criterion, and is justified only in and by itself. For this reason we speak of the fine tact, or scent, or instinct of the learned man." [15] A similar objection is sometimes urged against the scientific competence of geography, because it is unable to establish complete, rigid, logical control and perforce relies upon the option of the student. The geographer is in fact continually exercising freedom of choice as to the materials he includes in his observations, but he is also continually drawing inferences as to their relation. His method, imperfect as it may be, is based on induction; he deals with sequences, though he may not regard these as a simple causal relation.

If we consider a given type of landscape, for example a North European heath, we may put down notes such as the following:

The sky is dull, ordinarily partly overcast, the horizon is indistinct and rarely more than a half-dozen miles distant, though seen from a height. The upland is gently and irregularly rolling and descends to broad, flat basins. There are no long slopes and no symmetrical patterns of surface form. Watercourses are short, with clear brownish water, and perennial. The brooks end in irregular swamps, with indistinct borders. Coarse grasses and rushes form marginal strips along the water bodies. The upland is covered with heather, furze, and bracken. Clumps of juniper abound, especially on the steeper, drier slopes. Cart traces lie along the longer ridges, exposing loose sand in the wheel tracks, and here and there a rusty, cemented base shows beneath the sand.

---

[14] *Ibid.,* p. 39.

[15] Benedetto Croce, History, Its Theory and Practice (New York, 1921), pp. 109–110. The statement applies to the history that has the goal simply of "making the past live again." There is, however, also a phenomenologic history, which may discover related forms and their expression.

Small flocks of sheep are scattered widely over the land. The almost complete absence of the works of man is notable. There are no fields or other enclosed tracts. The only buildings are sheep sheds, situated usually at a distance of several miles from one another, at convenient intersections of cart traces.

The account is not that of an individual scene, but a summation of general characteristics. References to other types of landscape are introduced by implication. Relations of form elements within the landscape are also noted. The items selected are based upon "knowledge of the actual situation," and there is an attempt at a synthesis of the form elements. Their significance is a matter of personal judgment. Objective standards may be substituted for them only in part, as by quantitative representation in the form of a map. Even thus the personal element is brought only under limited control, since it still operates in choosing the qualities to be represented. All that can be expected is the reduction of the personal element by agreement on a "predetermined mode of inquiry," which shall be logical.

Extensiveness of areal features.—The content of landscape is something less than the whole of its visible constituents. The identity of the landscape is determined first of all by conspicuousness of form, as implied in the following statement: "A correct representation of the surface form, of soil, and of surficially conspicuous masses of rock, of plant cover and water bodies, of the coasts and the sea, of areally conspicuous animal life and of the expression of human culture is the goal of geographic inquiry." [16] The items specified are chosen because the experience of the author has shown their significance as to mass and relation. The chorologic position necessarily recognizes the importance of areal extensiveness of phenomena, this quality being inherent in the position. Herein lies an important contrast between geography and physiography. The character of the heath landscape described above is determined primarily by the dominance of sand, swamp, and heather. The most important geographic fact about Norway, aside from its location, probably is that four-fifths of its surface is barren highland, supporting neither forests nor flocks, a condition significant directly because of its extensiveness.

Habitat value as a basis for the determination of content.—Personal judgment of the content of landscape is determined further

---

[16] Siegfried Passarge, Die Grundlagen der Landschaftskunde, Vol. 1 (Hamburg, 1919), p. 1.

by interest. Geography is distinctly anthropocentric, in the sense of value or use of the earth to man. We are interested in that part of the areal scene that concerns us as human beings because we are part of it, live with it, are limited by it, and modify it. Thus we select those qualities of landscape in particular that are or may be of use to us. We relinquish those features of area that may be significant to the geologist in earth history but are of no concern in the relation of man to his area. The physical qualities of landscape are those that have habitat value, present or potential.

The natural and the cultural landscape.—"Human geography does not oppose itself to a geography from which the human element is excluded; such a one has not existed except in the minds of a few exclusive specialists." [17] It is a forcible abstraction, by every good geographic tradition a *tour de force,* to consider a landscape as though it were devoid of life. Because we are interested primarily in "cultures that grow with original vigor out of the lap of a maternal natural landscape, to which each is bound in the whole course of its existence," [18] geography is based on the reality of the union of physical and cultural elements of the landscape. The content of landscape is found therefore in the physical qualities of area that are significant to man and in the forms of his use of the area, in facts of physical background and facts of human culture. A valuable discussion of this principle is given by Krebs under the title "Natur- und Kulturlandschaft." [19]

For the first half of the content of landscape we may use the designation "site," which has become well established in plant ecology. A forest site is not simply the place where a forest stands; in its full connotation, the name is a qualitative expression of place in terms of forest growth, usually for the particular forest association that is in occupation of the site. In this sense the physical area

---

[17] P. Vidal de la Blache, *op. cit.,* p. 3.

[18] Oswald Spengler, Der Untergang des Abendlandes; Umrisse einer Morphologie der Weltgeschichte, Vol. 1 (München, 1920), p. 28: "Kulturen die mit urweltlicher Kraft aus dem Schosse einer mütterlichen Landschaft, an die jede von ihnen im ganzen Verlauf ihres Daseins streng gebunden ist, erblühen."

[19] Norbert Krebs, Natur- und Kulturlandschaft, Ztsch. d. Gesellch. f. Erdk. zu Berlin, 1923, pp. 81–94. Reference to p. 83. He states the content of geography as being "in the area (*Raum*) itself with its surfaces, lines, and points, its form, circumference, and content. The relations to geometry, the pure areal science, become even more intimate when not only the area as such, but its position with references to other areas, is considered."

is the sum of all natural resources that man has at his disposal in the area. It is beyond his power to add to them; he may "develop" them, ignore them in part, or subtract from them by exploitation.

The second half of landscape viewed as a bilateral unit is its cultural expression. There is a strictly geographic way of thinking of culture; namely, as the impress of the works of man upon the area. We may think of people as associated within and with an area, as we may think of them as groups associated in descent or tradition. In the first case we are thinking of culture as a geographic expression, composed of forms which are a part of geographic phenomenonology. In this view there is no place for a dualism of landscape.

THE APPLICATION OF THE MORPHOLOGIC METHOD

Form of induction.—The systematic organization of the content of landscape proceeds with the repression of a priori theories concerning it. The massing and ordering of phenomena as forms that are integrated into structures and the comparative study of the data as thus organized constitute the morphologic method of synthesis, a special empirical method. Morphology rests upon the following postulates: (1) that there is a unit of organic or quasi-organic quality; that is, a structure to which certain components are necessary, these component elements being called "forms" in this paper; (2) that similarity of form in different structures is recognized because of functional equivalence, the forms then being "homologous"; and (3) that the structural elements may be placed in series, especially into developmental sequence, ranging from incipient to final or completed stage. Morphologic study does not necessarily affirm an organism in the biologic sense, as, for example, in the sociology of Herbert Spencer, but only organized unit concepts that are related. Without being committed in any sense to a general biogenetic law, the organic analogy has proved most useful throughout the fields of social inquiry. It is a working device, the truth of which may perhaps be subject to question, but which leads nevertheless to increasingly valid conclusions.[20]

The term "morphology" originated with Goethe, and expresses his contribution to modern science. It may be well to recall that he turned to biologic and geologic studies because he was interested in

---

[20] The assumption "as if," advanced by Hans Vaihinger in his Die Philosophie des Als Ob, 7th ed. (Leipzig, 1922), *passim.*

the nature and limits of cognition. Believing that there were things "accessible and inaccessible" to human knowledge, he concluded: "One need not seek for something beyond the phenomena; they themselves are the lore (*Lehre*)."[21] Thus originated his form studies, and especially those of homology of form. His method of scientific inquiry rested on a definite philosophic position.

If therefore the morphologic method appears unpretentious to the student who is eager to come to large conclusions, it may be pointed out that it rests upon a deliberate restraint in the affirmation of knowledge. It is a purely evidential system, without prepossession regarding the meaning of its evidence, and presupposes a minimum of assumption; namely, only the reality of structural organization. Being objective and value-free, or nearly so, it is competent to arrive at increasingly significant results.

Application to social studies.—Morphologic method is not only the introduction to the biologic sciences, but it is steadily growing in importance in the social fields. In biology it is the study of organic forms and their structure, or the architecture of organisms. In the social field the continued synthesis of phenomena by morphologic method has been employed with greatest success perhaps in anthropology. This science can claim an honor roll of workers who have had the patience and skill to approach the study of social institutions phenomenologically, by the classification of forms, ranging from the concrete materials of clothing, housing, and tools to the language and customs of a group, thereby identifying step by step the complex structure of cultures. Spengler's brilliant and highly controversial thesis of history is far and away the most pretentious application of the method to the human field. Disregarding its elements of intuitionalism, it is in effect comparative morphology as applied to history, the second volume bearing that title. He characterizes the forms that, to his mind, compose the great historic structures, subjects them to comparison for different periods as homologies, and traces developmental stages. By however much the author may have exceeded his and our knowledge in his daring synthesis, he has shown the possibilities of a morphology of history, or of the study of history on a scientific basis other than the causal formula of historical rationalism.[22]

---

[21] Goethes sämtliche Werke, Jubiläumsausgabe, Vol. 39 (Stuttgart & Berlin [1902]), p. 72.

[22] Oswald Spengler, *op. cit.* The mathematico-philosophical thesis of the cultural cycle, the complete antithesis of Buckle, in particular is of such importance that it should be known to every geographer, whatever his position

The introduction of morphology into geography and the results.
—Method and term were first formally introduced into geography
by Carl Ritter, whose restoration of geography succeeded finally,
not in the idealistic cosmology he had espoused, but because after
all he laid the foundations for comparative regional study. Thereafter, perhaps because there was so much to do, the morphologic
studies were rapidly narrowed so as to regard only the surficial form
of the land. Grisebach's classic definition that "the morphologic
system illuminates, by regarding the relationship of forms, the obscurity of their descent" [23] was applied with fateful results to the
field of geography. The restriction of forms to relief, and interest
in the origin of these forms, shortly established, under the leadership of Peschel, von Richthofen, and de la Noë, the genetic inquiry
that was called geomorphology.[24] At first relying on the naïve descriptive classification of surface forms, as for example in Penck's
Morphologie der Erdoberfläche, which is chorologic morphology,
increasingly the trend was to classify on the basis of process, and to
trace these forms back to more and more remote forms. The genetic
historians of land form undertook increasingly the invasion of the
field of geology. The final step was that some of these specialists
lost sight almost completely of actual land forms and devoted themselves to the construction of theoretical forms deduced from individual physical processes. The defeat of geographic ends was
therefore almost complete and such geomorphology became a
separate branch of general earth science.

This autonomous genetic morphology inevitably led to an adverse
reaction among the chorologically-minded geographers, not because
the work was not carefully done, nor because it failed to develop a
valuable field of knowledge, but because it became unrecognizable
as geography.[25] Unfortunately a very general name was applied to a
very specialized discipline. Under a misapprehension of the term,
there has been a tendency to disregard in consequence the possibilities of the morphologic method. Vidal de la Blache perhaps earlier

---

may be with respect to Spengler's mysticism. There are at least three other
similar views of the structure of history, apparently independently discovered:
Flinders Petrie, Revolutions of Civilization (London and New York, 1911);
Henry Adams, The Rule of Phase in History, *in* The Degradation of the
Democratic Dogma (New York, 1919); and Leo Frobenius, Paideuma:
Umrisse einer Kultur- und Seelenlehre (München, 1921).

[23] August Grisebach, Die Vegetation der Erde nach ihrer klimatischen
Anordnung, Vol. 1 (Leipzig, 1884), p. 10.

[24] Albrecht Penck, *op. cit.,* pp. 5–6.

[25] Alfred Hettner, *op. cit.,* pp. 41–46.

than anyone else realized the situation and re-established morphology in its rightful position. The regional monographs that proceeded from his school expressed far more adequately than had been done before the full form content and structural relation of the landscape, finding in the cultural landscape the culminating expression of the organic area. In these studies, for example, the position of man and his works explicitly is that of the last and most important factor and forms in the landscape.

The perversion of geographic ends in the definition of morphology as the causal study of relief forms appears from the following considerations: (1) Relief is only one category of the physical landscape and ordinarily not the most important one; it almost never supplies the complete basis of a cultural form. (2) There is no necessary relation between the mode of origin of a relief form and its functional significance, the matter with which geography is most directly concerned. (3) An inevitable difficulty with a purely genetic morphology of relief forms is that most of the actual relief features of the earth are of very mixed origin. Behind the present forms lie processal associations, previous or ancestral forms, and almost inscrutable expressions of time. For the present at least, therefore, genetic morphology isolates those form elements that yield to causal analysis. In the selection of those relief facts that are legible as to genesis, it neglects some, even many, of the features of relief and abandons therefore the structural synthesis of even this segment of the landscape in so far as chorology is concerned.

In the late enthusiasm for studies of relief forms the climatologists were crowded into a relatively obscure position. Yet they, most largely, escaped the geographically sterile pursuit of the pure genetic method. Climatology has been phenomenologic rather than genetic. In spite of very scant knowledge of the origin of climatic conditions, the facts of climate have been summarized in terms of their geographic significance most admirably. In particular Köppen's series of trials at climatic synthesis, carefully developed as to biotically critical values, admirably restrained as to genetic explanation, are among the most important if not the most important contribution in this generation to geographic morphology. Yet such is the force of associations that few doubtless would name such climatic synthesis as a fundamental part of geographic morphology. It is more than a matter of mere nomenclature to object to the misapplication of the term morphology; it is a rut into which we have slipped and which has limited our range. Perhaps some of the cross-purposes in present-day geography may be traced to the failure to recognize that all the facts of the subject are to be organized by a general system, through which alone their relation may be determined.

PREPARATORY SYSTEMATIC DESCRIPTION

The first step in morphologic study.—Historically "geography commenced by describing and registering; that is, as a systematic study. It proceeded thereupon to . . . genetic relation, morphology." [26] The geographic study is still thus begun. The description of observed facts is by some predetermined order that represents a preliminary grouping of the material. Such systematic description is for the purpose of morphologic relation and is really the beginning of morphologic synthesis. It is therefore distinguishable from morphology not at all in principle but in that it lies at a lower critical level. The relation is not dissimilar to that between taxonomy and biologic morphology.

Descriptive terminology.—The problem of geographic description differs from that of taxonomy principally in the availability of terms. The facts of area have been under popular observation to such an extent that a new terminology is for the most part not necessary. R. D. Salisbury held that the forms of landscape had generally received serviceable popular names and that codification might proceed from popular parlance without the coining of new terms. Proceeding largely in this manner, we are building up a list of form terms, that are being enriched from many areas and many languages. Very many more are still awaiting introduction into geographic literature. These terms apply as largely to soil, drainage, and climatic forms as they do to land surface. Also popular usage has named many vegetational associations and has prepared for us a still largely unprospected wealth of cultural form terms. Popular terminology is a fairly reliable warrant of the significance of the form, as implied in its adoption. Such names may apply to single form constituents, as glade, tarn, loess. Or they may be form associations of varying magnitude, as heath, steppe, piedmont. Or they may be proper names to designate unit landscapes, as, for example, the regional names that are in use for most parts of France. Such popular nomenclature is rich in genetic meaning, but with sure chorologic judgment it proceeds, not from cause, but from a generic summation; namely, from form similarities and contrasts.

If systematic description is a desideratum for geography, we are

[26] Norbert Krebs, *op. cit.,* p. 81.

still in great need of enlarging our descriptive vocabulary. The meagerness of our descriptive terms is surprising by comparison with other sciences. Contributing causes may be the idiographic tradition of unrelated description, and the past predilection for process studies which minimized the real multiplicity of forms.

The predetermined descriptive system.—The reduction of description to a system has been largely opposed by geographers and not entirely without cause. Once this happens the geographer is responsible within the limits of the system for any areal study he undertakes; otherwise he is free to roam, to choose, and to leave. We are not concerned here with geography as an art. As a science it must accept all feasible means for the regimentation of its data. However excellent the individualistic, impressionistic selection of phenomena may be, it is an artistic, not a scientific desideratum. The studies in geomorphology, in particular those of the school of Davis, represent perhaps the most determined attempt to oppose uncontrolled freedom of choice in observation by a strict limitation of observations and of method. Different observations may be compared as to their findings only if there is a reasonable agreement as to the classes of facts with which they deal. The attempt at a broad synthesis of regional studies by employing our existing literature immediately runs into difficulties, because the materials do not fit together. Findings on the most important theme of human destructiveness of natural landscape are very difficult to make because there are no adequate points of reference. Some observers note soil erosion systematically, others casually, and still others may pay no attention to it. If geography is to be systematic and not idiosyncratic, there must be increasing agreement as to items of observation. In particular this should mean a general descriptive scheme to be followed in the collection of field notes.[27]

A general descriptive scheme, intended to catalogue areal facts broadly, without proceeding at this stage from hypothetical origins and connections, has been recently proposed by Passarge under the name *Beschreibende Landschaftskunde*.[28] It is the first comprehensive treatment of this subject since von Richthofen's *Führer für Forschungsreisende*, written just before the most flourishing period of geomorphology.[29] The work of Passarge is somewhat rough-

---

[27] Carl O. Sauer, The Survey Method in Geography and Its Objectives, Annals Assoc. Amer. Geographers, Vol. 14, 1924, pp. 17–33.

[28] Siegfried Passarge, *op. cit.;* Volume 1 has this expression as a subtitle.

[29] Ferdinand von Richthofen, Führer für Forschungsreisende (Berlin, 1886).

hewn and it is perhaps excessively schematic, yet it is the most adequate consideration by far that the whole matter of geographic description has had. Its express purpose is "first of all to determine the facts and to attempt a correct presentation of the significant, visible facts of area without any attempt at explanation and speculation." [30] The plan provides

for the systematic observation of the phenomena that compose the landscape. The method resembles most closely the chrie, a device for the collection of material in theme writing. It helps to see as much as possible and to miss as little as possible and has the further advantage that all observations are ordered. If earlier geographers had been familiar with a method of systematic observation of landscape, it would have been impossible for the characteristic red color of tropical residual soils to have escaped attention until von Richthofen discovered that fact.[31]

Passarge proceeds with an elaborate schedule of notes covering all form categories of the landscape, beginning with atmospheric effects and ending with forms of habitation. From these he proceeds to a descriptive classification of form associations into larger areal terms. For the further elaboration of the plan the reader is referred to the volume in question, as worthy of careful consideration.

The author has applied his system elsewhere to the "pure" as against the "explanatory" description of areas, as for example in his characterization of the valley of the Okavango, in the northern salt steppe of the Kalahari.[32] That he succeeds in giving the reader an adequate picture of the composition of area will probably be admitted.

One may note that Passarge's supposedly purely descriptive procedure is actually based on large experience in areal studies, through which a judgment as to the significant constituents of landscape has been formed. These are really determined through morphologic knowledge, though the classification is not genetic, but properly based on the naïvely generic forms. The capacious dragnet which Passarge has fashioned, though disclaiming all attempt at explanation, is in reality a device fashioned by experienced hands for catching all that may be wanted in an areal morphology and for deferring explanation until the whole material is sorted.

---

[30] Siegfried Passarge, *op. cit.,* p. vi.

[31] *Ibid.,* p. 5.

[32] *Idem,* Die Steppen-Flusstalung des Okawango im Trockenwald-Sandfeld der Nordkalahari, Mitt. d. Geogr. Gesellsch. Hamburg, Vol. 32, 1919, pp. 1–40.

FORMS OF LANDSCAPE AND THEIR STRUCTURE

The division between natural and cultural landscapes.—We cannot form an idea of landscape except in terms of its time relations as well as of its space relations. It is in continuous process of development or of dissolution and replacement. It is in this sense a true appreciation of historical values that has caused the geomorphologists to tie the present physical landscape back into its geologic origins, and to derive it therefrom step by step. In the chorologic sense, however, the modification of the area by man and its appropriation to his uses are of dominant importance. The area before the introduction of man's activity is represented by one body of morphologic facts. The forms that man has introduced are another set. We may call the former, with reference to man, the original, natural landscape. In its entirety it no longer exists in many parts of the world, but its reconstruction and understanding are the first part of formal morphology. Is it perhaps too broad a generalization to say that geography dissociates itself from geology at the point of the introduction of man into the areal scene? Under this view the prior events belong strictly in the field of geology and their historical treatment in geography is only a descriptive device employed where necessary to make clear the relationship of physical forms that are significant in the habitat.

The works of man express themselves in the cultural landscape. There may be a succession of these landscapes with a succession of cultures. They are derived in each case from the natural landscape, man expressing his place in nature as a distinct agent of modification. Of especial significance is that climax of culture which we call civilization. The cultural landscape then is subject to change either by the development of a culture or by a replacement of cultures. The datum line from which change is measured is the natural condition of the landscape. The division of forms into natural and cultural is the necessary basis for determining the areal importance and character of man's activity. In the universal, but not necessarily cosmologic sense, geography then becomes that part of the latest or human chapter in earth history which is concerned with the differentiation of the areal scene by man.

The natural landscape: geognostic basis.—In the subsequent sections on the natural landscape a distinction is implied between the historical inquiry into origin of features and their strictly morphologic organization into a group of forms, fundamental to the cultural expression of the area. We are concerned alone with the latter in principle, with the former only as descriptive convenience.

The forms of the natural landscape involve first of all the materials of the earth's crust which have in some important measure determined the surface forms. The geographer borrows from the geologist knowledge of the substantial differences of the outer lithosphere as to composition, structure, and mass. Geology, being the study of the history of these materials, has devised its classification on the basis of succession of formations, grouped as to period. In formations per se the geographer has no interest. He is concerned, however, with that more primitive phase of geology, called geognosy, which regards kind and position of material but not historical succession. The name of a geologic formation may be meaningless geographically, if it lumps lithologic differences, structural differences, and differences in mass under one term. Geognostic condition provides a basis of conversion of geologic data into geographic values. The geographer is interested in knowing whether the base of a landscape is limestone or sandstone, whether the rocks are massive or intercalated, whether they are broken by joints or are affected by other structural conditions expressed in the surface. These matters may be significant to the understanding of topography, soil, drainage, and mineral distribution.

The application of geognostic data in geographic studies is usual in a sense, areal studies being hardly feasible without some regard for the underlying materials. Yet to find the most adequate analysis of the expression of the underlying materials in the surface it is probably necessary to go back to the work of the older American and British geologists, such as Powell, Dutton, Gilbert, Shaler, and Archibald Geikie. In the aggregate, of course, the geologic literature that touches upon such matters is enormous, but it is made up of rather incidental and informal items, because landscape is not in the central field of interest of the geologist. The formal analysis of critical geognostic qualities and their synthesis into areal generalizations has not had a great deal of attention. Adequately comparable data are still insufficient from the viewpoint of geography. In briefest form Sapper has lately attempted a general consideration of the relation of geologic forms to the landscapes of varying climates, thereby illuminating the entire subject of regional geography.[33]

Rigorous methodologist that he is, Passarge has not failed to

---

[33] Karl Sapper, Geologischer Bau und Landschaftsbild (Braunschweig, 1917).

scrutinize the geographic bearing of rock character and condition, and has applied in intensive areal study the following observations (somewhat adapted) : [34]

> Physical resistance
>> Soft, easily eroded formations
>> Rocks of intermediate resistance
>>> much broken (*zerklüftet*)
>>> moderately broken
>>> little broken
>> Rocks of high resistance
>>> as above
> Chemical resistance and solubility
>> Easily soluble
>>> highly permeable
>>> moderately permeable
>>> relatively impermeable
>> Moderately subject to solution and chemical alteration
>>> as above
>> Resistant

In a later study he added provision for rocks notably subject to creep (*fluktionsfähig*).[35] An interpretation of geologic conditions in terms of equivalence of resistance has never been undertaken for this country. It is probably possible only within the limits of a generally similar climatic condition. We have numerous classifications of so-called physiographic regions, poorly defined as to their criteria, but no truly geognostic classification of area, which, together with relief representation, and climatic areas, is alone competent to provide the base map of all geographic morphology.

The natural landscape: climatic basis.—The second and greater link that connects the forms of the natural landscape into a system is climate. We may say confidently that the resemblance or contrast between natural landscapes in the large is primarily a matter of climate. We may go further and assert that under a given climate a distinctive landscape will develop in time, the climate ultimately cancelling the geognostic factor in many cases.

Physiography, especially in texts, has, largely, either ignored this fact or has subordinated it to such an extent that it is to be read only between the lines. The failure to regard the climatic sum of

[34] Siegfried Passarge, Physiologische Morphologie, Mitt. d. Geogr. Gesellsch. Hamburg, Vol. 26, 1912, pp. 133–337.

[35] *Idem,* Morphologie des Messtischblattes Stadtremsa, *ibid.,* Vol. 28, 1914, pp. 1–221.

physiographic processes as differing greatly from region to region may be due to insufficient experience in different climatic areas and to a predilection for deductive approach. Most physiographic studies have been made in intermediate latitudes of abundant precipitation, and there has been a tendency to think of the agencies in terms of a standardized climatic milieu. The appreciation even of one set of phenomena, as for example drainage forms, is likely to be too much conventionalized by applying the schematism of standardized physiographic process and its results to New England and the Gulf states, to the Atlantic and the Pacific coasts, not to mention the deserts, the tropics, and the polar margins.

But, if we start from the areal diversity of climates, we consider at once differences in penetration of heat and cold diurnally and seasonally, the varying areal expression of precipitation as to amount, form, intensity, and seasonal distribution, the wind as a factor varying with area, and above all the numerous possibilities of combination of temperature, precipitation, dry weather, and wind. In short, we place major emphasis on the totality of weather conditions in the molding of soil, drainage, and surface features. It is geographically much more important to establish the synthesis of natural landscape forms in terms of the individual climatic area than to follow through the mechanics of a single process, rarely expressing itself individually in a land form of any great extent.

The harmony of climate and landscape, insufficiently developed by the schools of physiography, has become the keystone of geographic morphology in the physical sense. In this country the emergence of this concept is to be sought largely in the studies in the arid and semi-arid West, though they did not result at once in the realization of the implied existence of a distinct set of land forms for every climate. In the morphologic form category of soils, the climatic factor was fully discovered first at the hand of Russian students, and was used by them as the primary basis of soil classification [36] in a more thoroughgoing manner than that which had been applied to topographic forms.[37] Under the direction of Marbut the climatic system has become basal to the work of the United States Bureau of Soils. Thus the ground was prepared for the general synthesis of physical landscape in terms of climatic regions.[38] Most

---

[36] K. Glinka, Die Typen der Bodenbildung, ihre Klassifikation und geographische Verbreitung (Berlin, 1914); revised and extended by E. Ramann, Bodenbildung und Bodeneinteilung (System der Böden) (Berlin, 1918).

[37] For desert forms there was in existence the synthesis of Johannes Walther, Das Gesetz der Wüstenbildung in Gegenwart und Vorzeit (Berlin, 1900).

[38] Excellently done by Sapper, *op. cit.;* but also strongly emphasized by

recently, Passarge, using Köppen's climatic classification, has undertaken a comprehensive methodology on this basis.[39]

The relation of climate to landscape is expressed in part through vegetation, which arrests or transforms the climatic forces. We therefore need to recognize not only the presence or absence of a cover of vegetation, but also the type of cover that is interposed between the exogenous forces of climate and the materials of the earth and that acts on the materials beneath.

Diagrammatic representation of the morphology of the natural landscape.—We may now attempt a diagram of the nature of physical morphology to express the relation of landscape, constituent forms, time, and connecting causal factors:

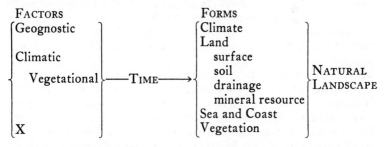

The thing to be known is the natural landscape. It becomes known through the totality of its forms. These forms are thought of not for and by themselves, as a soil specialist would regard soils, for example, but in their relation to one another and in their place in the landscape, each landscape being a definite combination of form values. Behind the forms lie time and cause. The primary genetic bonds are climatic and geognostic, the former being in general dominant, and operating directly as well as through vegetation. The "X" factor is the pragmatic "and," the always unequated remnant. These factors are justified as a device for the connection of the forms, not as the end of inquiry. They lead toward the concept of the natural landscape which in turn leads to the cultural landscape. The character of the landscape is determined also by its position on the time line. Whether this line is of determinate or infinite length does not concern us as geographers. In some measure, certainly, the idea of a climax landscape is useful, a landscape that,

W. M. Davis and G. Braun, Grundzüge der Physiogeographie, 2nd ed., Vol. 2, Morphologie (Leipzig u. Berlin, 1915), especially in the final chapters.

[39] Siegfried Passarge, Grundlagen der Landschaftskunde, Vols. 2, 3 (Berlin, 1921, 1922).

given a constancy of impinging factors, has exhausted the possibilities of autogenous development. Through the medium of time the application of factor to form as cause-and-effect relation is limited; time itself is a great factor. We are interested in function, not in a determination of cosmic unity. For all chorologic purposes the emphasis in the diagram lies at its right hand; time and factor have only an explanatory descriptive role.

This position with reference to the natural landscape involves a reaffirmation of the place of physical geography, certainly not as physiography nor geomorphology as ordinarily defined, but as physical morphology, which draws freely from geology and physiography certain results to be built into a view of physical landscape as a habitat complex. This physical geography is the proper introduction to the full chorologic inquiry that is our goal.

Forms of the natural landscape: climate.—In the physical structure of landscape, climate is first in importance. In the diagram it appears at the head of the list of forms and also as the major factor behind the whole category of forms. As a form, climate is an areal expression, the sum of the atmospheric features of the area. This is the sense in which it is treated in climatology. In American literature climates were first introduced prominently as areal forms, fundamental to geography in general, through Tower's chapters on climate in Salisbury, Barrows, and Tower's *Elements of Geography*.[40] The value of this view has been demonstrated by the steadily increasing role which climatology has played in the fundamental courses of instruction. In no respect are we as near to general agreement as in this.

Climatology is areal reality; meteorology is general process. The contrast is that between physical geography and physiography.

Land forms in the natural landscape.—The land includes four edaphic elements or properties analogous to the climatic elements; namely, surface or land form in the narrow sense, soil, drainage, and mineral forms. In the case of surface forms we are dealing with a body of fact that is of interest to geomorphology, to physiography, and to geographic morphology. The first is concerned with history, the second with process, the third with description and relation to other forms. For our purposes surface forms are to be regarded as climates are in climatology. Strictly we are concerned with the character of relief only; that is, with expressions of slope and exposure in relation to the other constituent forms of the landscape.

---

[40] Rollin D. Salisbury, Harlan H. Barrows, and Walter S. Tower, The Elements of Geography (New York, 1912), chapters 9–11, pp. 154–225.

The topographic map, interpreted in terms of use significance of different slopes, is in principle the complete chorologic representation of surface form. The relation of surface form to climate is so close that the grouping of surfaces by climates is warranted generally. Geognostic relation of surface also lends itself well to the areal grouping of land forms. The further penetration into genesis of forms leads increasingly away from geographic ends. Restraint in this respect is necessary and is attained through a proper realization of the goal of areal reality.

The areal differentiation of soils fundamentally is based on differences of productivity, or their habitat significance. Soils as areal form constituents are primarily grouped by climates; the secondary classification is geognostic and therefore also chorologically satisfactory. The placing of soils into the structure of landscape therefore presents little difficulty, the soil survey being in fact a highly specialized form of physical geography. Unlike some physiographers and geomorphologists, the field student of soils is not pursuing a nongeographic end, but is limiting himself to a small part of the geographic field.

Drainage forms are of course direct expressions of climate, and the most feasible classification of streams, swamps, and bodies of standing water is in climatic terms. For instance, moors are a type of high-latitude swamp, permanent features under conditions of low evaporation. Their growth is especially favored by the presence of certain plants, such as sphagnum moss. Their position is not restricted to lowlands, but they extend over fairly irregular surfaces by the expansion of a marginal zone of spongy vegetation. These swamps illustrate the interrelation of physical areal forms. Under them a distinctive soil is developed and even the subsoil is altered. This swampy covering also protects the land surface it has occupied from the attacks of running water and wind and molds it into broadly rounded forms. Where climatic conditions are not favorable to the development of such swamps, both in still higher and in lower latitudes, the forms of drainage, soil, and surface change markedly.

Mineral resources belong among the physical forms under the view of the physical landscape as a human habitat. Here the geognostic factor dominates genetically. The diagrammatic relation still holds in a measure, because of the concentration of minerals due to underground waters both at and beneath the surface. It would be pedantic to urge this point strongly, nor are we desirous to urge genetic relation as a necessary principle.

Forms of the sea in the natural landscape.—The relation of sea to land is organizable on the same basis of climate and geognosy. The seacoasts are in the main an expression of tectonic history and of climatic setting. Areally, climates afford the broader basis of classification, because elevation and subsidence of coasts have varied and are changing, as to direction and amount, so greatly, over short distances as to make a tectonic classification of seashores chorologically unsatisfactory. The seas themselves are obviously as intimately related to climate as is the land. Their currents, surface conditions, density, and temperatures are as certainly to be classified in climatic terms as land forms.

Vegetation forms in the natural landscape.—A. von Humboldt was the first to recognize, through systematic observations, the importance of vegetation in the character of the landscape. "However much the character of the different parts of the world depends on the totality of external appearances; though outline of mountains, physiognomy of plants and animals, cloud forms and transparency of the atmosphere compose the general impression; yet it is not to be denied that the most important element in this impression is the cover of vegetation." [41] The bonds between climate and vegetation are so direct and strong that a large measure of climatic grouping of vegetation forms is possible. Some plant geographers have found the classification of vegetational associations most desirable in terms of thermal or moisture belts.

Summary of the form relations in the natural landscape.—The large emphasis on climate in the previous statements does not mean that geography is to be transformed into climatology. The physical area is fundamental to any geographic study because it furnishes the materials out of which man builds his culture. The identity of the physical area rests fundamentally on a distinctive association of physical forms. In the physical world, generic character of area and its genesis are coupled so closely that the one becomes an aid to the recognition of the other. In particular, climate, itself an areal form, largely obscure as to origin, so largely controls the expression of the other physical forms that in many areas it may be considered the determinant of form association. An express disclaimer may be entered, however, against the notion of the necessity of a genetic bond in order to organize the phenomenology of the natural landscape. The existence of such bonds has been determined empiri-

---

[41] Alexander von Humboldt, Ansichten der Natur, Vol. 2 (Stuttgart & Tübingen, 1849), p. 20.

cally. By regarding the relationship of forms we have discovered an important light on "the obscurity of their descent," but as geographers we are not enjoined to trace out the nature of this descent. This remains the problem of geomorphology, which indeed now appears more complicated than ever, the validity of climatic control and of great secular changes of climate being accepted.

Thus far the way is pretty well marked. We know the "inorganic" composition of landscape fairly well, and, except for a somewhat excessive aloofness existing between plant and general geography, the place of vegetation in the landscape is properly cared for.[42]

The extension of morphology to the cultural landscape.—The natural landscape is being subjected to transformation at the hands of man, the last and for us the most important morphologic factor. By his cultures he makes use of the natural forms, in many cases alters them, in some destroys them.

---

[42] Alfred Hettner, *op. cit.,* p. 39, comments as follows on biogeography: "The great majority of studies in plant and animal geography have been made by botanists and zoologists, even though these works do not always completely satisfy our geographic needs. The botanist and zoologist are concerned with plants and animals, we with lands. . . . When they carry on plant and animal geography in this narrower sense, as, for example, Grisebach in his brilliant volume on the vegetation of the earth, they are doing geographic work, in the same manner as meteorologists who concern themselves with climatology; for the purpose is geographic, the results fit more closely into the structure of geographic instruction than into that of botany or zoology, and the whole process of thought and inquiry, oriented as it is about climate and soil, is geographic. We geographers are far from being jealous on that account; on the contrary, we acknowledge such aid gratefully; but rightly we have commenced also to do plant and animal geography, because certain problems concern us more than they do those who are not geographers and because we possess certain valuable preparations for such studies." The work of plant and animal geographers illustrates the partial artificiality of academic compartments. They require so specialized a training that ordinarily they are professionally classed as botanists and zoologists. Their method, however, is geographic to such an extent and their findings are so significant to geography that their work is more appreciated and perhaps even better evaluated by geographers than by biologists generally. Occasional field biologists, such as Bates, Hudson, and Beebe, have done work that encompasses so large a part of the landscape that they are really geographers of the highest accomplishment. It is, however, true that vegetation or fauna may be regarded somewhat differently as a part of the human habitat (economic plant and animal geography?) from the view of them as a part of botany or zoology. In this difference lies the justification of Hettner's recommendation of participation by the geographer in plant and animal studies. Now and then a geographer, as for instance Gradmann and Waibel, has mastered the field of biogeography to the enrichment of his whole position.

The study of the cultural landscape is, as yet, largely an untilled field. Recent results in the field of plant ecology will probably supply many useful leads for the human geographer, for cultural morphology might be called human ecology. In contrast to the position of Barrows in this matter, the present thesis would eliminate physiologic ecology or autecology and seek for parallels in synecology. It is better not to force into geography too much biological nomenclature. The name ecology is not needed: it is both morphology and physiology of the biotic association. Since we waive the claim for the measurement of environmental influences, we may use, in preference to ecology, the term morphology to apply to cultural study, since it describes perfectly the method.

Among geographers in America who have concerned themselves with systematic inquiry into cultural forms, Mark Jefferson, O. E. Baker, and M. Aurousseau have done outstanding pioneering. Brunhes' "essential facts of geography" represent perhaps the most widely appreciated classification of cultural forms.[43] Sten De Geer's population atlas of Sweden [44] was the first major contribution of a student who has concentrated his attention strictly on cultural morphology. Vaughan Cornish introduced the concepts of "march," "storehouse," and "crossroads" in a most valuable contribution to urban problems.[45] Most recently, Walter Geisler has undertaken a synthesis of the urban forms of Germany, with the deserved subtitle, "A contribution to the morphology of the cultural landscape." [46] These pioneers have found productive ground; our periodical literature suggests that a rush of homesteaders may soon be under way.

Diagrammatic representation of the morphology of the cultural landscape.—The cultural landscape is the geographic area in the final meaning (*Chore*). Its forms are all the works of man that characterize the landscape. Under this definition we are not concerned in geography with the energy, customs, or beliefs of man but with man's record upon the landscape. Forms of population are the phenomena of mass or density in general and of recurrent displacement, as seasonal migration. Housing includes the types of structures

[43] Jean Brunhes, La Géographie humaine, ed. 2 (Paris, 1912), pp. 62–66, 89–455; Amer. transl., Human Geography (Chicago and New York, 1920), pp. 48–52, 74–414.

[44] Sten De Geer, Karta över befolkningens fördelning i Sverige den 1 januar 1917 (Stockholm, 1919).

[45] Vaughan Cornish, The Great Capitals (London, 1923).

[46] Walter Geisler, Die deutsche Stadt: ein Beitrag zur Morphologie der Kulturlandschaft (Stuttgart, 1924).

man builds and their grouping, either dispersed as in many rural districts, or agglomerated into villages or cities in varying plans (*Städtebild*). Forms of production are the types of land utilization for primary products, farms, forests, mines, and those negative areas which he has ignored.

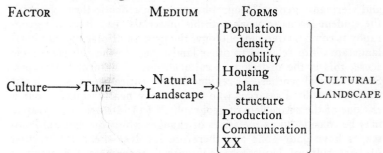

FACTOR   MEDIUM   FORMS

Culture ⟶ TIME ⟶ Natural Landscape → { Population density mobility Housing plan structure Production Communication XX } CULTURAL LANDSCAPE

The cultural landscape is fashioned from a natural landscape by a culture group. Culture is the agent, the natural area is the medium, the cultural landscape the result. Under the influence of a given culture, itself changing through time, the landscape undergoes development, passing through phases, and probably reaching ultimately the end of its cycle of development. With the introduction of a different—that is, an alien—culture, a rejuvenation of the cultural landscape sets in, or a new landscape is superimposed on remnants of an older one. The natural landscape is of course of fundamental importance, for it supplies the materials out of which the cultural landscape is formed. The shaping force, however, lies in the culture itself. Within the wide limits of the physical equipment of area lie many possible choices for man, as Vidal never grew weary of pointing out. This is the meaning of adaptation, through which, aided by those suggestions which man has derived from nature, perhaps by an imitative process, largely subconscious, we get the feeling of harmony between the human habitation and the landscape into which it so fittingly blends. But these, too, are derived from the mind of man, not imposed by nature, and hence are cultural expressions.

MORPHOLOGY AS APPLIED TO THE BRANCHES OF GEOGRAPHY

The consolidation of the two diagrams gives an approximation of the total scientific content of geography on the phenomenologic basis by which we have proceeded.[47] They may readily be expressed so as to define the branches of geography. (1) The study of the form categories per se in their general relation, the system of the forms of landscape, is morphology in the purely methodologic sense, and is the equivalent of what is called, especially in France and Germany, general geography, the propaedeutic through which the student learns to work with his materials. (2) Regional geography is comparative morphology, the process of placing individual landscapes into relation to other landscapes. In the full chorologic sense, this is the ordering of cultural, not of natural landscapes. Such a critical synthesis of regions for the entire world is the latest contribution by Passarge, who has thereby nearly rounded out a critique of the entire field of geography.[48] (3) Historical geography may be considered as the series of changes which the cultural landscapes have undergone and therefore involves the reconstruction of past cultural landscapes. Of special concern is the catalytic relation of civilized man to area and the effects of the replacement of cultures. From this difficult and little-touched field alone may be gained a full realization of the development of the present cultural landscape out of earlier cultures and the natural landscape. (4) Commercial geography deals with the forms of production and the facilities for distribution of the products of areas.

BEYOND SCIENCE

The morphologic discipline enables the organization of the fields of geography as positive science. A good deal of the meaning of area lies beyond scientific regimentation. The best geography has never disregarded the esthetic qualities of landscape, to which we know no approach other than the subjective. Humboldt's "physiognomy," Banse's "soul," Volz's "rhythm," Gradmann's "harmony" of landscape, all lie beyond science. These writers seem to have discovered a symphonic quality in the contemplation of the areal scene, proceeding from a full novitiate in scientific studies and yet apart therefrom. To some, whatever is mystical is an abomination. Yet

[47] The conclusions presented in this paper are substantially in agreement with Sten De Geer's article On the Definition, Method, and Classification of Geography, Geogr. Annaler, Vol. 5, 1923, pp. 1–37, with the contrast that a "concrete" *landscape* takes the place of De Geer's "abstract" *areal relation.*

[48] Siegfried Passarge, Vergleichende Landschaftskunde (Berlin, 1923); Die Landschaftsgürtel der Erde (Breslau, 1923).

it is significant that there are others, and among them some of the best, who believe, that having observed widely and charted diligently, there yet remains a quality of understanding at a higher plane that may not be reduced to formal process.[49]

DIVERGENT VIEWS OF GEOGRAPHY

The geographic thesis of this essay is so largely at variance with certain other views of the subject that it may be desirable to set forth in summary form what has been expressed and implied as to contrast in the several positions.

Geomorphology as a branch of geography.—German geographers in particular tend to regard geomorphology as an essential division of geography, and use largely the term *Oberflächengestaltung*, or the record of development of surficial form. The forms considered are ordinarily topographic only. The content of geomorphology has been most broadly defined by Penck,[50] who includes the following forms: plains, hill surfaces, valleys, basins, mountains, cavernous forms, seacoasts, seafloors, islands. These descriptive topographic terms are studied by geomorphology as to their derivation, not as to use significance.

Geomorphology being the history of topography, it derives present surfaces from previous forms and records the processes involved. A study of the geomorphology of the Sierra Nevada is a history of the sculpturing of the mountain massif, concerned with the uplift of the earth block and the stages of modification in which erosional processes, secondary deformations, and structural conditions are in complex relations. Relief features in this sense are the result of the opposition of orogenic and degradational processes through geologic periods of time. Certain features, such as peneplains and terrace remnants, thus have high diagnostic value in reading the record of modification of surface. These elements of the landscape, however, may be of little or no significance in the chorologic sense. To geomorphology the peneplain has been ex-

---

[49] A good statement of current searchings in this field is by Robert Gradmann, Das harmonische Landschaftsbild, Ztschr. d. Gesellsch. f. Erdk. z. Berlin, 1924, pp. 129–147. Ewald Banse has been publishing since 1922 a non- or anti-scientific journal, Die neue Geographie, in which numerous good items are enclosed in a repellently polemic shell.

[50] Albrecht Penck, Morphologie der Erdoberfläche, Vol. 2 (Stuttgart, 1894), pp. 1–2.

tremely important; the trend of geography has not been notably affected by its discovery. Out of the topographic complex the geomorphologist may select one body of facts illustrative of earth history, the geographer will use a largely different set of facts that have habitat significance.

The geomorphologist, therefore, is likely to be a specialized historical geologist, working on certain, usually late, chapters of earth history. Conventional historical geology is mostly concerned with the making of rock formations. The geomorphologist directs attention to erosional and deformational surfaces in the record of the rocks. To such an extent has this been the American orientation that we have in our country little geomorphologic work of recent date that is consciously geographic in purpose; that is, descriptive of actual land surfaces.

The geomorphologist can and does establish a connection between the fields of geography and geology and his labors further our own work. He advances our studies of landscape materially where he has preceded the geographer, and we properly regard him potentially as much a collaborator in geography as in geology. One of the present needs in American geography is a greater familiarity with and application of geomorphologic studies.

Physiography and physical geography.—When T. H. Huxley reapplied the term physiography he disclaimed expressly the desire to reform physical geography. He was not lecturing, he said, "on any particular branch of natural knowledge, but on natural phenomena in general." [51] The subtitle of his treatise reads "An Introduction to the Study of Nature." He chose the basin of the Thames as the area for his demonstration, not through chorologic interest, but in order to show that any area contained abundant material for the demonstration of the general laws of physical science. Huxley said:

I endeavoured to show that the application of the plainest and simplest processes of reasoning to any of these phenomena suffices to show, lying behind it, a cause, which will again suggest another; until, step, by step, the conviction dawns upon the learner that, to attain even an elementary conception of what goes on in his parish he must know something about the universe; that the pebble he kicks aside would not be what it is and where it is unless a particular chapter of the earth's history, finished untold ages ago, had been exactly what it was.[52]

[51] T. H. Huxley, Physiography: an Introduction to the Study of Nature, 2nd ed. (New York, 1878), p. vi.
[52] *Ibid.,* pp. vii–viii.

The two central ideas in his mind were the unity of physical law as shown by the features of the earth and the evolutionary march of the geologic record. It was the bright hour of dawn in scientific monism, with Huxley officiating at the observation of the lands. Physiography served in such a canonical role in elementary scientific education until a later age of machinery sent it into the discard in favor of "general science."

Physiography is still the general science of the earth, and concerns itself with the physical processes that operate at the surface of the earth and in the earth's crust. We still find the captions that Huxley introduced into his text: the work of rain and rivers, ice and its work, the sea and its work, earthquakes and volcanoes. These things have chorologic expression, but they are studied as general processes. As an investigator the physiographer must be above all things a physicist, and increasing demands are made on his physical and mathematical knowledge. The way of the development of physiography as research is through geophysical institutes. Academically it fits in best as a part of dynamic geology. The geographer probably needs to know little more of it than he should know of historical geology.

One may question, therefore, the propriety of such terms as regional physiography and physiographic regions. They contradict the essential meaning of the subject and ordinarily mean rather a loose form of geomorphology, which of necessity has areal expression. Physiography was conceived as a purely dynamic relation and is categorically incapable of consistent areal expression unless it becomes also a name applied to physical geography or to geomorphology.

Geographic morphology vs. *"geographic influences."*—The study of the physical environment was subjected to trenchant criticism by L. Febvre, with an equally incisive foreword by Henri Berr.[53] Both thoroughly relish the chance to riddle this geographic ambition. Geography as they see it is "to give an example of the true task of synthesis. . . . The effort of synthesis is a directed activity; it is not a premature realization." [54] Questions of environment "may have for the geographer their interest; but they are not his end. He must guard well against acclaiming as 'scientific' verities theories of adaptation 'simpliste' in character that more competent people are in process of completing or correcting." [55] "What is, then, the

[53] Lucien Febvre, La Terre et l'Évolution humaine (Paris, 1922).

[54] *Ibid.*, p. ix.

[55] *Ibid.*, p. 11.

commendable attitude in human geography? It can consist only in searching for the relations that exist between earth and life, the rapport which exists between the external milieu and the activity of the occupants." [56] Vidal de la Blache's thesis that in the relation of man to the earth there exists less of necessary adaptation than of "possibilisme" is worked out with skill and conviction. Excepting for their spirited devotion to the master of French geography, these authors are not really familiar with geographic thought. They do not fairly represent the tenets of geography, because they know chiefly the publicists of environmentalism, against whom they consider Vidal as the outstanding bulwark. Vidal will have an honored place in the history of geography, but we are no longer much impressed by his concern to establish decently good relations with rationalistic thought. Rationalism has seen better days than these; we no longer need to come to terms with it by diplomatic compromise. In spite of the deficient orientation in geographic thought, Febvre's volume directs a quality of dialectic at one geographic school which entitles it to high rank in geographic criticism.

In this country the theme that geography is the study of natural environment has been dominant in the present generation. It has come to be advertised abroad that such is the American definition of geography.[57] The earliest term was "environmental control." This was succeeded by "response," "influence," "adjustment," or some other word that does not change the meaning, but substitutes a more cautious term for the ringing declaration of control. All these positions are mechanistic. In some way they hope to measure the force that physical environment exerts over man. The land-scape as such has no interest for them, but only those cultural fea-tures for which a causal connection with the physical environment can be established. The aim, therefore, is to make of geography a part of biophysics, concerned with human tropisms.

Geographic morphology does not deny determinism, nor does it require adhesion to that particular faith in order to qualify in the profession. Geography under the banner of environmentalism rep-resents a dogma, the assertion of a faith that brings rest to a spirit vexed by the riddle of the universe. It was a new evangel for the age of reason, which set up its particular form of adequate order and

---

[56] *Ibid.*, p. 12.

[57] S. Van Valkenburg, Doel en richting der geografie, Tijdschr. v. d. K. Nederl. Aardrijksk. Genootschap, ser. 2, Vol. 41, 1924, pp. 138–140.

even of ultimate purpose. The exposition of the faith could proceed only by finding testimonials to its efficacy. To the true believer there were visible evidences of what he thought should be, which were not to be seen by those who were weak in the faith. Unless one has the proper temperament, his continued elaboration of this single thesis with the weak instruments at his hand becomes dreadfully monotonous. In such a study one knows beforehand that one will encounter only variants of the one theme of "influence."

The narrowly rationalistic thesis conceives of environment as process, and of some of the qualities and activities of man as products. The agency is physical nature; man responds or adapts himself. Simple as the thesis sounds, it incurs continually grave difficulties in the matching of specific response to specific stimulus or inhibition. The direct influence of environmental stimuli is purely somatic. What happens to man through the influence of his physical surroundings is beyond the competence of the geographer; at most he may keep informed as to physiologic research in that field. What man does in an area because of tabu or totemism or because of his own will involves use of environment rather than the active agency of the environment. It would, therefore, appear that environmentalism has been shooting neither at cause nor at effect, but rather that it is bagging its own decoys.[58]

CONCLUSION

In the colorful reality of life there is a continuous resistance of fact to confinement within any "simpliste" theory. We are concerned with "directed activity, not premature realization," and this is the morphologic approach. Our naïvely selected section of reality, the landscape, is undergoing manifold change. This contact of man with his changeful home, as expressed through the cultural landscape, is our field of work. We are concerned with the importance of the site to man, and also with his transformation of the site. Altogether we deal with the interrelation of group, or cultures, and site, as expressed in the various landscapes of the world. Here are an inexhaustible body of fact and a variety of relation which provide a

---

[58] A. L. Kroeber, Anthropology (New York, 1923), pp. 180–193, 502–503, scrutinizes the ex parte nature of environmental tenets in their relation to culture.

course of inquiry that does not need to restrict itself to the straits of rationalism.[59]

---

[59] Clark Wissler, The Relation of Nature to Man as Illustrated by the North American Indian, Ecology, Vol. 5, 1924, pp. 311–318. P. 311: "While the early history of the concept is probably lost to us forever, there are not wanting indications that the ecological idea was conceived in the same atmosphere as the theory of design, or of purposeful adaptation. However that may be, the effort on the part of the later professors of ecology has been to eschew all such philosophies except the fundamental assumption that plants and the rest of nature are intimately interdependent one upon the other." Thus "the anthropologist is not only trying to show what all the forms and forces of nature have done to man, but even with more emphasis what man has done to nature" (p. 312). This definition of anthropology includes a very large part of the social field, and is also a good definition for geography. At present anthropology is the study of culture per se. If our studies of man and of his work have large success in synthesis, a gradual coalescence of social anthropology and of geography may represent the first of a series of fusions into a larger science of man.

{ 17 }

Foreword to
Historical Geography

These remarks are directed to the nature of historical geography and to some of its problems. By preference I should present data and conclusions from my own work in Mexico. On second thought, however, I am moved to do what has been done so often in the annual address before this body: to set forth in some manner a confession of the faith that has stood behind one's work.

It is obvious that we who call ourselves geographers do not at present understand each other very well. We have more fraternal feeling of belonging together than common intellectual ground on which we meet freely and easily. We can hardly claim to be getting our chief intellectual stimulus from one another, to be waiting impatiently on the research of colleagues as needed for our own work. We are of various minds as to the fields in which we are engaged. So long as we are in such a condition of uncertainty about our major objectives and problems, attempts must be made from time to time to give orientation to ourselves along a common course.

AN AMERICAN RETROSPECT

This will not be another design for the whole of geography, but a protest against the neglect of historical geography. In the nearly forty years of existence of this Association, there have been but two presidential addresses that have dealt with historical geography: one by Ellen Semple and one by Almon Parkins.[1]

Annals of the Association of American Geographers, Vol. 31, 1941, pp. 1–24. Presidential Address given at the annual meeting of the Association of American Geographers, Baton Rouge, Louisiana, December, 1940.

[1] Ellen Churchill Semple, The Influence of Geographic Conditions upon Ancient Mediterranean Stock-raising, Annals Assoc. Amer. Geographers, Vol.

A peculiarity of our American geographical tradition has been its lack of interest in historical processes and sequences, even their outright rejection. A second peculiarity of American geography has been the attempt to slough off to other disciplines the fields of physical geography. Hartshorne's recent methodologic study [2] is an interesting illustration of both these attitudes. In spite of basing himself strongly upon Hettner, he does not take into account the fact that Hettner's own contributions to knowledge have been chiefly in physical geography. Neither does he follow Hettner into his main methodologic position, namely that geography, in any of its branches, must be a genetic science; that is, must account for origins and processes. Hettner's students have made many of the important contributions of late years to historical geography. Hartshorne, however, directs his dialectics against historical geography, giving it tolerance only at the outer fringes of the subject. I have cited this position because it is the latest and, I think, best statement of what is in fact, if not by avowal, a pretty general viewpoint in this country.

Perhaps in future years the period from Barrows' "Geography as Human Ecology" [3] to Hartshorne's late résumé will be remembered as that of the Great Retreat. This retraction of lines began by the pulling apart of geography from geology. Geography, of course, owes its academic start in this country to the interest of geologists. Partly in order to gain administrative independence in the universities and colleges, geographers began to seek interests that geologists could not claim to share. In this process, however, American geography gradually ceased to be a part of earth science. Many geographers have completely renounced physical geography as a subject of research, if not entirely as one of instruction. There followed the attempt to devise a natural science of the human environment, the relationship being gradually softened from the term "control" to "influence" or "adaptation" or "adjustment," and finally to the somewhat liturgical "response." Methodical difficulties in finding such relationships led to a further restriction, to

12, 1922, pp. 3–38; Almon E. Parkins, The Antebellum South: A Geographer's Interpretation, *ibid.,* Vol. 21, 1931, pp. 1–33.

[2] Richard Hartshorne, The Nature of Geography: a Critical Survey of Current Thought in the Light of the Past, *ibid.,* Vol. 29, 1939, pp. 173–658. Also as separate (Lancaster, Pa., 1939).

[3] H. H. Barrows, Geography as Human Ecology, *ibid.,* Vol. 13, 1923, pp. 1–14.

a nongenetic description of the human content of areas, sometimes called chorography, apparently in the hope that by and by such studies would somehow add up to systematic knowledge.

This thumbnail sketch of our generation, as to its dominant motifs, is simplified but, I hope, not distorted. Throughout this time, the desire has been to limit the field in order to secure its domination. There has been the feeling that we were too few and weak to do all the things which had been done in the name of geography, and that a sufficient restriction would mean better work and freedom from trespass quarrels.

Whichever way he has turned, the American geographer has failed to locate the uncontested field in which only professionally certified geographers might be found. Sociologists have been swarming all over the precincts of human ecology.[4] Odum and his North Carolina associates have been exploring with success the connotations of region and regionalism.[5] Economic geography has been approached from new angles by economists like Zimmermann and Mc-Carty.[6] Land planning can certainly not be claimed as the geographer's discipline, nor as a discipline in any sense, since it must obviously be primarily projected from a specific theory of the state. These errant years have not led us to the desired refuge. We shall not find our intellectual home in this movement away from our heritage.

The American geography of today is essentially a native product; predominantly it is bred in the Middle West; and in dispensing with serious consideration of cultural or historical processes it reflects strongly its background. In the Middle West, original cultural differences faded rapidly in the forging of a commercial civilization based on great natural resources. Perhaps nowhere else and at no other time has a great civilization been shaped so rapidly, so simply, and so directly out of the fat of the land and the riches

---

[4] E.g., Robert E. Park, Ernest W. Burgess, and Roderick D. McKenzie, edits., The City (Chicago, 1925); Howard W. Odum, American Social Problems: an Introduction to the Study of the People and their Dilemmas (New York, 1938), pp. 23–62.

[5] Howard W. Odum, Southern Regions of the United States (Chapel Hill, 1936); Howard W. Odum and Harry Estill Moore, American Regionalism: a Cultural-historical Approach to National Integration (New York, 1938).

[6] Erich W. Zimmermann, World Resources and Industries; a Functional Appraisal of the Availability of Agricultural and Industrial Resources (New York, 1933); Harold Hull McCarty, The Geographic Basis of American Economic Life (New York, 1940).

of the subsoil. Apparently here, if anywhere, the formal logic of costs and returns dominated a rationalized and steadily expanding economic world. The growth of American geography came largely at a time when it seemed reasonable to conclude that under any given situation of natural environment there was one best, most economical expression of use, adjustment, or response. Was not the corn belt *the* logical expression of soil and climate of the prairies? Did not its capital, Chicago, show in the character and energy of its growth the manifest destiny inherent in its position at the southern extremity of Lake Michigan, toward the eastern margin of the prairies? Did not the green sea of corn that overwhelmed the native prairie grasses represent an ideal realization of the most economical use of a site, as did the bending of the strands of communication to meet at the dynamic center of Chicago? Here the growth of centers of heavy industry at points of most economic assembly of raw materials was an almost mathematical demonstration of function of ton-miles, somewhat conventionalized in terms of freight-rate structures.

And so, in the simple dynamism of the Midwest of the early twentieth century, the complex calculus of historical growth or loss did not seem particularly real or important. Was it, in view of such "rational" adjustments of activity and resource, being very realistic to say that any economic system was nothing but the temporarily equilibrated set of choices and customs of a particular group? In this brief moment of fulfillment and ease, it seemed that there must be a strict logic of the relationship of site and satisfaction, something approaching the validity of natural order. Do you remember the studies that related land use to numerical sums expressing natural environment, that related intensity of production to market distance, that planned the "best" future use of land and "most" desirable distribution of population? Actors in the last scenes of a play that had begun in the early nineteenth century, the authors of these studies were largely unaware that they were a part of a great historic drama. They came to think that human geography and history were really quite different subjects, not different approaches to the same problem, the problem of cultural growth and change.

For those who would not follow in this train, the nineteen twenties and thirties have not been heartening for American geography. Those who found their work in fields of physical geography often have felt themselves scarcely tolerated. Particularly depressing has been the tendency to question, not the competence, originality, or significance of research that has been offered to us, but the admissibility of work because it may or may not satisfy a narrow definition of geography. When a subject is ruled, not by inquisitiveness but by definitions of its boundaries, it is likely to face extinction. This way lies the death of learning. Such has been the lingering sickness of American academic geography that pedantry, which is logic combined with lack of curiosity, has tried to read out of the party workers who have not conformed to prevalent definitions. A healthy science is engaged in discovery, verification, comparison, and generalization. Its subject matter will be determined by its competence in organization. Only if we reach that day when we shall gather to sit far into the night, comparing our findings and discussing all their meanings, shall we have recovered from the pernicious anemia of the "but-is-this-geography?" state.

A THREE-POINT UNDERPINNING FOR GEOGRAPHY

The business of becoming a geographer is a job of lifelong learning. We can teach a few skills, such as the making of maps of various kinds, but mostly, in the instructional period, the best we can do is to open doors for the student.

1. One of these, which is not sufficiently often thrown wide, is the history of geography. There is available to us a fine and great intellectual heritage. This is not simply the study of our subject as it has shaped up at various periods of its history, though this is stimulating enough. No one is likely to regret, for instance, becoming familiar with Greek thought in geography, as a background for his own thinking. Of especial value, however, to the development of the student is the first-hand study of the individual great and genial figures of our past. A student can hardly immerse himself for a period in following through the intellectual history of a Ritter or Humboldt without seeing wide horizons open up. This sort of thing, however, means learning to know these men through the whole range of their work, not by way of someone else's critique. A good knowledge of the work of one or more of our major personalities is about as important an induction into geography as I am able to suggest.

The list of these will vary with individual opinion. I should, however, like to bespeak a place on this shelf of classics for Eduard Hahn, as well as for Ratzel. Ratzel is best known to us, and that mostly at second hand, for the first volume of his *Anthropogeographie.*[7] There is far more in the unknown Ratzel than in the well publicized one. Hahn is our forgotten classic. For the viewpoint that I wish to develop in later paragraphs, he is perhaps the most important person in our history. At this point I shall simply submit the opinion that Hahn made of economic geography an historical science, that he opened up unimagined vistas of the origin and spread of cultures, and that he penetrated farthest, as well as first, into the concept of the economic region. From England I should like to nominate Vaughan Cornish and from this country George Marsh for full-length biographical inquiry. The half-dozen names offered will in themselves provide a truly liberal geographic education, provided each is taken as a whole, and not skimmed eclectically in terms of prearranged views as to what is and is not geographic.

2. American geography cannot dissociate itself from the great fields of physical geography. The ways that Davis, Salisbury, and Tarr[8] so clearly marked out must not be abandoned. A geographer, I submit, may properly be a student of physical phenomena without concerning himself with man, but a human geographer has only limited competence who cannot observe as well as interpret the physical data that are involved in his studies of human economies. It is a puzzling fact that American environmentalists have reduced attention to surface and soils, to climate and weather to most inadequate terms, whereas those who see in geography more than the relation of man to environment have continued to support by inquiry these physical observations. In addition, climatology, ecology, and geomorphology serve important methodologic purposes as disciplines of observation, the techniques of which may be applied to human geography.

3. Lastly, the human geographer should be well based on the sister discipline of anthropology. Ratzel elaborated the study of cultural diffusions which has become basic to anthropology, both as a means of inspection and as theory. This is essentially a geographic method. Its influence can be traced as a dominant theme through

---

[7] Friedrich Ratzel, Anthropo-Geographie, oder Grundzüge der Anwendung der Erdkunde auf die Geschichte (Stuttgart, 1882).

[8] William Morris Davis, Die erklärende Beschreibung der Landformen (Leipzig and Berlin, 1912); Geographical Essays, edited by Douglas Wilson Johnson (New York, 1909); Rollin D. Salisbury, Physiography (New York, 1907); Ralph Stockman Tarr, published under the editorial direction of Lawrence Martin, College Physiography (New York, 1918).

anthropology for the past half century, down to the current concern with the *Kulturkreis* and "culture area" concepts. Swedish geography gains part of its strength from its formal association with anthropology in the joint national society. In England the influence of Fleure and Sir Cyril Fox is that of a bond between the two disciplines, strongly shown by the active generation of geographers in that country.

Methodologically, anthropology is the most advanced of the social sciences, and one of its best developed methods is that of geographic distribution. Sten De Geer's essay on the nature of geography [9] is *de facto* a statement of a method in continuous use in anthropology. The forms of material culture with which the anthropologist deals are identical with those of human geography. His observations of culture traits, his synthesis of these into culture complexes or areas are, or should be, entirely familiar to us. His use of occurrences, discontinuities, losses, and origins of culture traits in terms of their localization as diagnostic of what happened to a culture is actually a mode of geographic analysis for genetic ends. It is precisely the same method of inferring cultural movement from distributions that August Meitzen introduced into continental historical geography many years ago.[10] It is also used in plant and animal geography to trace dispersals, retreats, and differentiations.

THE GEOGRAPHIC METHOD: TERRESTRIAL LOCALIZATION

The ideal formal geographic description is the map. Anything that has unequal distribution over the earth at any given time may be expressed by the map as a pattern of units in spatial occurrence. In this sense geographic description may be applied to an unlimited number of phenomena. Thus there is a geography of every disease, of dialects and idioms, of bank failures, perhaps of genius. That such a form of description is used for so many things indicates that it provides a distinctive means of inspection. The spacing of phenomena over the earth expresses the general geographic problem of distribution, which leads us to ask about the meaning of presence or absence, massing or thinning of any thing or group of things

[9] Sten De Geer, On the Definition, Method, and Classification of Geography, Geogr. Annaler, Vol. 5, 1923, pp. 1–37.

[10] August Meitzen, Siedelung und Agrarwesen der Westgermanen und Ostgermanen, der Kelten, Römer, Finnen und Slawen, 3 vols. and atlas (Berlin, 1895).

variable as to areal extension. In this most inclusive sense, the geographic method is concerned with examining the localization on the earth of any phenomenon. The Germans have called this the *Standortsproblem*—the problem of terrestrial position—and it represents the most general and most abstract expression of our task. No one has yet written this philosophy of geographic localization, but we all know that this is what gives meaning to our work; that our one general problem is the differentiating qualities of terrestrial space. Might one hazard the statement that in its broadest sense the geographic method is concerned with terrestrial distance? We are not concerned with universalized economic man, family, society, or economy, but with the comparison of localized patterns, or areal differentiations.

THE CONTENT OF HUMAN GEOGRAPHY

Human geography, then, unlike psychology and history, is a science that has nothing to do with individuals but only with human institutions, or cultures. It may be defined as the problem of the *Standort* or localization of ways of living. There are then two methods of approach, one by the study of the areal extension of individual culture traits and one by the determination of culture complexes as areas. The latter is the general objective of those continental geographers who speak of *genres de vie,* and of the English who lately are using the term "personality" as applied to a land and its people. Much of this sort of inquiry lies as yet beyond any systematic means of development.

We have available, however, an immediately useful restriction to the material culture complex that is expressed in the "cultural landscape." This is the geographic version of the economy of the group, as providing itself with food, shelter, furnishings, tools, and transport. The specific geographic expressions are the fields, pastures, woods, and mines, the productive land on the one hand, and the roads and structures on the other, the homes, workshops, and storehouses, to use the most generic terms, introduced mainly by Brunhes and Cornish.[11] Though I should not argue that these terms include all of human geography, they are the core of the things that we know how to approach systematically.

[11] Jean Brunhes, La Géographie humaine, ed. 2 (Paris, 1912); Amer. transl., Human Geography (Chicago and New York, 1920); Vaughan Cornish, The Great Capitals, an Historical Geography (London, 1923).

THE HISTORICAL NATURE OF CULTURE

If we are agreed that human geography is concerned with the areal differentiation of human activities, we are at grips at once with the difficulties of environmentalism. Environmental response is the behavior of a given group under a given environment. Such behavior does not depend upon physical stimuli nor on logical necessity, but on acquired habits, which are the culture of the group. The group at any moment exercises certain options as to conduct, which proceed from attitudes and skills that it has learned. An environmental response, therefore, is nothing more than a specific cultural option with regard to the habitat at a particular time. If we may redefine the old definition of man's relation to this environment as the relation of habit and habitat, it is clear that the habitat is revalued or reinterpreted with every change in habit. Habit or culture involves attitudes and preferences, which have been invented or acquired. There is no general environmental response in the wearing of straw hats. In Chicago they may belong to the summer wardrobe of the well-dressed man. In Mexico they are the distinctive badge of the *peón* in all weather; and the unmodified Indian wears no hat at all. Like every other culture trait, the straw hat depends on the acceptance by a group of an idea or mode, which may be suppressed or replaced by another habit. The design of science that Montesquieu, Herder, and Buckle forecast failed because we know that natural law does not apply to social groups, as eighteenth-century rationalism or nineteenth-century environmentalism thought. We have come to know that environment is a term of cultural appraisal, which is itself a "value" in culture history.

We know that habitat must be referred to habit, that habit is the activated learning common to a group, and that it may be endlessly subject to change. The whole task of human geography, therefore, is nothing less than comparative study of areally localized cultures, whether or not we call the descriptive content the cultural landscape. But culture is the learned and conventionalized activity of a group that occupies an area. A culture trait or complex originates at a certain time in a particular locality. It gains acceptance—that is, is learned by a group—and is communicated outward, or diffuses, until it encounters sufficient resistance, as from unsuitable physical conditions, from alternative traits, or from disparity of cultural level. These are processes involving time; and not simply chronologic time, but especially those moments of culture history when the group possesses the energy of invention or the receptivity to acquire new ways.

HUMAN GEOGRAPHY AS CULTURE-HISTORICAL GEOGRAPHY

The culture area, as a community with a way of living, is therefore a growth on a particular "soil" or home, an historical and geographical expression. Its mode of living, economy, or *Wirtschaft* is its way of maximizing the satisfactions it seeks and of minimizing the efforts it expends. That is perhaps what adaptation to environment means. In terms of its knowledge at the time, the group is making proper or full use of its site. However, these wants and efforts need not be thought of in monetary or entirely in energy terms, such as units of labor performed. I dare say that every group of men has built its habitations in the spot that for them has been most suitable. Yet to us—that is, for our culture—many such sites appear queerly selected. Therefore, as preliminary caution, every culture or habit must be appraised in terms of its own learning; and also habitat must be viewed in terms of the occupying group. Both requirements place a severe tax on our ability as interpreters.

Every human landscape, every habitation, at any moment is an accumulation of practical experience and of what Pareto [12] was pleased to call residues. The geographer cannot study houses and towns, fields and factories, as to their where and why without asking himself about their origins. He cannot treat the localization of activities without knowing the functioning of the culture, the process of living together of the group; and he cannot do this except by historical reconstruction. If the object is to define and understand human associations as areal growths, we must find out how they and their distributions (settlements) and their activities (land use) came to be what they are. Modes of living and winning a livelihood from their land involves knowing both the ways (culture traits) they discovered for themselves and those they acquired from other culture groups. Such study of culture areas is historical geography. The quality of understanding sought is that of analysis of origins and processes. The all-inclusive objective is spatial differentiation of culture. Dealing with man and being genetic in its analysis, the subject is of necessity concerned with sequences in time.

Retrospect and prospect are different ends of the same sequence.

---

[12] Vilfredo Pareto, The Mind and Society, Vol. 2, Theory of Residues (New York, 1935), pp. 508–511 and *passim.*

Today is therefore but a point on a line, the development of which may be reconstructed from its beginning and the projection of which may be undertaken into the future. Retrospection is concern with origins, not antiquarianism; nor do I have sympathy with the timorous view that the social scientist may not venture to predict. Knowledge of human processes is attainable only if the current situation is comprehended as a moving point, one moment in an action that has beginning and end. This does not constitute commitment as to the form of the line, as to whether it has cyclic qualities or shows no regularity; but it does guard against overemphasizing the importance of the current situation. The only certain advantage of studying the present scene is that it is most fully accessible to inspection. Yet out of the contemporary data in themselves it is not possible to find the means of selecting what is diagnostic of important process and what is not. I am inclined to say that geographically the two most important events of my lifetime have been the settlement of the last of the prairie lands and the coming of the Model T Ford: one an end, the other a beginning of a series of cultural processes. Yet how well did we, whose business it was to do so, pick out these critical processes at the time of their happening, or link them with the changes derived from them? And why did we miss them, if not because we were unaccustomed to thinking in terms of processes?

HISTORICAL GEOGRAPHY DEMANDS REGIONAL SPECIALIZATION

The reconstruction of past cultures is a slow task of detective work, as to the collecting of evidence and weaving it together. The narrative historian may accept anything out of the past as grist at his mill, but not so the culture historian; and I wish to reckon historical geography as a part of culture history. Our obligation is to glean classified data on economy and habitation so that a valid filling of gaps of area and of time can be made. Let us take, for example, the reconstruction of Mexico at the moment of the Spanish conquest. Here we need to know as well as is possible the early sixteenth-century distribution of population, urban centers, urban economies, types of agriculture, sources of metal and stone, provision of plant and animal materials from wild lands, and lines of communication. The early authors who drew a picture of pre-Spanish as against Spanish conditions, such as Torquemada's famous *Monarquía Indiana*,[13] unfortunately made general rather than localized state-

---

[13] Juan de Torquemada, *Veinte y un Rituales y Monarquía Indiana*, 3 vols. (Madrid, 1723).

ments, or took a situation that was true at one place and applied it
as though it were general. One cannot rely, therefore, on most of
the accounts that were intended to be synoptic, but must turn to the
minor records that give local data. The reconstruction of critical
cultural landscapes of the past requires (*a*) knowledge of the functioning of the given culture as a whole, (*b*) a control of all the
contemporary evidences, which may be of various kinds, and (*c*)
the most intimate familiarity with the terrain which the given culture occupied.

The historical geographer must therefore be a regional specialist,
for he must not only know the region as it appears today; he must
know its lineaments so well that he can find in it the traces of the
past, and he must know its qualities so well that he can see it as it
was under past situations. One might say that he needs the ability to
see the land with the eyes of its former occupants, from the standpoint of their needs and capacities. This is about the most difficult
task in all human geography: to evaluate site and situation, not from
the standpoint of an educated American of today, but to place oneself in the position of a member of the cultural group at the time
being studied. It is, however, a rewarding experience to know that
one has succeeded in penetrating a culture that is removed in time or
alien in content from ours.

Such work obviously cannot be done by sample studies ranging
widely, but may require a lifetime given to learning one major context of nature and culture. One may thus extend one's learning outward to the limits of a culture area and explore the contrasts on the
other side of the boundary line. Or one may undertake excursions
to areas characterized by important kindred qualities. But always
there must be the base, the area for which the observer is making
himself the expert. The human geographer cannot be a world tour-
ist, moving from people to people and land to land, and knowing
only casually and doubtfully related things about any of them. I
doubt whether a human geographer can ever be a continental authority. Should we not get rid of the habit of writing regional text-
books about areas we don't know, with materials we copy from secondary sources that we are unable to evaluate? Nor are a thousand
so-called type studies, individually quasi-photographic records of
spots on the earth, likely to add up to anything significant. We recognize expertness among ourselves in physical geography, but do we
have anything of the sort in human geography? If we do not, is not
the difficulty that we have been concerned with non-genetic forms of
presentation rather than with intensive and analytical observation?

We have a full company of Ph.D.'s duly trained in human geography, teaching hundreds of classes to thousands of students; but how little they are adding to the substance of the science they represent!

Historical regional studies of the kind indicated are in the best and oldest geographic tradition. Cluverius, in the seventeenth century, did some extraordinarily acute reconstructions of ancient Germany and Italy,[14] skillfully uniting knowledge of the classics and knowledge of the land. Humboldt's *Essay on New Spain*[15] is still the classic of historical geography of Mexico. The stimulus of Humboldt and Ritter was pointed up through the work of Meitzen in the mid-nineteenth century into an adequate discipline of historical geographic study. Meitzen's approach affected all continental geography greatly. Historical regional specialization is well expressed in the great repository of the *Forschungen zur deutschen Landes- und Volkskunde*. The influence of Fleure and Miss Taylor is evident in the studies of the younger English geographers. It is about time that we in this country become actively conscious of this, the great tradition in human geography.

THE NATURE OF THE CULTURE AREA

In all regional studies—and we equate regional geography and historical geography—a serious problem is in the definition of the term "area." There has been so much inconclusive discussion of the term "region" or "area" that apparently no one definition suffices.

Most commonly the attempt has been to proceed from the "natural area." Yet it is hard to know what constitutes a natural area, unless it be an island, for climates, land forms, and soil provinces are likely to diverge widely. Hence the preference for the study of islands and areas that simulate insular conditions in their sharpness of outline. If we can agree on what is a natural region, we are still faced by the fact that cultural units are likely to straddle the boundary zones of physical contrasts. Boundaries rather than centers of physical regions are likely to be centers of culture areas.

We often employ the term "natural region" to designate any

---

[14] Philippus Cluverius, Germaniae Antiquae Libri Tres (Lugdunum Batavorum, 1616); Italia Antiqua (Lugdunum Batavorum, 1624).

[15] Alexandre de Humboldt, Essai Politique sur le Royaume de la Nouvelle-Espagne, 5 vols. (Paris, 1811); Engl. transl., Political Essay on the Kingdom of New Spain, 4 vols. (London, 1811).

areal division of simple habitat qualities that may facilitate study by reducing complexity. Quite subjectively we indicate that "natural" region A is a coniferous forest land, that region B is characterized by a certain climate, that area C is a land of mountains, that region D is a province of coal and oil. Consistently we mix terms in designating natural regions, selecting a major quality of habitat for each. We are therefore likely to conceal, rather than to answer, the dilemma of area by calling it a natural unit.

In human geography we are mainly interested in the connotation of the cultural area. The unit of observation must therefore be defined as the area over which a functionally coherent way of life dominates. The most satisfactory illustration we have to date is in Eduard Hahn's basic economic regions of the world.[16] We are, however, still far from knowing how to determine a culture area beyond saying that it has intimate interdependence of living. Nevertheless we have a simpler task than the anthropologist in his all-inclusive culture areas, though perhaps we too in the end must build up our areas by finding a sufficient accordance of common traits. A culture area of one order may be recognized by the dominance of a single economic complex. A culture area of a superior order may be determined by the interdependence of a group of areal economies. The traits of making a living are for us the dominant things to observe. Until we know much more about them we do not need to concern ourselves much with other qualities of culture.

Economic areas rarely have fixed or sharp boundaries. Historically they may experience shifts of centers, peripheries, and changes of structure. They have the quality of gaining or losing territory and often of mobility of their centers of dominance. They are fields of energy, within which changes in dynamism may show characteristic directional shifts. It is also possible to imagine a culture area which in the course of time shifts away completely from an earlier location and still maintains organic continuity.

We are interested in the origin of a cultural system as to place of birth. This we may call the theme of the culture hearth, the inquiry into the localization of culture origins. The classical formulation of the problem still is that of the places of origin of agricultural systems. Next, we are concerned with the energy that a growing culture shows as to manner and rate by which it occupies land, including the nature of the extending frontiers. Next, we are interested in the manner of stabilization of one culture area against another. Finally,

---

[16] Eduard Hahn, "Die Wirtschaftsformen der Erde" [map] *in* Die Haustiere und ihre Beziehungen zur Wirtschaft des Menschen (Leipzig, 1896).

there are the problems of decline or collapse and of succeeding cultures. The homologues of all these questions are well known from plant ecology in the study of plant societies.

THE RELEVANCE OF ALL HUMAN TIME

A dissent may now be registered against that view of geography which considers geography as exclusively or peculiarly concerned with present economies or cultures. One of the fundamental questions in all social study is how to account for the rise and loss of institutions and civilizations. The birth or fall of a great state or culture will always claim the attention of students of civilization. One is no less a geographer if he is engaged in knowing the rise and passing of a culture that lies back at the dawn of history than if he is concerned with the growth of industrial Chicago. There may be as important things to learn about human geography in the archeology of the Mississippi Delta as in its fields of sugar cane. Any topic in the social sciences is important, not by reason of its date, but by the light it throws on the nature of culture origins and changes. This assertion is basic to the present position. If it is correct, all human time is involved in the field, and any predilection for considering the present as intrinsically most important misses the expressed aim of human geography as a genetic science.

Here and there geographers have concerned themselves with prehistoric settlements and culture. In Louisiana, Kniffen and Ford are providing a good illustration of what may be learned by archeogeographic study.[17] There is, indeed, a specifically geographic dimension to archeology, that of the complete distribution of the traces of a culture, essential to the reconstruction of its population pattern and its economic geography. Even in our best known area, that of Pueblo culture, this approach has been carried out only once, by Colton and his associates at the Flagstaff Museum, an approach which I should like to recommend as a model of workmanship.[18] English geography is today most largely indebted to Fleure, who

---

[17] Fred B. Kniffen, The Indian Mounds of Iberville Parish, Louisiana, Louisiana Dept. of Conservation, Geological Bull. No. 13, 1938, pp. 189–207; James A. Ford, Analysis of Indian Village Site Collections from Louisiana and Mississippi, Louisiana Dept. of Conservation, Anthropological Study No. 2, 1936.

[18] Harold S. Colton, Prehistoric Culture Units and their Relationships in Northern Arizona, Museum of Northern Arizona, Bulletin 17, 1939.

has concerned himself primarily with the farthest corridors of time.[19] In this field there is hardly a question of continuity with the present culture area, but an approach to the general problem of the specialization and viability of culture. To some of us, at least, the geography of Basketmaker Man or of the Bell-beaker Folk is as revealing and absorbing as anything in the present-day world. Those of us who are completely historical geographers are concerned with human origins and changes throughout all human time. Let no one think, therefore, that we are in any sense offside from the main theme if we work at the farthest reaches of time, the childhood of our race. We think, rather, that the human geographer who works on the short-time dimension of the contemporary scene is held by a peculiar obsession.

THE ARCHIVE IN HISTORICAL GEOGRAPHY

The first step in reconstruction of past stages of a culture area is mastery of its written documents. The discovery of contemporaneous maps is the first thing hoped for, but rarely realized. We have, however, scarcely exploited the documentary possibilities in the United States of old land surveys as to notations on the character of vegetation and of "improvements" early in the period of settlement. There is a fair amount of valuable material in the Land Office plats and in the older records of land grants that give glimpses of the pioneer landscape. Factual data, precisely localized, of enumerations of persons and goods, of land titles, assessments, production, lie neglected in various archives to await exploitation. There is an embarrassment of such riches in the old Spanish records for New Spain, from parish records up to summary reports that were sent to the king in Spain. There are diaries and accounts of early explorations, the *visitas* made by inspecting officials who reported in detail on condition of the country, letters of missionaries, the so-called geographic relations ordered for all Spanish America at several times in the sixteenth and eighteenth centuries, records of payments of taxes and tributes, data on mines, salines, and roads. Perhaps no other part of the New World has as elaborate a documentation on settlements, production, and the economic life of every part as do the Spanish colonies, but it is certainly an exceptional area for which

[19] Harold Peake and Herbert John Fleure, series of 10 volumes under the collective title "The Corridors of Time" (London and New Haven, 1927–1956).

documentary sources will not yield a large part of the data needed to reconstruct the geographic pattern of living through successive stages of its history. Familiarity with such records, however, takes much time and search.

FIELD WORK IN HISTORICAL GEOGRAPHY

Let no one consider that historical geography can be content with what is found in archive and library. It calls, in addition, for exacting field work. One of the first steps is the ability to read the documents in the field. Take into the field, for instance, an account of an area written long ago and compare the places and their activities with the present, seeing where the habitations were and the lines of communication ran, where the forests and the fields stood, gradually getting a picture of the former cultural landscape concealed behind the present one. Thus one becomes aware of the nature and direction of changes that have taken place. Questions begin to take shape as to what has happened to local site values. It is real discovery thus to take old documents into the field and relocate forgotten places, to see where the wilderness has repossessed scenes of active life, to note what internal migrations of inhabitants and of their productive bases have occurred. There comes a time in such study when the picture begins to fit together, and one comes to that high moment when the past is clear, and the contrasts with the present are understood. This, I submit, is genetic human geography.

This may be hard and often difficult work physically, because there are trails that must be followed if one is to get the answers. One must go over the ground of former activity, no matter what its present accessibility or facilities, or lack thereof, for the comfort and health of the student. It isn't a question of learning to know a country by modern means of transport. There is an exaction of intimacy with out-of-the-way places which historical geography often imposes that modern economic geography does not. This sort of inquiry demands that the field worker go where the evidence requires him to go. Hence the importance of those brief and precious younger years when he is physically able to follow his clues through the chosen area. There are all too few field seasons that will be available to him. At best, when the days of insufficient physical strength come upon him, he will wish that he had been in the field longer and more often, to secure the observations which he needs.

The first objectives of historical field work are to value the habitat in terms of former habit, and to relocate the former pattern of activity as indicated in the documentary record. To these are added more specific tasks of field observation. The chief of these may be called the location of the cultural relicts and fossils.

Cultural relicts are surviving institutions that record formerly dominant, but now old-fashioned, conditions. Familiar illustrations are (1) types of structures, (2) village plans, and (3) field patterns surviving from former days. Every student of European geography knows how house type, settlement plan, and field systems have yielded knowledge of the spread of different kinds of settlement forms, often where the written record is silent. Scofield, Kniffen, and Schott have well shown how such data may be used in this part of the world.[20] (4) Some of us have been engaged in tracing the distributions of varieties of native crop plants as indicators of cultural spreads. Similar work remains to be done with Old World plant and animal domesticates to trace routes of cultural dissemination. (5) Little has been done in the study of old forms of plant and animal husbandry. We lack inquiries into native hoe husbandry or *milpa* agriculture, into old traits of backwoods farming still surviving among us, into the old basic elements of our stock ranching, into the historic functions of the barn, into types of different immigrant agricultures. Such type studies, recording in faithful detail the year-round calendar of old-fashioned agricultural communities, would be of great value, especially if they can be carried out so as to show what modifications have come in with time. (6) Similarly, there still are archaic forms of placer, pit, and even lode mining, and (7) old ways of felling timber and getting out logs. All such archaisms which help to understand former processes operative in localizing settlement and use of resource should be recorded while they still exist. (8) The old-fashioned water- and animal-powered mills, and (9) the survival of old transport methods by water and land are other instances in point.

It may be objected that such inquiries are technologic and not geographic. However, every organized activity is a skill that has been learned or developed by a group or community, without the understanding of which the geographer cannot interpret the pro-

---

[20] Edna Scofield, The Evolution and Development of Tennessee Houses, Journal of the Tennessee Academy of Sciences, Vol. 11, 1936, pp. 229–240; Fred B. Kniffen, Louisiana House Types, Annals Assoc. Amer. Geographers, Vol. 26, 1936, pp. 179–193; Carl Schott, Landnahme und Kolonisation in Canada am Beispiel Ontarios, Schriften des Geogr. Instituts der Univ. Kiel, Vol. 6, 1936, pp. 201–210, 271–274.

ductive occupation of his area. If there is no such thing as direct adaptation in human geography, there can be no human geography that does not concern itself with communities as associations of skills. The field geographer, then, must observe the expression of such skills in the cultural objectives of a group occupying a given site, and the historical geographer must recover the survivals of old skills that explain older dominant forms of land occupation.

Moreover, the geographer as field worker has the opportunity to make observations of how material cultures worked that other social scientists are not likely to secure, because mostly they are not accustomed to field observations. Not even anthropologists give attention to the husbandry of their primitive peoples in the sense that should be expected from a geographer observing the same people. It is difficult to imagine a human geography that fails in expertness in the processes of getting a livelihood. If pack trails are geographic phenomena, the pack trains that use them are also; the feeding places that the animals use involve a knowledge of the fodder or forage on which they depend; then why not also the utility of the animal as to the distance it can cover and the load it carries, and the whole process of loading and driving? Let protest fall where it may, I should not be interested in historical geography or in human geography except as helping to understand the differentiation of cultures, and I cannot get understanding of this sort except by learning the ways and devices men have used for making a living out of their homelands.

Fossil forms may be considered those that are no longer functioning, but which still exist, either obsolete or as ruins. The field study of ruins is important, for it alone will show in some cases localization of production or settlement that has failed. There are the direct ruins of habitation that give clues as to why people once lived there, from hearth places of early man to abandoned farmsteads. There are the curious and persistent alterations of soil where once an earthen floor stood, or the refuse of settlement was dumped, often expressed by characteristically different vegetation. There are the escaped plants of the household that may propagate themselves indefinitely in its vicinity, the lilac bushes of the Northeast, the Cherokee rose of the Southeast, pomegranate and quince in Spanish American lands. There are ruins of land use in abandoned fields that may be identified from prehistoric surfaces of tillage to the boom agriculture of two decades ago. The evidence may be in particular plant successions, in changes in the soil, even in ancient furrows. In the Old South, it is well known that the exact limits of old fields may be determined by stands of old-field pine, and the time of abandonment approximated by the age of the trees.

There are lesser lines of historical field work, the place names that have connotations of olden days, folk customs and dialectic turns that reveal traditions of times when tradition was a living part of the economy, the memories that still belong to the oldest members of the group. The oddments one thus turns up by living with a people are not inconsiderable, and occasionally there is a lead that is most revealing. I may refer to the illumination that Eduard Hahn got out of considering unconsidered trifles about food and drink habits in Europe, especially vestigial mannerisms that no one had considered before him.

In all historical geography, field work demands most acute observation, constant alertness to clues, flexibility in hypothesis. It is not comfortably routinized as may be the mapping of current land utilization.

There is urgency in such field observations. Year by year the sweeping hands of modern industry and commerce brush away more and more of what is old. Traditions die with the old people; documents are destroyed; weather, storm, and flood erase the physical remnants; science and market standardization destroy old crops. Now is a better time than will ever be again for both student and the records, before the years invalidate both.

Thus a science of comparative regional geography may grow up among us, which will shun the following fallacies: (1) that geography has substance as a science of contemporaneous activity; (2) that historical geography can be done by adding the missing environmental notations to the works of historians; (3) that historical geography is only library work; (4) that a geographer can acquire expertness by knowing a little about a lot of unrelated localities; (5) that descriptive studies, done without regard to process, i.e., genesis and function, can add up to a science, either physical or social; (6) that geography can deal with relations of culture and site without understanding the nature of cultural process, growth, and differentiation; and (7) that there is some way of compensating for lack of curiosity and dearth of knowledge by devices of style and organization.

SOME THEMES IN HISTORICAL GEOGRAPHY

A number of general problems are suggested as the sort of comparative knowledge we should be advancing:

1. Certain processes of physical geography, involving secular change, may affect man. (*a*) The most important is the problem of climatic changes or cycles. The other sciences of man expect us to get the answers as to facts, nature, and direction of climatic alteration in human time. The areally specialized geographer has the opportunity to shed light on this controversial subject. In all the dry margins of the world, this topic is of major concern; especially, have their boundaries expanded since the beginning of agriculture? Methods and results in using noninstrumental climatologic data might well constitute a recurrent symposium at meetings of this Association. (*b*) In part connected with this question is the problem of natural changes in vegetation since glaciation; few problems should be more interesting to the geographers of the interior United States than that of the prairies, or of the humid grasslands in general. (*c*) Another topic is that of natural changes of coast line and drainage in the period of human occupation. In these meetings, Russell has pointed out drainage changes of the Mississippi, some since the crossing of De Soto. Marsh's classic *Man and Nature* [21] outlines a lot of such problems.

2. Man as an agent of physical geography. (*a*) At present we incline to deny all effects of settlement and clearing on climate, in contrast to the attitude of an older generation, as shown by the literature of early American forestry. Indeed, the science of forestry began largely on the hypothesis that trees diminished climatic extremes. We are hardly sufficiently well informed to dismiss this topic entirely. There is, in terms of our present information, no assurance that in certain climatic tension zones, as of dryness, radical alteration of the ground cover cannot affect critical relations of temperature, humidity, and moisture availability at and near the ground level. I should not be entirely sure that man has not extended the limits of deserts by altering the climatic condition of the lowest film of the atmosphere, which may be called the intravegetational climate.

(*b*) Geographers have given strangely little attention to man as a geomorphologic agent. Soil erosion is the popular name for the processes of surface removal that man has released or accelerated. The incidence of soil erosion may be a major force in historical geography. Did soil losses sap the Mediterranean civilizations? Were the Virginians great colonizers because they were notable soil wasters? Geographical field work should embrace thorough search for full, original soil profiles and note the characteristic diminution

[21] George P. Marsh, *Man and Nature; or, Physical Geography as Modified by Human Action* (New York, 1864).

or truncation of soil profiles in fields and pastures. Thus only can an understanding of the age, nature, and extent of wastage of productive surfaces be secured, and thereby the changing fortunes of human agricultural regions registered. The strange blind spot of geography to this, one of its most basic problems, may illustrate the result of dodging the historical approach.

The aggradation of waste on surfaces below the slopes of cultural denudation is, of course, the complementary part of the situation. Gullies mostly are advanced, acute symptoms of soil erosion, including some that have served in text-books as illustrations of normal youthful valleys. How often have geographers distinguished between natural ravines and man-induced gullies, or found the latter of interest as to their incidence and life history? Surely nothing could be more geographic than critical studies of the wastage of surface and soil as expressions of abusive land occupation. On the one hand are the pathologic physical processes; on the other, the cultural causes are to be studied. Next come the effects of continued wastage on survival of population and economy, with increasing tendency to degenerative alteration or replacement. Finally, there is the question of recovery or rehabilitation.

The theme was clearly indicated as a formal problem of geography three-quarters of a century ago by Marsh.[22] Geographers have long given lecture courses on conservation of natural resources and considered the evils of soil erosion. But what have they done as investigators in the field, which may actually lie at the doorsteps of their classrooms? Is the answer that soil students should study sheet wastage, geomorphologists gullies, agricultural economists failing agriculture, rural sociologists failing populations, and the geographer prepare lectures on what others investigate?

(c) All results of destructive exploitation must be regarded as involving changes in habitat. The presence of civilized man has often meant changes in the regimen of streams and of underground charge of water. Irrigated areas show here and there the creeping paralysis of alkali accumulation or of waterlogging. The forms of dissipation of natural capital are many, their causes are cultural, their results are slow crises in the affected areas; their connotation is therefore a matter of human geography.

(d) A special problem of the alteration of the land by man is the relation of culture to plant and animal ecology. There are questions in this field that may be reserved to the plant or animal specialist. The historical geographer, however, must take this topic

[22] *Ibid.,* pp. 8–15, 214–252, and *passim.*

into account so far as he is able to deal with it; and, since he works deliberately with historical data, he may encounter evidence that the ecologist will not. In Mexico, for instance, it is apparent that civilized and primitive men have modified the vegetation rather differently. Primitive husbandry was far less bound to low slopes than is modern agriculture. Given certain conditions of climate and soil, hoe agriculture was in effect a long-term forest-crop rotation, usually on hill and mountain slopes. Under such a system, in effect as it has been for thousands of years, the whole of the present wild flora may represent locally a type of old-field succession. The coming of the white man introduced in certain areas a new form of pressure on the native vegetation through heavy grazing. About the mines in particular, he effected complete deforestation through the needs of wood and charcoal in the mines, as well as by persistent pasturing of stock about the mining camps. The old mining camps may now be surrounded by open country for many leagues where once there were forests and brushlands.

These are some of the themes which the historical geographer may well develop. In the process he will probably learn something about the suppression of certain vegetation elements because of their superior utility to man, because of their low ability to reproduce, or because of their sensitivity to an ecologic balance. There is nothing particularly esoteric about learning the important constituents of a native flora, or even in observing their habits of reproduction and growth. One observer may go further with this theme than another, but its appropriateness can hardly be questioned, and the cultural approach may sharpen observation of the biotic association as to time elements. In climatic tension zones in particular, it is possible that human interference may operate characteristically to displace widely former vegetation boundaries. Any area with a long grazing history, in particular, should be examined in this respect as to the replacement of palatable browse and grass by unpalatable, probably woody, or bitter, succulent elements. The role of fire, especially in the hands of primitive man, needs much additional observation, undertaken with the knowledge that long-continued burning may have opposite effects on vegetation from those that result from a short series of burnings.

3. Sites of settlements. The location of a settlement records the particular preferences as to habitat that concerned the founders. Since a settlement once established is not readily transferred, subsequent culture changes alter the site value, and confront the people of the town with the alternative of moving or of meeting developing

handicaps. Perhaps if we were locating our cities *de novo* we should place relatively few of them in the exact sites which they occupy. Consider the towns that grew up on once-navigated streams, on portages, and under other site selections that have lost their significance, but which have imposed repeated problems on later generations as transport, supply, and municipal services have changed. If California were being settled today, San Francisco would probably be a middle-class suburb of a major city across the bay. Yet in the 1840's San Francisco was the most eligible site for a port at which ocean and river transport met. It has successfully maintained a large number of urban functions in which it acquired initial dominance, and has on the whole overcome the handicaps of a transverse peninsular position as these have developed.

At the time a settlement is made, it may generally be regarded as combining in its site the best means of satisfying the wants of the founding group. It is necessary, therefore, to regard the site in terms of the original wants. In one case protection may be important, in another indifferent. Food and domestic water needs and transport advantages vary with the founding culture. Site classifications in terms of cultural attitudes at the time of origin of settlement have rarely been made, yet here is the basic chapter in a science of urban geography. Next would come revaluations of the site and accommodations under change of culture: the site viewed under successive stages.

4. Settlement patterns. We do not have a great deal of comparative historical knowledge about (*a*) dispersal or agglomeration of habitations, (*b*) the spacing and size groups of clusters of settlements that develop under particular cultures, (*c*) functional specialization as between town and town within one culture area, or (*d*) functional differentiation within a major town. These are some of the most obvious problems of localization of habit that need inquiry in historical and regional terms.

5. House types. Americans have given little attention to the unit of dwelling, which commonly approximates the social unit, or the family in its inclusive connotation rather than in the marital sense. Is the dwelling unit single or multi-family, does it provide for its dependents and retainers, does it include arrangements for the domestic animals? Does it include formal provisions for the storage of primary necessities or for the exercise of crafts or trades? What is the functional generalization of the house plan? The study of house types basically is the study of the smallest economic unit, as that of village or town is that of an economic community. In both

cases description seeks the meaning of structure in relation to institutionalized process, as an expression of the culture area. Houses are historical geographic records. They may date from a former historical stage, or they may, as current buildings, still preserve conventional qualities which once were functionally important (fireplaces, porches, shutters) on American houses.

6. Land occupance studies with regard to the historic structure of the culture area. At any given time, in theory, there is a momentary equilibrium of habitat evaluation and habit wants. Environmental advantage or disadvantage should then always be relative to the moment or stage of the particular culture, and land use an accommodation of the wants and energies of a community, which changes as these change. Change, however, usually is slow, partly because of the difficulty of revising property lines. The rationalization of land use meets the opposition of the design of fields and other land holdings of earlier days. At any one time land rights and land use are likely to conserve a good deal of the past. Settlement patterns, house types, field systems, and land ownership are the best-recognized observational items used in reconstructing changes and continuities.

7. What of cultural climaxes? Is there in human societies something like an ecologic climax, a realization of all the possibilities inherent in that group and its site? What of limits of population growth, of production attained, of accumulation of wealth, even of increment of ideas beyond which the matured culture does not go? We may be skeptical of the more extreme hypotheses of the cyclic character of all culture, but we too are concerned with the recurrence of cultural peaks, of stabilization, and of cultural decline. The rise and fall of cultures or civilizations, which have interested most historically-minded students of man, cannot fail to engage the historical geographer. A part of the answer is found in the relation of the capacity of the culture and the quality of the habitat. The case is relatively simple if destructive exploitation can be shown to have become serious. There is also the knotty problem of overpopulation (which may be very much a reality in the culture-historical sense though a heresy to the theoretical social scientist), involving diminishing opportunity and sharing for the individual. There may arise loss of productive energy by maldistribution of population as between country and town, between primary producers and those who are carried as leisure class. There may be shift of comparative advantage to another people and area. A melancholy and stimulating subject is this scrutiny of the limits of culture.

8. Cultural receptivity. A new crop, craft, or technique is introduced to a culture area. Does it spread, or diffuse vigorously, or does its acceptance meet resistance? What are the conditions that make a certain group eager to accept innovations, whereas another chooses to continue in its old ways? This is a general problem of social science, which in part can be examined by geographic studies.

The geographer, in the first place, is best able to determine the existence of physical barriers or corridors. Perhaps a crop does not spread because it encounters an unsuited climate, perhaps the soil it requires is not of a type that a particular husbandry has learned to utilize.

In the second place, the geographer presumably has kept track of the presence or absence of material culture traits. He should know whether a crop or a skill is confronted by a satisfactory alternate already established in the area. The dissemination of wheat growing in Latin America has been considerably affected by the food habits of the people with regard to other starch and proteid crops. It is only true in terms of world markets, and hence of strictly commercial production, that the yield of a given plot as to wheat or corn will determine which will be grown. I should like to add that even the current world market price is only an expression of cultural demand from a dominant purchasing group, not a real expression of utility of the several grains.

It may well be remembered that Ratzel founded the study of the diffusion of culture traits, presented in the nearly forgotten second volume of his *Anthropogeographie*,[23] and that Eduard Hahn came upon the great problem of his life work by asking himself why some peoples engaged in dairying and others would have nothing to do with milk or its products.

9. The distribution of energy within a culture area. Here we may refer to the great thesis of Vaughan Cornish, that of the cultural "march." [24] His view is that every growing civilization has had an active frontier: an actual frontier, on which the energies of the people become massed, where power, wealth, invention are most highly developed. This has some resemblance to Turner's thesis of the frontier,[25] though it does not involve the necessity of continued expansion. It begins with expansion, but the energies of a culture

---

[23] Friedrich Ratzel, Anthropogeographie, Vol. 2, Die geographische Verbreitung des Menschen (Stuttgart, 1891).

[24] *Op. cit.,* pp. vii–ix, 26–27, and *passim.*

[25] Frederick Jackson Turner, The Frontier in American History (New York, 1920).

once localizèd on such a border may continue to manifest themselves by leadership in many ways long,after expansion has ceased. Historically, therefore, it is not in the central parts of a culture area that the great developments take place, but on what was both the most exposed and the most alluring border. There is a lot to be done in considering the dynamic fields (*Kräftezentren*) within the whole expanse of a given culture area. There is much to be said for the thesis of Cornish. The dynamic front of Mexico, for example, has been the northern border throughout its history. Archeology, in both New and Old World, shows many illustrations of the flowering of culture at the far margins of a culture complex.

10. Cultural stages and succession. Turner made an unfortunate error when he accepted an ancient, deductive view that human progress advances through an identical series of stages, which he thought he could recognize as general stages of the American frontier. We know that there is no general cultural succession, but that each culture must be traced separately through its history of acquisitions and losses. Hahn's great work,[26] in particular, warns against deductive approaches to cultural stages, as, for example, by his denial that pastoral nomads derived from hunters rather than from older agricultural backgrounds. Since cultural change by no means follows a general or predictable course, it is necessary to trace back each culture through its historical steps.

It is not generally appreciated that the first and dominant pattern of Spanish settlement of the New World was the formal organization of all Spaniards into town corporations and their permanent domiciling in such a *villa* or *real*. From this basic knowledge that the Spanish pioneer was a member of a town corporation at all times, the nature of Spanish penetration and economic organization acquires a very different form from that of the settlements by the other colonial powers of the New World. On our American frontier there was no such uniformity as in Spanish America, but a considerable number of first stages from north to south, dependent on colonizing group; nor was there one type of frontier in the westward movement. Might it not be time for geographers to try to characterize the culture complexes and successions in the settlement of the United States? It should provide substance for some of the future meetings of our Association.

11. The contest for area between cultures. Certain cultures have been notably aggressive; some such can be determined for almost any part of the human past. The contest for dominance in the meet-

---

[26] *Op. cit.,* pp. 32–33.

ing zones of cultures, the manner in which a balance is established and a boundary takes form, express cultural energy and adaptability. Ratzel had in mind this sort of study in his political geography, which stressed the historical struggle for space.[27] Whether by conquest, absorption, trade, or superior adaptability, all cultures have been marked by ground-gaining or ground-losing qualities.

CONCLUSION

The human geographer has the obligation to make cultural processes the base of his thinking and observation. His curiosity is directed to the circumstances under which groups or cultures have diverged from, or been assimilated to, others. Most of the history of man has been a matter of differentiation of culture and of reconvergences. We cannot even point to a uniform human culture back in the dawn of Paleolithic time. The Tower of Babel is almost as old as man. In the literal meaning there are very few "common-sense" qualities about living habits; that is, things that are most sensibly done in one way only, general logical or psychological necessities. I fear that the more theoretical social sciences, like economics, are likely to lose sight of this truth. In this country, we are likely to forget this because we happen to be part of a tremendously vigorous and widespread culture, so confident of itself that it is inclined to regard other ways as ignorance or stupidity. The terrific impact of the modern western world, however, does not repeal the old truth that the history of man has been markedly pluralistic, and that there are no general laws of society, but only cultural assents. We deal not with Culture, but with cultures, except so far as we delude ourselves into thinking the world made over in our own image. In this great inquiry into cultural experiences, behaviors, and drives, the geographer should have a significant role. He alone has been seriously interested in what has been called the filling of the spaces of the earth with the works of man, or the cultural landscape. His primarily is the difficult job of discovering the meaning of terrestrial distributions. The anthropologists and he are the principal social scientists who have developed field observation as a skill.

The themes suggested for our work may represent a task beyond our immediate individual or joint ability, but they are at least a design of the quality of knowledge we seek. Our several efforts may build consciously toward the understanding of the differentiation of

[27] Friedrich Ratzel, Politische Geographie (München and Leipzig, 1897).

the earth at the hands of man. We shall not get far if we limit ourselves in any way as to human time in our studies. Either we must
admit the whole span of man's existence or abandon the expectation
of major results from human geography. Either we must produce or
warm over what others have prepared. I see no alternative. From
all the earth in all the time of human existence, we build a retrospective science, which out of this experience acquires an ability to
look ahead.

{ 18 }

Folkways of Social Science

The divisions of knowledge and the methods of acquiring it are mainly organizational conveniences and alternative descriptive techniques. The master craftsman can work with simple and even indifferent tools; a main advantage of processing equipment is that it enables the use of the less skilled and increases the volume of the materials processed. Our present hazard is rather that the mechanisms of investigation become so complicated, immobile, and costly as to tie the investigator to processing centers and to require more and more technicians.

In American social science it has indeed become a dominant folkway to associate progress with putting the job of inquiry into large-scale organizations, under formally prescribed methods, and with limited objectives. Having adopted the name "science," we are impressed by the "method of science" as inductive, quantitative, experimental. We are even told that such is the only proper method. We should be grateful to those mathematically and experimentally talented persons among us who have found significant problems to be resolved by such approaches. Experimental inquiries into human behavior are giving new insight into social attitudes and tensions. Machines that count and compute are superior aids to inspection at the hands of those who can ask significant questions about data that are actually quantitative. Statistical and experimental procedures are, however, tools, limited to certain purposes and dependent as to product upon the quality of the problem that has been set up. The more we get committed to keeping counts and tests going in ever lengthening series, and to adding suitable items as additional series, the more do the limits of social science become defined by what may be measured. And thus the more restricted does the range of per-

The Social Sciences at Mid-century: Papers Delivered at the Dedication of Ford Hall, April 19–21, 1951 (Minneapolis, 1952), pp. 100–109. Copyright, 1952, by the University of Minnesota.

sonalities and temperaments become who are attracted into social studies. There is further risk that we attach such merit to quantification as to confuse means and ends, industriousness with intellectual achievement.

No field of inquiry can be properly defined by any specific means or methods of gaining knowledge. A person may devote himself to the mastery and use of a particular technique, but knowledge is eclectic and grows by using any means that add to understanding. Geography, for example, has a vested interest in what is called by everyone the "geographic method." In simplest terms, this is placing on a map the distribution or variation of anything that is spatially localized or varying. Geographers should be making more use of this method of inspection than they do, for many questions of distribution cannot be studied without it. I should not admit, however, as has been claimed, that all the data that concern geographers are mappable, or that their conclusions are necessarily derived therefrom. Therefore I cannot agree that geographers can be recognized by their own method. Some can be, and some good ones cannot be.

Many other investigators use the geographic method. It is much employed in the study of biota and in interpreting the dispersal and evolution of organisms. It is an important tool in comparative linguistics. It is peculiarly the three-dimensional representation of phenomena; it may yield otherwise undisclosed information about the fourth dimension, time in a relative sense. It is used for continuously varying distributions, as, for example, climatologic data. By it are recorded limits, gaps, overlaps, gradients. No plant geogpher would approach the study of the evolution of pines without charting as exactly as possible the recognized entities of the genus. Out of this mapping he can then draw inferences as to limiting environmental factors, but he can also get insight as to migration and variation. An anthropogeographer, Friedrich Ratzel, opened up new vistas to comparative, historical ethnology by studying the diffusion of culture traits through charting their distributions. He thereby initiated a long, now unhappily languishing, inquiry into the incidence of inventiveness as against the borrowing of culture traits. The method has very many and largely unrealized possibilities in social studies, and is to be well recommended as an aid to discovery. It is, however, only a good tool, congenial to some temperaments and revealing for some purposes. No method is more than that.

If social scientists cannot be identified by any particular manner of working, we may know them only by the things they think about in common, or which concern some of them as questions in which there is a convergent interest. If "physics is what physicists work at," we also shall be known by our works, and saved by them alone. In any field there are a few persistent questions, which each generation asks in its own manner. The course of inquiry changes in part by following the directions of greatest success in discovery. It changes also with the cultural climate of the time and place.

We are all trying to know more of the nature of human society. Immediately, however, we find that there is a division of interest between "society" in the singular and in the plural. For the latter we often prefer to use the name "cultures." At the present moment, and especially in this country, this division has become sharp, and to my thinking overstressed. In part, this is the result of notable returns from the use of quantitative approaches. In part, I think, it results from the fact that we are overinclined to universalize our own position and moment. We all hope that the knowledge of the basically human, freed of time and place, will continue to grow. We must also remember that this generalized "social man" carries genetic, physiologic, and cultural modifiers, which are most difficult to isolate. May the experimentally disciplined neo-Spencerian science of society have every success; but let it not cast off those who work in other directions and ways. To this present and growing danger I shall refer again.

At mid-century the social sciences have moved far away from where they stood at the beginning of the century. In numbers of workers they have multiplied greatly. Thousands fill the places manned by a few score in those early years. When memory calls the roll, however, of that elder generation, we look up to them with respect and admit that they opened up wide horizons that we in part have lost. I think of George Vincent and his Socratic seminar in Public Opinion, carried on without benefit of random sampling; of the gentle sage of Michigan, Henry Adams, and his misgivings about the coming day of the experts; of Franz Boas, impatient of speculative constructions while time was running out for getting the record of the primitive and basic cultures; of Sumner's relentless dissection of the social institutions of the past and the "phantasms" of the day. The men were few, but they had stature; they had wide learning and the long insights of history. They came to build the social sciences from backgrounds ranging from oceanography to biblical science, and they came to pioneer their new fields because of slowly matured interest. They read freely in various languages and were familiar with other cultures than our own. They worked mostly as individuals and felt free to change their directions and approaches. They remind me of what Sumner said about his Göttingen professors: that they "seemed bent on seeking a clear and comprehensive conception of the matter under study (what we call 'the truth') without regard to any consequences whatever."

Most of those I knew were detached observers, unconcerned about choosing or directing their work in terms of social or political ends. (The reform element came along somewhat later. In my Chicago days this intrusion of emotional drive was noticeable only in some students of sociology, then already in some numbers refugees from divinity schools, seekers for a new faith in social welfare. In economics I saw the welfare motivation come in with the young labor economists.) The theses of social evolution of Spencer, Morgan, and Sumner were discussed, with due reserve about the existence of a "natural" order and succession in society. I did not become aware until later that the analogy was a misuse of the biologic concept. Geographers were attracted by environmental determinism and familiar with Buckle's theory of history. We were also beginning to see the ecologic unbalance that came through industrialization, and listened to the early conservationists, especially to Van Hise. There was no talk of interdisciplinary training because we did not think of confining ourselves to our particular discipline and were welcome wherever we went.

Today our great educational structures are much more formally organized and more partitioned. The social studies have seen an especially large growth in student numbers. They have elaborated curricula in terms of sequences and specializations; so we must admit the gibe that the student has been learning more and more about less and less. We have been trapped by our numbers, and we have sought a way out by devising more ways of processing more students. The equally bedeviled administrations then distribute staff increases by noting where the enrollment is piling up, and so more courses must be added, to build up still more enrollment in these areas of academic congestion.

Also we are expected to be scholars. We have less and less time for thinking, and again we turn to organization to simplify and regulate that part of our activity that is left for research. We acquire space, equipment, man power, and budgets, and put them into a table of organization as research bureaus and institutes. Obviously, long-term projects are favored, planned in terms of an orderly series of steps in the acquisition of data and of processes for their analysis. Workers are assigned to designated posts and tasks. Again we have set up an assembly line for mass production, resembling the operations of industry and government. In some cases the product is subjected to scrutiny, even to policy clearance. And often a distinction develops between directing staff and working staff.

Institutes of research first appeared in the natural sciences, as associations of independently operating scholars. With the development of experimental work, some of them came to be built about a greatly gifted individual, a master craftsman whose own work had outlined so large a field that he needed younger workers to extend the rate and field of common exploration. This *primus inter pares* ideal has been achieved occasionally in the social studies, for instance by Wesley Mitchell and Carl Alsberg. I think we must admit, however, that more often the idea of an institute has come first, thereafter the question as to who should run it, and last of all the matter of why it was needed. Should not the question be, Is there a problem that has become so complex and sufficiently far advanced that an organized and concerted effort is necessary for further advance, and is it to be under the direction of the man who has thought himself farthest into this matter? I fear that not many institutes originate or are maintained thus. We tend to raise up career administrators, able at finding funds, tactful, energetic operators, who at best have been scholars too briefly and who by temperament and the course of their lives become more and more removed from the contemplation and concentration that are needed for creative work. Thus they may lose even the sensitiveness and understanding by which they know who a scholar or what a piece of creative work is.

Of all fields, we have perhaps become most given to conferences and committees for the planning of research. We agree as to division of labor, as to preventing duplication of research, as to priority of topics, as to assembling specialists for a cooperative project. In these and other ways are we unwittingly going about shackling freedom of inquiry. Borrowing a term from the engineers, we recommend "pilot studies," serving as models to be reproduced until another design is approved for another series of studies. Conferences require agenda, and these have offspring that result in further conferences. The common variety of scholar is awkward, bewildered, and often bored by these uncongenial procedures, which pass into the control of our entrepreneurial colleagues. Thus we develop hierarchies of conference members who speak a common language, obscured from us by its own ceremonial terms. They become an elite, fashioning increasingly the directions and limits of our work, as they become more and more removed from the producers.

A serious and delicate problem is posed by the growing role of the national research council and foundation, the last years having seen a continually increasing concentration of influence. Although there are more and more individual workers, there is no such rise in diversity of interests. With the growth of central advisory, planning, and granting agencies, perhaps simply as a matter of economy of attention, it has come about that a reduced number of directions are selected for approval and support. Thus is introduced a grave and growing disorder into the body of our scholarship. When preferments and rewards are being posted for doing certain things and not doing others, the pliable and imitative offer themselves most freely, and the stubborn ones hold out. Local authority is impressed by the objectives expressed by the distant patron. He who is not deflected from his chosen direction to take part in the recommended enterprise is the unhappy guest who sits out the party. Thus conformity to a behavior pattern comes to prevail. Yet the able researcher will always know best how he should employ his mind, and his inclination will be to seek his own way. The dependent and complaisant ones do not matter. Paved with good intentions, the roads down which we are being urged do not lead toward the promised land of freedom of the spirit. No group can or should wish to be wise and farseeing enough to predetermine the quest for knowledge.

Another contemporary attitude is that better social scientists are made by experience in governmental offices. My own services in the Army of the Potomac were brief, but I doubt that it is a good thing for most of us to be long on that firing line or to perform staff duties. A good service record may mean enthusiasm to carry out the policies set up by superiors. A comradeship of like-mindedness develops, or the professor becomes one of the policy makers and hence a politician. Such affiliations and successes bring rewards of prestige that he takes back with him to his own campus. He retains his status in the official reserve and is occasionally recalled. He is a man of influence and probably a dispenser of patronage to his junior colleagues, particularly when academic jobs are hard to get. He practices the virtues of pump priming, and naturally he is likely to preach them.

Continued and dominant concern with current events that touch us strongly, and especially with those affecting political decisions, is a mounting strain on scholarly detachment. We have lived in a disturbed world for a generation. Having moved from crisis to crisis within this country and abroad, we are crisis-minded and inclined to be fervent.

My first experience of the force of political emotion was in the

Bull Moose campaign, when I heard the first Roosevelt voice the call to stand at Armageddon and battle for the Lord, the audience breaking into the battle song, "Onward, Christian Soldiers." Even at that moment of exaltation, this seemed to me a somewhat less than scientific description of the actual situation. I shall not recall the later, more numerous and more notable appeals that have been answered by mass affirmations of righteousness. We do appear to have become more responsive to social issues and more ready to identify ourselves with political groups. Courses that deal with current events are strongly attractive to present-day youth looking for guidance to a better world. They hope the professor is the true prophet they are seeking, and gradually the teacher becomes accustomed to wearing the robe of the prophet. Research programs are set up in terms of social goals, and it is assumed that professional training provides the deep insight needed. Having set up schools for the training of prophets, it gratifies us to hear that the great task of social science is to remake the world. Sumner was born a half-century too soon; there is no one to speak to us about the "phantasms" of our time. The only emotional drive we should acknowledge, and should choose our work and workers by, is the esthetic one of the satisfaction derived from better understanding.

Of late years social science has been occupied with removing time from the pattern of our thoughts, and similarly also, place. The "here and now" claims almost the whole of our attention, in so far as it is not projected into the future. Kronos, eldest of the gods, and the Fates have been supplanted by newer household gods, such as Keynes and Freud. Yet psychology cannot examine what is in the past or what lies beyond repeatable and verifiable observation. The New Economics deals with *ad hoc* solutions of current situations, recent as to origin and of uncertain viability. Statistical analyses are restricted to very short runs of time. In economic history the industrial revolution seems at a dim distance, interesting largely because of its expression in classical economic theory. It has become commonplace to think that the social sciences face up to contemporary problems, that the humanities or others deal with the past.

This turning away from the meaning of time and place is a rather peculiarly American folkway of the day. I should derive it from our unique national history and geography, the late and rapid exploitation of the most richly and variously endowed land mass in the world. The older Western world has not similarly simplified the study of society to universalize its present self.

A German sociologist, Alexander Rüstow, successor to Alfred Weber, has dealt with the present as a moving point on the million-year long line of human history.[1] Why indeed should the study of society wish to be anything less than a study of the origins, development, mingling, and extinctions of human institutions and values throughout all human time and among all humankind? In our day, in particular, one might be hesitant about being indifferent to the flow of time, for time has come to have vertiginous acceleration. If I take my life span as a yardstick, at one such interval removed Goethe was creating his Faust, and the source of the Mississippi was yet unknown. Two spans removed, Voltaire and the Encyclopedists were opening the Age of Reason, and France had just lost control of North America; at six, the Reformation was under way, and Cortés was building New Spain upon the ruins of the Aztec state.

Do we think that we dominate time, as an upward spiral that we have under control, our increasing knowledge confidently shaping its development? Or is this faith that we are shaping progress by material skills and building an ever expanding system in truth the great "phantasm" of our day, the "brave new world"? Have we set up an economy of waste, which we call the miracle of American production? Can we disregard our deficit spending of natural resources because we shall continue the triumph of mind over matter? Are other times and other places of importance only in so far as they can be related to our egocentric and ephemeral position? Are we the cleverest people of all time or the blindest because we think neither of whence we came nor whither we are bound?

Our needs have little to do with more refined techniques or with research planning. We need to make the social sciences, as indeed the academic life, more inviting to more good young minds, and more diverse ones, and then we should protect, not confine, their growth. We are getting too limited a selection of temperaments and talents, we are educating them too narrowly, and we tell them too much how and at what they should work. I want to see the young fellows given the freedom of range that we had when we were young. I want to see us give back the search for truth and beauty to the individual scholar, to grow in grace as best he can.

Fifty-nine years ago William Osler came from the Johns Hopkins Medical School to address your own young medical faculty and students.[2] He then said: "It is so difficult to be still amidst bustle, to be quiet amidst noise; yet 'es bildet ein Talent sich in der Stille'

---

[1] Alexander Rüstow, Ortsbestimmung der Gegenwart, I, Ursprung der Herrschaft (Erlenbach-Zürich, 1950).

[2] William Osler, Aequanimitas, with other Addresses to Medical Students, Nurses and Practitioners of Medicine, ed. 2 (London, 1908). References to pp. 41 and 419.

alone, in the calm life necessary to continuous work with high purpose." (It would seem that at that time it was unnecessary to identify or translate Goethe.) Through the years this was a favored
theme of his. At a valedictory to the "new world" he reaffirmed it:
"It is hard to get the needful seclusion, on which account it is that
our educational market is so full of wayside fruit. I have always
been impressed by the advice of St. Chrysostom: 'Depart from the
highway and transport thyself in some enclosed ground, for it is
hard for a tree which stands by the wayside to keep her fruit till it
be ripe.' "

The evolution of the organism has been toward ever growing
diversity of forms. Through the ages the earth has grown richer in
the variety of living things. An organism may have an innate tendency to produce variation in its offspring, but the new form rarely
gets established in the midst of the many from which it is a deviate.
If the mutant finds a different and secluded spot away from the mass
of its kind, it may have a chance and reproduce. The great, rich
plains of the world are dominated by a few species, in large numbers; the uncommon plants grow in broken terrain and on uncommon soils. It is up to us to see that the promising variant gets
sheltered ground. It is those who differ from us that are needed, not
the mass production of our own kind. We are doing too much line
breeding, too little selection of hopeful diversity.

In my experience, the talented, original student is the only one
for whom it is difficult to find a place. He may be as likable as another and as willing to work at the customary tasks of his trade.
But it is usually safest not to call attention to any unfamiliar direction his mind is taking. What the market wants and gets is persons
who can fill job specifications neatly. We dislike having juniors
around who think about matters beyond our ken and reach. We
build sheltering walls against the unknown by making organizations
and methods, curricula and research programs. And we get no more
than we make room for.

Will those who come after us say that we offered protection and
encouragement to young minds differing from our own, that we
raised no barriers to seeking and thinking, that we blocked no paths
into the unknown, that we turned no one from whatever most roused
curiosity and gave delight, that we "have loved no darkness, sophisticated no truth"?

The Education of
a Geographer

ON ORIGINAL BENT AND EARLY PREDILECTION

As professionals we claim only that we are privileged to devote ourselves to the field of geography. Neither we nor our academic predecessors discovered the field, nor have we ever been the only ones who have tilled it, nor is it likely to be properly attended should it be thought restricted to those who claim privilege and competence from appointment and title. The first professor of geography in the world was named in 1820; I am of the early second generation in the United States. We of the vested succession must always remember that we have never been more than a few of those who contribute to the growth of geographic knowledge. The interest is immemorial and universal; should we disappear, the field will remain and it will not become vacant. We may draw no invidious distinction between professional and amateur; both are needed as cherishing and contributing to geographic knowledge. The gloss is here: An association of minds is not determined by a committee on credentials.

The geographer partly is born, partly shaped by his early environment, and comes rather late into our professional care. This is the usual and proper condition. We are also recruiting officers, and we do need to recognize good material in the raw state. I suspect that we have more than ordinary difficulties as talent scouts. How common is a boyhood ambition to be a geographer? It is an unlikely interest to assert itself early, or to be admitted to one's mates or oneself in school age. In college, we know too well, a professed and actual liking for taking courses in geography (and success in getting good grades) is an indifferent indication of future promise. The

Annals of the Association of American Geographers, Vol. 46, 1956, pp. 287–299; address by the honorary president of the Association at its annual meeting, April, 1956.

student may be beguiled by his temporary contacts and surroundings, such as the attractive qualities of an instructor. When he is detached from such stimulus he may sink into inaction and after a time no more may be heard of him. How can we discover aptitude, emergent interest, and the promise to continue in independent growth? This is our first concern. If we select well, half of our problem is solved.

Let me not appear to discount the value of the great school, but let us also not overrate it. Whoever shared in those golden early days at Chicago knows the stirring of the spirit in the group Salisbury assembled. Salisbury had great clarity of exposition and the ability to develop a theme by rigorous questions, but what I cherish most in him is that he respected curiosity and doubt on the part of the student. He liked the informed dissenter. Hettner, Philippson, and Fleure will be remembered as masters of instruction; from their schools have come a considerable number of the best of our European colleagues. Their students were drawn from and continued to develop along quite different directions, and were not shaped over one last by their student training.

What one learned in class may be forgotten, but what is remembered is the stimulation by association of related yet varied personalities and interests. The invitation of the student period should be greater than the discipline. I should not like to think of anyone as the product of a particular school, but as having been found and nurtured at the right time by good gardeners. And thus we get back to the young plants that may flourish in our care, or may do so without it.

We are not a precocious lot, nor should we wish to be. We are unlikely to start early and we need a long time to mature. Ours is a task of slow accumulation of knowledge, experience, and judgment; techniques and formal processes of analysis and of generalization are subordinate. We do not gain competence quickly, nor by the learning of one special skill. We are subject to shifts of focus as we learn more about whatever we are working at. The start on one theme may turn into a different one. It is either distressing or exciting, according to one's nature, to find that the trail one expects to lead toward a certain point may carry one into unexpected directions. It seems to be a quality of our particular kind that we always require more readiness to learn what is relevant than to perfect ourselves by specific training and method.

It is proper, therefore, that we have been reluctant to accept a general formal discipline, that in our more confident moods we imagine ourselves with the power to explore in many directions, and that we admit to our group different temperaments and diverse interests. It has always been characteristic that we have been made up of individuals of many backgrounds, having some denominator in common. That our departments and institutes have multiplied in later years has not altered our plural origin and, I hope, will not do so.

It is, I think, in our nature to be a heterozygous population. Despite the line-breeding now available by extensive series of courses in geography, running from the freshman year to the Ph.D., we still get much of our best blood from those who come from quite other academic stocks and backgrounds. These join us not because they have been inadequate in their previous commitments but because it took time for them to find their place over on our side. A revealing history of geographers and of geographic thought might be written about this theme of convergence of individuals out of different origins and conditions.

May a preselective bent toward geography be recognized before it asserts itself as deliberate election? The first, let me say most primitive and persistent trait, is liking maps and thinking by means of them. We are empty-handed without them in the lecture room, in the study, in the field. Show me a geographer who does not need them constantly and want them about him, and I shall have my doubts as to whether he has made the right choice of life. We squeeze our budgets to get more maps, of all kinds. We collect them from filling stations to antique shops. We draw them, however badly, to illustrate our lectures and our studies. However little a member of your institution may know what you are doing as a geographer, if he requires map information he will call on you. If geographers chance to meet where maps are displayed (it scarcely matters what maps), they comment, commend, criticize. Maps break down our inhibitions, stimulate our glands, stir our imagination, loosen our tongues. The map speaks across the barriers of language; it is sometimes claimed as the language of geography. The conveying of ideas by means of maps is attributed to us as our common vocation and passion. Even in the most fundamentalist period of this Association those devoted to maps were admitted to the elect.

A map invites attention alike synoptically and analytically. What kind of a road is marked; through what kind of country does it run? Its symbols are translated into images, and these are assembled in the mind's eye into meaningful associations of land and life. We use them as actual guides and we enjoy them in armchair travel. Who has not journeyed by map to Tibesti or Tibet, raised the peaks of Tenerife or Trinidad on the western horizon, or sought the Northwest Passage? Who has not been with Marco Polo to Cathay, with Captain Cook to the Sandwich Islands, and with Parkman over the Oregon Trail? Who reads fiction for plot, suspense, or psychologic conflict, or to be transported to tropical shores with Stevenson or Kenneth Roberts, to India with Kipling or Masters, to know Florida with Marjorie Rawlings or New England with Esther Forbes?

The geographer and the geographer-to-be are travelers, vicarious when they must be, actual when they may. They are not of the class of tourists who are directed by guidebooks over the routes of the grand tours to the starred attractions, nor do they lodge at grand hotels. When vacation-bound they may pass by the places one is supposed to see and seek out byways and unnoted places where they gain the feeling of personal discovery. They enjoy striking out on foot, away from roads, and are pleased to camp out at the end of the day. Even the urban geographer may have in him the need to climb unpopulated mountains.

The geographic bent rests on seeing and thinking about what is in the landscape, what has been technically called the content of the earth's surface. By this we do not limit ourselves to what is visually conspicuous, but we do try to register both detail and composition of the scene, finding in it questions, confirmations, items or elements that are new and such as are missing. This alerting of the mind by observing what composes the scene may derive from a primitive survival trait when such attention meant the avoidance of peril, want, getting lost. In my days of field work in back areas of Mexico I learned to accept confidently the geographic and natural history competence of the native guides. They knew how to interpret the lay of the land, to keep a mental map, to note almost any change in the scene. They were usually able to identify the plants and were right as to systematic grouping and ecologic association.

Geography and natural history are indeed related by their manner of observation. Much of what both identify and compare lies outside quantitative analysis. Species are not recognized by measurements but by the judgment of those well experienced in their significant differences. An innate aptitude to register differences and similarities is joined to a ready curiosity and reflection on the meaning of likeness and unlikeness. There is, I am confident, such a thing as the "morphologic eye," a spontaneous and critical attention to form and pattern. Every good naturalist has it, and many of them are also very good at geographic identification and comparison.

The term "morphology" came into the study of land forms a hundred years ago; it is at the very heart of our being. We work at the recognition and understanding of elements of form and of their relation in function. Our forms and their arrangements are grossly macroscopic and infinitely numerous, so that we have always to learn about selecting what things are relevant and eliminating the insignificant. Relevance raises the question of why the form is present and how it is related to other forms. Description is rarely adequate and even less often rewarding unless it is tied to explanation. It seems necessary therefore to admit to the geographic bent the fourth dimension of time, interest in how what is being studied came to be.

Some of us have this sense of significant form, some develop it (and in them I take it to have been latent), and some never get it. There are those who are quickly alerted when something new enters the field of observation or fades out from it. One of the rewards of being in the field with students is in discovering those who are quick and sharp at seeing. And then there are those who never see anything until it is pointed out to them. At this time screening of recruits may begin, if geography is a science of observation. The premise here is that we build from things seen and analyzed, however provisionally, to a comparison with data from elsewhere, from someone else, or inferred by necessity from a past that cannot be seen.

ON BEING UNSPECIALIZED

Geography as explanatory description of the earth fixes its attention on a diversity of earth features and compares them as to their distribution. In some manner it is always a reading of the face of the earth. We professionals exist not because we have discovered a line of inquiry or even own a special technique but because men have always needed, gathered, and classified geographic knowledge. The names we apply professionally to the items or forms that we identify and perhaps even to the processes we pursue are commonly and properly derived from many vernaculars; we organize them into a vocabulary of wider and clear intelligibility. Often the languages of primitive peoples and the dialects of our own cultures provide us with more meaningful terms than does literary speech. A familiar illustration is in the meaning of land, vegetation, and cultural forms for which we borrow from local speech and extend their application to other areas.

In addition to such naming of geographic categories, both physical and cultural, out of popular speech, we derive retrospective knowledge of past conditions from the study of geographical proper names. The topical and local geographical vocabulary of languages in particular is a substratum of learning that still awaits exploitation, both for the identification of kinds of our phenomena and for comparative cultural insights.

In this sermon, as one may do in a sermon, I return to the opening text that geographic content, relations, processes—in sum, geographic awareness—are of reason and necessity wider than what we, the professors of geography, work at. Beyond and around what we study today lies an area of interest, of identification and concepts, which we do not intend to appropriate only to ourselves. The subject is and will be greater than the sum of our disciplinary efforts. We do claim a superior obligation to contribute in all the ways in which we are able, asserting no prior rights or competence that derive only from our profession. The Association of American Geographers was begun and was carried through its earlier years by that notable group of founders who met together because of their affection for the subject, though their professional jobs were elsewhere, in geology, biology, history. Those were very good days, followed by a time of restrictive association when those who held jobs in geography were chosen over those who brought ideas and observations. Happily this time seems to be past and we again are broadening the compass of our fellowship.

If we shrink the limits of geography, the greater field will still exist; it will be only our awareness that is diminished. Though the individual limits his own efforts, he may not ask the same limitation of others, nor deny his approval of efforts that go in another direction. A geographer is any competent amateur—in the literal sense —of whatever is geographic; may we never wish to be less than that.

A particular method of inspecting data is known to all scholars as the geographic method, based on charting the limits or range of phenomena, features, or traits that have a localized distribution on the earth. The mapping of distributions was begun by natural historians, or natural philosophers as they were called in the eighteenth century, who were interested in the limits of species and thus in the spread or dispersal of organisms to the extremity of their ranges.

This cartographic description is always topical and analytic: what qualities of environment, dispersal routes, elapsed time, and interdependence or competition established the boundaries beyond which a particular animal or plant does not occur? A century and a quarter ago Berghaus extended such topical mapping to include not only biotic and physiographic data, but also cultural ones, as of peoples, economies, and languages. Ratzel examined the distribution of culture traits, as of primitive technology, and was largely responsible for the attention given since then by ethnologists to the spread or diffusion of specific learnings or skills.

An arduous and rewarding art of detection is offered by these distributional studies: They are geographically descriptive because they are concerned with terrestrial extension; they are geographically analytic because they demand proper identification of the items under scrutiny and comparison with other distributions; they are geographically dynamic because they seek clues from distribution for explanation of presence or absence, of origins and limits. Distribution is the key to process. The intellectual satisfactions of such inquiries are inexhaustible. Their pursuit will continue to be carried on by workers in many disciplines, from which we may gain knowledge but in which we also must participate more than we do.

It is neither necessary nor desirable that we consider the totality of region as the common basis of geographic study. Individual interest and competence begin and may remain with specific elements of nature and of culture and with the meaning of their spatial relations. If we say that our job is only to synthesize, we are likely to become dependent in all things on others for the validity of what we assemble and interpret.

Though the analytic distributional method thus called geographic is employed with skill and penetration by others than ourselves, it is also the one most rewarding to our purposes. We must individually try and hope for competence in learning more or most about the distribution of some thing or group of things. I do not accept the idea that anyone can do the geography of a region, or comparative geography, when he knows less about anything he assembles than others do, as I do not accept the notion that every geographer must be concerned with regional synthesis. The ineptly named holistic doctrine leaves me unmoved; it has produced compilations where we have needed inquiries. This is no counsel of despair but rather I wish to say that geography, like history, resists any overall organization of interests, directions, or skills, yet does not lose thereby an acknowledged position of its own kind of knowledge and of valid process of discovery and organization. In a time of exceedingly great increase of knowledge and techniques we remain in a measure undelimited and, I may add, unreduced to a specific discipline. This, I think, is our nature and our destiny, this our present weakness and potential strength.

We continue properly to be, as I have said that we have been always, a diverse assemblage of individuals, hardly to be described in terms of dominance of any one kind of aptitude or temperament, mental faculty, or emotional drive, and yet we know that we are drawn together by elective affinity. It is about as difficult to describe a geographer as it is to define geography, and in both cases I am content and hopeful. With all shortcomings as to what we have accomplished, there is satisfaction in knowing that we have not really prescribed limitations of inquiry, method, or thought upon our associates. From time to time there are attempts to the contrary, but we shake them off after a while and go about doing what we most want to do. There are institutional and curricular pressures, but these are not intellectual directives. One of the wisest of university administrators has said that any department is largely a budgetary convenience.

It seems appropriate therefore to underscore the unspecialized quality of geography. The individual worker must try to gain whatever he can of special insights and skills in whatever most absorbs his attention. Our over-all interests, however, do not prescribe the individual direction. We have a privileged status which we must not abandon. Alone or in groups we try to explore the differentiation and interrelation of the aspects of the earth. We welcome whatever work is competent from whatever source, and claim no proprietary rights. In the history of life the less specialized forms have tended to survive and flourish, whereas the functionally self-limiting types have become fossils. Perhaps there is meaning in this analogy for ourselves, that many different kinds of minds and bents do find congenial and rewarding association, and develop individual skills and knowledge. We thrive on cross-fertilization and diversity.

THE TRAINING PERIOD

In the training period we have our different ways of selecting and conditioning the prospects. The comments here offered are those of one weather-beaten coach who has watched many a player from spring practice through midseason performance.

In the first place, I doubt that undergraduate majors in geography are to be recommended as those who should continue as graduate students. The bigger the major program gets and the more prerequisites get hung onto it, the less is likely to remain of a properly balanced liberal education, and the less leeway exists for the student to delve into areas of knowledge that he needs for his individual education. We too have been swept along by the current specializing academic trend that is narrowing the higher educational process almost everywhere on our side of the Atlantic and is pushing academic departments into applied and technical orientations.

Putting labels on beginners herds them into premature profession. Registrars and other administrators like such facilities of identification and advancement; we are caught because departments depend on budgets, enrollments, and other kinds of numbers that have little relevance to the ends of learning. A good undergraduate diet for us would be a sharply limited number of geography courses (limited especially as to the number of regional ones), one enriched in the staples of liberal arts, and especially in natural and cultural history. A big departmental curriculum is probably a sign of bloating, not of fecundity.

What benefit of training and insight comes out of regional courses? After many years I am no closer to an answer. I think we give far too many such courses, that they may be given for indifferent reasons, and that too often they contribute little to learning or to skills. More and more the concern with regional classifications and regional boundaries leaves me cold. I find that I like my courses on Latin America better since I have given up any system of geographic regions. Who can, or wants, to remember a lot of regional subdivisions anyway? In our own operation we decided long ago that we should give a regional course only if the instructor had prior and major preoccupation with such an area, and especially if it was based on continuing field studies, topical rather than inclusive in content.

A good regional course is largely an individual creation out of long application, involving physical discomforts and pleasures, muscular, cutaneous, and gastric, and has been nursed on much meditation. It demands some ability and interest in physical geography and an understanding of other ways of life and how they came about. A really intimate association with other cultures is needed and slow to be acquired. To me it is a study in historical geography. Such a course may indeed open new vistas to the young student and leave a lasting impress on his education. Such a course, however, grows slowly and is not built on any generally applicable, nor on a symmetrical or encyclopedic, organization of subject matter. If it is truly instructive, it can hardly be reproduced or revised by someone else, nor serve as a model for the construction of parallel courses for other regions. Thus the area study programs, much promoted and subsidized in the last years, have of necessity relied on pre-planned organization, on methodologic unity, and on derived data rather than on experienced observation. Similarly, we have a lot of regional courses that are organized assemblages of industriously collected facts, taken at second hand. *A* writes such a book, *B* uses it as a text, and thus regional courses proliferate.

If we prune out a lot of the regional work now spread through our curricula, we shall also urge ourselves to move the topical courses out of their present obscure corners. Topical courses have the advantage that they are analytic, and their elements may be scrutinized at any scale of inspection and by more or less adequate techniques. In the education of the student and in his postgraduate development the topical inquiry is attainable and rewarding.

I am becoming more and more doubtful that regional studies are for the beginner in research. The more I see of regional theses, with their descriptions and classifications and dot maps, which are possibly useful but are mainly secondary collections of presumed facts, the more do I wish that this time and energy had been focused on some topic which is a problem. What problems are stated and at least partly resolved in an average regional thesis? The incipient regional geographer is either sadly at a loss to determine what he wishes to describe, or else follows a routine grouping of data that depresses his job to pedestrian performance. One end of geographic knowledge *is* comparative regional understanding; I don't agree in the least that it must be the only end, to which topical studies are considered only as building stones. I shall commit myself further and say that if most younger students stayed on the trail of themes rather than of regions our contributions to knowledge would be more numerous and of a higher order.

Once most geographers in America did physiographic or geomorphologic studies as a matter of course. They still do so in other parts of the world, and, as we have seen here, in Canada. We have lost in insight by abandoning them. Any kind of a geographer profits by knowing how processes of weathering, transport, and deposition fashion any part of the face of the earth he studies. We have also abandoned a strong, and perhaps the most available, incentive to field observation and for training the eye to recognize features diagnostic for explanatory description. The morphology of land forms links form to process; it requires selective observation and critical judgment as to what has happened to the surface studied. I would not have missed what I learned from Salisbury and Leverett and others in recognizing glacial land forms, setting up multiple hypotheses, and coming to a conclusion as to the meaning of the evidence. When we dropped land forms as our business, we lost a major stimulus to get into the field, to see and think, to state and solve problems. We replaced a lively and promising science with pedestrian schemes of description, perhaps designed even so as to circumvent curiosity. And we are denying the young student one of the best and most generally present means of training the eye to see and the mind to develop generalization. It is hardly accidental that so many of those who have contributed most to human geography also, at least in their earlier years, made original contributions to physical geography.

The field of biogeography requires more knowledge of biology than can be demanded of most of us. It is, however, so important to us and so inadequately cultivated from almost any side that we should encourage the crossing of geography with natural history wherever the student is competent. In particular, we need to know much more of the impact of human cultures on plant cover, of man's disturbance of soil and surface, of his relation to the spread or shrinkage of individual species, of human agency in the dispersal and modification of plants. To these questions a few of us are, and more should be, addressing ourselves. This advice means, of course, again that I do not see our future in a retraction within limits that set us apart from other disciplines. Especially do we need more workers who like and are able to live on frontiers, such as those of biology. Nor does this mean that we are trying to wrest territory from others. Plant distributions and the intervention of man in the rest of the organic world we know to be major themes of geography. Brunhes made that lesson clear to all. We cannot fail to be concerned with man as a steadily increasing dominant of the living world; and therefore we need more familiarity with natural history, including its modes of field study and how it sets up its problems. Homer Shantz is our finest example of significant contribution in this manner; what he brought to meetings of this Association in specific insight and general wisdom will long be remembered. In Europe the tradition is old and general. In Germany, for example, geography has been biogeographically enriched from the days of Humboldt through Gradmann, Waibel, and Troll to Wilhelmy.

These and others have been better geographers, whether they turned to land forms or human cultures, because they were able to make sense out of *Standort* or localization of biotic data. Waibel, fondly remembered by a number of us here, transferred the sense of problem he developed in biogeography into economic and population geography.

Underlying what I am trying to say is the conviction that geography is first of all knowledge gained by observation, that one orders by reflection and reinspection the things one has been looking at, and that from what one has experienced by intimate sight come comparison and synthesis. In other words, the principal training of the geographer should come, wherever possible, by doing field work. The important question here is not whether he gets practice in mapping techniques but whether he learns to recognize forms that express function and process, to see problems implicit in location and areal extension, to think about joint or disjunct occurrence. The class of forms, be they of land, vegetation, or culture, is optional; the important thing is to get this awareness of form started up, to recognize kind and variation, position and extent, presence and absence, function and derivation; in short, to cultivate the sense of morphology.

The field excursion and the field class need not be concerned with a predetermined organization of observations, such as is contained in a synoptic map legend. Leads in plenty—physical, organic, or cultural—will turn up in the course of walking, seeing, and exchange of observations. A successful field experience may well result in a different topic for each participant. To some, such see-what-you-can-find field work is irritating and disorderly since one may not know beforehand all that one will find. The more energy that goes into recording predetermined categories, the less likelihood there is of exploration. I like to think of any young field group as on a journey of discovery, not as a surveying party.

Such excursions and field courses are the best apprenticeship. The student and the leader are in running exchange of questions and promptings supplied from the changing scene, engaging in a peripatetic form of Socratic dialogue about qualities of and in the landscape. Locomotion should be slow, the slower the better, and be often interrupted by leisurely halts to sit on vantage points and stop at question marks. Being afoot, sleeping out, sitting about camp in the evening, seeing the land in all its seasons are proper ways to intensify the experience, of developing impression into larger appreciation and judgment. I know no prescription of method; avoid whatever increases routine and fatigue and decreases alertness.

It is one of our oldest traditions to start by observing the near scenes; it is equally in the great tradition that the journeyman goes forth alone to far and strange places to become a participant observer of an unknown land and life. An interesting test of American geography is being tried and with unexpected response in the new grants that have been set up for the purpose of getting young persons out into distant and poorly known ends of the earth, as leisurely observers. One of the finest experiences of youth is to go where none of your kind has been, to see and learn to make some sense out of what has not been known to any of us. The nestling of classroom, drafting table, and library needs all the encouragement we may give to develop the power of ranging and solitary flight.

The training of the geographer should give attention, finally, to the history of geographic thought, to the ideas that have prompted and focused geographic inquiry, and to the circumambient intellectual climates within which geography has lived at different times and places. We, as little as any group, can be content with current literature, or with what is available to us in English. Complacency as to our own language means the exclusion of a great, probably the greater, part of what has been well learned and well thought about. Can anyone say that he chooses to remain ignorant in his own work because it requires exertion to find out what has been done in other times or written in another language? A scholar does not limit himself to what is most convenient, least of all to such arbitrary reduction of language. A monolingual Ph.D. is a contradiction of terms, one who has not been stirred by the history of ideas, their persistence, alteration, or fading, and who condemns himself to live in needless poverty.

Mainly I have been leaving the trail unmarked by any arrows of methodology. We live in a day when method is being sought, thought, and professed, especially by those who call themselves social scientists. We still stand uncommitted, though we are being advised that we too should have a properly defined methodology. A little of this is a tonic, but it easily becomes habit-forming and diverts the addict from productive work. I should rather recommend that we can learn more from the study of dominant ideas and problems as they have arisen in geographic work, from the objectives and changes of interest shown in the lives of those who have contributed most. What I think geography should be illustrates only my own preferences. What geography is is determined by what geographers have worked at everywhere and at all times. Method is means; the choice is with the workman for his particular task; the critic may object to incompetence but not to what the author has sought. Let us ask "What is geography?" by looking for and appreciating whatever has been done well and with new insight.

DESCRIPTION FOR WHAT?

I hope to get through this presentation without any dictum as to what geography is. We begin by selecting the kinds of things proper to be described for the inquiry in hand. The theme in each case provides the screen for the data, and guards against excessive and irrelevant scattering of attention. The conventional areal study may be an encyclopedia but it is not a synthesis. Are we not under a form of inductive fallacy if we collect lots of data on lots of subjects, thinking these will somehow acquire meaning? Such humility is, it would seem, hope unduly deferred from the plodding collector to someone else who may at some future time make use of the pieces of wood that have been hewn and stacked. I know of no general or inclusive descriptive system for regional study that has the promise of a real taxonomy.

There is at present enthusiasm for field mapping and its techniques. The geographer, we are told, should get into the field and map and map. But map what and to what purpose? Is not this possibly another horn of the dilemma? Topically, as for land forms and plant assemblages, mapping is feasible and may be rewarding, if it is morphologic and not merely morphographic. Lately we are getting a spate of land-use surveys, urban and rural. Having been one of those responsible for starting these up (dualistic, if you wish, but "holistic" never), I have become increasingly doubtful about them as means of discovery. Setting up the legend should be fine mental exercise; executing it by mapping soon runs into diminishing returns, except for revision of the legend. Revision of the scheme in some measure invalidates what has been mapped before; it is therefore resisted as delaying the job. The legend is apt to become master of the observer, depressing and limiting his observations to predetermined routine. Routine may bring the euphoria of daily accomplishment as filling in blank areas; but the more energy that goes into recording the less is left for the interplay of observation and reflection. Don't commit your field season to a mapping stint unless you know it is demanded by a real and present problem. Time-consuming precision of location, limit, and area is rarely needed; sketch maps of type situations, cartograms at reduced scales, serve most of our purposes. Field time is your most precious time; how precious you will know only when its days are past.

The "unit area" scheme of mapping may be a useful cataloguing device, like the decimal systems of librarians (though I doubt it), but as a means of research I should place it below almost any other expenditure of energy.

These misgivings about mapping programs and their techniques rest on a growing conviction that we must not strain to make geography quantitative. Quantification is the dominant trend in our social sciences, which are imitating the more exact and experimental sciences; it happens to be fostered at the moment by the liking of those who dispense funds for long-term programs and institutional organizations. I think we may leave most enumerations to census takers and others whose business it is to assemble numerical series. To my mind we are concerned with processes that are largely non-recurrent and involve time spans mainly beyond the short runs available to enumeration.

BEYOND FORMAL SCIENCE

Beyond all that can be communicated by instruction and mastered by techniques lies a realm of individual perception and interpretation, the art of geography. Really good regional geography is finely representational art, and creative art is not circumscribed by pattern or method. We are unduly embarrassed to let ourselves appear in public without the identifying insignia of our cadre. Vidal de la Blache freed French geographers from such qualms, and French geography has been notable for vivid and meaningful regional portrayal. We may have more latent artistic talent than we know, but we don't encourage it, and so it becomes suppressed. Many a letter is written from the field that enlivens and enlightens the study, but no trace thereof gets into the finished report. Why can't a geographer working in the Great Plains convey to the reader the feel of horizon, sky, air, and land that Willard Johnson did? Or what Shaler and Ellen Semple did for Kentucky and its people? Why make our regional studies such wooden things which no one may read for the insight and pleasure they give?

Esthetic appreciation leads to philosophic speculation, and why not? Are not the compositions of nature, the lines and colors of terrain and of mantling vegetation proper things to consider? How almost inevitably right are the rural scenes wherever simple folk have designed and placed their habitations! The structures of man express function in adaptation to site, with the identifying stamp and preference of each particular culture. There is an esthetics of the assemblage of forms, an esthetic morphology of landscape, latterly often violated by industrial civilization. Is not this question of the harmonious landscape also something proper to think upon?

We need not say that it is not for us to cross the threshold of value judgments. We are largely committed to the study of human behavior; it is proper and reasonable that we are troubled about how man has acted for good or evil. Social science as practised today has not replaced moral philosophy. As we study how men have used the resources available to them we do distinguish between good and bad husbandry, between economical or conservative and wasteful or destructive use. We are distressed by the progressive impoverishment of parts of the world. We do not like soil erosion, forest devastation, stream pollution. We do not like them because they bring ugliness as well as poverty. We may cast up accounts of loss of productivity; but we also think that misconduct is more than a matter of profit and loss. We are aware that what we do will determine for good or evil the lives of those who will come after us. And therefore we geographers, least of all, can fail to think on the place of man in nature, of the whole of ecology. Man's intervention in and disturbance of the organic and inorganic world has become so accelerated that we may be tempted to escape from the present into a future in which technology has mastery over all matter, and thus promises forgiveness and redemption. But will it? Is that our fated way? Is that the sort of world we want? The moralist lives apart from the quotations of the market place and his thoughts are of other values.

There is nothing wrong with academic geography that a strong coming generation cannot take care of. We can have the needed succession if we free it as much as we may to do what each can do best and wants most to do. It is not for us to prescribe by definition what they shall work at or by what method they shall do so. Academic freedom must always be won anew.

Published Writings of
Carl Ortwin Sauer

1915-1962

Published Writings of
Carl Ortwin Sauer
1915–1962

1915

Exploration of the Kaiserin Augusta River in New Guinea. *Bulletin of the American Geographical Society*, Vol. 47, pp. 342–345.

Outline for Field Work in Geography [with W. D. Jones]. *Ibid.*, pp. 520–526.

1916

† Geography of the Upper Illinois Valley and History of Development. *Illinois Geological Survey, Bulletin* No. 27. 208 pp., ills., pls.

1917

The Condition of Geography in the High School and Its Opportunity. *Journal of the Michigan Schoolmasters' Club, 51st Annual Meeting, 1916*, pp. 125–129; reprinted, *Journal of Geography*, Vol. 16, pp. 143–148.

Proposal of an Agricultural Survey on a Geographic Basis. *Michigan Academy of Science, 19th Annual Report*, pp. 79–86.

1918

Geography and the Gerrymander. *American Political Science Review*, Vol. 12, pp. 403–426.

A Soil Classification for Michigan. *Michigan Academy of Science, 20th Annual Report*, pp. 83–91.

Starved Rock State Park and Its Environs [with G. H. Cady and H. C. Cowles]. *The Geographic Society of Chicago*, Bulletin No. 6. 148 pp., ills., map.

The present volume includes the full text of items marked with two daggers (††) and excerpts from those marked with a single dagger (†).

1919

Mapping the Utilization of the Land. *Geographical Review,* Vol. 8, pp. 47–54.
The Role of Niagara Falls in History. *The Historical Outlook,* Vol. 10, pp. 57–65.

1920

The Economic Problem of the Ozark Highland. *Scientific Monthly,* Vol. 11, pp. 215–227.
The Geography of the Ozark Highland of Missouri. *The Geographic Society of Chicago, Bulletin No. 7.* 245 pp., ills., pls.

1921

The Problem of Land Classification. *Annals of the Association of American Geographers,* Vol. 11, pp. 3–16.

1922

Notes on the Geographic Significance of Soils—I, *Journal of Geography,* Vol. 21, pp. 187–190.

1924

The Survey Method in Geography and Its Objectives. *Annals of the Association of American Geographers,* Vol. 14, pp. 17–33.

1925

†† The Morphology of Landscape. University of California Publications in Geography, Vol. 2, No. 2, pp. 19–53.

1927

Recent Developments in Cultural Geography. In *Recent Developments in the Social Sciences* (New York, Lippincott), pp. 154–212.
† Geography of the Pennyroyal. *Kentucky Geological Survey, Ser. 6,* Vol. 25. 303 pp., ills., maps.
Lower Californian Studies. I, Site and Culture at San Fernando de Velicatá [with Peveril Meigs]. University of California Publications in Geography, Vol. 2, No. 9, pp. 271–302.
Vereinigte Staaten. In *Stielers Handatlas,* 10th ed. (Gotha, Justus Perthes), sheets 95–100.

1929

Land Forms in the Peninsular Range of California as Developed about
Warner's Hot Springs and Mesa Grande. University of California Publications in Geography, Vol. 3, No. 4, pp. 199–290.
Memorial of R. S. Holway. *Annals of the Association of American Geographers,* Vol. 19, pp. 64–65.

1930

Basin and Range Forms in the Chiricahua Area. University of California
Publications in Geography, Vol. 3, No. 6, pp. 339–414.
†† Historical Geography and the Western Frontier. *In* James F. Willard and
Colin B. Goodykoontz, edits., *The Trans-Mississippi West: Papers Read
at a Conference Held at the University of Colorado June 18–June 21,
1929* (Boulder, 1930), pp. 267–289.
Pueblo Sites in Southeastern Arizona [with Donald Brand]. University of
California Publications in Geography, Vol. 3, No. 7, pp. 415–459.

1931

Geography, Cultural. *Encyclopedia of the Social Sciences,* Vol. 6, pp. 621–624.
Prehistoric Settlements of Sonora, with Special Reference to Cerros de
Trincheras [with Donald Brand]. University of California Publications
in Geography, Vol. 5, No. 3, pp. 67–148.
Review of H. E. Bolton, Anza's California Expeditions. *Geographical Re-
view,* Vol. 21, pp. 503–504.

1932

Aztatlán: Prehistoric Mexican Frontier on the Pacific Coast [with Donald
Brand]. University of California Publications: Ibero-Americana, No. 1.
92 pp., ills., maps.
Correspondence [on physical geography in regional works]. *Geographical Review,* Vol. 22, pp. 527–528.
Land Forms in the Peninsular Range. *Zeitschrift für Geomorphologie,* Vol. 7,
pp. 246–248.
†† The Road to Cíbola. University of California Publications: Ibero-Americana, No. 3. 58 pp., map.

1934

The Distribution of Aboriginal Tribes and Languages in Northwestern
Mexico. University of California Publications: Ibero-Americana, No. 5.
94 pp., map.

Peschel, Oskar. *Encyclopedia of the Social Sciences,* Vol. 13, p. 92.

Ratzel, Friedrich. *Ibid.,* pp. 120–121.

Ritter, Karl. *Ibid.,* p. 395.

Semple, Ellen Churchill, *Ibid.,* pp. 661–662.

Preliminary Recommendations of the Land-Use Committee [with C. K. Leith and others]. *Report of the Science Advisory Board, 1933–1934,* pp. 137–161.

Preliminary Report to the Land-Use Committee on Land Resource and Land Use in Relation to Public Policy. *Ibid.,* pp. 165–260.

1935

Aboriginal Population of Northwestern Mexico. University of California Publications: Ibero-Americana, No. 10. 33 pp., map.

Review of G. C. Shattuck and others, The Peninsula of Yucatan. *Geographical Review,* Vol. 25, pp. 346–347.

Spanish Expeditions into the Arizona Apacheria. *Arizona Historical Review,* Vol. 6, pp. 3–13.

1936

†† American Agricultural Origins: A Consideration of Nature and Culture. In *Essays in Anthropology Presented to A. L. Kroeber in Celebration of His Sixtieth Birthday, June 11, 1936* (Berkeley, University of California Press), pp. 279–297.

1937

Communication [in reply to one by Ronald L. Ives regarding Melchior Díaz]. *The Hispanic American Historical Review,* Vol. 16, pp. 146–149.

The Discovery of New Mexico Reconsidered. *New Mexico Historical Review,* Vol. 12, pp. 270–287.

Discussion [of Isaiah Bowman, Influence of Vegetation on Land-Water Relationships]. In *Headwaters Control and Use, Papers Presented at the Upstream Engineering Conference Held in Washington, D.C. September 22 and 23, 1936,* pp. 104–105.

The Prospect for Redistribution of Population. In *Limits of Land Settlement: A Preliminary Report to the Tenth International Studies Conference, Paris, June 28–July 3, 1937,* pp. 7–24.

1938

Destructive Exploitation in Modern Colonial Expansion. *Comptes Rendus du Congrès International de Géographie, Amsterdam, 1938,* Vol. 2, Sect. 3c, pp. 494–499.

†† Theme of Plant and Animal Destruction in Economic History. *Journal of Farm Economics,* Vol. 20, pp. 765–775.

1939

Man in Nature: America before the Days of the White Men. A First Book in Geography (New York, Scribner's). 273 pp., ills., maps.

1941

†† Foreword to Historical Geography. *Annals of the Association of American Geographers,* Vol. 31, pp. 1–24.
†† The Personality of Mexico. *Geographical Review,* Vol. 31, pp. 353–364.
The Credibility of the Fray Marcos Account. *New Mexico Historical Review,* Vol. 16, pp. 233–243.

1942

The March of Agriculture across the Western World. *Proceedings of the Eighth American Scientific Congress Held in Washington May 10–18, 1940,* Vol. 5, pp. 63–65.
The Settlement of the Humid East. *Climate and Man, Yearbook of Agriculture, 1941,* pp. 157–166.

1944

†† A Geographic Sketch of Early Man in America. *Geographical Review,* Vol. 34, pp. 529–573.
Review of Paul Rivet, Les Origines de l'Homme Américain. *Ibid.,* pp. 680–681.

1945

The Relation of Man to Nature in the Southwest. *The Huntington Library Quarterly,* Vol. 8, pp. 116–125; discussion, pp. 125–130, 132–149.

1947

†† Early Relations of Man to Plants. *Geographical Review,* Vol. 37, pp. 1–25.

1948

Colima of New Spain in the 16th Century. University of California Publications: Ibero-Americana, No. 29. 104 pp., ills., map.

†† Environment and Culture during the Last Deglaciation. *Proceedings of the American Philosophical Society,* Vol. 92, pp. 65–77.

1950

Cultivated Plants of South and Central America. In *Handbook of South American Indians* (Smithsonian Institution, Bureau of American Ethnology, Bulletin 143), Vol. 6, pp. 487–543.

Geography of South America. *Ibid.,* pp. 319–344.

Grassland Climax, Fire, and Man. *Journal of Range Management,* Vol. 3, pp. 16–21.

1952

Agricultural Origins and Dispersals. (Bowman Memorial Lectures, Series 2. New York, American Geographical Society). 110 pp., maps.

†† Folkways of Social Science. In *The Social Sciences at Mid-century: Papers Delivered at the Dedication of Ford Hall, April 19–21, 1951* (Minneapolis, University of Minnesota Press), pp. 100–109.

1954

Comments [on Paul Kirchhoff, Gatherers and Farmers in the Greater Southwest]. *American Anthropologist,* Vol. 56, pp. 553–556.

Economic Prospects of the Caribbean. In A. Curtis Wilgus, edit., *The Caribbean: Its Economy* (Gainesville, University of Florida Press), pp. 15–27.

Herbert Eugene Bolton (1870–1953). *The American Philosophical Society, Year Book 1953,* pp. 319–323.

1956

The Agency of Man on the Earth. In William L. Thomas, Jr., edit., *Man's Role in Changing the Face of the Earth* (Chicago), pp. 49–69.

Summary Remarks: Retrospect. *Ibid.,* pp. 1131–1135.

†† The Education of a Geographer. *Annals of the Association of American Geographers,* Vol. 46, pp. 287–299.

Time and Place in Ancient America. *Landscape,* Vol. 6, No. 2, pp. 8–13.

1957

†† The End of the Ice Age and Its Witnesses. *Geographical Review,* Vol. 47, pp. 29–43.

1958

†† Man in the Ecology of Tropical America. *Proceedings of the Ninth Pacific Science Congress, 1957,* Vol. 20, pp. 104-110.

A Note on Jericho and Composite Sickles. *Antiquity,* Vol. 32, pp. 187–189.

Review of Harold Gladwin, History of the Ancient Southwest. *Landscape,* Vol. 8, No. 2, p. 31.

1959

Middle America as Culture Historical Location. *Proceedings of the 33rd International Congress of Americanists, 1958,* Vol. 1, pp. 115–122.

Age and Area of American Cultivated Plants. *Ibid.,* pp. 213–229.

Homer LeRoy Shantz. *Geographical Review,* Vol. 49, pp. 278–280.

1961

Sedentary and Mobile Bent in Early Societies. In Sherwood L. Washburn, edit., *Social Life of Early Man* (Viking Fund Publications in Anthropology, No. 31), pp. 256–266.

1962

†† Fire and Early Man. *Paideuma,* Vol. 7, pp. 399–407.

†† Homestead and Community on the Middle Border. *Landscape,* Vol. 12, No. 1, pp. 3–7.

†† Seashore—Primitive Home of Man? *Proceedings of the American Philosophical Society,* Vol. 106, pp. 41–47.

Terra firma: Orbis novus. In *Hermann von Wissmann-Festschrift* (Tübingen), pp. 258–270.

Index

Index

Abbott, Charles Conrad, 199, 208
Abilene culture, 207–208; sites, 227, 258
Acadia, 230
Acaponeta, 57–58; Acaponeta River, 60
Acapulco, 58
Acheulian culture, 160, 262
acorns, processing of, 284
Adams, Henry Carter, 382
Africa: early man in, 164–165, 184, 290–294, 297; in volcanic like country, 291–294, 297, 300–302, 304; along coastal areas, 293, 297, 304–305, 311; climatic history, 302–303
Aftonian interglacial interval, 202, 218
agave, 135
"Age of Surveys," 319
Agiabampo, bay of, 65
agricultural machinery, 16, 35; plows, 13, 15–16, 35, 38, 143; drills, 16; harvesters, 16; mowing machines, 16; threshers, 16
agriculture, New World: pioneer Midwest, 15–17, 32, 34–38, 41, 142–143; aboriginal, 33, 80, 87, 94, 100–102, 109–111, 122–126, 129–132, 136, 142–143; California, 50–51, 141; temporal, 63, 109; aboriginal and modern compared, 140–141; balanced, 149; commercial, 149. *See also* plant domestication
agriculture, Old World, 122, 127, 128–129, 136–140, 259, 268–269. *See also* plant domestication
agriculture, origin of, 164, 364; desert thesis, 120–124; mountain valley thesis, 125–126; climatic conditions, 129–131; soil conditions, 131; competitive or alternative domestication, 136–137; single or plural origin, 136–139; conditions adverse to primitive farming, 140–144; in forest lands, 143. *See also* plant domestication
Ahome, *see* Oremy

Ahrensburg people, 278
Ahuacatlán, 57
Ainu, blood groups of, 237, 239
Ajos, Sierra de los, 99
Álamos, Pueblo de los, 65, 70
Álamos River, 64
Alaska: during Ice Age, 164, 199, 203–205, 224, 241, 280, 285–286; corridor from, 205; wildlife in, 285
Alcaraz, Diego de, 72, 88, 97; massacre of, 89, 95, 99
Algonkin tribes: blood groups of, 239; language of, 243; moccasins of, 244
Algonquin beach, human sites on, 255
Alps, glaciation in, 288
Alsberg, Carl Lucas, 384
Altamont moraine, 273
Altar, 91
Alvarado, Pedro de, 114
amaranth, 135, 138
Amazon basin, 229; climate of, 182–183, 190; tropical rain forest of, 184; agricultural tribes of, 185; archeologic sites in, 185; primitive tribes of, 186, 235; languages of, 242–243
Amazon land, legend of, 55–56, 58, 61
Amazonids, 235
Ameca, 56
Ameghino, Florentino, theory of, 199
Ames, Oakes, 177–179
Andes, 229; *ceja de la montaña* of, 182, 190
animal domestication, 146, 265
Antevs, Ernst, 206
anthropology, 356–357
Apache tribe, 66
Aquihuiquichi, 64
Araucanian people: blood groups of, 238; language stock of, 242; huts of, 244
Arawaks, 191, 243
arcabuco, 191